DAKOTA SQUADRONS IN ACTION

FROM D-DAY TO V.E. DAY

AIRBORNE, SUPPORT AND SUPPLY OPERATIONS IN THE LIBERATION OF EUROPE

CLIVE BENNETT

AIR WORLD

First published in Great Britain in 2025 by
Air World
An imprint of
Pen & Sword Books Ltd
Yorkshire - Philadelphia

Copyright © Clive Bennett, 2025

ISBN 978 1 03612 119 8

The rights of Clive Bennett to be identified as the Author of this work has been asserted by him in accordance with the Copyright, Designs and Patents Act 1988.

A CIP catalogue record for this book is available from the British Library.

All rights reserved. No part of this book may be reproduced, transmitted, downloaded, decompiled or reverse engineered in any form or by any means, electronic or mechanical including photocopying, recording or by any information storage and retrieval system, without permission from the Publisher in writing. No part of this book may be used or reproduced in any manner for the purpose of training artificial intelligence technologies or systems.

Typeset in INDIA by IMPEC eSolutions
Printed and bound in the England by CPI Group (UK) Ltd, Croydon, CR0 4YY

The Publisher's authorised representative in the EU for product safety is Authorised Rep Compliance Ltd., Ground Floor, 71 Lower Baggot Street, Dublin D02 P593, Ireland.
www.arccompliance.com

For a complete list of Pen & Sword titles please contact

PEN & SWORD BOOKS LIMITED
47 Church Street, Barnsley, South Yorkshire, S70 2AS, England
E-mail: enquiries@pen-and-sword.co.uk
Website: www.pen-and-sword.co.uk

or

PEN AND SWORD BOOKS
1950 Lawrence Rd, Havertown, PA 19083, USA
E-mail: uspen-and-sword@casematepublishers.com
Website: www.penandswordbooks.com

Dedicated to all the men and women who served with
46 Group RAF and with RAF Transport Command.

Contents

Foreword by Flight Lieutenant Seb Davey   ix

Introduction   xi

Chapter 1	Daks Arrive at Down Ampney (February 1944)	1
Chapter 2	Intensive Training and Joint Exercises (March–May)	8
Chapter 3	Something's Afoot (June)	20
Chapter 4	Service Français (July, August)	69
Chapter 5	Time to Shine – Market Garden (September)	88
Chapter 6	Keeping up the Support (October, November)	155
Chapter 7	Winter Tales (December, January 1945)	161
Chapter 8	One Last Hurrah, Operation Varsity (February, March)	169
Chapter 9	War Drawdown, End of Hostilities Within the European Theatre (April, May)	183
Chapter 10	The Flying Nightingales	194
Chapter 11	Aircraft and Crews	200

Acknowledgements   269

Endnotes   270

Index   276

Foreword by Flight Lieutenant Seb Davey

Air Transport, in the military context, is often regarded as a less glamorous capability compared to others within the scope of non-civilian aviation. I suspect that if the population were to be asked to imagine the iconic military aviation machines of the 1940s, their responses would mostly contain the beautiful Spitfire and Hurricane fighters, or the mighty heavy bombers of the era, the Lancaster, Halifax and Stirling. While they were vital to the war effort and, in their own way pivotal, none of them featured in General Eisenhower's list of the four main war winners. It would be easy to counter this with 'he was an American though' but their USAAF equivalents didn't feature either. The Dakota, however, did.

In my opinion, the most startling aspect of military air transport is the range of activities that this role encompasses. The non-exhaustive list of these includes logistical movement of personnel and freight to supply these assets to the front line rapidly, aeromedical evacuation to expeditiously move the wounded to more suitable medical care, aerial delivery by parachute of cargo (such as ammunition, fuel and food) to where it is needed without the requirement for an airfield, and airborne assault using paratroopers, delivering a large, effective fighting force in a very short timescale.

As a modern-day Royal Air Force pilot in the air transport role flying the Airbus A400M Atlas, and previously the Lockheed Martin C-130J Hercules, I have employed the techniques, tactics and strategies described in this wonderful book every day of my working life. To a great degree, they are unchanged from the methods employed by the outstandingly brave men (and, unusually for 1940s wartime aviation, women) during the period covered by this book. I also have the great honour of being able to follow in the footsteps of the aviators of the time as a modern-day Dakota captain for the Royal Air Force Battle of Britain Memorial Flight.

'Our' Dakota is the third oldest aircraft in the Royal Air Force inventory. She is a delight to fly. She is responsive, relatively powerful (thanks to her Pratt and Whitney Twin Wasp radial engines) and has a variety of roles with BBMF that echo her operational versatility in times gone by. Her primary role is as a training aircraft for the bomber pilots as the skills required for handling a large tail dragger are absent from today's RAF. But also, she is used as a display aircraft in her own right, a paratrooper-dropping aircraft and occasionally as engineer transport. Every time I fly her, I think of those that went before me. It is humbling.

In this book, Clive Bennett has recorded the contribution of No. 46 Group, its Dakotas and their crews in exceptional detail. As a modern-day equivalent, albeit not having yet experienced the same extreme operational environment, I thoroughly hope you enjoy reading and learning about the sacrifices made by, and the effect of, this Royal Air Force group. The airfields mentioned in this book are now just farmers' fields but as you will gather from reading, were thriving hubs of activity in those times. I implore you to consider what these brave personnel did in delivering the effect that they did and in providing a huge contribution to the liberation of Europe and the return of peace.

Lest We Forget.
Flight Lieutenant Sebastian Davey
BBMF Dakota Captain

Introduction

On 17 January 1944, 46 Group Transport Command was established to provide glider towing and to deploy parachute troops and supplies to the front lines, primarily once the Allied invasion of mainland Europe had begun. The six squadrons comprised 48 and 271, which operated out of RAF Down Ampney, Gloucestershire; 233 and 437 (RCAF), which flew from RAF Blakehill Farm, Wiltshire; and 512 and 575, which called RAF Broadwell, Oxfordshire, their home. Two additional units were aligned to the group, 107 (Transport) Operational Training Unit at RAF Leicester East, as well as 1697 (Air Despatch Letter Service), which operated a small fleet of modified Hawker Hurricanes to deliver urgent secret mail and small specialised equipment to the beachheads post-June 1944.

Chapter 1

Daks Arrive at Down Ampney (February 1944)

No. 512 Squadron had been operating the Douglas Dakota since June 1943, primarily on supply flights to destinations throughout the United Kingdom and Allied countries, normally, within the Mediterranean from its base at RAF Hendon in north London. They were the most prolific users of the aircraft in the RAF and had good experience of its capabilities. On 15 February 1944 aircraft and crews started to relocate to RAF Broadwell in Oxfordshire. Ten aircraft transferred initially and flying operations commenced upon arrival on local sorties. Sister squadron 575 started the transition from Hendon to Broadwell on the same date, although they had sent an advance party on 11 February under the command of Squadron Leader Sproule. 'A', 'B' and 'C' flights were established on 15 February under the command of Squadron Leaders, Cragg, Pascall and Horsfall. The following day, 512 continued with familiarisation flights, although these were undertaken at night. Training continued for 512 over the next few weeks, as more aircraft arrived for 575 Squadron over the period 19 to 24 February. Cross-country flights, including map reading and circuits, quickly followed, and air crews were getting acquainted with their new home as the flying intensified on a daily basis.

The first four Dakotas for 48 Squadron arrived at Down Ampney airfield on 26 February, these aircraft were used for cockpit familiarisation and general training procedures. The squadron was back on English soil after a sojourn and operations in Gibraltar. Re-formed at Down Ampney, it consisted of a total of 66 officers, 161 Senior NCOs and 325 airmen, with only 24 officers, 71 senior NCOs and 135 airmen actually being transferred from the original squadron, the balance being transferred from Transport Command. General training and converting on to the Dakota began in earnest during the early stages of March 1944, and all squadrons were achieving good amounts of flying time, both by daylight and night time. This gave their command a good indication of the progress made by all the squadrons.

The second squadron allocated to Down Ampney was 271, moving from RAF Doncaster to their new home on 29 February 1944, just three days after 48 Squadron. Departing at 09.10 with twenty Dakotas, they touched down just before lunchtime, and began the squadron's relocation to their Gloucestershire base. As with all fellow squadrons within 46 Group, the training format was going to be intense, with 400 flying hours scheduled each month. This was aimed at bringing all crews up to speed before operations began in earnest later in the year.

Fifty-two crews were allocated to 575 Squadron's 'A', 'B' and 'C' flights at Broadwell, and thirty aircraft allocated. A modification procedure was set up at RAF Hendon to bring all new Dakotas up to the same standard and for them to be able to release paratroopers. Two Oxfords also arrived at Down Ampney to act as hacks for general flying duties and functions for units at the base.

At RAF Blakehill Farm building work was still progressing ready to receive 233 Squadron. An advance party headed by Wing Commander Morrison and Squadron Leader Mackenzie arrived on 28 February to ensure readiness to accept the squadron, who were due to arrive on 5 March. The first aircraft were not due to take up residency until early March, but a small detachment from 271 Squadron's 'A' Flight was on base by late February, and the airfield was declared open and operational from 9 February 1944.

On 1 March 575 employed ten aircraft on glider towing and a cross-country exercise. This was mirrored by 512, who put up sixteen aircraft for a large formation flight. This route took the crews from base–Rushden–Pershore–base–Basingstoke–Chippenham–base. These types of practice flights were to become a normal process for all the squadrons within the group, along with glider towing. Exercises were in abundance during March and both 512 and 575 were heavily involved daily in cross-country, formation, low-level flying, and glider towing. These were by day and night, and took crews to unfamiliar locations around the general area bordering Oxfordshire.

The main party from 233 arrived on 5 March at Blakehill and the station was officially opened by Group Captain W.M.C. Kennedy, commanding officer for the station. This was duly followed on 6 March with the arrival of some of the crews, the remaining on the 7th, along with twelve Dakotas for the commencement of flying training.

All 46 Group's squadrons and their crews needed to be fully operational as soon as possible, and were involved in similar syllabus training, so all tended to be trained with their sister squadrons at their home airfields. There were exercises that did involve all 46 Group's assets training together when required, with all five (later six) of the squadrons following the same basic operating principles of Transport Command and the operation of the Dakota.

Operation Snowshoe was scheduled to take place later in March and would involve training for 240 men of assault units (to be airborne simultaneously) and practice in supply dropping. This though was carried out after 10 March, when more crews were in situ.

Separately, ten air crews and twenty-two service personnel were sent to Netheravon from 48 Squadron. Crews were changed every other day, but ground crew remained for a seven-day period; this was to allow for paratrooper training to take place and to give consistency with the servicing of aircraft allocated. Information was subsequently received that all administration personnel and glider pilots were to be transferred from 38 Group and allotted to Netheravon, to create a more central hub and make it easier to be able to collect gliders from Downham Market and deliver them to Netheravon. This was maintained over the next three to four days, with up to six gliders a day being collected and delivered. The last of three new Dakotas were collected from Doncaster on 10 March and duly welcomed into 271 Squadron's care. On the 12th there was the collection and arrival of a further eight gliders, with two Oxfords going from Down Ampney to St Mawgan for radar modifications as well as an additional aircraft from Broadwell.

General squadron strength now totalled thirty-eight allocated to the four main units at Ampney and Broadwell. Blakehill Farm was not far behind, but their training was a few weeks adrift of the other squadrons. Gliders were also becoming more prolific at airfields, on average twenty-four being present. This presented an issue as there were as many as two Dakotas or three gliders on one hard standing, a problem when you do not have enough locations available for both. Thankfully construction was advancing and soon these issues would be resolved! Parachute modifications continued apace on all the aircraft, with another twelve aircraft delivered to Hendon on 14 March.

Also that day, several crews were sent to Hampstead Norris[1] from 48 Squadron to be trained in the first tranche to learn the skill of glider towing. No problems were encountered, a great relief to all involved. The glider towing detachment lasted for several more days during the middle of the month, along with regular familiarisation flights, until the next phase of training was introduced.

No. 512 completed its first squadron exercise on the 16th, which was deemed a success when fifteen aircraft flying in five 'Vic[2] formations' and spaced within 30-second intervals deployed a parachute drop of 225 troops from the 5 Parachute Regiment at the DZ[3] located at Winterborne Stoke. Unfortunately, only 223 of the troops were dropped, and all except one landed within the DZ. The sole individual who did not reach the target area got his foot entangled in the lines and by the time he had realised and freed himself he had drifted and was 3 miles away. Nos 512 and 575 Squadrons were involved in three days of exercises at Netheravon: on the 16th, Operation Faith, on the 17th, Operation Hope, and on the 18th, Operation Charity. These operations had other squadrons taking part, notably 271 Squadron, and their training began in earnest on the 16th when fifteen aircraft performed a practice mass take-off and landing, which was completed in four and ten minutes respectively. Fifteen 271 Dakotas carrying fifteen paratroopers were airborne on the 17th to take part in Exercise Hope, routing out over Honeybourne, Banbury, High Wycombe and Andover for the DZ and then on to Ampney. Troops were from the 12 Battalion Paratroopers and they jumped on to the DZ at Winterbourne Stoke, but trooper number nine (the padre) who was travelling in the twelfth aircraft, experienced a slight issue! Caught by the previous jumper's straps, he was quickly grabbed and pulled back into the aircraft by one of the crew supervising. The aircraft did a circuit and once over the DZ the padre and the rest of the troops made a successful jump. God was clearly watching over this particular member of his flock that day!

A repeat of the previous day's exercise was carried out (Operation Charity), although with a slightly different route: Winchcombe, Brackley, Aylesbury, Andover, DZ and return to base. This was carried out with aircraft from RAF Broadwell, from where both squadrons supplied fifteen aircraft, and involved the dropping of 7 Battalion Paratroopers. All successfully dropped with no issues reported. Upon landing, the captains and navigators were interrogated by intelligence officers to gain instant feedback that was used to report back to 46 Group on the success of the exercise.

Pilots and navigators were sent to South Cerney to view instructional films on the operation of Gee,[4] Rebecca[5] and Eureka[6] on the morning of the 19th, followed by glider tugging training to complete the day. Crews were sent to Netheravon over the next couple of days for various training missions, supply dropping (roller conveyers[7]) on the 20th and pannier dropping on the 21st.

Dakota KG366 took off from Broadwell on the 20th on an authorised flight to Doncaster piloted by Flight Lieutenant Mountford. The following day, on the return flight the aircraft crashed near Watlington, Oxfordshire, and all the crew perished. These included Mountford, Flying Officer Levings, Flying Officer Beck, Flying Officer Robertson and Flying Officer Falloon. This was the first fatal accident that had happened since the transition to 46 Group of the five squadrons; it would not be the last.

Six aircraft from 'A' Flight, 271 Squadron left Down Ampney for Errol between Perth and Dundee, Scotland, on the morning of the 23rd for their participation in Exercise Snowshoe (supply dropping to the Army). The DZ was set up in a valley roughly 6 miles north-west of Ballater Bridge. The first morning trip on the 24th was somewhat disrupted as the DZ location was changed, but the message did not get relayed to all crews from the previous evening briefing. Five aircraft got airborne for the first run, two made a good drop, their supplies straight on to the DZ, while the remaining three identified the DZ as the weather was clear, and dropped their panniers in the correct location. It was just a shame that the DZ location was changed to approximately 1½ miles away from where their panniers had landed. That afternoon's operation was somewhat different as the correct DZ was known by all crews and experience gained on the morning run gave valuable knowledge that they shared before take-off. All aircraft successfully dropped all their panniers on to the DZ.

The next task for 271 Squadron was Exercise Bizz II, the object of which was to drop elements of the 3rd Parachute Brigade on to the DZ near Watchfield. Ten aircraft were involved in paratrooper and container drops out of Down Ampney, for which the Dakotas were fitted with containers loaded on to bomb racks[8] on the outside of the wings. The route was Christchurch, followed by an out to sea leg, feet dry at Bridport GRV, Wotton Basset RV, DZ then return to Ampney. No. 271 Squadron dropped 148 troops, who all landed safely on to the DZ, although there were two refusals who did not jump and were taken back to the airfield. RAF Broadwell squadrons also took part with thirty-three Dakotas; sixteen from 512 Squadron and seventeen from 575, these crews flew in three Vic formations at thirty-second intervals. Their task was to deploy 175 troops along with containers and bicycles. Take-off was at 17.10, with dropping scheduled for 19.00. Following the same route as 271 Squadron, they arrived over the DZ on time and the first paratrooper jumped at 19.00 exactly. Even though the weather was not particularly good, with a slight haze above the DZ, the conditions for the jump were near ideal as there was none or little wind. Containers were released with no issues, but the loaded bicycles were proving a might problematic to get out of the aircraft successfully! All aircraft returned to their home base, via the same outbound route.

An accident occurred on the 25th at Purton, Gloucestershire, when a Dakota flown by Sergeant Moody was in collision with another aircraft flown by Flight Sergeant Sanderson. Moody managed to get his aircraft safely back to base, even though it was slightly damaged. However, Sanderson's Dakota lost control and took a direct path earthbound, killing all those onboard instantly. Flight Sergeant F.A. Shakespeare, Sergeant G.T. Fennell, Flight Sergeant J.H. Sanderson, LAC H.A. Stone, AC2 J. Winder and AC2 J.E. Markey were the crew who perished on that fateful day.

No. 233 Squadron were kept active on the 27th when they sent fifteen aircraft to RAF Cottesmore, where 290 troops from the 1 Division were flown to DZ ref 605672-61595 for a timed jump at 11.34. The Dakotas then landed at Netheravon, where the same troops emplaned for the return flight to Cottesmore, arriving at 16.00. This operation was repeated on the 31st, when once again 15 aircraft were sent to Barkston Heath for 269 paratroopers to be dropped at Netheravon at 12.34, both drops deemed successful.

Night flying was introduced to 48 Squadron during the 25th to increase the number of crews from a total of twelve who were proficient in this activity. This progressed well and by the month end the total flying hours were at a credible fifty-two hours and twenty minutes. The first of many lectures was held on the last day of the month.

The subject was instruction on MI9 techniques and instruction if ever anyone was in the unfortunate position of being shot down over enemy-held territory. Half the squadron attended this first lecture due to limited space and flying activities. Flight Lieutenant Hartley as Station Intelligence Officer, delivered the necessary information.

On the 26th, 575 Squadron put up thirteen aircraft for low-level cross-country formation flying, while 512 Squadron continued with glider towing. This type of training continued for the rest of the month, while both squadrons at Broadwell received and sent more aircraft to RAF Hendon and RAF Doncaster for modification work.

While March was productive for 48 Squadron, there were two taxiing accidents that marred an otherwise perfect start to operations. That said though it was somewhat surprising that there were not more accidents because the airfield was still in a state of construction, with various added obstacles scattered around the location that caused additional hazards for the crews.

The 27th brought more bad news as an Oxford[9] that was conducting night Gee training had found that bad weather was enclosing in on Down Ampney and that there were weather diversions in place to use RAF Little Rissington as an alternative landing field. However, this was incorrect and fog was in evidence at Rissington, where visibility was poor. The Oxford continued on its approach but crashed into buildings, killing the three crew, Pilot Sergeant Reynolds, first Navigator Flight Lieutenant Shannon and second Navigator Sergeant Dorn.

On the 29th, 512 Squadron received Dakotas KG407, KG480, KG486 and KG422 from Doncaster and the modifications unit, but had allocated FL603, FL627, FL630, FL632, FZ548, FZ550, FZ556, FZ563, FZ568, FZ569 and FZ627 to be sent out to Hendon for modification work to begin.

For the remainder of the month, it was a case of crews and aircraft being transferred around between different squadrons, some being posted out of 46 Group. General flying training continued at bases and was focused on Netheravon for any paratrooper DZ flights, while glider collections did continue to bolster requirements at all groups' respective airfields. A photographer from South Cerney visited Down Ampney to take the crew's pictures for their fake identity papers, in case of capture at any time in the future. This task would soon be carried out for all crews associated with and based at any of the squadrons at Broadwell and Blakehill Farm.

Chapter 2

Intensive Training and Joint Exercises (March–May)

No. 233 Squadron at Blakehill Farm were progressing well with their training, rapidly attaining the same levels as the other squadrons within group. The construction work was almost complete and flying activities were not impeded by these final stages of the build.

April continued in the same vein as March ended, with more continuation training and glider towing. This also involved a dummy trial that took place for Operation Otis, this was due to take place on the first of April and was to have involved all squadrons. The activities took a whole day of preparation, but it was decided that the gliders required modifications and fittings to be carried out before participation. Unfortunately, none were available, so the operation was cancelled. Bad weather curtailed flying on the first day and when the same thing happened on the second day Otis was cancelled permanently.

Nine aircraft from 233 Squadron took part in Exercise Heth V on the 7th, the dropping of 147 paratroopers of the 1 Division in Vic formations of three lines astern. The drop was made on to the DZ and it was a success. The weather was fine, crews also using this as a navigational exercise.

Exercise Dreme was under way to get crews fully capable with their individual navigation and accurate timings by moonlight. This involved aircraft from four squadrons, fifteen crews being allocated from each at Down Ampney and Broadwell. All aircraft were launched from their home airfields in quick succession but quickly recalled as the operation was cancelled straight after take-off due to bad weather and cloudy skies. The objective of this exercise was to perform a simulated night-time glider towing training scenario, but other factors had come into play to curtail ops.

When the weather allowed, general flying continued by day and night until 9 April. Exercise Tour was carried out, with 48 Squadron putting up seventeen aircraft, and 271 Squadron supplying one more at eighteen. They were once again joined by aircraft from 512 and 575 Squadrons, who supplied eighteen and eleven aircraft respectively. The aim of Tour was to practise night-time navigation and timings, as Dreme had intended. This time the aircraft progressed further than completing a circuit and landing, as they were airborne for three hours and forty-five minutes on a route Down Ampney/Broadwell–Rothwell–Westley–Bury St Edmunds–Braintree–Aylesbury–Harford Bridge–Andover Aerodrome–Netheravon. One of 512 Squadron's Dakotas, KG369, crashed at 02.02 near Chedworth, Gloucestershire, and all the crew were killed. These were Flying Officer Brummwell, Sergeant Eastell, Pilot Officer Teed and Sergeant Smith.

Nos 48 and 271 Squadrons launched all aircraft within half a minute, although the weather was not the best and two aircraft failed to reach their targets and drop zone. A further six aircraft were up to a minute late from the timings, the rest of the group arriving shortly after. Some of the Dakotas from 48 Squadron found that they had drifted and were over London, to their surprise. They were fortunate as there were no raids on the capital that night and therefore the barrage balloon[10] defences were set at a low altitude and did not interfere with the aircraft routing through! Thirty-four aircraft made their return to base and landed. Even though there were some issues during the exercise, overall it was assessed as a success.

More crews were despatched to Netheravon for supply drop training and the South Cerney photographer visited Down Ampney to complete the fake identity cards with crews, who were dressed in their civvies.

There was a slight incident with a glider at Down Ampney on the 6th. While being towed aloft during a training flight, the glider separated from its tug aircraft at 100ft as the tow rope had come adrift from the Dakota, and the glider was left to its own devices. Thankfully the pilot was alert and made an instant crash-landing, although this happened outside the airfield perimeter. No one was injured, but the glider did suffer some damage.

Local glider tugging was conducted on the 10th during daylight hours at Ampney and Blakehill. It was intended to carry on into the night, but once again the weather had different ideas and flying was curtailed for the day. Broadwell did manage to put fourteen aircraft up in the afternoon to demonstrate the whole squadron performing a mass supply container dropping exercise and 233 Squadron continued with glider towing into the night.

One bit of information was shared with crews by the station armourer at Down Ampney, namely the art of placing a destruction bomb aboard the Dakota if the need arose to destroy the aircraft following a crash-landing in enemy-held territory. This was well received by all who attended, but nobody ever wanted to be in this situation!

Captain Instone of MI9[11] arrived once again at Ampney to give a lecture on escape and evasion tactics. He gave two talks to crews, one in the morning, the other an afternoon affair. The lecture was rather poignant, as Instone had managed to escape from the enemy. This seemed to go down well with everyone, as they felt somewhat privileged to be given the talk by somebody who knew his subject well. There was a lot of emphasis on making sure that security was maintained, and that all imparted information should remain with the crews. There were a few souls who felt they had to talk or write about this, but the powers that be quickly became aware and the matter was swiftly dealt with.

Nos 512 and 575 Squadrons were flying almost daily operations involving cross-country glider towing, day and night, as well as low-level cross-country flights to hone their skills further. Navigation flights were also performed and during the middle of April they were starting to perform container dropping on to DZs.

On the 13th five crews from 'A' Flight, 512 Squadron were involved in carrying out container dropping, while crews from other flights were also engaged in formation flying including light and heavy glider tows. Crews then flew short cross-country and simulated troop drops at dusk. There was good weather and visibility with no cloud and with a direct route from the DZ to base as aircraft were scheduled to land and arrive, three aircraft every five minutes. The whole squadron was airborne and, in the circuit, 'A' Flight called up exactly on time and filtered into the stream to land successfully. Sergeant Turnbull, who was piloting Horsa LG696, managed to undershoot the flarepath upon landing at Down Ampney and crashed into the corner of the squadron drying room. This burst the boiler as well as wrecking the corner of the building. Luckily, even though the glider was severely damaged, no injuries were sustained, but the building was out of commission for a time while repairs were carried out.

The first operational mission for the Dakotas of 46 Group fell to three aircraft from 575 Squadron, when on the 17th a leaflet dropping mission was undertaken. The target was the Vire river area just south-east of Cherbourg. The Dakotas used were FZ695, crewed by Flying Officer P.R. Sandford, Flying Officer J.V. Chitty, Warrant Officer P. Siddons and Warrant Officer E.T. Fennell; KG402, Wing Commander T.A. Jefferson, Flight Lieutenant R.E. Charlton, Flying Officer C.F. Plimmer and Pilot Officer E.F. Waight; and the third Dakota KG310 had Flying Officer J.W. Furley, Flying Officer R.T. Hamlyn, Flight Sergeant W.F. Watts and Pilot Officer W.A. Stacey. The weather was good for this first mission, but there was cloud cover at 3,000ft preventing any view of the ground over the target area. The crews, though, did manage to drop 400,000 leaflets in the general vicinity of the target area.

Flying activities continued at pace both by day and night until the 17th, when Exercise Roger commenced. This was a joint venture between 48 and 233 Squadrons and both units put up eighteen aircraft respectively. No. 233 Squadron put up twenty-four aircraft for large-scale formation flying on the 15th to practise for exercise Mush, which was scheduled to start in a few days.

No. 271 Squadron experienced another accident during night-time flying on the 17th. Dakota FZ552 took off on glider towing training when the aircraft took a steep climbing turn once airborne. The glider found it impossible to keep up with the Dakota and the glider pilot released his craft and managed to make a safe landing. Unfortunately, the Dakota went into a dive and hit the ground, killing all on board. Flight Sergeant F.E. Moody, Flight Sergeant H.J. Ralph, Warrant Officer J.A. Brown, and Sergeant R.J.F. Sackarley were lost that night. The same day an aircraft from 575 Squadron crashed while undergoing glider tugging, with the three crew injured and hospitalised.

On 20 April came the next phase for the squadrons when Operation Mush was initiated. This was a large-scale co-operation with the Army, with many different units involved. No. 48 Squadron were dropping paratroopers from 1 and 4 Brigades near Southrop Airfield, while 271 Squadron were releasing airborne troops in the same location. Timings for the drop were very specific, set for 08.34 to 08.37 on the morning of the 21st. Twenty aircraft were utilised for the dropping of paratroopers and an additional ten were in use for roller conveyor supplies. The morning drop was conducted successfully, all troops landing safely, with containers of arms and ammunition. It was intended that ten aircraft from each squadron were to drop panniers later that night, but the weather closed in, and the visibility deteriorated so the drop was brought forward to 18.00. Even though the change in time did make the drop somewhat easier, it was still an achievement for all the crews involved and the exercise was deemed successful, with all tasks completed.

More squadrons took part in their first operational mission under their new alignment to Transport Command. Starting on the 22nd and every night through to the morning of 26 April, aircraft were tasked with leaflet-dropping raids over enemy-occupied territory, under the mantle Operation Nickel.

The first nights raids for 271 Squadron were carried out by Dakota FZ549 piloted by Wing Commander M. Booth, Flight Lieutenant R. Johnson, Flying Officer J. Wallis and Flying Officer R.H.J. Horner, who dropped leaflets on Laval. Dakota KG340, piloted by Flight Lieutenant D.S. Lord, Flying Officer D.C Agar, Flying Officer D.I. Macdonnel and Pilot Officer E. Ballotyne, targeted Argentan from 8,000ft. Dakota FZ634 Piloted by Major P.S. Houbert, Flight Lieutenant R. Fellowes, Flight Lieutenant D. Grant and Sergeant M. Butterworth, dropped their leaflets on to Bayeux.

These drops were repeated the following night, and again on the 23rd and 24th when a group of aircraft took to the skies to perform leaflet drop over Tours. The weather closed in at Ampney, with all three aircraft diverting into Harwell upon their return.

Aircraft used on the 24th were:

KG367: Flight Lieutenant G. Crawford, Flying Officer J.C. White, Flying Officer J. Orr and Flying Officer J.C. Jarvis.
FL364: Flight Lieutenant J.C. Cooke, Pilot Officer J.S. Sargent, Pilot Officer W. Early and Warrant Officer H.K. Robertson.
KG340: Squadron Leader R.O. Altmann, Flight Sergeant Shearwood, Flying Officer R.H.J. Horner and Squadron Leader Bridgewood, the target was Bayeux, once again nothing to report and all aircraft making a successful return to base.

The last night of the operation (25th) saw the last of the leaflet-dropping missions, when three aircraft took off, one to drop on to Laval and the other two to Tours. Dakotas and crews assigned were:

KG365, Flying Officer Flather, Warrant Officer Oakley, Sergeant Hope and Flying Officer Miller, flew a successful mission and dropped on to Laval. KG444, Flying Officer Edwards, Flight Lieutenant Wallis, Flight Sergeant Green and Flight Sergeant Randall experienced problems with navigation equipment and did not reach Tours, so discharged its load on to the Sarthe area and took an additional two hours before returning to base. The final aircraft of the flight, KG347, crewed by Flight Lieutenant McLoed, Flying Officer Bodwin, Flying Officer Shannon and Flying Officer Mundy, also had difficulties with its Gee equipment over the Channel and as instructed returned to base without dropping leaflets.

No. 48 Squadron also took part in the operation and the first night (22nd) was the only one when aircraft saw anything of significance when crews witnessed tracer and star shells[12] off the coast of Cherbourg. Two aircraft encountered difficulties with their Gee apparatus and had to turn back, while the remainder of the force continued to their target with no reports of anything untoward taking place.

Fires were also seen around Mayenne and an air raid was observed at Southampton, where two enemy aircraft were seen crashing into the sea. The mission was scheduled to take place again for the third consecutive night, and the targets this time were Argentan and Laval. Again one aircraft returned to base with Gee issues, but the remaining four continued on and completed the mission.

No. 575 Squadron continued their Nickel missions to drop leaflets over northern France on the 22nd, with four aircraft taking part: KG402, KG327, KG363 and FZ695. KG402 and KG327 again focused on the Vire river south of the Cherbourg peninsula, where they dropped 92,000 leaflets. The other two aircraft concentrated on the area around Saint-Lô, where 52,800 leaflets were successfully released. All aircraft returned successfully.

On 28 April, twenty aircraft from 48 and 271 Squadrons released gliders over Down Ampney in honour of the AOC in Command Transport Command, Sir Frederick Bowhill GBE KCB CMG and DSO, who visited the base. All aircraft got airborne within twenty-six minutes and all crews and ground staff were duly congratulated by the commander-in-chief on the way the display was presented and carried out.

Operation Bullseye was held on the 30th and involved the sobering task of fitting stretchers and practising loading and unloading casualties into and out of the aircraft, a precursor to what the future would hold for all squadrons within the group.

April was also the month that crews started to train in earnest on their other task of glider towing. Aircraft and crews obtained valuable experience in this objective, both during day and night, all crews completing this part of their training.

No. 512 Squadron were involved in night flying from 1 May, six of their crews employed in light and heavy glider towing. Twenty-four aircraft were busy in the afternoon on an NF test[13] in preparation for their next exercise. No. 575 Squadron were also gainfully employed with two aircraft on air test, another on a cross-country navigational flight and one other doing practice Rebecca training. Exercises Firefly and Bullseye were in operation for 271 Squadron for both day and night from the 1st, although the night flying was curtailed because the weather was too wet and windy. This was a mixture of Gee navigation and cross-country flights. The weather did not improve and by the 3rd the exercise was cancelled.

Shrewton on Salisbury Plain was used for an exercise, where 48 Squadron simulated drops on 3 May. A new type of drop zone was tried but insufficient information was given to the squadron, the aircraft approached the target from the wrong end and confusion abounded. It showed the need for more detail to be afforded to the crews from higher authority prior to future operations. All the aircraft were airborne for three hours after a 22.00 take-off. No. 575 Squadron arrived at Netheravon on the afternoon of the 3rd with fifteen gliders in tow, this was for a glider and troop-dropping exercise, which was carried out successfully.

On 5 May, Exercise Confirmation II which was carried out during the night, with 271 and 48 Squadrons putting up fifteen aircraft, as well as the Blakehill Farm and Broadwell squadrons. The purpose of this was for every aircraft to drop a container at a specified DZ (Map Ref. 2215635) at a height of 300ft above MSL.[14] One of 271 Squadron's aircraft did not reach the DZ, so returned to base. The drop was only under moonlight conditions with no ground aids, take-off commencing at 00.15 and 01.42 and with the drops taking place at 02.35 to 04.02. The route was Base–Gillingham–Taunton–Hartland Point–St Govan's headland–Berrow–TRV–[15]DZ and return. All aircraft returned safely to their respective airfields. The exercise was deemed successful, but the accuracy was recorded as not particularly good.

Paratroopers of the Polish 1st Independent Paratrooper Brigade were the next customers for 48, 271, 512 and 575 Squadrons on the 7th and 8th of the month. Fifteen aircraft were in use on the 7th from 48 and ten from 271, 512 supplied nine and 575 added a further fifteen. They dropped the Poles on to the DZ at Kelmscott Airfield between 08.00 and 09.00 under the mantle of Exercise Noggin. The route taken was Base–Alcester–Huntington–Berkhamsted–TRV–DZ. There was an exceptionally early start on the 8th when Exercise Nark got under way at 02.28, dropping the Poles from both the 1st and 22nd Paratrooper Battalions on to a DZ near to Langford. Pathfinder aircraft from each squadron were assigned and took off thirty minutes prior to the main force. The routing was the same as Operation Noggin, only the DZ being different. The Pathfinder aircraft despatched their troops on target and on time, although the main force did encounter some difficulties due to a delay in setting up the DZ, as the markings to guide the main force into the target zone led to a bit of speculation among the air crew. That said, all managed to drop their paratroopers accurately. Unfortunately, an aircraft from 271 Squadron flown by Flight Sergeant Fletcher flew in low and four of the paratroopers were killed and a large number were injured upon hitting the ground. No. 233 Squadron were starting to be more involved in routine training, glider towing and formation flying, with these key operations being performed and honed. The 2nd Battalion, Polish Paratrooper Brigade, were actively involved with 233 Squadron at the beginning of the month, being transported to and inserted into their respective DZ for training, with 162 paratroopers being successfully transported.

There was an instructional day on 9 May, when crews were handed a series of escape aids. Compasses, magnetic buttons, collar studs and escape boxes were issued to all for future operations. On receiving the crews these knew only too well that they would soon be called upon to put all their recent training to good use.

Nos 512 and 575 Squadrons were involved in Exercise Noggin II, which involved nine and ten aircraft respectively from each on a cross-country flight to deploy paratroopers into a specified DZ. A further exercise, Nark II, was instigated for early on the morning of the 11th. Aircraft from every squadron within the group were assigned, and all were airborne between 02.41 and 03.27. Wing Commander Booth (271 Squadron) acted as pathfinder for the flight. The weather was initially misty but cleared as the aircraft approached the DZ at Kelmscott airfield.

Two crews from 271 Squadron were sent to 107 OTU[16] at Leicester East to assist in the training of new crews for 46 Group squadrons. No. 512 Squadron employed twelve crews on night-time map reading. This exercise was to enhance the skills of the crews, who had to perform as a cohesive unit, flying individually at one-minute intervals from Broadwell. All excelled.

The next major milestone in the daily life for 48 and 271 Squadrons took place on 15 May. The order of business was the squadron's bi-monthly aircrew meeting, held in the briefing room. Wing Commander T.F.U. Lang started proceedings by detailing that all duty crews were to be on call twenty-four hours a day, sleeping was to be in the crew room and in the operational requirements they were to render all assistance in gathering crews for briefings and interrogation.

Intelligence officer Flying Officer Dollin then took centre stage and briefly outlined that everyone needed to abide by the strict censorship measures in place, stressing the need to maintain security at all costs. Dollin then turned his attention to something that had been reported and duly mentioned. There had been instances on recent Nickel raids of one or two cases of packaged leaflets that had been discharged from aircraft without first having their paper wrappings removed. This was obviously intended to hasten the unloading, but to throw the whole bag in one swoop would have done very little in spreading the message contained in the leaflets over a large area. It would also have the potential of inadvertently hitting a hapless individual on the ground and at least giving him one hell of a headache. If though it did have the good fortune to land on the head of a German soldier and break his neck, it would have been a worthwhile achievement, but this was not a practical way to deal with the enemy, or a good way to spread the cause among the locals. Either way, Dollin added, this practice must stop and the leaflets were to be distributed over the largest possible area, so the packages must be unwrapped and dropped as small parcels!

During the middle part of May, RAF Broadwell saw an increase in the number of flying hours. Day flying was still exceeding night flying by an average of three to one, but the intensity was starting to increase towards the end of the month. Loads that were being carried also changed as more flights were taking place, with panniers being despatched from the aircraft. Modifications were continuing at Hendon, and the aim was for all squadrons to have aircraft of universal capabilities as soon as possible.

The next few days were quiet for all, with local flying for most. This helped to keep the number of flying hours up, with cross-country flights on a crew-by-crew basis for individual training programmes. Squadrons continued with cross-country glider towing during the days, while night flying was cancelled due to the weather playing its hand from the 17th. Lectures were also held out in the morning by Flight Lieutenant Dean relating to Allied prisoners and the interrogation methods employed by the Germans, sharing most valuable advice for a prisoner of war. The tactics changed on the 18th as 271 Squadron started pannier dropping on the local DZ during the days and went back to glider towing at night.

Things started to change somewhat on the 19th, with censorship fully in place within 46 Group, following field censorship a few days previously. Each flight was assigned an officer to assist with the daily task of ensuring all letters were fully censored prior to 11.00, as per the regulations. There was certainly no delay with personnel getting their letters despatched before the time deadline came into force. Exercise Charlie was held, which involved formation flying. There were ten aircraft from 271 Squadron and nineteen from 48 Squadron, with all gliders landing safely back at base. There was a slight incident during the flight when one aircraft was hit by lightning, although damage was minimal.

Nos 575 and 512 Squadrons were employed in the afternoon on the demonstration Operation Exeter. Both employed fifteen aircraft to show their paratrooper deployment capability, which was witnessed by the King, Queen and Princess Elizabeth and officers from SHAEF.[17]

Squadrons were involved in glider towing and pannier drops on the local DZs close to their own airfields. The Station Defence Scheme was implemented on State C readiness for all personnel allocated to Down Ampney. Later in the day a Whitley crash-landed on the base with its starboard engine on fire.

The undercarriage was damaged and duly failed, with the aircraft continuing to travel down the runway on its belly before finally coming to a stop. The fire was quickly dealt with, all exited safely and nobody was injured.

The next day Exercise Consternation took place, which involved seventy-five Horsa gliders that landed over a ten-minute window at Netheravon airfield. Fifteen of the gliders were towed by aircraft of 48, 271, 512 and 575 Squadrons, which represented 46 Group. The exercise was deemed a success, even though the weather was not favourable. The release of the gliders was made between 16.59 and 17.07, with the aircraft continuing to Down Ampney to drop their tow ropes in a five-minute window of 17.25–17.30. The route was Tetbury–Cirencester–Banbury–Aylesbury–Hungerford (TRV)–Netheravon, with a return route of Trowbridge–Base. One aircraft had to turn back almost immediately after take-off as requested by its glider pilot due to technical issues. Once the ropes were dropped the aircraft continued straight into another exercise, Gulliver, a navigational operation that lasted well into the night. This was to allow wireless operators the training required to employ their skills to aid with the route and course of the aircraft. The route taken for Gulliver involved flying from base to Warminster–Newquay–St Mary's Isle–Chicken Rock, Isle of Man–Rhyl, then returning to base. This exercise was a first as nursing orderlies were carried to give them experience of long flights, a precursor to what they would be experiencing soon.

Something was brewing and talks seemed to be taking greater importance around the various units. RASC[18] personnel were starting to be given air experience flights, ranging from local circuits to cross-country sorties. This was obviously to prepare them for missions that would become more apparent as time dictated.

Things began to change from 27 May. All leave was cancelled until further notice and the only flying that was now deemed necessary was local and air testing as all training was considered complete with all crews fully qualified. Crews who had not had their intelligence photographs taken were instructed to proceed to either Boscombe Down or Pershore to get the matter resolved as soon as possible. Crews were told to ensure they had all their vaccinations an inoculations and that they attended all lectures. Lastly, more nursing orderlies (Flying Nightingales) were detailed to gain air experience flights, various aircraft being employed from the Avro Anson through to the Oxford and Dakotas if available.

With no flying and no leave, crews started using the time to inspect all their personnel kit, ensuring they had their escape aids and photographs suitable stored.

Another lecture took place for 48 and 271 Squadron crews on the 13th, this time in ASR[19] and was given by Flight Lieutenant Fletcher, a controller with 11 Group during the Battle of Britain. The talk discussed those difficult times when the Allies were in a completely different situation to the current one. As a prelude to Germany's potential invasion of England, Britain's air defences had to be destroyed prior to any landing attempt. Fletcher said that was not going to be the case for the invasion of the Continent as the Allies' massive air campaign had destroyed most of the German defences and driven the Luftwaffe from the coastal areas and pushed them further inland. While the belief was possibly considered to be genuine, history has shown that the invasion was not going to be a pushover and the Germans were by no means a defeated nation. The will to fight was still strong and the Allies were going to encounter a determined foe.

Chapter 3

Something's Afoot (June)

June started with good weather. Security was also on the agenda and the crews were advised to use and practice Rebecca as much as they could. ALO[20] Captain Ormsby-Gore explained the latest signalling code now in place for all air-to-ground communication going forward.

All crews were subjected to a night vision check and testing. Bases were also sealed,[21] which confirmed to many that Zero Hour was close, although nobody knew when. Censorship was further tightened, with all mail now being sent to the base censor to be screened before being forwarded. Telegrams and registered letters were also subjected to the rules of censorship, and telephone calls were closed for all.

There was time for all crews to concentrate on their own personal fitness as well as any other medical issues. The dental van appeared outside the crew room at Ampney and this proved to be popular and its services were in high demand. Of course, this had no relevance to the two attractive nurses, or the fact that the van served the best cup of tea that had been seen at the base for quite a time! The crew's enthusiasm to let the dentist loose was a small price to pay for the rewards on offer. Morale was extremely high during these few days of the dentist's visit.

On the 2nd the last few personnel were flown out to Pershore by 512 Squadron Dakota FZ690 from Broadwell for inoculations, etc. At Down Ampney, there was an air of expectation circling the airfield. Rumours abounded that there was a big operation imminently, and that the intelligence officer had been tipped off and knew about the plan. The lack of any training for all units, no leave and all the recent lectures, was definitely leading to something. Every time the intelligence officer was seen, there were whispers between any assembled personnel. The braver ones actually confronted him and asked him outright if anything was planned. The intelligence officer kept his lips fully closed, as he was expected to. It wouldn't have mattered though if he had spoken; he did not know anything anyway!

Everyone's curiosity was pricked even further at 14.00 when the message came through that all three airfields, Blakehill Farm, Broadwell and Down Ampney, were fully sealed and nobody was allowed to leave until further notice. Any personnel who were out of the camp at this time were rounded up by the local constabulary and returned to base. A few of the officers involved in the repatriation later revealed that when they were accosted by the local bobbies, they had to make quick recollections of any potential misdemeanours that they may have any knowledge of. They were very relieved that they were only being taken back to their airfield! By the end of the day the bases were quiet with a full complement of personnel all confined and waiting for the next announcement.

The following day, 3 June, news started to be released to certain crews as to the next phase for the squadrons. These were first operations of D-Day, the opening up of the second front. Crews were on hand to receive the first set of briefings at 09.00 then 10.00, an understanding of the roles that all the squadrons were going to play during this important operation. Crews were shown general maps of the area, as well as given specific maps on individual DZ with full descriptions and explanations. Crews were also taken in small numbers into the intelligence libraries to view scale models (12ft × 4ft) of their intended DZ, along with photographs and maps. This was intended to aid the crews in identifying the correct area for the gliders to set down. Another aid that afforded the crews from 48 and 271 Squadrons at Down Ampney was the running in the afternoon of a film that was continually on which showed the approach to their respective DZ, as well as other DZs within the local area. This was screened at three times normal speed, with one approach having a night filter on to show differences during the hours of darkness. Crews did feed back that this film was useful, but only showed one run over another DZ, and that more time dedicated to DZ V would have given more time for the crews to concentrate on their respective target.

Aircraft were then painted with two thick black and three white stripes on both the upper and lower wings and fuselage. This were the standard markings for all aircraft operated by the Allies over enemy territory and was being rapidly applied to every one that was to venture over the Normandy coast and inland areas. The need for cleaning brushes was never as high both before and after this time around early June 1944, as that was the easiest way to apply the paint quickly!

On 4 June a final lecture was held for aircrew on the subject of security by the squadrons' intelligence officers. There was an 09.00 start and all assembled flying crew were issued with escape purses.[22] They were then told to stand by for final instructions that were due to be issued in the afternoon. AOC Air Commodore Fiddament DFC addressed all later in the afternoon, congratulating the crews on their training, which was carried out in a much-reduced timeframe. He passed on his words of encouragement and stressed the need for security, but wished them all Godspeed for the upcoming operation.

Unfortunately, due to adverse weather conditions that night's operation was going to have to be postponed for twenty-four hours until the weather cleared over the Normandy coast. The crews, eager to get things into motion, used the time wisely to study the model and maps to improve their understanding of the area of the operation. Understandably, there was no flying on this particular day. Some aircrews were taken to a paratrooper transit camp that was close to their bases and met the troops they would be carrying over to France.

On 5 June all crews attended refresher briefings in the morning. Operation Tonga (D-Day) was scheduled to take place that night and continue into 6 June, weather permitting. In the afternoon the CO of the 3rd Parachute Brigade, Brigadier J. Hill, addressed all the crews at Down Ampney on the upcoming operation and gave good cheer and confidence to all participating in that evening's tasks. He said that the superiority of the Allies over the enemy's forces was so great that they were not going to stop them in their activities and duties.

Operation Tonga Objectives

No. 48 Squadron were allocated thirty aircraft to be configured for paratrooper operations, and these were scheduled to deploy their passengers at DZ V. Their route out of Down Ampney would take them to Chedworth–Enstone–Fairoaks–Worthing (GRV). Once Worthing was reached, they would continue to position 4959N 0000W, then to TRV on the coast of France, position 4917N 0008W, then on into the DZ. Once the DZ was reached and all troops were despatched, the aircraft would fly through positions 4914N 0000W and 4929N 0030W to cross the French coast to the north of Ypreville–Biville, after skirting Le Havre and its well-known flak belt on its southernmost point.

Seven crews from 271 Squadron were allocated to tow gliders across to France. A 15.00 briefing was held that detailed the mission, with take-off down for an early morning departure for a civil twilight release time of minus 4.35 hours before D-Day. The weather looked decidedly suspect for the mission, although the men from the Met Office gave great confidence that all would work out fine, which all duly did.

The night of 5 June and the early part of the following morning brought together all the crews who had been training intensely for the past months. Prior to the launch the commanding officer raced around to the assembled aircraft and delivered a personal message from General Eisenhower, which relayed good wishes and good luck to all taking part. The thirty aircraft from 48 and 271 Squadrons got airborne from Down Ampney between 23.20 and 23.33 and headed out on their prescribed track. The mood in the aircraft was one of excitement and nerves. The squadrons had 517 paratroopers, with a full complement of kit and 92 containers of arms and ammunition aboard, with all bar four managing to make the jump on the DZ. Glider tugs were also detailed to tow gliders down to Normandy, although they carried very few men but were packed with equipment including, jeeps, guns, motorcycles etc.

From the beginning of June all crews at Blakehill Farm had been put on to general readiness, with all aircraft air tested on the 2nd to make sure that everything was ready for the upcoming operations. It was a captain's responsibility to ensure that his crew had all the necessary equipment available. At 16.00 on the 3rd the base was completely sealed with nobody allowed to enter or leave, unless on official business and with the authority of the commanding officer. Guards were posted around the base and the camp had limits in place around the boundary lines. Orders were received the following morning from Group HQ and crews were assigned their part in Operation Tonga. Major General Browning, Air Commodore Fiddament, Air Vice Marshal Collier and Air Vice Marshal Edmonds attended the briefing and were made aware of the targets for 233 Squadron, who were to deploy with thirty aircraft, six towing gliders while the remaining twenty-four carried paratroopers from the six airborne divisions.

On the morning of the 5th crews with paratroopers and both groups then preceded to the briefing headquarters to ascertain their duties once in France. Crews had memorised details of the drop zone, understanding every minute part of the route to complete a successful mission. Air Chief Marshal Sir Trafford Leigh-Mallory accompanied by Air Commodore Fiddament visited the base and spoke briefly to aircrews. They stressed the fact that the record of the squadron during its period since converting and training to their new role had surpassed all expectations and as a result 233 Squadron had been given the envious choice of DZ K, the furthest inland drop zone within Normandy. The squadron were to drop their paratroopers directly on to the DZ and as this target was of great importance their drops needed to be accurate and on time. The squadron must and would not fail the confidence of the airborne forces.

Final briefing commenced at 20.00 for the operation, all preparations being carried out and checked with crews assembling by their aircraft, which had been marshalled earlier that day, Gliders were hooked up to their tugs and all paratroopers started to board. At 22.50 the first of six glider-towing Dakotas, Captained by Wing Commander Morrison AFC got airborne, followed in quick succession by the remaining five. Aircraft carrying the paratroopers and led by Squadron Leader Miller got airborne at 23.11 and all twenty-four were airborne within five minutes. They routed out from base to Chedworth, then Littlehampton, and positioned off the coast of Normandy at TR7, then on to the DZ.

The gliders were released over the area between 00.50 and 00.53 and the paratroopers jumped between 00.54 and 00.58½, 407 of them complete with kit bags and containers dropping into the area north-west of Touffréville. Light flak was encountered and seen over the French coast, especially in the Le Havre and Cabourg areas and inland in the Caen area. Two Dakotas were lightly damaged, and another two aircraft failed to complete the mission and returned to base. These aircraft were piloted by Flying Officer H.E. Jones and Warrant Officer McCannell. Dakota KG356, which was captained by Flight Officer Jones, along with his crew, Flight Sergeant J.A. Daldorph, Flight Officer I.N. Williams and Warrant Officer C. Engleberg, were approaching the area near to Caen at a height of approximately 600ft and were met with heavy anti-aircraft fire, roughly 4 miles from the DZ. The aircraft was hit and ablaze, but undeterred the aircraft continued on its flight and Jones signalled for the paratroopers to jump, which they all successfully did. He then turned and gave the order for the crew to abandon the aircraft. Jones could have saved himself by exiting the aircraft through the pilot's escape hatch. Refusing his parachute when brought to him, he stayed piloting the Dakota to keep it level and allowing his crew to jump to safety. Flying Officer Jones went down with his Dakota and perished in the ensuing crash. Engleberg was also still on the Dakota when it crashed and it appears that Jones had made an attempt to crash-land to try to save them both. Even though Jones was killed instantly upon impact, Engleberg was still alive and was pulled to safety by local farmers Alice Duhamel and her son Arthur. They took the injured flyer back to their farm and treated him the best they could. They were joined by two others from the crew, Daldorph and Williams, who were later picked up by an Allied unit, who took them to hospital. Engleberg sadly passed away at the farm and the Duhamels buried him on their land, adorning the grave with flowers. This though did have consequences, for the SS imprisoned both Alice and Arthur, later murdering the son for his part in caring for Engleberg.

Warrant Officer M.M. McCannell, flying Dakota KG429 with his crew, Flight Sergeant A.R. Porter, Flight Sergeant A.T. Downing and Warrant Officer N.I. Berger, got airborne from Blakehill at 23.16 with their paratroopers from 8th Battalion, Parachute Regiment. The route took them close to the canal shipyard near to Colombelles, France, which was heavily defended with flak guns. These took their toll on the aircraft and a direct hit brought it down. All bar one of those on board died in the crash and were interned in a communal grave near to the church of Saint Martins.

The route out followed Chedworth–Littlehampton and positions towards the French coast, which was crossed at Le-Hôme-sur-Mer, then on to Touffréville for the dropping zone. The route back was Ypreville-Bivelle–Életot–Littlehampton–Base. Light flak was seen along the coast of France, especially in the Le Havre and Cherbourg areas and inland towards Caen. Aircraft KG430, captained by Flight Lieutenant Mackie, got held in German searchlights for approximately fifteen to twenty seconds and was subjected to bursts of flak that were to port and around 50 yards from the aircraft, although no hits were registered. Another Dakota, FZ688, piloted by Flying Officer Vince, was slightly damaged over the drop zone by flak. A lot of crews, when passing the French coast, saw many of the coastal batteries at Merville being bombed and later on their return saw the power factory at Caen receiving similar treatment. The crew of KG415, flew by Captain Flight Lieutenant Cody, appeared to see two aircraft going down in flames off the French coast.

No. 512 Squadron were also carrying members of the 6th Airborne Division into Normandy and started getting airborne from 23.15 onwards with the thirty-two aircraft allocated. Its sister unit, 575 Squadron, supplied twenty-one aircraft although these were equipped with paratroopers from the 3rd Parachute Brigade.

No. 512 Squadron's main operation was to drop the 9th Parachute Brigade and members of the 3 Paras (6th Airborne Division) at night on to the DZ behind enemy lines. The target DZ was located 3 miles inland of the coastal entry point approximately halfway between Cabourg and Ouistreham, on the Normandy coast. A heavy coastal battery unit was situated roughly 2 miles in a north-westerly direction from the DZ, and this was the intended target to be destroyed. No. 575 Squadron were also going to be dropping troops, the 13 Brigade, on to a DZ that was slightly south-west of DZ V, the target for troops dropped by 512 Squadron. The 13th (Lancashire) Parachute Battalion were to capture and hold two bridges, one over the canal and the other over the river to the north of Caen. Operation Neptune was the code name assigned to this part of Tonga (Overlord) and was due to commence at 07.00 local.

The lead Dakota, piloted by Wing Commander Coventry, took off at 23.15, followed quickly by the rest of the squadron. The thirty-two aircraft formed up into vics of three aircraft, each in thirty-second intervals. Their route took them towards Enstone and Fairoaks, crossing the coast at Worthing. Aligning on to the beacon at Worthing, the Dakotas started emitting the Letter V to identify the flight. Good visibility was on offer, although there was 10/10ths cloud that had obscured the moon, which made map reading difficult. The next turning point was a DR[23] position a few miles off the north-west tip of Cap D'Antifer, from where they flew towards the coastal entry point for DZ V. Twelve miles from the English coast the Dakotas extinguished all lights to aid self-protection, although because the moon was still obscured formation flying was proving difficult for the crews. However, the black and white stripes painted on the fuselage and wings of all the aircraft participating in Operation Overlord did prove advantageous during low-light conditions. A force of 100 Lancasters had been bombing the gun battery approximately twenty minutes prior to the airborne force appearing over the area, and during the final run large explosions were seen. Light flak was also experienced, coming from the direction of Le Havre, but this tended to fall short and did not affect the formation. Other streams of aircraft entered the coast at similar points and were running up the same channels and entry points towards DZ V. The flak took its toll on one aircraft, and it was seen to crash in flames on the coast. The DZ was clearly identified by most of the flight and crews started to make their first runs on to the target. Troops were dropped on time and within the centre of the DZ. A couple of aircraft had to make second runs to discharge their passengers, and Wing Commander Coventry was forced to make three as on the first two runs a trooper had slipped in the doorway and the jump light had returned to red before they could exit. This third run caused congestion over the DZ and this was quite a problem as some crews reported taking avoiding action to prevent collisions with other Dakotas. There were estimates of 250 aircraft dropping troops in the area at the same time. The target deadline time was 00.50 for the squadrons to drop their troops, 568 in total, which most achieved, although timings to the minute were slightly delayed if crews had to make additional runs. Once complete the formations tended to break and aircraft made their own way back to base. With no injuries or damage reported, the mission was a success.

Twenty-one aircraft were detailed to drop paratroopers and their equipment from the 3rd Paratrooper Brigade at DZ N. This was located on the eastern side of the River Orne between the villages of Ranville, Amfreville and Le Mariquet. The first aircraft were over the DZ between the hours of 00.57 and 01.12 early on 6 June, with all troops dropped successfully. Slight enemy opposition was encountered, with five aircraft sustaining damage from flak, but all returned to Broadwell.

The first glider-tugging aircraft from 48 and 271 Squadrons commanded by Wing Commander Booth got airborne at 22.48 and all were eventually airborne by 23.33. The route down to the DZ was uneventful, until the French coast was reached. Once above enemy-controlled ground a few aircraft experienced light flak and some damage was incurred but all the squadron continued on towards their target. Dakota coded WG (KG414), flown by Pilot Officer Hull, received damage to its rudder, port engine and wing, while aircraft AD (KG338), piloted by Flying Officer McCreanor, was struck in the starboard wing. Dakota AS (KG436), piloted by Flight Lieutenant Smith, was also hit by flak, the port engine taking the hit and subsequently rendered useless. Smith elected to carry on with the operation, bringing the aircraft back across the Channel to make a forced landing at West Malling after some skilful flying. Once on the deck the aircraft's entire electrical system failed, with it becoming totally unserviceable. Aircraft UY, flown by Flying Officer Mackay, was also damaged by flak in the starboard mainplane and fuselage, and Dakota AZ, flown by Flight Lieutenant Stone, was similarly damaged.

All bar one of the aircraft assigned that night carried twelve 20lb bombs and these were dropped upon crossing the French coast. The intention was to force the German gunners to keep their heads down and not to shoot at the approaching force of Dakotas on their journey to the DZ. How much this actually achieved is open to debate, but it certainly would have helped the morale of all on board knowing that this small act was striking a blow against the enemy.

Once at the drop zone the Dakotas released their cargo of paratroopers out into the dark French night, even though three of the men could not jump as one was sick, another was hit in the leg by a stray bullet and the third, the unluckiest of all, was knocked down by his eager companions in the rush to exit the aircraft and was subsequently trampled and knocked unconscious.

When the drop had concluded, all aircraft returned to England by the route prescribed, and once landed all crews were subjected to interrogation and fed back their experiences and the part they had played in the biggest land invasion of all time. The drop zone had been subjected to poor visibility due to smoke from a recently blitzed battery. That, aligned with there being no lights on the DZ or any assistance from Rebecca/Eureka plus the report of an off-track Stirling flying across the path of the Dakotas, did cause some general concerns and was noted in the debrief.

Flying Operations June 5/6 Operation Tonga, the Dropping of Paratroopers

There were several incidents involving flak and machine gun fire that did have an impact on the Dakotas of 48 Squadron. AJ KG321, flown by Squadron Leader McVeigh, received hits to both the wings and body, while AH KG409, flown by Flying Officer Murray. All the aircraft landed safely with no injuries.

Squadron Leader Wheatley-Smith, flying AY KG346, was to experience many hits during the operation and these were so severe that upon crossing the English coast on the return leg his starboard engine cut out and he had to make an emergency landing at Ford Airfield. Despite the substantial damage his aircraft received, there were no injuries. Three more Dakotas received slight damage: AZ KG423, flown by Flight Lieutenant Stone; AR KG417, Flying Officer Wills; and UC KG337, Pilot Officer Pearson. All returned to Ampney.

Additional to the operations at Down Ampney, ten Dakotas were repositioned to Blakehill Farm as 'A' Flight, 271 Squadron, to provide capacity for more paratroopers who were going to be deployed to protect the left flank for the British Second Army landing on the beaches at Normandy.

On 6 June Operation Mallard was under way, which involved thirty-seven Dakotas from 48 and 271 Squadrons towing Horsa gliders containing airborne troops to form an air landing brigade for release at DZ N. This was going to be a very similar operation to Tonga the previous evening, although the personnel and the transportation method would be different. The force was met mid-Channel by overwhelming fighter cover. One pilot said, 'The whole show seemed a damn sight easier than exercises of earlier days!'

There was an incident during take-off involving a glider being towed by Dakota AP KG401, which was being piloted by Flight Lieutenant Alford. All onlookers gasped as it parted company with its starboard wheel just as it got airborne. The combination carried on to its designated target, jettisoning its other wheel when safe and clear over the coast. It went on to land safely at its destination.

The Dakotas taking part in Operation Mallard did not encounter any enemy air activity. There was some light flak though, but although a number of aircraft were hit in the fuselage and wings, all aircraft returned safely. They carried 133 airborne members of the 1st Battalion, Royal Ulster Rifles, along with eleven jeeps, fourteen trailers, twelve motorcycles and thirty-seven bicycles.

During this period 48 Squadron experienced its first loss with the death of wireless operator Sergeant Carr, from the crew of Flying Officer Le Huray on Dakota UV KG426. The aircraft was hit at 21.09 just a couple of minutes after releasing its glider. The impact caused the Dakota's starboard engine to catch fire, which in turn made the aircraft lose considerable height. Le Huray gave the order to jump and he and his co-pilot, Flying Officer Farrell, ran towards the back of the aircraft to exit through the main side access door. Upon reaching the door, they noticed that Flying Officer Woodcock and Sergeant Carr had already exited the aircraft. They also realised they were too low to complete a successful jump, so they elected to stay with the Dakota and crash-land. Quickly returning to the cockpit, they saw that smoke was filling the area and they had difficulty seeing the instruments. Le Huray went to lower the flaps to aid with the impending crash-landing, only to inadvertently lower the undercarriage. This hit the ground, causing the aircraft to ground loop. The shock threw the fiery starboard engine away from the main bulk of the aircraft, which came to a stop a mere 75 yards away from the initial impact! Both Le Huray and Farrell make a swift exit from the burning wreck and bolted towards a safe point approximately 50 yards away, in case the bulk of the fuel within the aircraft took hold and exploded. Once safe, Farrell realised that he had some damage to his leg, and on closer inspection found it had broken in two places. Meanwhile, the two crew members who had jumped clear, Woodcock and Carr, had successfully deployed their parachutes, but they both landed in the Caen Canal. Woodcock saw that Carr was struggling and shouted over to him asking him to hang on, Woodcock freed himself from his parachute and started to make his way to Carr but as he got near, Carr was suddenly dragged below the surface by his chute and was not seen again. After swimming to the bank, Woodcock was helped out of the water by some locals and taken to a nearby house, where he was given whisky, milk and a change of clothes while his own were set to dry. Woodcock did return to the canal the next morning to see if he could see any signs of Carr's parachute or even his body, alas to no avail. Woodcock was led back to the British lines and eventually arrived at the beach. He was taken aboard a landing craft that was heading back to England with returning glider pilots. Transported back to Down Ampney, he met up with Le Huray on this return leg and described the terrible news of what happened to Carr. As for the other incumbent of Dakota KG426, Farrell had been left at a casualty clearing station, but made his way back to Ampney, where he arrived on 17 June.

For Operation Rob Roy four aircraft and crews from 271 Squadron were assigned to drop supplies over DZ N over the night of the 6th and into the morning of the 7th. This took the same routing as Operation Mallard. The aircraft dropped sixty-four panniers weighing 22,400lb and were deployed close to the target area. Once again there was no enemy airborne activity but there was light flak and anti-aircraft fire from friendly forces.

Nineteen aircraft were detailed to deploy troops from the 6th Airlanding Brigade that were being transported across in Horsa gliders, destined to land on LZ N to the east of the River Orne. The Dakotas were over the LZ at approximately 20.57 and released the Horsas on time. Enemy ground fire was experienced, and three aircraft were hit by small round fire that was coming from a wooded area on the western bank of the river. Once the Dakota and glider combinations were over the south-east of Renouville they started to turn to starboard and the gliders were released towards the LZ. A total of 304 troops of the 6th Airborne Division were successfully deployed, including all equipment, jeeps, cycles, trailers and motorcycles. Five Dakotas then returned to base.

Operation Rob Roy

In addition to those aircraft from 271 Squadron, five from 512 Squadron were also detailed to drop supplies on the night of the 6th on to DZ N, which was located east of the River Orne and was in the area between the villages of Ranville, Amfreville and Le Mariquet. On approach to the DZ aircraft were fired on from ships at anchor on the coast. Two Dakotas received damage and had to jettisons their supplies and return to base. The remaining three aircraft continued on to the DZ and successfully despatched fifty-eight panniers of supplies to the ground forces before returning to Broadwell.

Twenty-one aircraft from 233 Squadron were detailed to carry out a resupply mission to the forces of the 6th Airborne Division, which had been deployed the previous night. The DZ was located to the east of the River Orne, the actual dropping area slightly east of Barville, north of Le Mariquet and south-west of Amfreville. Supplies were contained in 371 panniers and included food, ammunition, petrol, radio sets and explosives. There were also eighty-eight bundles of bedding, medical supplies and stretchers. Routing out from Blakehill Farm to Bognor Regis for a Channel crossing, the French coast was intercepted at Franceville-Plage, and on to the DZ. The return leg followed the same track across the French coast, with the Dakotas flying towards Littlehampton and then back to Blakehill.

There was intense but light anti-aircraft fire, which was believed to emanate from friendly vessels that had been subjected to an airborne attack moments before the Dakotas passed overhead. About 1 or 2 miles off the French coast inbound, KG341, piloted by Warrant Officer Bailey, reported the first and second aircraft of the leading vic being hit. KG424, flown by Squadron Leader Wright and crew, were seen taking a turn to starboard and then went down in what looked like a controlled dive, with smoke emitting from both engines. The second Dakota, KG329, containing Flying Officer Wood and crew, were seen to take a direct hit and burst into flames, with the debris falling towards the ground.

Another Dakota, KG441, flown by Flight Lieutenant Lestang and crew, suffered unserviceable electrical systems. The crew persevered and attempted to make the DZ but failed and returned to base. Dakota KG433 (Warrant Officer Saunders) was hit in the fuel tanks and the starboard wing, FZ688 (Warrant Officer Vines) had trouble with the trim tab control, and FZ672 (Squadron Leader Mackenzie) encountered flak in the area around Ouistreham, Le Havre and Cherbourg.

6 June, Operation Neptune – the Insertion of Troops via Parachute and Glider Ops

Overlord[24] was the code name for the operation to secure a foothold on continental Europe, with the aim of inserting a driving force that could ultimately fight its way through France, Belgium, Netherlands and eventually Germany.

Neptune's part was to combine both seaborne and airborne assaults in the general areas of Caen and the Cherbourg peninsula with the objective to capture airfields and other targets within the Caen area of operations. Also, the main objective was to take the port at Cherbourg and protect its use as a future embarkation point for troops and resupply from the UK. The plan was to split these responsibilities into two, with the British to take care of the Caen sector while the US were allocated Cherbourg.

The British Second Army was to carry out an assault on the sector between Asnelles and Ouistreham. The left flank of the British sector was going to be protected by the 6th Airborne Division, which would rest on the Canal de

Caen and would have given the Germans' high ground with which to overlook the area and bring artillery fire on the British forces. The 6th Division were therefore were tasked with denying the enemy the area between the rivers Orne and Dives, north of the road that linked Troarn–Sannerville–Colombelles, which gave advantage in delaying any enemy reserves and reinforcements moving in from Caen, east to west.

Other minor taskings were the capture (intact preferably) of bridges over the Canal de Caen and River Orne close to Benouville, the destruction of bridges over the River Dives, as well as the capture of the fortified coastal battery at Merville, which overlooked the landing beaches near to Ouistreham.

The RAF's role in supplying troops and equipment to lift the 6th Airborne Division into theatre was split between 38 and 46 Groups. The number of aircraft needed for such an operation as this (including glider ops) made it impossible for the RAF to complete alone, so additional resources were supplied by the US Army Air Force.

The lift for the 6th Airborne Division (comprising the 3rd and 5th Parachute Brigades and the 6th Airlanding Brigade) was commanded by Air Vice Marshal L.N. Hollinghurst CB, OBE, DFC and Air Commodore A.L. Fiddament DFC. The glider contingent was under the control of Colonel G.J.S. Chatterton DSO. The aim was to put a formidable force into theatre in one lift, but to place the whole division would entail a two-day operation.

The planning stage for Operation Overlord and Operation Neptune was a joint affair with very close cooperation between the staff allocated to 6th Airborne Division and 38 and 46 Groups. A special secure HQ was allotted at Milston close to Netheravon airfield.

Early in February 1944 the planning had been focusing on the Caen area, which offered the best terrain for airborne landings. The process for setting out DZ and LZ were carried out in a reverse order, the first criteria that needed to be met was the Army's and RAF's requirements. This planning firstly allocated the size of the forces into area, and the airborne requirements to deliver into theatre considering the navigation and the landing issues associated with the gliders. When the DZ and LZ had been selected and the forces allocated this directed the flight plan, which in turn dictated the airfields to be used, ensuring the necessary range of aircraft, weights, number of troops, etc. and so the departure point of the task force.

As stated, Caen had been at the forefront of the planners' minds for Neptune. The area had large clear, level fields that were ideal for landings, although there were two specific targets that had to be covered during the operation. These two places of extreme importance were the bridge at Benouville and the gun battery at Merville, which did not appear to cause any real concerns.

The defences within the areas of the drops were reasonably light with flak positions scattered around the locale. There was the ever-present danger of flak barges around the Canal de Caen, something that was noted to pass on to the crews and forces being deployed.

The plan to insert the 6th Airlanding Brigade in gliders on the night of D-Day minus one, along with one of the two Parachute Brigade groups, all appeared sound. Unfortunately the terrain that led to the LZ and DZs being selected had also featured in the minds of the Germans as obvious places to insert an attacking force. Photos obtained during a reconnaissance sortie on 13 April revealed extensive work taking place over the selected grounds. The fields showed obstructions being placed in those proposed for the landing of the gliders. These were confirmed as anti-air-landing obstacles[25] and forced a radical change from the original plan of insertion on D-Day minus one, to a daylight landing on D-Day itself. The revised plan entailed the 6th Airlanding Brigade being given the additional task of clearing the obstructions from the landing grounds and lanes for the gliders to arrive in the early evening of D-Day.

The airborne plan consisted of the 3rd and 5th Parachute Brigade groups and their objectives, the 5th to land after midnight on the morning of 6 June by jumping into DZ N to operate in the Benouville–Ranville region to hold the area and capture the battery (map reference 107765), then to protect LZ N for glider landings. The 3rd jumped at the same time but on to LZs K and V, protecting the line Troarn–Varaville and hitting the enemy battery at Merville (map reference 155776).

The 6th Airlanding Brigade also had an Airborne Armoured Reconnaissance Regiment aligned with them during the evening of D-Day under the code name of Mallard and at 21.00 a force of 220 Horsa gliders on LZ N and W. They were also accompanied by thirty Hamilcars[26] carrying the recon regiment, who landed on a special strip on LZ N. There were also four additional Hamilcars assigned to carry additional equipment that followed the main force into the area. Stirling tugs also carried containers, which they duly dropped once the main glider force were on the ground and they had despatched their respective gliders. This then completed the landing phase of the 6th Airborne Division on to continental Europe on D-Day. The resupply mission would now take place under the code name of Rob Roy using DZ N as its main focus.

The Flight Plan

Requirements for the allocations of aircraft and gliders to the DZ and LZ being already agreed, the heights and position of glider release points had to be determined. There were a few key facts that had to be addressed prior to the decision being finalised: avoidance of flak and small arms fire, map reading, and the use of ground aids to help the tug aircraft in deciding their position for as long as possible for release. As per most glider operations, the height of 1,500ft AGL[27] was normal, adhered to and selected. Latitude was given to the glider crews for their exact release, and detailed information on the forecast of winds were issued if known, but principally the operation was that as per the training manual. Exceptions were made in respect of the gliders landing on the bridges at Benouville and the battery at Merville. These were allowed to be released at 6,000ft AGL as this gave a much more exact glide path and approach to allow for an extremely difficult landing. In the event of cloud cover the tugs were to stay on the glider track at maximum height until the gliders were within gliding range.

The routing was then planned taking into account the following requirements:

The minimum of turns and the maximum straight run-in for drop and release.
Best use of radio aids (GEE).
Avoidance of flak (big concentration around Le Havre) and of friendly naval forces.
Minimising risk of enemy radar and its detection rate.
Ground aids in friendly territory.
Coordination of forming up tracks allowing for large US airborne forces in the UK and coordinating of all routes with other commands.

All aircraft that were operating within 38 and 46 Groups were fitted with Gee to aid navigation to guide them to their approximate target areas when used in conjunction with Rebecca II as a short-range homing device to pinpoint targets (DZ and LZ). Other aids (Occults[28] and Pundits[29]) were also available and special coded lights that supplemented Eureka beacons at Group RVs.[30] Certain gliders that were on task for special operations were also fitted with Rebecca. Routes were planned where possible to use most of Gee lattice lines and new frequencies were introduced on D-1 to reduce the risk of jamming.

To aid the main force, an advance party from the 22nd Independent Parachute Company were on site to arrange the Eureka beacons at all DZs and LZs. Checks were made and the station homing signals[31] for the beacons were fully utilised to ensure proper functioning prior to the final runs taking place. A concern was oversaturation of the area by the numbers of aircraft in the sky, so all aircraft kept their Rebecca units switched off until 10 miles from the DZ/LZ sites.

Air Support

On D-Day-1 there was a lot of extra activity in the skies over Normandy as 100 Lancaster bombers attacked the battery at Merville, this taking place ten minutes before the main body of 38 and 46 Groups' aircraft arrived overhead. The bombing raid was only partially successful, although the battery had been attacked on previous operations to try to disable the facility.

Support operations were conducted to try to curtail enemy interceptions from German night fighters further inland, and standing patrols were in operation from 23.45 (D-Day-1) until 04.30 on D-Day. Patrolling fighters strafed ground targets in and around the DZ/LZ to try to draw any flak and ground-based light arms fire prior to the main air insertion. These aircraft were clear of the area before the first landings.

Confusion was also a key factor in the support operation, and at the last possible moment ten Window-dropping[32] aircraft commenced a simulated attack near to the Seine estuary to confuse the enemy radar.

The six tug aircraft of the advance party (Coup-de-Main) for the bridges at Benouville were all allocated two 500lb general-purpose bombs to be dropped on a powder factory near to Caen on the south-eastern corner of the town.

This was supposed to give the impression of a small force just targeting targets of choice and not to alert the enemy to the fact that this was indeed a small insertion force.

Lastly, there was a small psychological support force of bomber aircraft from No. 3 Group that had to deploy and drop small dummy parachute troops. These were intended to draw enemy troops away from the main force and tie up the Germans into thinking a force had been dropped away from the real targets and therefore create confusion. This was also aligned with the same force using noise simulators to create both panic and fear within the enemy as to what was happening. This part of the Operation used the slightly tongue in cheek code name of Operation Titanic; even in these highly stressful and dangerous days there were still moments of humour around.

The evening of D-Day the air support was more generic, and for the squadrons of 38 and 46 Groups there were close fighter escorts by twenty-five squadrons from 11 Group, high- and low-level fighter cover off the beachhead as a matter of routine and escorted bomber operations and fighter sweeps to the south and south-east of the beachhead areas.

Order of Battle

Nos 38 and 46 Groups were made up of the following squadrons based at the following airfields:

- 38 Group – Brize Norton, 296 Squadron – Twenty-two Albemarles with four reserves
- 38 Group – Brize Norton, 297 Squadron – Twenty-two Albemarles with four reserves
- 38 Group – Harwell, 295 Squadron – Twenty-two Albemarles with four reserves
- 38 Group – Harwell, 570 Squadron – Twenty-two Albemarles with four reserves
- 38 Group – Keevil, 194 Squadron – Twenty-two Stirlings with four reserves
- 38 Group – Keevil, 299 Squadron – Twenty-two Stirlings with four reserves

- 38 Group – Fairford, 199 Squadron – Twenty-two Stirlings with four reserves
- 38 Group – Tarrant Rushton, 298 Squadron – Eighteen Halifaxes with two reserves
- 38 Group – Tarrant Rushton, 644 Squadron – Eighteen Halifaxes with two reserves
- 46 Group – Broadwell, 512 Squadron – Thirty Dakotas, no reserves
- 46 Group – Broadwell, 575 Squadron – Thirty Dakotas, no reserves
- 46 Group – Down Ampney, 48 Squadron – Thirty Dakotsa, no reserves
- 46 Group – Down Ampney, 271 Squadron – Thirty Dakotas, no reserves
- 46 Group – Blakehill Farm, 233 Squadron – Thirty Dakotas, no reserves

This made an assault force totalling 340 aircraft with a reserve fleet of twenty-five over the fourteen squadrons allocated to the groups.

Overall, for D-Day operations, the glider force totalled 1,040 Horsas with an additional eighty Hamilcars that were allocated to Halifax squadrons because of the type's ability to handle these larger gliders.

The 6th Airborne Division would take up to 360 Horsa gliders, 10,000 X Type parachutes and roughly 3,000 containers on the operation. Another 10,000 containers would be required for further resupply after the main assault.

On the evening of 5 June, two Albemarles were allocated to each of the three DZs (N, K and V) to drop the Pathfinder force. Their target time was 00.20 DBST[33] Cloud was 10/10ths and visibility was good at 4,000ft; the wind direction was 295/28 and 230/10 over the DZs. Arrivals were on time, although there were difficulties in exiting for four of the six aircraft involved, and exactly half the force had to complete at least double runs on the zones. Troops were dropped with an error of +two minutes, but one aircraft had to make three runs and finally dropped its troops fourteen minutes late. All Albemarles flew their missions and returned to their respective airfields with no issues.

The success of this mission was vindicated when the subsequent aircraft carrying the main force of the 6th Airborne Division reported back that the lights and ground aids were functioning and fully operational when approaching the DZ/LZs. Eureka was not working over DZs K and N, and it was damaged on DZ V even though two sticks[34] of troops were dropped on the DZ with no concerns. There was an error with one of the Pathfinder Albemarles as it dropped its Eureka beacons for DZ K on the southeastern corner of N, where it was put into use. Unfortunately troops who were to be dropped on to N ended up being dropped on to K; not the last men to be placed in the wrong location over the following couple of days!

In preparation for the gliders to land at their allocated LZs X and Y, arrestor parachutes were fitted to six of them to decrease the stopping distances at these locations. Visibility was good and all gliders were released between 4,500 and 5,500ft and approximately 5–6 miles from the LZs. Estimating the percentage success of this part of the glider operation, if a glider landed within 1 mile of the centre of the LZ it was deemed a success. No account was taken of gliders that landed farther out, even though they played a significantly useful part in the attack and subsequent battle.

Landing zones X and Y, where the Coup-de-Main party were deployed, was the domain of the Halifax/Horsa combination from 644 and 298 Squadron respectively. Three-ship formations were scheduled to release their gliders at 00.20, and arrester parachutes were attached to the gliders for the other LZs. Visibility was good over 10 miles, with cloud coverage at 6/10ths – 9/10ths at 5,000–6,000ft. Wind direction was 290 to 312 degrees, wind gusting up to 18 mph when they entered the run on to the LZ, the tugs releasing at 4,500–5,500ft at 5–6 miles. However, one glider was released blindly east of Houlgate, and this meant a landing 8 miles west of the LZ near to Périers-en-Auge, which did resemble the LZ to some degree. The other five gliders, three for LZ X which all landed within yards of the bridge and the two for LZ Y, both reported 150 and 400 yards of the bridge and LZ. There was no flak at all either observed or encountered by any of the gliders, and their arrival probably meant they were not identified until overhead the LZ itself.

Dropping the advance parties of 5th Parachute Brigade on DZ N was again conducted by Albemarles, three from 297 and two from 296 Squadron, at 00.20. The weather conditions were 10/10ths cloud at 4,000ft, with good visibility. Exit difficulties were experienced by two of the aircraft, causing an additional run by one. Out of the forty-seven troops on board, forty-six jumped and one returned to base. All thirteen containers were successfully jettisoned from the aircraft and landed near the DZ.

The advance party of the 3rd Parachute Brigade on DZ K was again allocated to two Albemarles of 295 and 570 Squadrons with the aim of dropping the pathfinders at 02.00, without any ground aids. Once again visibility was good, with broken cloud at 1,500ft. Timings were running late at three and a half minutes but drops were accurate. The second runs to jettison containers went well but only with one aircraft as the second could not identify the DZ accurately and did not drop its containers. The drop on to DZ Y by the 3rd Parachute Brigade was conducted by fourteen Albemarles, equally split at seven apiece from 295 and 570 Squadrons, with the same timing of 02.00 and once again without ground aids. Visibility ranged from 1–6 miles at 10/10ths at 1,500 to 7/10ths at 2,000ft. The wind was variable with speeds recorded at 12 gusting to 41mph. There was exit trouble for a few of the aircraft involved and two only dropped three and six troops respectively, while one Albemarle had six troops jumping without warning over the coast, while four more were dropped on to the DZ. One aircraft experienced enemy machine gun fire above the DZ and had to make a second run to despatch its troops. Two others experienced failure of their Gee equipment, which affected their ability to locate the DZ successfully. One of these flew along the coast trying to find the entry point to the DZ and lost time, while the other did not find the entry point at all after seven unsuccessful attempts. It was hit by flak and number two paratrooper was knocked into the exit, jamming it so others could not jump. The aircraft returned to base with nearly a full complement. A total of 140 troops were allocated to be dropped between 00.21 and 00.29, and out of these 106 were dropped correctly, 16 were dropped incorrectly and 18 did not drop at all. Regarding the supporting containers, out of fifty-six, forty-two dropped correctly, eight incorrectly and six were not dropped at all.

The landing of six gliders on to LZ K was in the hands of Dakota from 233 Squadron out of Blakehill. The time for release was scheduled for 00.45 at 1,500ft above ground level. Weather over the LZ was reported as good, with visibility at 3–5 miles, cloud at 10/10ths at 4,000ft, and a westerly wind. The glider pilots did report quite bumpy conditions and encountered heavy smoke obscuring the approach to the LZ. The tug pilots released correctly at heights ranging between 500 and 1,700ft over a time period of 00.45–00.48. Out of five of the glider crews, only two reported reaching the LZ K, three landed close or on LZ N. Two of the latter had been released on instruction of the tug, as they thought they were on a course to land on K. The error was linked to the previous mix-up of beacons, with K wrongly operational on N LZ. One glider did not report at all.

Landing eleven gliders on LZ V was another Dakota tug squadron with seven aircraft, with the assistance of four Albemarles from 38 Group. These were scheduled to release at the same time of 00.45. The glider crews reported rather an unpleasant crossing experiencing, with low cloud in patches as well as bumpy conditions. The tug pilots gave good reports over the LZ, with visibility at 10/10ths cloud at 3,000ft, lowering to 1,000ft in places. The glider crews reported smoke obscuring the area, which appeared to be from the bombing of the battery just prior to the insertion. Three tugs lost their gliders in cloud just off the French coast, while the remaining eight tugs reported release between 00.44½ and 01.05, between 1,000 and 1,700ft approximately 1 mile north-east-west of the LZ. All tug pilots recalled they recognised the LZ from both the maps and models shown prior to the operation.

The dropping of the main force of the 5th Parachute Brigade on DZ N was allocated to the main·force, 131 aircraft were detailed, 110 from 38 Group and 21 Dakotas from 46 Group. There were 2 unserviceable aircraft from 38 Group, but the remaining 129 did get airborne to carry out the mission. Visibility was good with cloud ranging from 7/10ths to 10/10ths at 2,000 to 4,000ft, and Eureka and lights were functioning on the DZ.

A total of 123 aircraft reached the DZ between 00.48½ and 01.12, although one aircraft reportedly reached it at 01.43. The remaining aircraft (five Stirlings, one unidentified) were all reported as missing. Some 2,026 out of the 2,125 troops were dropped from the 123 aircraft, along with 702 out of the 755 containers. Reports from the field were that the drop was very successful and accurate.

No. 46 Group allocated thirty-seven Dakotas to transport the main party of the 3rd Parachute Brigade to DZ K with a drop time of 00.50. Visibility was 10/10th at 3–5 miles, 4,000–6,000ft. All lights and Eureka were functioning on the DZ. Two aircraft from 233 Squadron, KG356 piloted by Flying Officer Jones and KG429 flown by Warrant Officer McCannell, did not make the drop and were reported missing. Later the information came through that they had both been shot down close to the French coast with all souls on board lost. The remaining 35 aircraft dropped 615 troops between 00.48 and

01.00. The total allocated to drop was 617 but one was killed before the DZ and another refused to jump. A total of 151 containers out of the allotted 163 were also dropped. Again, the error of dropping the incorrect Eureka beacon on to DZ N instead of K meant that the formation leader actually dropped his troops on to N and was followed by a few of the following Dakotas, who also dropped their troops on the wrong DZ. The error was rectified before all troops were dropped by turning off the beacon and lights. Confirmation by the 3rd Parachute Brigade after the drop stated that thirteen sticks were dropped on N and eight on K!

The drop of the main party of the 3rd Parachute Brigade on to DZ V by seventy-one Dakotas of 46 Group was scheduled for 00.50. Visibility was good at 7–10/10ths at 2,000ft. No ground aids were on at the DZ and seventy of the Dakotas reported dropping their troops between 00.49¾ until 01.17. The remaining aircraft reported missing the DZ. There were 1,294 troops transported to the DZ but only 1,287 dropped as 4 had exits problems, 2 were injured and could not jump, with 1 remaining on board due to being sick. There were 223 containers dropped out of a total of 235.

Landing gliders on the coastal battery was entrusted to three Albemarle/Horsa combinations of 297 Squadron, with gliders detailed to land at 04.30. Because this mission was deemed extremely dangerous, one that called for volunteer glider pilots, all craft were fitted with Rebecca and arrester gear. Ground troops who were attacking the battery lit the area using star shells to aid navigation for the gliders. The weather was not helping the insertion, with cloud at 1,000ft and almost complete coverage at 10/10ths only adding to the difficulties that were experienced. One of the three gliders managed to part company with its tug while still over England, again in dense cloud, and made a successful forced landing. Another glider experienced the arrestor parachute[35] becoming deployed in mid-stream and this caused the combination to rapidly lose height. A quick decision was made to jettison the chute and control was thankfully regained, although the deployment of the chute had put strain on the tail assembly of the glider and the controls were sloppy and somewhat less responsive to the inputs made by the pilot. Another result of this action was that the starboard undercarriage had been carried away. The journey from the coast to the LZ was fraught, with constant flak encountered, which damaged both gliders and wounded four passengers. When they arrived at the

LZ neither crew could distinguish the battery and had to make four circuits until being released at 04.24½ and 04.25½ at 1,800 and 1,200ft respectively. There was some confusion in identifying the target, as one glider crew mistook a bombed village for the battery and attempted to land. At 500ft they realised their mistake and took evasive action, managing to land in a field 600–800 yards from the battery. The other glider crash-landed into an orchard a mere 50 yards from the battery and both gliders were subjected to intense machine gun and mortar fire. The battery was finally silenced at 04.45 by the 9th Parachute Battalion party before the incumbents of the gliders could get into the action.

Sixty-eight Horsa and four Hamilcars were the main force of gliders that landed on LZ N. The combinations were handled by aircraft from 38 Group and were detailed to land at 03.20 on strips cleared from all obstructions. Visibility was fair but a low stratus belt covered the French coast with light rain at 2,000ft. The lights from the LZ were clearly identified and the wind averaged 290/94. Fifty out of the sixty-eight Horsas were released over the LZ between 03.24 and 03.34 at heights ranging from 1,500 to 1,600ft. Of the balance of gliders that did not make the LZ, three cast off in cloud en route, four cast off over England and seven cast off between the French coast and the LZ itself. Out of the latter seven, three were engaged by flak, along with a total number of twenty-five gliders that encountered flak on their way into the LZ, although no one was injured, passengers or crews. Glider pilots confirmed that forty-eight landed close to the LZ, although the crosswinds did make for many collisions with other gliders as well as natural and manmade obstacles. Of the four Hamilcars, one had to make a forced landing in England after breaking the tow rope, another had the same experience a mile from the LZ but landed safely, while the other two managed to land directly on the LZ.

Summary of Results: Operation Tonga

Parachute Sorties
266 aircraft detailed
264 aircraft took off
255 aircraft reported successful drops
7 aircraft missing

4,512 troops carried
4,310 troops were dropped
1,315 containers carried
1,214 containers dropped

Glider Sorties
98 combinations detailed, all got airborne
74 gliders successfully released
57 gliders confirmed as reaching near or on the LZ
22 gliders reported missing
Out of the 196 glider pilots, 125 returned to the UK, four were killed, 14 wounded and 53 were missing
611 troops carried, 493 reported as successfully released
44 out of the 59 jeeps, 55 out of 69 motorcycles, 15 out of the 17 quarter-pounder guns and one bulldozer were successfully released. The one tank was not dropped.

Operation Mallard – evening of 6 June

This phase of the deployment of Allied troops on the Normandy front used LZs N and W.

For the landings at N a task force of 116 Horsa and thirty Hamilcars were transported by eight squadrons from both 38 and 46 Groups (four each). The weather was primarily good with visibility at some 10–15 miles with little or no cloud at the release heights and wind direction at 320 degrees, speed 10–15 mph. Eureka was employed and available on the LZ, although very little was reported by any of the crews. A total of 142 out of the force of 146 landed successfully, one crashing on the LZ. The remaining three gliders were subjected to the following difficulties: one combination crashed into the sea, all crew safe; one crashed upon take off; with the other making a forced landing after the tow rope broke over England. The total landing period was 20.51–21.23; 32 minutes for 142 gliders to conduct safe landings averaging over four a minute on to the LZ.

LZ W was detailed to receive 112 Horsas transported by 6 Stirling and Albemarle squadrons from 38 Group. Of the 112, only 110 took off, the other two becoming unserviceable prior to launch. Weather conditions were good with a 10–15-mile visibility available, the wind very similar to that seen on LZ N. Some crews reported seeing smoke over the LZ but contradictions were received by other crews, who stated no issues, Eureka was available for use on the LZ. Two gliders cast off while still over England and force landed, two more had difficulties over the Channel that caused one to ditch, but the other managed to land safely. Figures later reported from the LZ stated that 110 gliders reached it and landed, although there is clearly a discrepancy with these totals that was not clarified. The landings were completed in twenty-eight minutes, between 20.52 and 21.20, the area becoming quite congested with up to six gliders landing line abreast at times.

Summary of Results: Operation Mallard

258 Combinations
256 Combinations airborne
246 Gliders landed successfully on or near the LZ

The plan to retrieve as many of the gliders as possible for reuse was established prior to the operation taking place. Unfortunately, the position on the ground did not present itself well for a good source to retrieve as many gliders as initially thought. Most of the LZs had become battle grounds for a few weeks, although LZs N and W did yield up to forty Horsas that were pulled out from the areas by Dakota tugs and the help of the HGSU.[36] Out of these, only thirty-nine landed safely back in England, with the other one ditching in the Channel. Both LZs, though, did manage to produce roughly 1,200 tons of glider spares that were salvaged for potential reuse.

When the whole operation was reviewed to ascertain any lessons learned or opportunities to improve for future operations, a range of constant issues were seen as in the hands of the gods and something the air force could not influence in any way. Firstly, the aircrews could promise a good proportion of success providing two things were in their favour, reasonable visibility and good ground aids. If only one of these existed, they could offer a merely cheerful attempt at delivering, and no extra training would improve upon the rate of success in this circumstance, with the state of the equipment available to the aircrews. While it has always been stated that the radio aids that were afforded to most crews were just aids, some crews depended heavily on them when in operational situations. Thus error in their use as navigational aids meant the system broke down. Then there were the crews who flew and put the navigation on to the flight lead, which was open to any errors that the lead may have incurred during the mission. The only true way to get greater confidence that the target would be reached by the force would be for every crew to rely on their own navigation, using both aids and the old-fashioned method of maps and waypoint markers.

Of the aircraft that did not make accurate landings on the DZs, it if fair to say that the drops were very detailed and it was not particularly easy to achieve a high degree of success. There were no radio or visual aids to assist them, as well as the fact that they had to place their troops only 4,000 yards away from coastal batteries that were still operational at that time.

The landing of gliders by day and night was also reviewed, detailing the different risks and challenges that these operations carried. The daytime risks were far more from the flak in and around the LZ area as well as any encountered from the coast. This was countered by a greater reduction in hazardous landings and possible crashes, something that was more common in night-time landings, although at a far-reduced impact of flak. Of course, every case did have its own merits and was judged accordingly, although it was necessary for both types of landings to take place to keep a force deployed behind enemy lines, something that could not happen unless missions were flown around the clock.

One other complication of both the paratroopers' and gliders' insertions was the four different types of aircraft allocated to the two groups (38 and 46) and their different characteristics and performances. This was apparent in the carrying loads and speeds and weights afforded to each. This impacted greatly on the army's load and flight planning, which was also complicated by the different speeds of paratrooper flights and glider tugs in the formations. Slower aircraft potentially entered the wake of preceding aircraft, causing handling issues as well as bunching up of aircraft over their respective DZs/ LZs and either creating more activity, or in the case of slower aircraft, creating larger gaps on arrival. Mixed formations were kept to a minimum wherever possible, but this could not always be granted due to the need to move such a large body of men and equipment in such a short time window. The ideal was, of course, to reduce the number of variants of aircraft for the operation, but with such a drain on resources the RAF were dealing with for fighter, bomber and transport aircraft, there were types that should have been withdrawn that were still giving service, along with the USAAF aircraft also involved in this deployment.

Glider separation from tug aircraft continued to be the biggest cause of abortive glider sorties. The primary failure was down to the breakage of the tow rope, commonly caused due to the combination of flying through the wake of other aircraft or becoming out of position with the tug in cloud and putting excessive strain on the rope, which would induce the failure. This though was an acceptable risk as retaining the formation tightly condensed and was a safe way to getting the task force on target, so the occasional positional issues and trouble in cloud were out of the control of the pilots and down to mother nature. The strength and integrity of the tow ropes were something that could be investigated prior to the next major glider deployment.

Lastly, the LZs were deemed to be suitable for the gliders, allowing plenty of room for landing safely when aligned to the landing lights and radio aids. The enemy's obstructions proved to be weak in their ability to stop the landing force, as most of the poles that were inserted into the ground were short and the Horsas' wings travelled straight over the top of them in most circumstances. A few did cause some damage, and collisions took place that also caused minor injuries to crews and troops.

Overall, the operation was deemed successful, with air- and glider-borne troops arriving on time and in the correct areas as scheduled. The postponement of the operation by twenty-four hours may have caused a slight disruption with crews being briefed in a slightly more hurried fashion than ideally planned. This when also aligned to the films and models available to view and aid, which were not even completed in the correct form, could only give an incomplete picture for those taking part. Low priority was given to the aircrews from both groups as they only had one model per airfield to view and very little photographic material to consult. The importance of supplying as many visuals aids to all those taking part was drastically underestimated.

In conclusion, although Operation Neptune may not have been the ideal model on which to base all future airborne invasion operations, it did demonstrate that a large spearhead could be conducted with successful results. As for the next airborne operation, there were certainly lessons learned that could be put into practice to ensure a more robust exercise, wherever that may be on the road to finally defeating the Germans and the liberation of Europe.

Personal Stories – Tonga: Flying Officer J. Le Huray (55070)

Briefed for Operation Mallard, myself (skipper), Flying Officer Linn Farrell 2nd Pilot, Flying Officer Bill Woodcock Navigator and Sergeant Charlie Carr Wireless Operator. We were scheduled in tug seventy-two out of the seventy-four tasked for the op. Our glider was carrying twenty-eight troops and one trailer full of ammunition.

    Take-off and the journey over to France was uneventful without any issues, the weather was beautiful as we crossed the coast at 1,000ft and made our run down the river. The glider released directly over the bridge as intended, I could see another glider on fire on the LZ and to starboard there were three kites under light flak fire in front of me, roughly 3 miles north-west of Caen. Three bursts of flak then suddenly hit us, firstly in the tail and running up the fuselage, the second burst hit the starboard engine, setting it ablaze, finally the last burst caught the fuselage and wings, filling the cockpit with smoke and fumes. Height was roughly 700ft and decreasing rapidly. I pressed the feathering button on the starboard engine, which enabled me to gain some height, told Linn to tell the blokes jump! Bill and Charlie managed to get out and Linn got halfway down the fuselage and I left the controls to join him. As I reached the Nav's door the kite was on her side and started to take a right-hand spiral, again descending quickly, so a return to my seat and managed to regain partial control by closing the port throttle and reducing speed. At 150ft the starboard fell out, which gave much better control. A field was spotted out to starboard about 100 yards long, so the flaps were put down, the ignition was switched off and I went in for a landing downwind. The port wing tip touched the ground first, which ended up with us performing a ground loop!

    With the wreck still burning, myself and Linn rushed out and made a dash of roughly 50 yards away into a ditch. Linn turned to me and mentioned that he had hurt his foot. A couple of Tommies hailed us and were quickly followed by a major, who arrived and took us to a first aid post. There an Australian medical officer dressed Linn's foot, gave him a morphine shot and put him to bed.

I was then taken by the major to the HQ for the 6th Airborne Division, where I met with the GOC General Gale. It was then I received some tea and a chair to sleep in for the night. During the night I saw the supply dropping operation in full flow. There was flak, sometimes quite intensive, and I saw one kite take a hit and catch fire. I could see the lights on the panniers as they fell on to the DZ, approximately 100 yards from where I sat. In the morning I saw the general again, and he informed me where Linn had been taken to. A sergeant took me to the hospital, which was located in a local village. Once at the village we stopped for a quick whisky that had been specially made for the German troops. At the hospital we learned that Linn had already been moved to a Casualty Evacuation Centre, so we turned back and travelled on to the HQ. Once we arrived back, I met General Gale once again and he offered me to join him for breakfast consisting of bacon, eggs and marmalade. Later that day I met Leonard Mosley of Kemsley House, who arranged to take me to the beaches. This was where all the war correspondents were taking their despatches for transmissions to the UK. Arriving at the beaches was a miserable affair, the weather was cold and miserable. There were dead strewn all over, their bodies lying in grotesque attitudes, although there had been some attempts to start to collect the bodies and sort into two heaps, British and German!

There was a group of German prisoners who were encircled by a single strand of barbed wire, two guards looked very browned off having been gripped for the job! A senior German officer stood somewhat further away with a British officer escort. The high tide was lapping over the steel mesh road that had been laid the previous day, the 15 yards, or 10 of sand between the sea and dunes had not yet been cleared of mines and presented a scene of utter confusion. Terrifically congested, mainly with the wrecks of assault craft, jeeps, light guns and tanks. Landing craft were making regular runs up to the beach to disgorge troops, who floundered in the 4ft deep water, the surf breaking over them, most managing to keep their rifles dry, but many forgetting to take the same care of their cigarettes!

I was joined by another pilot, Flying Officer Anderson, a Canadian from 38 Group who had bailed out on the eve of D-Day from a Halifax. He boasted that he had liberated a German helmet and rifle as souvenirs of his trip! After an hour or so, we were allowed to board one of the LCIs.[37] This meant a wade out to the gangway and once on board we sat out on the open deck drying out in a biting wind. The only form of heat offered to us was by drinking the innumerable self-heating cans of soup. Our convey of LCIs totalling seven craft took hours to form up and were ready for the off when everything was scattered as bombs from three Fw 190s appeared. Thankfully they were hotly pursued by roughly twenty Spits. Another two hours to re-form and get ready to go, followed by a twenty-hour crossing! Disembarking at Newhaven at 8am, Anderson and I were lucky enough to be taken to the mess of the embarkation personnel, where we were welcomed by the CO. Bacon and eggs duly followed.

Transport back to base then became the next target for me. I met Major Jackson, who took me along to meet an old friend, Bill Woodcock, who told me of the bad news around Charlie Carr and his death in the Caen Canal. Luckily though Major Jackson had his own transport and offered me a lift as he was going to Down Ampney. I was very pleased to be able to join him. On route we had to call in at Fargo, where the glider pilots were to be debriefed, and where after a summary debriefing, I managed to grab another bacon and eggs. Finally, I arrived at base at 18.15, 45 hours after my crash-landing in Normandy.

Personal Stories : Flying Officer J.M. Woodcock (J11505)

Flying in Dakota KG426, we were airborne and towing a glider on the evening of the 6 June towards our destination of a DZ in Normandy, the seventy-second aircraft in a large formation. Proceeding along the prescribed route, turning south 5 miles off Le Havre, a relatively quiet flight with nothing noted until just at the mouth of the River Orne flak was noticed bursting around us! No notice was paid to this, and we continued to travel up the River towards our DZ, glider dropped and I observed his release from the Astro Dome. The radio operator, Sergeant Carr, was sitting in the back just aft of the starboard engine and watching for any activity from below. Suddenly flak raked us from the rudder to the starboard engine! I noticed that the operator was in the back, so I dashed through the communicating door to find the whole compartment filled with smoke, several ragged holes along the starboard side of the aircraft and Carr lying face down on the floor, partially on his hands and knees. I immediately returned to advise the pilot, then went back to Carr to see how he was. When I got back Carr was standing up and I asked if he was ok. At this exact moment we were hit again, this time the starboard engine burst into flames. Both of us immediately snapped our parachutes on as the aircraft made a steep dive. Both Carr and I were standing at the door, but with the aircraft going down at such a rate it made it impossible to jump. The pilot appeared to get the aircraft under some control and attained some more height, about 700ft I believe. Carr wished to jump, but I said no, I think the pilot will make it. At that moment the engine blazed, flames appeared to lick over the cockpit and under the fuselage towards the port engine. Carr and I were standing side by side at the door, my right arm preventing him from jumping until absolutely necessary because of the low altitude. I glanced at the second pilot, saw him getting up from his seat and indicating to jump. As we exited the aircraft we watched as she slowly started to turn on to her back, so Carr and I went out!

Parachutes opened instantly and in a matter of seconds we were landing in the Caen Canal. Carr landed roughly 25 yards ahead of me and about 10 yards from the bank. I released my chute and saw Carr floating in the distance and calling for help. My parachute was billowing in the water, but I couldn't see any sign of Carr's chute. I called to him, and he answered, but after I had swum a few strokes, I could not see him as he disappeared under the water. I then swam to the bank and was helped out of the water by two local Frenchmen. I immediately asked them if they had seen Carr, they both replied he has gone! I spent a few minutes examining the water, but it was too dark as dusk had fallen and I had no success. The Frenchmen took me with them to their families, where I was given whiskey and milk, and more importantly a change of clothing while mine dried out. In the morning, I went back down to the canal but could not see anything. One Frenchmen then led me across some fields to where some British troops were heading for Caen. There I met some glider pilots heading for the beaches, so I tagged along with them. After many detours we made it to the beaches. In a nearby field I met Major Jackson of the Airborne troops, who suggested I joined with him, which I did gladly. Boarded a landing craft at 11.00, sailing at 15.00 and disembarking at Newhaven the next day at eight thirty. I then met up with Le Huray, who had a miraculous escape from his aircraft with Farrell, the latter being left at a casualty clearing station with a broken ankle. We travelled to Down Ampney with Major Jackson in his car, arriving approximately forty-five hours after take-off. Reported to the station Intelligence Officer, Station Commander and Squadron Commander, in that order, then off to bed, so ending an interesting period, although unhappy in one sense at the loss of Sergeant Carr.

Report on Operation Mallard, 6 June 1944, Flight Lieutenant Williams in Dakota FZ690, 512 Squadron

We took off at 18.37 on 6 June 1944 with a strong 80-degree cross wind and were airborne after a run of the full length of the runway of 2,000 yards. We had 43 minutes to assemble both squadrons in the air and a course was set for Coventry. On turning at Coventry for the station RV, it was found that only one glider was behind us besides our own. On arrival at the station RV the remainder of our squadron was waiting, and a course was set 30 seconds early for our first turning point. The trip out to the English coast was uneventful but we had difficulty in keeping to our times owing to a strong tail wind and to the fact that it was dangerous to throttle back with a heavy glider behind us. We did a 'Dog Leg' near the English coast and crossed outwards 46 seconds early. The fighter cover was waiting for us, and we set course for the French coast at 20.01. We ran down the French coast north of Le Havre about 10 miles out and although we had a clear view of the coast no opposition was encountered. Shortly after leaving Le Havre we could see the invasion fleet off the French coast and our course took us over the capital ships which were shelling the beaches. Our height was 800ft so we had a good view of the proceedings. We turned down the river for our release point and climbed to 1,000ft when the glider released itself, we then lost height and proceeded to the rope dropping DZ. On turning to starboard for the run out we were coned in crossfire from three ships lying in the docks off the river and although we took violent evasive action we were repeatedly hit with medium flak. The wireless operator and the navigator were both wounded and two shells exploded in the cockpit between the pilot and myself, doing considerable damage. We set course for England but we dare not lose too much height as we didn't know how badly we were hit.

Glider Pilot D-Day Flight

At 18.37 on D-Day, 6 June 1944, the first glider took off from Broadwell towed by Squadron Leader Rae AFC of 512 Squadron. There was quite a crosswind and most of the take-offs were of a 'shaky do'. The forming up of gliders took time but when we crossed the coast of England heading south, the stream was complete. The French coast north of Le Havre was sighted at 20.25, and as we had been briefed to land at 21.00 most of the pilots expected to be intercepted by enemy fighters. We had our own escort of Spitfires and Mustangs, which had been with us since we left England and I should imagine that they were thinking that if the sight of this glider fleet doesn't bring them up then nothing will. At 20.45, we saw the fleet ahead, and what a sight, lights were flashed at us, good luck messages by the score, it bucked everyone up no end. The beach at Ouistreham was being shelled by Jerry and as our track lay directly over this piece of beach, quick calculations as to the height of the trajectory of the shells were being made, but before any satisfactory answers could be arrived at we were passing over the beach and then the panic started, where were the bridges, where was the pull off point,[38] where was the LZ, were the poles down? A quick look at the target map just to make sure that everything was in its right place and then we pulled up the knob and released our glider from the tug. Two thoughts were now uppermost in my mind, get down quickly and get down in the right place. The glider ASI[39] was showing 110 mph when I was cross wind of the LZ. Half flap was put on and then the turn to the LZ. The speed was around the 100 mark when full flap was applied. The glider was losing height rapidly when the poles came into view. There was no clear lane and as there was not the slightest wish or chance of going around again the glider nose was heading between two of the poles. Ahead of us there was a house, so I put on my brakes (wheel) in midair and as the glider touched down there was a screaming of brakes, a pole was missed by inches and then by using full left rudder another pole missed the cockpit and was knocked by the right wing. I understand myself that before I had got out of the cockpit, the passengers who were members of the RUR's[40] were out of the glider and had already taken up defensive positions around the glider. I climbed out feeling very relieved at getting down safely and had a quick look around. The sky was black with aircraft, tugs of all kinds, gliders both Horsa and Hamilcars, fighters by the score. Some tugs were hit. I saw three Albemarles, from one of which four jumped, one Dakota which later we learnt had force-landed successfully. All were hit by flak from the Caen area. In twenty minutes my glider had been unloaded and the eighteen soldiers headed by a major were on their way to their RV. We had our own RV to get to, only about 440 yards away, but what a distance it looked. Mortar shells were now bursting on the LZ. One Horsa piloted by Flight Sergeant Tarbitten was hit and burst into flames, one gunner was killed, a Hamilcar was hit by another shell and several were killed in that one. By 22.00 all but three crews from our squadron had reported to the RV. Defensive positions were taken up by 23.00 and everything was in good order. At 01.30 the order to stand down, except for double sentries, was given. Containers had been dropped on the LZ at midnight and most of the pilots had managed to get hold of a parachute to sleep in. At 04.30 we were all standing to again. Things had been fairly quiet during the night, but now the fun was starting again. At 05.00 we heard that No. 3 Commando, who had been the first people in from the beachhead, were taking over our positions and that all glider pilots were going back to the beachhead to be taken back to England. We were all fairly glad to leave that area as Jerry was getting his mortar fairly well ranged in, and there was quite a lot of throwing oneself flat on the ground as the shells came over. Three unexploded shells dropped quite near to one section's post. We were now on our way back and except for one hold-up by a sniper in a church, who we later found out was a Jerry parachutist dressed up as a Roman Catholic priest, everything went off quite well. We marched about 7 miles to the beachhead and then to get on an LCY we had to wade into the sea, everybody moaned like hell about this, but they were all glad to be going back. We took some time to form up into a convoy and by the time we had disembarked in England we had been on board for 22 hours. Back in England we learnt that the three missing crews had turned up so that there had been no casualties at all. In all the operation was very successful and most of the glider pilots considered that it had been easier than exercises that they had taken part in during training.

Captain Thomas (Glider Pilot)

On 7 June Operation Rob Roy was the resupply mission to DZ N and entailed six aircraft from 48 to drop eighty-eight panniers and eight containers of various supplies to the deployed troops. Take-off time was scheduled for 22.25 and the drop was an eight-minute window between 23.50 and 23.58. Crews involved encountered none or very little fire from enemy sources, although their intolerance to friendly fire instances was becoming more of a dangerous nuisance to all. Both the aircraft recognition of Allied ground forces and the Royal Navy left a lot to be desired, so much so that crews started to fire off Very[41] cartridges and lowered their undercarriage to show they were indeed friendly forces! Both actions did little to dissuade their comrades from continuing to fire on them. Three out of the six aircraft were hit, although thankfully not badly and returned safely. Looking at the issue of being fired on, the crews were somewhat understanding of the eagerness and confusion of some that may have contributed to these actions, especially in the first few hours following the invasion, and did pay tribute to the accuracy of the anti-aircraft gunners and their persistence in trying to bring an aircraft down, although, it was true to say that they hoped that further experiences might be unnecessary going forward! The mission was a success, all supplies being dropped in the correct areas and all aircraft returned to Down Ampney between 01.35 and 01.40.

No. 271 Squadron took the 7th as a rest day. The intention was for the squadron to be on alert, which some were allotted in the afternoon in case of emergency calls for their services. No flying was required.

The following day and after completion of Rob Roy the squadrons had a day of rest, the only flying seen was Dakota AY KG346 flown by Pilot Officer A.M. Smith and crew, who were returning from Ford after they made their forced landing the day prior. All were interrogated and subsequently released to maintain their duties. The afternoon allowed representatives of the press into camp to talk with the crews and to listen to experiences that were shared. The concert party gave a performance, its first since returning from Gibraltar, among the many acts and entertainment on offer. The biggest cheer was saved for the station commanding officer (Group Captain Bradbury DFC) and his announcement that the station was no longer sealed, and everyone could enjoy the local amenities once again!

June eighth was another down day for the squadrons, even though a small amount of test flying did occur with the different units. Most of the crews did express a slight anti-climatic feeling following the hectic few days around

D-Day, and crews felt they would still be busy flying troops, etc. into theatre. The Commanding Officers did express their thoughts that all personnel must be ready and prepared for periods of inactivity at times but must remain alert and ready to go at a moment's notice, assignments would be at very short notice. It was also stated that crews should try to always maintain a good high state of morale. The evening saw the arrival back at Down Ampney of Le Huray and Woodcock, who filed their reports and were then given five days' leave, although they had to travel to London for an interview with the AOC[42] before they could take some well-earned rest.

Similar flying activities were in place for the next couple of days, with only local/test flying taking place. The afternoon welcomed the Commanding Officer of the Glider Regiment, Major Jackson, who relayed his personal experience of June the sixth on Operation Mallard. His tales managed to keep the assembled crews from 48 and 271 entertained and interested in his thoughts around the success of the tug aircraft as they towed gliders towards France. Thankfully all were very impressed as he thanked them for the way they had delivered all personnel to their destinations, although he did state that his own personal flight had given him a smile when the tug released his glider and he saw the Astro Dome of the Dakota fit to bursting point with inquisitive crews who wanted to watch the behaviour of the glider upon release. A collective roar of laughter came flooding from the audience at this juncture! In the evening another visitor to the camp was welcomed when the Secretary of State for War The Right Honourable Sir Archibald Sinclair Bt, KT, CMG, MP, visited the entire based crews and passed on the thanks of the Prime Minister, Winston Churchill for all their hard work shown with the D-Day operations. The third visitor to attend the camp within a short time period, was the Marshal of the Royal Air Force, Lord Trenchard GCB, GCVO, DSO, DCL, LDD, who attended on 12 June. Keen to visit all squadrons, where he was received and had informal chats with various flying crews, listening intently and showing interest in their recent exploits and operations conducted. It goes a long way in the minds of the active-duty crews and was fully appreciated that this VIP was welcomed so easily into the fold and all the retinue was left the other side of the gate and this Grand Old Man of flying became one of the squadron while he was with the crews.

On the ninth the glider pilots returned to the respective bases following their recent French visit. Everyone was keen to hear how things had gone and for their experiences, which some were eager to share, but not all! The camps were finally fully unsealed from the pre D-Day lockdown.

Hopes of further operations were high for 48 when on the 13th crews were called for a briefing at 14.00, however, this was short-lived as cancellation came through at 12.30. The 14.00 slot though was still put to good use as the station Medical Officer Wing Commander Mundell gave a lecture on the Air Evacuation of Wounded from the front. No. 233 Squadron were called into action on the 13th with aircraft detailed to carry pickets to B.2 (Basenville, northern France). Their route took them from Blakehill Farm to Selsey Bill–Amelles-sur-Mer–B.2, then the same route back to base. Heavy flak was encountered some 5–6 miles south of the landing strip, but no other enemy activity was seen by the squadron. Four tons of the screw pickets were unloaded on arrival and twenty casualties (fourteen stretcher and six walking) were flown back to England. The return flight and their passengers were unfortunately going to be the main workload and routine for the Dakotas for the foreseeable future! The sorties were going to work in such a manner that outbound aircraft would be loaded with various freight destined for continental airfields and would return with wounded personnel back to Down Ampney, Blakehill Farm and Broadwell. It was very apparent that the morale of the crews needed to remain high as this next phase of their operations was not going to be the most pleasurable for all concerned.

A Flight and Squadron Leader A.B.J. Pearson from 271 became the first British Transport pilot and aircraft to land on French soil since the capitulation of the country back in 1940 when he arrived at Basenville on 8 June.

More aircraft were detailed from 233 to aid with the transportation of HQ personnel from 83 Wing (RAF Thorney Island) to B.2, escorted by six Spitfires on both flight legs, no enemy opposition seen, and it was duly noted that the town of Caen was ablaze. Only Dakota KG440 brought back three stretcher cases of casualties. No. 233 Squadron were called upon to supply seven aircraft to transport personnel and equipment of 144 Wing from Ford to B.3, close to Sainte-Croix-sur-Mer, routing from base to Ford, then onto Selsey Bill–Estuary of the River Orne–B.3 and return. On the 15th the squadron detailed aircraft to carry VIPs and others to B.2, returning with more VIPs and passengers (inc two fighter pilots) as well as seated casualties to Northolt, the Dakotas continuing onwards to Blakehill. Another six aircraft were assigned to aid in the transportation of a Fighter Wing from Tangmere to Landing Ground B.2. Their route took them from Blakehill to Tangmere, then on to Selsey Bill–Estuary of the River Orne and return via the same route to base. Total number of personnel and kit successfully deployed was 104, including the Canadian official photographer. The return leg of the flight was also loaded with casualties, 111 in total including twenty-nine sitting and eighty-two stretcher cases. Two of these were German prisoners. Two Dakotas were assigned to carry out screw pickets and ammunition to B.5 (Cauilly), routed from Base–Selsey Bill–B.5–B.2–Selsey Bill–Base. Within 5 minutes of landing at B.5 the Germans started shelling the strip, Stores were quickly unloaded, and the aircraft took off and flew to B.2. They evacuated twenty-four stretcher cases and five seated back to the UK.

Broadwell's Dakotas were also gainfully employed as they were scheduled to partake in transport duties to Normandy. 575 had a tasking on the seventeenth when eight aircraft were detailed to move 137 RAF personnel from Holmsley South to L.9 (north of Camilly), with the return flight repatriating casualties. Unfortunately, this flight did suffer the collision of two of the Dakotas (KG343 and unidentified) when they were landing. Dust was obscuring the view and the aircraft collided. Shelling was also experienced on the landing ground while casualties were being loaded, the remaining six aircraft, including the crews of the unserviceable aircraft, took off for B.2, where more wounded and two pilots (shot down over Normandy) were all loaded aboard for the return flight.

No. 512 Squadron were also active on the seventeenth, they were due to make their first forays on to Normandy soil. They along with their sister squadron were to fly to RAF Holmsley South to collect seventy-six passengers and transport them to France. All kit and personnel loaded for a rendezvous at Selsey Bill with a squadron of Spitfires, who were going to act as escorts for the unarmed Dakotas on their crossing. Intersecting the French coast at Ouistreham and encountering no enemy aircraft or surface vessels, the squadron flew up the estuary of the River Orne, turning right and a direct landing on to B.5, a 1,700-yard landing zone roughly around 3 miles from the enemy lines. With the passengers disembarking and wounded being loaded, the Germans started to open up and shelled the landing zone. The risk to the aircraft was such that an immediate evacuation was ordered and all aircraft made a hasty departure, heading for B.2 that was closer to the coast and further away from any pending danger. The ambulance convoy arrived about 1 hour later with the rest of the wounded for onward transport, once they had taken off and made contact with their escorts for the return flight.

The eighteenth saw five aircraft detailed to cover the transportation of bombs to B.2, the route being the tried and tested one of Selsey Bill, the mouth of the River Orne and back. Once on the ground in France 4,500lbs of bombs were unloaded and seventy-two stretcher cases and eighteen walking casualties were loaded for the return flight to England. There were also two prisoners of war within this total. Dakota KG441 did suffer an engine failure while landing at B.4. Luckily the aircraft touched down without incident and managed to unload its cargo of eight 500-pound bombs! For the rest of June the details were very similar, with aircraft taking general stores out to France, including bombs, ammunition, blankets, food, periodicals, etc. and returning with casualties, both stretcher cases and walking wounded, including the occasional prisoner of war. The return flights were now using both RAF Blakehill Farm and RAF Down Ampney to repatriate the wounded.

The lack of operations over the next five days or so did create the need for some activity to take place. Luckily on the eighteenth 48 Squadron received orders to provide five aircraft and 271 another five to assist the move of 126 Wing RAF from Tangmere to a landing strip in Normandy (B.4) Bény-sur-Mer. Dakotas proceeded to Tangmere, where they were loaded with personnel, kit and various stores and duly departed at 15.00 and made course for France. Low cloud made the crossing somewhat difficult, the leader of the formation found it challenging to locate the airfield in Normandy (B.4), and inadvertently arrived at B.5 Le Fresne-Camilly, along with other Dakotas within the formation. Once the aircraft had come to a halt, it became quickly apparent that they were in the wrong location. Tin helmets adorned the heads of troops sat in slit trenches and the occasional shell burst on the end of the runway confirmed this to the crews, so the aircraft quickly took to the air once again to find the correct forward landing ground! One of the aircraft (AF KG364) developed engine trouble and had to divert into B.2 (Bazenville), where repairs were carried out and the aircraft reached its destination of B.4 along with the other Dakotas in the formation. Three of the formation reported being fired upon by friendly forces during this operation, although with no injuries sustained by any crew members Four aircraft were allocated to return ninety-five casualties, the fifth Dakota returned empty.

More activity did occur on the twenty-second of the month, this time another fighter squadron move from Harrowbeer in Devon to Detling. The squadrons involved were 1 and 165, with the support of 6001 and 6165 serving echelons. Confusion in the organisation resulted that there would be no air support available and that they would have to use rail transport, so a lot of kit was already packed up and shipped this way when the transport aircraft arrived at Harrowbeer. This resulted in estimates that out of the fifteen aircraft assigned, only nine would be required, which offered the opportunity for 132 airmen to be transported by air. Three aircraft then transitioned to Predannack to collect six Merlins and transport to Detling. On arrival at Detling two Dakotas did come together as wingtips made contact. This luckily only resulted in light damage and both aircraft were on their way in due course.

With the Allies getting a foothold in France, a number of different flying assets nearer the front line could operate from ALGs.[43] While 48 and 271 Squadrons had already played their part in moving two such units, they were used once again on the 27th when the movement of personnel and general stores was required for 247 Wing to move from Hurn to B.6 Coulombs (Normandy). The initial idea was for the crews to deploy to B.9 (Lantheuil), but the serviceability of this landing ground was unprepared, so they diverted to B.6 instead. Take-off at 07.32 for arrival at Hurn at 08.10, where all aircraft were loaded with freight and personnel. Total weight of 35,720lb carried to Normandy, with an arrival time of 13.42. An uneventful flight, although the weather closed in and severe rain caused visibility to reduce, but all aircraft successfully landed at 13.42, and unloaded, then reloaded with 115 casualties and then took off at 16.22, arriving and landing back at Down Ampney just after 18.00.

As the end of June came, 48 had one more task to undertake for the month. Seven aircraft were allocated to cross the Channel to ferry personnel and equipment from 91 FSP[44] to Advanced Landing Ground B.2 (Basenville). The weather delayed take-off time until the skies cleared, but all aircraft were airborne by 10.45 with a total weight of 24,908lb, aircraft touching down at B.2 at 12.31. One aircraft had though managed to get airborne earlier and relocated to Northolt to collect a VIP and staff, although after an hour sat on the ground the order came for the aircraft to get airborne as the VIP was not going to show. At 11.13 the Dakota was on its way with only the Staff on board! After another delayed return flight, due to the fifty-five casualties being sent to the incorrect field at B.8, all were eventually repatriated to England.

A few days earlier there had been feedback that troops in Normandy were not receiving their bread allowance. This became quite a concern, so every flight out and across the Channel carried on average 500lb of bread to be distributed to the troops in theatre. No. 48 Squadron benevolent fund also carried out a certain amount of digging about and provided cigarettes, papers, magazines, etc. sent along with the bread.

Base to Normandy to Base

On the twentieth of June we left Broadwell at 10.53 in Dakota KG322 (Pilot Flight Lieutenant Clarke) en route for Hurn with instructions to land there and pick up a load to be transported to landing strip B.6 in Normandy. We landed at Hurn at 11.22 and were given lunch. At 13.00 we commenced loading with ground staff and equipment of 121 Wing RAF. Loading was complete by 13.45 and we took off with the other aircraft of our squadron at 14.05 for Selsey Bill, our RV with our fighter crew. At 14.35 we linked up with our Spitfire escort over Selsey Bill and set course for the mouth of the River Orne.

The weather was good for a major part of the Channel crossing, there being no cloud with a wind of 35/40 mph. from east-north-east. Although our aircraft were flying in echelon part formation in fours, there was far too great a distance between the leading aircraft and the last, in my estimation about 4 miles. I think that had we kept closer together we should have derived far greater protection from our escort in the event of an attack by enemy aircraft. We kept a continuous watch from the astro-dome for enemy fighters and at one time were puzzled to identify two aircraft which appeared to be overhauling us from the rear. As they drew nearer, we identified them as two Ansons who presumably thought our fighter escorts were a 'good thing'. They joined us and eventually passed us just before the French coast. About 15 miles out from the coast the weather suddenly deteriorated, strata – cumulus cloud at 400/500 and visibility about 3 miles. We descended below the cloud and lowered the undercarriage, losing sight temporarily of the aircraft ahead. The approach to the mouth of the River Orne was a little awkward. We were now forming line astern and one of the Ansons cut in ahead of us to starboard. We were about 400ft ASL and in order to keep in line our airspeed dropped to 100/110 mph and we used a ¼ flap. There were masses of balloons to our starboard flying from ships, the beaches and from the town of Ouistreham, and they were partially hidden by the cloud. We watched the Anson on our starboard with some anxiety as it appeared to be flying straight into the balloons but at the last moment the pilot spotted them and made a sharp turn to port. From the estuary to the landing strip the visibility was poor, being not much more than 1 mile. On our approach we crossed another line of Dakotas at right angles who subsequently turned out to be our own machines in the circuit. At 15.28 we landed, taxied off the strip and unloaded. It was fairly quiet, our only sight of enemy activity being a single Fw 190 hedge hopping about 600 yards away. I was standing at one of the gun sites (Bofers) at the time but the aircraft was so low that they were unable to fire on it. They informed me that they were awaiting confirmation of a 'kill' from a few days before.

We remained at B.6 until 19.15 when, as no wounded had arrived, we prepared to take off to RV at B.4 with an escort home. Three minutes before take-off an orderly rode up and gave us instructions to land at B.4 and pick up casualties. This was unknown to the Wing Commander, who had already taxied out to take-off position. At 19.35 hours we landed at B.4 together with Flight Lieutenant McLeod, who had received similar instructions, while the remainder of our aircraft, having picked up their escorts, set course for home. At B.4 we found everything in readiness and within 15 minutes we were loaded with twenty-five walking casualties. Flight Lieutenant Clarke communicated with operations and an escort of four Spitfires was given to us from the same strip. At 20.25 we took off proceeded by the Spitfires. The weather had now cleared considerably and we had no difficulty in finding our route out over the River Orne. We flew in close touch with Flight Lieutenant McLeod and all went well until twenty minutes out from the coast as Flight Lieutenant Clarke saw one of the Spitfires dive into the sea, although the pilot did bale out. Two of the remaining three Spitfires dived over him and as there was a ship in the vicinity we carried on our way.

The rest of the journey was uneventful. We reached Selsey Bill at 21.20 and parted company from our one remaining Spitfire and arrived back at base at 21.55, where the wounded were quickly unloaded and taken away.

Flying Officer James (512 Squadron)

Impressions of E.1 (the first casualty evacuation mission to Europe)

E.1 was like having your house burned down – it happens to everyone else but yourself – at least that's the way it seemed to me. We had read reports of Dakotas landing in France to evacuate wounded – heard pilots and crews describe their trips on the radio, even seen the aircraft landing there on newsreels, but somehow it never seemed to happen to us. We'd been standing by for so long ('it's on, it's off') that it was with more than a little surprise that I heard early one morning – very early one morning – that at last we were to land on the 'other side'. Of course, I knew it couldn't happen all the time, and when the trip was scrubbed after that 03.30 rise and shine, it was only what was expected. The following morning – 17 June – was to have been much the same (I thought) but even though I still felt sure that something would interfere with our leaving, the 06.00 take-off really happened. We flew empty to Holmsley South except for two passengers, a WAAF[45] medical orderly (very WAAF and very orderly) and a two-stroke motorcycle. Holmsley South was fairly well organised, the dispersal was arranged with numbered flags so that the aircraft (which were also numbered) had no difficulty in finding the exact spot at which to park. Our passengers too found this system very helpful and whilst we were at briefing, they assembled at their allotted aircraft and loaded their kit. We found that we were to move the ground personnel of a Typhoon squadron and from the amount of kit some of the lads were carrying it looked as if they were taking their Typhoons with them. Each man carried amongst other things a streamlined bomb carrier and we were told that the squadron's aircraft were due to start operating from their new base that very afternoon – almost a breath of organisation in the air. The situation map in the briefing room showed us that the German line lay only about 2 miles from the strip on which we were to land, so it was evident that circuits were out and OTU flying was not to be the order of the day. We took off late – almost ten minutes late – thanks to the time it took the squadron to form up on the end of the runway, but a little corner cutting got us to the fighter rendezvous right on time.

The formation was pretty gruesome until well out over the sea. At one time there were three quite separate streams flying in parallel, but eventually everyone settled down and things looked reasonably neat – fourteen Dakotas in vics of three, vics in line astern. There were to have been fifteen but 'E' Easy had dropped out at Holmsley South with magneto trouble. Our Spitfire escort flew very close and was very thrilling to watch – they obviously had great difficulty in coping with our relatively slow speed and throughout the trip flew round and round the formation whilst a few stayed right on the flanks and some kept several miles to the rear. I looked for the top cover but the sun was too bright and made my eyes water so I gave up and just hoped they were up there somewhere. It seemed a long way to France that morning in spite of the fact that there was so much to see – I was surprised to find that the large convoys of all shapes and sizes of ships looked exactly as they had done in newsreels – there must have been millions of 'em. The odd balloon here and there just completed the picture. I wondered if there had ever been convoys like that before and when yet another flock came into view I knew that there never had. We took no chances with the Navy – a cartridge had been in the Very pistol since before leaving the coast of England – the Aldis lamp was plugged in ready for use – but above all we avoided wherever possible flying over anything larger than a rowing boat. I stood in the Astro dome and lapped it all up as we drew closer to the French coast, getting more and more thrilled. The lowering of the wheels and the losing of height speeded things up quite a bit – we now seemed to be racing towards France at a terrific rate and I found myself looking forward more and more often, until eventually taking up a position looking straight ahead. The haze got worse for a few moments and then suddenly – with a dramatic effort far better than could have ever been arranged by any human agency – the haze cleared slightly and there lay France. The navigation was super. As soon as it was possible to make out details off the coast we could see that we were aimed straight at our proper point of entry. That strip of coast had become very familiar to us from the maps and models we had studied for the paratrooper drop on D-Day and I looked along the coast for our landfall of that eventful night – it was too distant to be recognised at that height but as we drew closer to the land the visibility improved still more and we saw the houses of Caen quite clearly.

We turned very sharply over the lip of land near Ouistreham where the River Orne reaches the sea – the terrific battle that I'd expected to see so much was not very evident. I guess it must have been noisy down there on the ground but to me it was rather an anticlimax to find things so quiet. I'd expected to see a few fires and gun flashes, but on the east side of the river there was no sign of life. DZ N looked terrific, with dozens of gliders lying all over the place, as did another DZ on the west side of the river. The first impression of these DZs was one of havoc and wreckage, but as we passed over them we could see that quite a few gliders were undamaged and that their crashed appearance was due only to the fact that the whole of the rear part of the fuselage had been detached from the rest to facilitate quick exit of the troops they'd carried over. I looked at the sky – it was busy, with small groups of Spitfires and Thunderbolts in every corner – no doubt as to whom the air over the beachhead belonged. The ground too, I could see, was crammed tight with equipment and big dumps – every field seemed to be full of lorries, tanks, guns and men. We passed over a crashed P.38 lying on its belly – it looked pretty whole, I guessed it could have been there only a few days. Out on the beaches the landing craft were hard at work with balloons riding in the sunshine above them. Just off the beach was a huge semicircle of ships sunk end to end so that they were a solid breakwater – an artificial harbour just for the occasion. And in the shelter of the ships dozens of smaller craft were milling around looking fully busy and rather vicious.

The aircraft seemed to speed up again and I realised we were getting lower and lower – I turned again and looked forward, and as I did, I could see that we were just off the end of the runway at B.5. No circuit, just a turn and we were there. The site of the strip quite shook me, it looked as big and firm as a normal runway at home and had taxi tracks leading off into dispersal areas in the neighbouring fields. By this time I could see that there were men working on the runway – dozens of 'em – and as they saw we were landing direct, they ran out of the way as hard as they could with little trails of yellow dust following them. The metal strip was obviously not yet complete, so we landed on the clearing on the starboard side. Even before we touched down huge clouds of dust bellowed up behind us blotting out everything. We'd expected dust but not like that – it was worse than a desert airfield, the dust much finer and more clinging. I wondered how much of this sort of flying we would do before our aircraft were fitted with tropical filters and dust traps. The runway behind was invisible so I went to the back to fix the door – and to be the first of 512 to tread the fields of France! We seemed to be taxiing for miles and the dust got steadily worse but eventually the fans stopped and I jumped out as the rest of our aircraft were taxiing up to a standstill in a long line behind us. We were first in, in spite of all those threats to beat us to it. Good oh!

I didn't think much of France – the drome was little different to what any strip of English countryside would look like if it were suddenly turned into an aerodrome. I pictured the mud that would come with the rains and thought of Base – there would have been little to choose between them. But the dust – surely there couldn't be dust like this anywhere else but here? A crashed Thunderbolt stood over near the runway and as the dust cleared, we could see that two of the aircraft in our formation were stuck on the runway. We found that they'd had a mild collision on landing and were being examined before taxiing away in case of undercarriage damage. Our passengers offloaded quickly and we helped the WAAF to fix the stretcher fittings already for our load back. A small crowd of soldiers and airmen gathered around each aircraft to greet new arrivals and to see if we had brought any newspapers, cigarettes of magazines with us. They looked very oily and dusty – as if they'd been there for months – and in reply to our anxious queries about bombing and strafing told us that they'd never yet seen a German aircraft in daylight, though they were often on the prowl during the night. They did say that the strip had been shelled only the day before and mentioned – just in passing – that the Jerries had advanced slightly since then, the line being 1,500 yards from the strip. Everyone seemed quite cheerful about being so close – except us. We could see that the aircraft were hidden from view by a small wall of earth and a small wood that we had parked behind, but the clouds of dust must have shown them exactly where we had stopped.

The ambulances arrived and just before they reached the line of aircraft the shelling started. Being completely unused to anything so warlike, we just couldn't judge how bad it was, but the blokes who lived there said that there was nothing to worry about at all – most reassuring if you could only believe them! Shells came over at odd intervals – we ducked at the same odd intervals till we gradually got used to it and got back to loading the aircraft. I wondered what was going to happen when we tried to take off as the bursts were all on or around the runway – the two Dakotas on it had well and truly evacuated and were eventually hit and destroyed. The CO went off in a jeep to examine the take-off run and the quickest way out of the place. Our wounded passengers were slowly loaded until each aircraft had about six on board and it was then decided not to risk the aircraft any further and arrangements were made to fly to another strip where we could complete loading unmolested – the patients going by road. That take-off defies description. One moment we were in dispersal, the next the engines were started and the next we were in the air, it was as quick as that, The passengers were looking very pleased to be out of it and the same goes for the crew. It would have been rather unpleasant to have had to spend the night at B.5, particularly as we had brought no spades! It took only a few minutes to get to the new strip – B.2 – and what a difference we found at this one! It was as if we had gone a hundred miles away instead of just four. Not a sign of anything hostile – only the faint rumble of gunfire that was only a vague background noise. We fed our patients tea and sandwiches whilst waiting for the rest of our complement and talked to them whilst the CO fixed up another fighter escort as we were already too late to meet the one previously arranged. The lads were a pretty mixed lot and all from the Caen sector of the front, where the fighting had been fairly severe in the previous 10 days. One lad with an arm injury was from the 7 Armoured Division – old friends from the desert who'd done so well in the Wavell push of 1940–41. We talked of those hectic days until the heat of the sun on the aircraft made everyone sleepy. We left them in the very capable hands of the orderly and explored the field whilst they slept. It looked very organised and in odd corners crashed Spitfires and Thunderbolts were being repaired by RAF servicing personnel. Two Liberators were dispersed amongst poppies, one with a very beautiful Varga girl painted on its nose. They looked fully serviceable, but I don't suppose they were there for fun. We picked some poppies for the WAAF as she was rather busy and got back to the aircraft just in time to greet the rest of the casualties who had just arrived and were being loaded. There was room for everybody in spite of the fact that we'd lost two aircraft and their crews, who would be travelling back as passengers also. Take-off was quite normal this time and we were soon well out over the sea on the way home. I contacted base on the radio and told them of our estimated time of arrival and the number of casualties we were carrying.

The trip back was soon over and in spite of a bumpy ride only one person was ill, the WAAF medical orderly, who sat on a box looking very poorly while the patients did their best to comfort her! I guess the excitement had been a bit too much for her. She'd had a very busy day and had done a terrific job – just by being there she helped the boys quite a lot. We waited with them after we had landed until the ambulance and medical officers took over. We wished them 'Good Luck' and pushed off to supper – E.1 was over.

Chapter 4

Service Français (July, August)

The beginning of July heralded more evacuation flights as well as general flying duties required by transport squadrons. Normality now for the Dakotas was these flights across the Channel due to their carrying capability for delivering supplies and personnel to mainland Europe and bringing the wounded back to England for medical treatment and care. This was the first time that this kind of support was available to the British military in any major war, and it was fully utilised.

On 1 July two crews from 271 Squadron embarked on the first cross-Channel flight using the new corridor, number seven, which used the route Christchurch–Pointe de Barfleur, the mouth of the river Vire. This route was chosen as a relatively safe transit into northern France. The first aircraft from 271 took off at 14.50, piloted by Squadron Leader Squires in KG515, and although the weather was somewhat wet, he made the out and return trip to B.6 Coulombs in just four hours, including loading casualties. A second aircraft (FZ592), captained by Warrant Officer Quin, also got airborne at the same time as Squires, but elected to stay overnight at B.8 Sommervieu and returned the next day. Alas though, the weather got substantially worse and the aircraft had to land at Ford at 16.05 and discharge its wounded. Broadwell was unfortunately suffering from poor weather conditions, so a very limited number of flights got airborne for both 512 and 575, primarily a couple of local flights during the day and a few navigational taskings for the night.

Four crews from 271 Squadron, six from 48 and two from 233, aided in the transportation of 39 Wing from Odiham to B.8 on the 2nd. The Dakotas used by 271 were FZ628, KG512, KG444 and KG564, 48 using KG414, KG350, KG439, KG411, KG317 and KG394, with 233 supplying KG410 and KG403. The weather was unsettled with heavy showers, and this also involved an overnight stay for the crews. Two scheduled flights were introduced from

Down Ampney to B.8, the first departing at 08.00 arriving at 09.30, returning from B.8 at 11.00 and arriving at Down Ampney at 12.30. The second flight left Ampney at 11.00, arriving at Northolt at 11.45, then leaving Northolt at 14.00 and arriving at B.8 at 15.30. The return via Northolt was carried out the following day, with arrival back at base at 11.00. The object of this flight was to carry out VIPs and return with casualties.

The following day, 3 July, continued with casualty evacuation for 48, with very little flying activity for 271, except the second scheduled run via Northolt. Flown by Flying Officer Hirst in KG345, the crew stayed overnight in France and returned to base the following morning. 'A' Flight was still operating from Blakehill Farm and one aircraft (KG562) took off for B.8 at 11.21 loaded with shells and two passengers and returned with casualties. Support for this was also carried out by a 233 Squadron Dakota (KG566), which also flew out of Blakehill.

The following day there was a change to the operating schedule for the runs to B.8. Three aircraft were to leave Down Ampney at 08.00 with medical supplies and Army freight, returning the same day with casualties aboard and arriving by 12.30. The stop via Northolt had now been cancelled. Additionally, a further afternoon flight of three aircraft would depart base at 14.00 with Army freight and return for a 19.00 arrival, once again with casualties. No. 48 Squadron carried out Operation Balbo, which involved towing gliders for a period of one hour to keep the crews current. This was repeated on the 5th but no operational flying took place for the French run. On the 6th five Dakotas transited the short distance to Netheravon to pick up gliders and return to base. The B.8 run was carried out by three Daks (KG397, KG386, KG419) carrying freight comprising blood, penicillin, yeast, copper fuses and bread, while as usual the return flight brought home casualties. No. 271 Squadron also carried out flights to B.8, and again three aircraft (FZ639, KG362, FZ660) were designated. Only two of these aircraft returned the same day, again loaded with casualties. The remaining one stayed the night at B.8 but moved to a new landing strip of B.14 (Amblie). A flight out of Blakehill sent a Dakota (KG345) to B.14 to deliver mail (6,000lb) to the invasion forces and bring home letters (5,000lb) on the return leg.

With the regular flights to France now becoming well established, all squadrons were now heavily involved in delivering supplies to the front. On 7 July 48 Squadron despatched three Dakotas (KG386, KG406, KG439) carrying a mixture of spares, yeast, blood and other medical supplies to B.14. Five Dakotas from 512 Squadron were involved in pannier dropping, with another three on the French trip and further aircraft on local duties. No. 575 Squadron were just as gainfully employed with training and air tests. No. 233 Squadron only despatched one aircraft during the day, when FZ679 flew out to B.6 on a mail run. Finally, 271 Squadron flew three aircraft to France, but their loads consisted mainly of soap! The sad fact was that the main load for all the Dakotas who flew out and back to France on this day were still high numbers of casualties to bring home.

A number of high-ranking visitors arrived at Down Ampney, including BOAC[46] officials. Within the ranks of guest were Lord Knollys, Sir Harold Howitt, Robert Maxwell and Lloyd Taylor. They witnessed flying demonstrations carried out by both 48 and 271 Squadrons, including quick take-off and glider balbos. There were ground exhibits of various aircraft that were loaded with different supplies and fits, including, bombs, panniers, jeep and trailer, as well as a normal ambulance aircraft with stretchers and a WAAF orderly.

The weather was showery on the 8th. Bombs with tails were ordered for B14 and aircraft of 271 Squadron (KG545, KG516 and KG367) were specified for the resupply flight. No. 48 Squadron supplied medical supplies and army freight to the forementioned landing ground, utilising Dakotas (KG350, KG439 and KG395), 271 bringing back forty-seven cases on stretchers and twenty-eight who could sit. The Princess Royal visited Down Ampney to meet wounded troops from Normandy. She had a tour of the base and was escorted by the Station Commander, Group Captain J. Bradbury DFC.

Both 48 and 271 Squadrons transported their first POWs[47] among the troops repatriated on the 10th. Two crews from 'A' Flight, 271 Squadron, Blakehill Farm, left at 08.00 on that day and proceeded to Bolthead to transfer the personnel and kits for a Typhoon squadron that was being transferred to Hurn. Sparrow Ambulance flights with Ansons operating out of RAF Jurby (Isle of Man) were visited by eight 271 Squadron crews, who flew in equipment to keep the flight stocked to perform its duties. Another Royal visitor to Ampney was Her Majesty Queen Mary. The Queen was shown the type of actions and workload that the squadrons were at present conducting. She inspected a Dakota fitted out for the evacuation of casualties, which was shown to her by the captain, Warrant Officer Christie of 48 Squadron.

No. 233 Squadron had inherited the role of delivering the mail from and to England during the early to mid-part of July. They carried vast loads almost daily (weather permitting) across the Channel, keeping this important service running and the communications open for all serving personnel from their families, friends and loved ones. Typically, a single aircraft could accommodate over 3,000lb of mail when loaded at Blakehill, similar weights being returned from the front. There were even occasions when two Dakotas were assigned to this tasking.

Things were settling down for the squadrons at Broadwell (512 and 575) during July, with routine flights to the landing strips in and around Normandy, delivering various freight and passengers and repatriating casualties on the return. Other taskings performed were glider towing, pannier dropping, navigational flights and general transport duties. The normality that these two squadrons were experiencing was the same for most flying the Dakotas with 46 Group at this time in the war; the occasional special duty, VIP visits and similar that was afforded to the few.

No. 271 Squadron were involved in transporting 313 (Polish) Squadron, with six aircraft flying from Lympne to Skebrae and Sunbrough on the 11th. The return trip was carried out the following day when 118 Squadron made the journey in the reverse direction.

No. 48 Squadron despatched three aircraft (KG426, KG411 and KG439) on the 17th for the usual flight to Normandy (B.14), but unfortunately they had to be recalled due to bad weather. Two managed to return to base, while the third (KG426), crewed by Squadron Leader R.D. Daniells, had to divert into an American strip in the Cherbourg peninsula (A.15) and remain there until the weather cleared. Once possible it made it safely to B.14. A rather bizarre event took place when the aircraft arrived at A.15 as the Secretary of State for War Sir James Gregg, was due to be visiting, and he was meant to be travelling on a 48 Squadron aircraft. When the crew stepped out of the aircraft, they were met by a barrage of cameras being pointed in their direction. The Americans had certainly pushed the boat out for this occasion, it's just a shame that their intended VIP was not a passenger. Even though the mistake was soon explained, the hospitality shown towards the crew left nothing to be desired.

The 18th provided a slight change for 271 Squadron as fourteen crews were involved in the night exercise Seekout, which provided twelve aircraft to locate an unknown position and try to detect the Eureka location, although no reported success or failure of this has come to light. Another repeat exercise was also in place for the 18th, when fifteen crews took part in a balbo[48] exercise. This entailed the short route from Little Rissington–Cirencester–Thornbury–Base and did give some relief to the scheduled routing to France and B.14, although these flights were still happening. Exercise Highland I was carried out on the 21st and involved both 271 (three aircraft from 'A', Flight Blakehill Farm) and 48 Squadrons, which both supplied nine aircraft and twelve respectively. Also joining them were 233 Squadron from Blakehill Farm, which supplied a further nine aircraft. The exercise involved the 52nd Infantry Division and was a resupply mission in the Swindon, Lambourne and Malborough areas by day, with satisfactory results. Routing was from base(s)–Swadlincote–Sleaford–Bletchley–Didcot–DZ and return to base.

One of 48's aircraft returned on the 24th after carrying an enemy mine across from France. It landed at Thorney Island for examination by the Royal Naval authorities. Another new travel corridor[49] (eight) was opened up from Cap de la Hague to Lulworth Cove, while the existing corridor number seven continued to be used for all outward transportation flights to Normandy. A briefing was also held for squadrons to participate in Exercise Independent. This involved six crews from each taking off in the early morning and dropping on to a specified DZ routing, which was via Harwell, Oakham, Evesham, Didcot and DZ. The exercise was rated as successful, but a small number of paratroopers did drop in a nearby wooded area close to the DZ. Thankfully there were no injuries. Dakota (KG439) carried British and French officers and the Prefect of Bayeux from B.14 on the 27th, along with other returning personnel, one American, three Army and two RAF officers, who were transported back to England.

There was another important visitor to Down Ampney on the 28th when the Inspector General toured the base. A mass take-off was shown with aircraft getting airborne to show the capability available.

Normandy Detachment (Crews Flight Lieutenant Cough, Flight Lieutenant Williams, Flight Lieutenant Lee, 512 Squadron)

At 08.00 on Monday, 18 July 1944, we were airborne from base in Anson NK489 en route to Northolt to pick up Wing Commander Strange. At 10/10ths low stratus was spreading inland from the east, and approaching the Chilterns we were obliged to climb up through it as the base was well down and covering the hills. Contact was made with Northolt on VHF[50] but reception was bad. Some 20 minutes were spent trying to obtain a bearing from Northolt with reception getting worse until the set packed up completely. We had managed to get the cloud base at 4,000ft and visual of 2 miles, although we were uncertain of our exact position to an accurate degree at this time. We set a course of 250 degrees and proceeded in the direction of the base, where we knew the cloud coverage had been 8–9/10ths. After 10 mins flying frequent gaps in the clouds were observed and as the base was soon to be fairly high, we descended through one of the gaps and soon pinpointed ourselves at Reading. Course was once again set for Northolt, where we arrived at 09.50 and stood by for Wing Commander Strange. A message was received during the morning to say that he would be delayed and consequently the crew stood by in the mess. We left Northolt at 14.10 and made our way to Thorney Island, where two passengers were to emplane. We arrived there in good time and finally made our way to B.14 strip at 15.10 with our full complement of passengers. The weather was heavy in the London area but as we moved south it became fine with a visibility of 2–4 miles in slight haze above the Channel.

The crossing was uneventful, only the sight of a large convey which was heading for France and stretching for as far as the eye could see off our port beam. When within sight of the Cherbourg Peninsular we altered course to starboard to avoid a convoy of escorted landing craft which were heading north, and from then on we flew parallel to the coast on the peninsular and on into the estuary of the Vire. The visibility by this time had become very thick in haze, on either side large concentrations of ships were seen anchored, the vast majority seen flying balloons at about 500–600 ft. We then turned to port and set course for strip B.14 approx 30 miles distant. We had already lowered our wheels in accordance with procedure and the slow speed at which we were now flying gave us an excellent opportunity to have a look around. The fields as far as one could see in all directions were literally crammed to capacity with stacks of supplies, thousands upon thousands of crates in orderly array. Large concentrations of vehicles here and there supplemented this gigantic array of equipment while the main roads to and from Bayeux had a continuous stream of traffic mostly moving up towards the front. We landed at B.14 at 16.20 booked in at Flying Control, ADRU[51] and the Security Police and immediately located the cook house, where we received a very welcome cup of tea and some sandwiches.

Later when the aircraft had been dispersed, we set about getting ourselves a tent and getting dug in. We were in luck as the lads from the cook house had only that day dug a substantial trench next door to the tent we were given, and they handed this over as our official shelter. It wasn't long before we had drawn our bedding, filled our palliasses[52] from straw and dried grass from a nearby field and settled down. We had our supper consisting of biscuits, cheese and sardines, washed down with hot camp tea and as it was still light decided to explore the local village of Banville before turning in. There was nothing of interest to be found here apart from the church, which had earlier harboured an enemy sniper and the top of the tower had been knocked off in a determined and successful effort to remove him.

We had been warned earlier of the possibility of an odd Hun strafing the area at dusk and 23.00 found us wandering around, tin hat in hand and not far from the dugout, expecting the worst. Sure enough, an aircraft was soon heard flying fairly low in the area but by this time a terrific shower of light flak was on its way up and although the machine was seen there was no beat up in our direction. For the next half hour occasional bursts of flak heralded a new intruder but by 23.50 all seemed quiet enough and we turned in.

Up in the morning around 08.00 to tinned bacon and sausages and lashings of hot tea, only to find the weather very dull with heavy low stratus but nevertheless quite warm. There was no flying to be done, so we amused ourselves by playing cricket with a length of rubber hose for a bat. We had been told of a Canadian Mine School at Banville and had been invited to go along and have a look around. We jumped at the opportunity and arrived sharp on time at 13.30 and were met by the Commanding Officer, a Canadian lieutenant, who showed us a large collection of mines, booby traps and explosives which he had collected for the school. He explained how each weapon worked and, what was especially interesting, how to neutralise each one in turn. We left with a feeling of great admiration for these engineers whose job it is to clear mines and small booby traps and with the knowledge that the most tricky and dangerous part of that task is to locate the infernal things! It was apparent that every mine that the Hun had produced has at least one device on it for the attachment of a booby trap or trip line.

We then decided to try to get into Bayeux about 17 miles distant and as we were already on the right road soon managed to hitch a lift from a 15 cwt army truck which was going most of the way. The journey, interrupted occasionally by a traffic block, lasted about an hour, during which time we were able to get a closer view of the masses of supplies and equipment stacked in the fields alongside the road. One field we passed contained about thirty burned out and damaged Allied tanks which had been salvaged from earlier fighting in the area. About 3 miles from Bayeux we got into a large open lorry which was going into the centre of the town and standing up in the back had a good view of the surroundings. The traffic congestion was increasing, and more frequent halts were made, one opposite a prisoners' cage where we could see about 200 enemy in their field grey uniforms lying around in the sun. We finally arrived in the centre of the town to find it crowded with sightseeing soldiers and the local inhabitants busy about their shopping with an occasional group clustered around the latest news bulletins which were pinned up here and there. Most of the shops seemed to have plenty to sell, clothing being extremely expensive, while hardware and furniture were of an inferior quality. Camembert cheese at 11 francs per box abounded in all grocery shops and even the chemists displayed a few cosmetics. We noticed one young woman whom we took to be a one-time enemy collaborationist as she had her hair shaved off and seemed to have been roughly handled recently as her legs were badly cut about. We rounded off our short visit by walking around the cathedral, a truly magnificent piece of architecture, and reminiscing how fortunate it was that this wonderful work was untouched by the tide of war. Shortly afterwards we were on our way home at speed, having got a lift in a jeep driven by an MP officer, who took us to within 3 miles of our base and we were able to get another lift in a jeep almost immediately right to B.14.

I had made up my mind that on the following day I would endeavour to get a lift through to the Airborne Division, who were still in the line just across the River Orne. It wasn't a good day for flying so I set off around midday and managed to get a lift almost immediately to La Deliveranoc, a few miles east of the strip. There was a colossal congestion of traffic here and in dodging about avoiding all types of vehicles from tanks to jeeps I took the wrong road – in fact the one to Caen! When halfway to Caen I managed to get another lift in a jeep with some army people who were going straight to the newly won

Carpiquet aerodrome. With that plan changed I decided to accept their offer and go along and have a look around. Anyhow, driving through country lanes and smashed villages finally brought us to the airfield. During the journey one became extremely conscious of the danger of mines as all the roads and lanes were marked off as having been cleared of mines for the verges and for some distance of 26ft from the roads and lanes' edges. All buildings and hangars at the aerodrome were completely demolished and the whole area was known to be sown with shoe mines, a type of mine encased in a wooden box which could not be detected by the normal mine detector. Lying amongst the debris were a considerable number of heavy tanks and what appeared to be the relic of an Me 410 abandoned by the enemy when they withdrew from the airfield. This ground over which the Canadians fought so bitterly for 3 days showed signs of the desperate nature of the fighting, especially the village of Carpiquet which lies at the foot of the aerodrome on the northern side. Not one building remained habitable – a pathetic disarray of ruined clothes, furniture and household equipment littered the roads and hung on to the shattered walls of the houses. What had once been an attractive little village was now completely dead! The return journey proved even more interesting as it took us through a part of the city of Caen, which had only just been won from the enemy. Again, the same story of destruction but here the people were endeavouring to salvage what little remained of their homes.

And so back to B.14 to learn that we were to leave with Wing Commander Barritt for Northolt in the morning. The return trip proved uneventful, and we arrived back at base during the afternoon, looking forward to a good hot shower and a couple of pints of beer to wash down the Normandy dust.

The third occasion that VIPs were carried by 48 Squadron occurred on the 29th, when, among others, Admiral Preston of the Royal Navy and two air commodores returning from B.14 were above the Channel in degrading weather aboard KG404. Taking off from B.14 at 08.28 and soon into cloud cover at 10/10ths, the flight settled on to its predicted route back to England. However, after a short while a couple of the passengers became concerned about reaching landfall due to the state of the weather. The aircraft was using another corridor (ten) towards Selsey Bill and the pilot (Pilot Officer Warwick) was getting slightly anxious about his own navigation, especially considering the high-ranking officials that were his cargo! Undeterred, he pushed on, keen to show that the RAF could display that navigation was a key factor for every airman in the service, and confirmed to the air commodore that this was so, and they would reach landfall at Selsey Bill as specified. After a few moments the navigator whispered into the pilot's ear to descend through the clouds, which he did only to find they were right above Selsey Bill and so continued on to Thorney Island and an impeccable landing. The commodore and his fellow VIPs were so impressed with the crew that they invited them to join in the mess for drinks and congratulations of an outstanding job well done, which was warmly received. Much later, Pilot Officer Warwick did share that there was no one more surprised than himself to find out that when they broke cloud they were exactly as specified on their route; a little unkind on his navigator perhaps!

During the 26th, 512 was one of the squadrons that were detailed take part in Exercise Rowanberry, which was intended to be carried out, but due to bad weather all aircraft were unable to reach their destination of Tealing until the following day. One aircraft (FZ610) crashed on landing. The crew consisted of Flying Officer Payne, Flight Sergeant Horaburgh, Flying Officer Mattocks and Warrant Officer West. Unfortunately, both Mattocks and West were killed and Horaburgh was badly wounded. This exercise was to be a twenty-four-hour pannier-dropping resupply operation at a local DZ carried out by four different crews over the allotted time period. The exercise was subsequently postponed to a later date and was rescheduled for briefing on the 28th. Once again, after a further twenty-four-hour period of delay occurred, Exercise Rowanberry eventually took place on the 29th and the first phase was to lift the 52nd Division from Tealing (Scotland) to base and get the assembled troops comfortable in the loading and unloading of equipment from aircraft quickly and accurately. Crews from 48 Squadron took part in the initial stage of the exercise, which then saw Down Ampney provide thirty machines for the main event: twelve from 271 and eighteen from 48. No. 512 Squadron allocated fifteen aircraft to the exercise, with three acting as spares if required. Not enough lashing equipment had been sent up with the aircraft when they deployed, so an additional aircraft had to travel up to Scotland to take more. This was of great importance as the 52nd Division had vehicles that needed to be secured within the aircraft to stop any movement. This caused more than two hours of delay before all the aircraft could take off on their flight back down south. The move down from Scotland was deemed a success, even though a belt of adverse weather had been encountered across the middle to upper areas of England. Formations of ten aircraft were due to fly down to Down Ampney, although because of the bad weather aircraft were despatched from Tealing in one-minute intervals. During the 30th eight crews from 'A' Flight, Blakehill Farm, took part in the exercise, which ended on the 31st with the 52nd Division being ferried back to Tealing, again after expediting their rapid loading and unloading of the aircraft.

There were a couple of interesting flights for 48 Squadron on the 30th and 31st. The first was when a returning flight from Normandy on the 30th had a war correspondent aboard, P.H. Walker. He had travelled back to England on KG404, one of the daily returning aircraft, and had in his possession a multitude of captured enemy war material weighing 510lb destined for the eyes of MI10[53] and A12G.[54] Alas, this was kept close to his person and was not for general release. Upon touchdown in the UK he was briskly whisked off to an unknown destination. Lastly, the most interesting and certainly the most unusual visitor was brought back aboard KG439 when it departed B.14 at 08.33 on the 31st. This passenger was a German guard dog that was captured injured in Normandy and brought back to be compared to a British dog for its performance and handling, etc. Imaginarily christened Fritz upon arrival, it transpired that the animal's wounds were received during a patrol at Rouville, south-east of Caen, and it was lucky enough to be given first aid by its captives. Again, this hound was quickly transported away on reaching the base, onward for interrogation by the British War Dog School.[55] It is interesting to note that the school quickly found out that Fritz had been trained to attack anyone with a firearm, something that the unlucky reporter from the *Daily Mail* discovered when he pointed his camera towards the dog, who instinctively thought it was a gun!

Another aspect of 48's duties that were allocated during July was the formation of a VIP flight that was outstationed at RAF Northolt. Its main function was the transportation of said VIPs between London and the Continent and the advanced landing grounds. A total of eight crews were allocated for a period of several days and covered the various tasks. The breakdown for July and early August was:

1–6 Jul Flying Officer Wills and Crew
2–15 Flight Lieutenant Keiller and Crew
6–20 Flight Lieutenant Whitfield and Crew
12–26 Squadron Leader Drummond and Crew
17–31 Flying Officer McCreanor and Crew
20–3 Aug Flight Lieutenant P.W. Smith and Crew
26–8 Aug Flight Lieutenant Alford and Crew
31–11 Aug Flying Officer Finlay and Crew

Memoirs of Flying Officer Mackay (48 Squadron) and His Time on Detachment in Normandy

During a recent detachment in Normandy, I was very fortunate in having to do next to no work for practically a whole week. Consequently, days off were numerous and my navigator and I used these to their fullest. Our method of travel was the time-honoured hitch-hike and on our first 'Charleying'[56] trip up to the American front south of Saint-Lô we probably hitched more than twenty rides – almost everyone on a different type of vehicle. We found the American forward sections dug in 15 miles south of Saint-Lô, after about half a dozen MPs had told us we would be killed if we went another hundred yards up the road and an American colonel had greeted us joyfully and seemed altogether to take a good view of seeing anyone in a different uniform. Our first realisation of being in the front line was when a couple of Americans leapt across the road and disappeared into a hedge. My navigator and I gaped and put out our pipes and then it dawned on us we had better do likewise. A few yards further down on we found the company commander in a farmhouse in a little hollow, and 75yds further up the road were the Germans on the brow of the next hill. Things were fairly quiet at that time of the afternoon – one mortar shell landed about 10yds off in the farmyard where we had been admiring some very juicy ducks, but Jerry was polite enough to wait until we had just got back into the farmhouse before he dropped it. We were only able to stay an hour with the Yanks, who were in grand form although from what we picked up from them they must have had a very tough time from shells, mortars and bombing up to that period. Just as we were leaving on top of a truck, a machine gun opened up on us, but they were lousy shots! The next day we were taken by an airborne Colonel to see the Sixth Airborne Division, but although we saw the DZ and LZ, and in particular the quite uncanny effort put up by those six gliders dropped on D-Night to take the bridge (the nearest glider finished within 10ft of the bridge and the other five were bunched up behind him), we were unable to stay as long as we would have liked, and it was really a very quiet day. We spent the afternoon and evening of two subsequent days with a North Country Regiment who were an absolutely magnificent bunch – perhaps the most thrilling event was when a platoon sergeant (the only member of his platoon left since his battalion landed on D-Day) showed us exactly how a PIAT[57] gun should be used. He bet the platoon commander a quid that, without sighting or ranging the gun, he could drop a bomb on a Spandau[58] position about 75 yards away, which had been troublesome earlier in the day. It was grand to watch the bomb travel and land exactly slap on top of the Spandau. My navigator and I were thrilled, but the sergeant only seemed to be worrying about when he'd get his quid from the platoon commander!

I could write chapters about those two days, but I feel I should devote the rest of this line to our last day. As usual we hitched up to the front, and first of all ran into an artillery captain, who took us up to Regimental HQ, where we were told we could stay as long as we liked. However, we still wanted to get up to the front so we left as soon as we politely could and made our way past streams of stationary MT[59] until we found the CO of the infantry battalion in that area, and he greeted us warmly. It appeared that a tank had just been caught on a mine on the road although the forward infantry company had gone through them, and were about 300yds ahead of our position. The battalion were just beginning a big attack so another tank tried to get up the road but met with the same fate. The RE[60] then blew a gap in the hedge so that a third tank could try to get forward of the attack. The tank went through the gap – and was blown up in the next field. After that the flail tanks were brought up and sent down the road to clear it of any remaining mines. Just about that time a German prisoner was brought in – I was surprised when he appeared and started nattering in French, and, as none of the Army types there spoke French, I acted as interpreter (not a very good one, but it was fun). He appeared to be an Alsatian and was keen to tell us everything, but unfortunately didn't know even the strength of his own company. We stayed on at Battalion HQ and I managed to squeeze into the flail tank in which the

CO went up to reconnoitre – got a hell of a bouncing around but didn't see a thing. At dusk Jerry started shelling us, and we made a dive for the carrier, which was the nearest shelter. It wasn't really much help so in a short lull we leapt for a shell hole, where we sat and prayed for about fifteen minutes. There were seven of us in that hole, and the Army types were grand. One, a tall, very mild-looking man of about thirty-five, whom I would say took the lower Fourth for Greek before the war, complained, 'Really, this is AWFULLY undignified, I get so dirty, and it happens so often – I seem to have spent weeks crawling round on my tummy.' Another folded his arms behind his head and sang 'This is a lovely way to spend an evening', but most of the remarks were lost because of the din. Nothing could worry blokes like that and they made us laugh till we wept. That strafe ended after about quarter of an hour, and apart from the odd mortar or shell things were quiet until midnight when we had half an hour that I shall never forget – Jerry appeared to be after a crossroads a hundred yards to one side of us, a wood a hundred yards the other side, and the farmhouse we were in as Battalion HQ. The shelling started suddenly and at one point I counted about 110 shells landing around us in under 2 minutes. Plaster was falling off the ceiling most of the time, and I curled up to the size of a field mouse. It stopped suddenly as it had started and what amazed me was that only one bloke even bothered to pass a remark about it – and he wasn't really bothered. The CO produced a bottle of whisky and said, 'Well chaps, it's my birthday'! We were sorry to leave those chaps early in the morning to get back to our strip – they were absolutely grand, and quite unbeatable.

August dawned with the same tasks continuing from the previous month. All of group were busy taking supplies out to the front and returning with injured personnel for medical treatment. No. 233 Squadron had an interesting mission on the 1st, when Dakota KG447 operated a flight to B.8 to collect and bring back a captured German miniature tank.[61] The tank was loaded aboard under extreme caution as it was still loaded with explosives, although the detonators had been removed prior to take off!

'A' Flight, 271 Squadron, returned to Down Ampney on the 2nd after their two-month stay at Blakehill Farm. Their replacements were in the shape of 'B' Flight, who took up residence on the same date with their allocation of twelve aircraft. This also encompassed all the ground crew, who changed locations for each flight.

No. 512 Squadron were assigned to transport a VVIP on the 2nd when Lord Trenchard and aide, Wing Commander Geddes, flew from Northolt to fly to Landing Ground A.7. Dakota KG432 was selected for this mission and duly set off late in the evening to relocate to Northolt for their important passenger to embark the next morning. The flight was crewed by Squadron Leader B. Smith, with Flying Officer M.F. Porter, Flight Sergeant T.W. Payne and Warrant Officer F.A. Prior. Getting airborne, they set course for the French coast but as they got close the weather was too bad and the crew elected to return back to England and divert into Thorney Island. Taking off again later in the day, they tried once again to get into A.7 but the weather had not improved, so as directed by Lord Trenchard they proceeded to land at B.12 with onward movements to B.14 and finally A.7. This had taken until the 5th, when they finally returned to Northolt and onwards to Broadwell.

On the 3rd, Exercise Extraction took place to enhance crews' navigational skills, especially in the field of homing in on Eureka equipment markers. Also, the crews were dropping the 5th Parachute Brigade by day on to the DZ. No. 271 Squadron supplied seven aircraft out of the sixteen taking part, the remaining coming from 512 Squadron out of Broadwell. The route was Netheravon–Cirencester–Thame–Doles Wood–DZ–Base, and was reported successful.

The loads for the Dakotas varied from day to day, although there were staples being transported to France such as mail, ammunition, blood, bread, general military spares, wireless equipment, etc. One of the more unusual but very well-received loads, and some would say most important, was ten barrels of beer. These were handled with extreme care upon loading and on arrival!

As the front continued to expand, the scope of operating landing zones within the near Continent also grew for the five squadrons to fly into. This would continue growing as the months wore on. Danger was still a part of everyday flying operations, and Dakota FZ674 struck the ground in northern France during a resupply flight and all the crew perished. The crew were Flight Lieutenant Morrison, Pilot Officer Hakansson, Flying Officer Lomas. Flight Sergeant Guy and Nursing Orderly Corporal Brennan.

The 6th saw two Dakotas, one from both 48 and 271 Squadron, perform an unusual flight to Iceland in conjunction with the Venturas of 251 Squadron that had moved into RAF Reykjavik. At 16.20 Major P.S. Joubert and crew got airborne on the outbound leg of their special transport journey. With stops made at Tain and Wick, Reykjavik was reached during the afternoon of the following day. Passengers and freight were uploaded for the journey from Wick to Iceland. The return flight departed on the 8th with passengers and freight being transported to Prestwick, two aircraft landing back at home on the morning of the 9th.

Nos 512 and 575 Squadrons took part in Operation Mole on the 9th, a night-time glider-towing exercise taking aircraft from their base to perform a mass landing at Netheravon. Ten aircraft were assigned to 575 and eight from 512. All aircraft were ready and took off at 01.00 from Broadwell. Five aircraft were duly despatched from Broadwell to Netheravon the following morning to collect the gliders and return them to Broadwell. Exercise Consternation II was active, and this provided training for both aircrew and glider pilots to fly in parallel streams roughly half a mile apart. This also gave the glider pilots experience in landing en masse. Forty-two aircraft were involved in the exercise and came from all the squadrons allocated to 46 Group. Routing was via Newbury, Aylesbury, Shipston-on-Stour, Hungerford, to an LZ at Netheravon. Also, on the 7th, four Dakotas performed the daily run to France, but a fifth Dakota was employed transporting the personnel staff of General Eisenhower from England to A.22 (Colleville-sur-Mer).

The pressure of the repatriation of casualties along with prisoners of war was taking its toll on Down Ampney. Seventeen aircraft returned on the 8th and a proportion of them landed at Broadwell and Blakehill Farm to ease the situation at Ampney. This was something that would prove necessary going forward. The Dakotas of the five squadrons reached a milestone when on the 9th they carried a record 527 wounded back to Ampney, Blakehill and Broadwell.

Exercise Lemon was planned to train air despatchers (RASC) in their supply at night scenario. This though had to postponed by twenty-four hours due to availability issues with aircraft and crews, and was subsequently cancelled on the 11th as well due to unfavourable weather conditions. One of 48 Squadron's Ansons was employed on a cross-Channel mission to transport WAAF personnel from Northolt to B.14 and an empty return flight to Ampney.

One of their Dakotas flew out empty to B.3 (Sainte-Croix-sur-Mer) and returned with RAF personnel directly to Middle Wallop. The weather played its part in curtailing this trip at Fairwood Common and it finally arrived back at Down Ampney during the morning of the 12th.

Rumours started to circulate within the group that there was a big event planned and an increase in training would soon be happening, although there was nothing of any note to add credence to this! There was, though, an increase in dinghy training for crews at their local swimming baths. This could have been for the general flights happening daily over the Channel to France, or training for another operation that would be carried out overwater. Either way, it was a welcome relief for most at that particular time. None of the crews thought too much about why the training was increased, they just took it all in their stride and continued doing the job at hand. Glider towing practice was increased, as well as the general French supply flights, while Dakotas on the Normandy run continued with each squadron sending out aircraft daily and repatriating casualties on the return, and a whole host of various personnel from every service were carried to and fro.

The airborne corridors from England to France were revised again from the middle of the month, crews were advised of the following:

Corridor seven – South traffic; Selsey Bill–Barfleur.
Corridor eight – North-bound traffic; Cap de la Hauge–Christchurch.
Corridor ten – North-bound traffic; proceeding to Thorney Island and Northolt–Mouth of River Vire to Selsey Bill.

Information was received about Operation Transfigure, the object of which was to drop paratroopers and land gliders in and around the Rambouillet area to cut off escaping German troops on the Orleans–Paris line. The briefing was scheduled for the 16th at 14.30, but this was postponed for an additional twenty-four hours. All Normandy flights were put on hold for the duration of the period 14–18 and only 233 Squadron operated to France during this time. Two Dakotas from 48 Squadron did fly from Manston to B.6 on the 17th carrying RAF freight, while Ansons were operating back and forth to France if required. Transfigure was postponed again on the 17th for another twenty-four hours, although crews were allowed off their confinement at 20.00.

On the 18th, Transfigure was finally cancelled, and crews from all squadrons that were scheduled to take part were quickly back into the full operation of resupply flights to Normandy.

With things generally settling down, the transportation from various points in England to France and the never-ending stream of unfortunate casualties being returned meant the workload for squadrons was relentless. The number of flights being performed daily, and the varied types of freight being carried, was still the main focus. On the 20th, Group Captain J. Bradbury DFC gave a talk detailing and emphasising that the way the war was being fought on mainland Europe would see cancellations and delays of all kinds of operations that had been planned by the Allies. He stated that the rapidly changing face of the war and the fluidity of the fighting would mean that the transport boys would be called on for all kinds of assistance, sometimes at short notice, and sometimes in a more planned format.

A slight change to activities on the 21st saw Army staff and ammunition being transported to Vannes and assistance given with the evacuation of French paratroopers. Six Dakotas from 48 Squadron and four from 271 Squadron were also called upon to fly a resupply mission to Chambois with panniers loaded with tank and anti-tank shells. The Polish 1st Armoured Division were in a corridor of the Falaise Gap and the Germans were counter-attacking with the 5th Panzer Group to allow their troops to escape at the mouth of the gap. The aircraft were joined by another ten from 233 Squadron as there was an urgent request to support the Poles, who were running low on ammunition. Low cloud was unfortunately covering most of northern France, with heights reported from 100 to 900ft. Visibility was so poor that only four out of ten Dakotas from 233 Squadron managed to find the DZ, dropping sixty panniers of equipment. The aircraft that did not manage to deploy their supplies returned to base. One aircraft (KG447), piloted by Flying Officer J. Byrnes, landed at B.14 and returned the following day. One Dakota (KG421), piloted by Wing Commander J.A. Sproule, did not return from the mission. It was found to have crashed with slight injuries sustained by the pilot and Flight Lieutenant B. Cobcroft. The navigator, Flight Lieutenant W.G. Owen, was more seriously injured but thankfully all four managed to return to England with Flying Officer Byrnes and crew. Flight Lieutenant Owen was hospitalised for a prolonged period of time, and on the 26th, Wing Commander Sproule was enticed into hospital to have shrapnel removed from his leg, after much persuasion!

Exercise Shuttle I was carried out on the 25th. This was a practice for the Airborne Forward Delivery Airfield Group and consisted of loading and unloading aircraft equipment quickly. No. 271 Squadron supplied fifteen crews, who took part in three sorties to Southrop, via Chipping Sodbury and Westbury. Another exercise, Ubique, was planned for the following day but cancelled at short notice as crews had to be available for a large transport detail on the 27th. Ubique had been intended to test the accuracy of night navigation.

The recovery of parts from Wing Commander Sproule's crashed aircraft took place on the 26th when a Dakota carrying a small truck and 15-cwt trailer was sent out to France. The salvaged parts were returned to Down Ampney.

The weather was fine and sunny for the morning of the 27th, when crews were detailed for special transport duty. Twelve aircraft from 271 Squadron and eighteen from 48 Squadron were scheduled to take food and general supplies to the people of Paris. No. 233 Squadron were tasked with sending twenty-four aircraft with fuel, their route being Selsey Bill–Pointe de Barfleur–Montebourg–Carantan and their final destination, Orléans. One Dakota suffered hydraulic failure but was nursed to the ground by its crew, where American personnel already stationed at the French base soon initiated repairs. This operation was a massive undertaking for the RAF, as 500 aircraft from a number of bases were assigned similar roles and missions. On the following day, 575 Squadron were also employed to take 75,448lb of biscuits into Paris aboard fifteen Dakotas. Their return leg did warrant a call into B.14 to bring back casualties, but none were available so they returned empty. Taking such a number of aircraft away from the front-line support did hamper the normal day-to-day activities, although the Dakotas were still able to perform their daily French runs, at slightly reduced capabilities. The destination for the food flights was still Orléans-Bricy airfield, these continued until the last day of the month, when the flights were cancelled for certain squadrons, although they did continue at a much-reduced level for other squadrons within the RAF. The Dakotas from 46 Group were going to have a much more important role to fulfil during the month of September.

Chapter 5

Time to Shine – Market Garden (September)

September 1944 was a momentous month for the aircraft and crews within 46 Group. There would be heroes defined as well as sorrow and sadness that would affect everyone linked to the squadrons. The biggest airborne armada was going to be concentrating on the area around Arnhem in the Netherlands and the RAF Dakotas of 46 Group were going to be at the forefront of this operation.

From the start of the month operations continued in the same vein as they ended in August. Dakotas were employed on the French run from every squadron, taking general freight to France and now Belgium, as the Allies had broken through and were making inroads north towards the Netherlands. Aircraft from 48, 271, 512 and 575 Squadrons were primarily on the ground ready to receive long-range fuel tanks. Wing Commander Sproule had stated that 48 and 271 Squadrons would be taking part in an operation from Africa, so all crews were issued with tropical kit. However, the operation was subsequently cancelled so the long-range tanks were only fitted to a few Dakotas.[62] The date of this operation was not yet defined, although this was not due to take place until after the airborne operation in the Netherlands, which was not common knowledge among the crews at this time.

Operation Linnet was planned for the 2nd. This was to drop an element of the 1st Airborne Division on to an LZ near to Tournai via gliders over two lifts. At the last moment this was postponed by twenty-four hours. No. 271 Squadron had allocated nineteen aircraft for the first lift and seventeen for the second, with 48 Squadron providing similar quantities. The operation was finally cancelled on the 3rd as the military situation around Tournai was deemed satisfactory. All long-range fuel tanks were subsequently removed from aircraft thus fitted. 'B' Flight, 271 Squadron, out of Blakehill Farm, performed general transport duties out of Northolt to Brussels, Le Bourget and Coulombs with ten aircraft. Some crews that overnighted at B.14 were keen to get airborne early on the 5th for the return fight. Unfortunately a message had come through stating that they must remain in situ as seventy-five Dakotas of various American squadrons were being loaded at Down Ampney throughout the morning with supplies and there was no room available to take home-based aircraft until this task was completed.

Dakotas from 512 and 575 Squadrons were involved in conveying troops to Beauvais, France, with nine and thirty-one aircraft taking part respectively. The front line was advancing so quickly that their destination airfield had changed, so the Dakotas actually aimed for Douai, Amiens and Vitry to unload the troops and the supplies and freight carried. Logistically this meant that the Dakotas could not complete the trip out and back within a day, so they night stopped in France. On the 5th they conveyed further freight back to Beauvais, Vitry and Douai before proceeding back to Broadwell.

The 6th brought the news that Operation Comet[63] was planned for a date in September, yet to be confirmed. There was a lot of activity with crews receiving vaccinations and inoculations, and ground crews also finished kitting out in preparation for deployment. Information was quickly relayed throughout the higher echelons in all squadrons on the 7th that the operation involved airborne troops being deployed via gliders in the Arnhem, Nijmegen and Grave areas in the Netherlands. Once inserted it would be the troops' job to hold all strategic bridges that crossed the Rhine. The principle was very similar to the cancelled Operation Linnet that was meant to take place a few days earlier. Again, the flights would be in two lifts, with take-off times scheduled for a morning departure as well as an afternoon sortie, with the date of the 8th being specified. Late in the evening though the operation was postponed for twenty-four hours.

For the next couple of days airfields remained relatively quiet, the operation being postponed a couple more times. Gliders were regularly repositioned during this time as the wind direction kept changing, necessitating the different use of runways for getting airborne. Crews were allowed to leave their bases on the afternoon of the 9th. They had been kept confined due to security reasons. All the personnel involved with Operation Comet were certain that the time had come after the numerous cancellations that had been so prevalent over the last few days, but alas the word came through that there would be another forty-eight-hour delay. This affected all the squadrons within the group, although a few aircraft were still taking part in the French resupply runs and the casualty return legs. No. 437 Squadron were starting to form up at Blakehill Farm during the first couple of days of September. This was a Royal Canadian Air Force squadron that was under the control of 46 Group and made up the full complement of six squadrons.

No. 271 Squadron were assigned to carry out transportation movements on the 10th, when twenty-four aircraft were airborne at 07.00 with petrol destined for Brussels (Melsbroek, B.58). This was followed in the afternoon by another eight Dakotas that were moving a similar load to the same destination. Also, fifteen aircraft were assigned to transport 34 Wing from Northolt to B.48. All returned to Down Ampney empty. 'B' Flight at Blakehill were busy in both the repatriation of injured and shipping various freight out to B.6 and B.14. Similar flights were also undertaken by the other units from Broadwell and Blakehill. The amount of supplies needed to fight the war on the European front was a momentous requirement and the Dakotas of 46 Group had to keep on delivering. Flights to Brussels had become well established, this new destination as well as France being operated on a daily basis carrying supplies and the occasional VIPs to and from the UK. There was a change in the commands. Wing Commander Sproule was posted to Blakehill Farm to take charge of newly allocated 437 (Canadian) squadron, while Wing Commander M. Hallam was transferred from 46 Group HQ to take the helm of 48 Squadron on the 11th.

It seemed certain that Operation Comet would be cancelled as all available crews were linked to other transport jobs on the 12th. All the squadrons were not detailed to fly at all between the 14th and 16th as preparations were under way for Operation Market Garden (Comet renamed), which was scheduled to take place from the 17th, although there was demand for some flights to continue to France and Belgium. Very limited numbers of Dakotas were used, and all had to be back at base by 23.59 on the 14th. The only exception was 512 Squadron, who did assign nine aircraft to fly out to B.6 on the 15th early in the morning and returning the same day. Even though there were no operations scheduled, a few aircraft movements did take place on the 15th and 16th, primarily aircraft testing and relocating personnel for the upcoming airborne operation, as well as getting key personnel in place for the newly formed second squadron at Blakehill Farm (437), who had managed to get enough crews active to form 'A' Flight just in time for Market Garden. By the end of the 16th all Dakotas were at their respective bases, fuelled and loaded ready for the off the following day.

With all aircraft and gliders marshalled in readiness for the operation to begin, all camps were sealed, and briefings held on the 16th at all bases. Details were divulged around the main purpose of the exercise to insert elements of the 1st Airborne Division to establish bridgeheads over the Rhine at Arnhem, seize the bridge and await the arrival of 30 Corps. This was meant to outflank the Germans and speed up the crossing of the Rhine into Germany. The briefings were conducted by the Station COs, who outlined that the Army could not carry out their tasks until the airborne forces had landed and assured the bridge and subsequent surrounding area.

The route that was conveyed to all aircraft was:

Base–Hatfield
Position B Antigua 52 18 20 N 01 36 15 E
Position C Bermuda 51 43 15 N 03 41 30 E
Position D Columbia 51 38 15 N 04 05 52 E
TRV 51 38 15 N 05 18 40 E
LZ Arnhem Area (ref. 657814)

Market Garden – The Plan

In mid-September 1944 the enemy was fighting on the defensive along the line of the Albert and Escaut Canals from Antwerp to Maastricht. Reports were received that the remnants of good divisions including parachute troops and new arrivals from the Netherlands were in theatre. The push from the Allies was slowly weakening the German defences, but despite having few reserves and a reduction in armour their resistance was still holding firm. Behind, the three rivers of the Maas, Waal and Neder Rijn and the Maas-Waal Canal provided a natural line of defence against any northward advance to break through the Germans. A plan was being conceived to outflank the Siegfried Line and to cut the enemy forces off in the western Netherlands, the intention of the Commander-in-Chief, 21st Army Group, being to cross via the three rivers and form a bridgehead at Arnhem, then to continue north through the Netherlands and turn east into the Reich.

The main axis of the advance would see troops engage from Eindhoven–Grave–Nijmegen–Arnhem and these men were duly allocated to 30 Corps. The task of capturing and holding the main river and canal crossings were going to be given to the newly formed First Allied Airborne Army and three airborne divisions, one British and two American, to form an airborne carpet of troops from Eindhoven to Arnhem inclusively. The first day expected to see the airborne operation and the Allied landing ground forces to be in the area just south and west of the line Breda–Tlburg–Eindhoven–Aachen, with small armoured and motorised columns.

Airborne forces were made up from:

HQ 1 (British) Airborne Corps, commanded by Lieutenant General F.A.M. Browning CB, DSO
1st Airborne Division – Maj. Gen. R.E. Urquhart DSO
1st Polish Independent Parachute Brigade Group – Gen. Maj. S. Sossabowski CBE
Special Air Service (SAS) troops
2nd Air Landing Light AA Battery
52nd (Lowland) Division (Airportable)
Glider Pilot Regiment – Col G.J.S. Chatterton DSO
Airborne Forward Delivery Airfield Group (AFDAG)
HQ XVIII (US) Airborne Corps
82nd (US) Airborne Division
101st (US) Airborne Division
878th (US) Aviation Engineer Battalion

The Air Force contingent was made up from the following:

38 Group RAF – AVM L.N. Hollinghurst CB, CBE, DFC
Ten squadrons consisting of two Albemarle, six Stirling, two Halifax, with Horsa and Hamilcar gliders
46 Group RAF – Air Commodore L. Darvall MC
Six squadrons consisting of Dakotas with Horsa gliders

IX US Troop Carrier Command – Maj. Gen Paul L. Williams
Fourteen groups and Pathfinder School Dakotas and Hadrian (CG-4A) gliders

No. 46 Group's involvement with the operation involved all squadrons fully employed with the transportation of troops (paratroopers and glider-borne) and the main plan of inserting an airborne force within the area of Arnhem, Nijmegen–Grave and Eindhoven. The most northerly sector (Arnhem) was the broad area designated to the British forces, although a few exceptions did apply. The 1st British Airborne Division were to seize and hold the bridges at Arnhem with bridgeheads to allow the 2nd Army to cross via road, rail and pontoon crossings. The US airborne divisions were to seize and hold similar targets to the British at Nijmegen and Grave as well as the high ground between Nijmegen and Groesbeek. Advanced Airborne Corps HQ were designated to fly in with the first glider lift of the division. The 101st Airborne Division were to seize bridges in the Eindhoven area. No. 878 (US) Aviation Engineer Battalion and the 2nd Air Landing Light AA Battery were to be flown in via glider to prepare and defend the landing strips north of the Arnhem area. Finally, the 52nd (Lowland) Division were to be flown into the same area as the 878th by Dakotas if the situation allowed. All the lifting of the airborne forces for the Arnhem sector was entrusted to the RAF's 38 and 46 Groups, including all glider towing and pathfinder dropping. All paratrooper drops would be undertaken by the US IX Troop Carrier Command and latterly transporting airfield engineers and defence units. Nos 38 and 46 Group would be responsible for all resupply missions.

The military tasking for this operation was designated to be in three sectors and these were deemed to be interdependent: if the forces in the Eindhoven and Grave–Nijmegen should not be able to seize and hold their designated objectives (bridges), the force at Arnhem would be cut off. The control of the Arnhem bridges would protect the Nijmegen forces by preventing the move of enemy forces from moving southwards. Arnhem was the pivotal point of the operation and an early relief of the forces via ground would be essential for a successful operation. A single airborne division inserted 60 miles behind enemy lines could realistically not be expected to operate unsupported for any length of time. Air tasks were also going to operate interdependently:

joint flight plans were necessary to ensure complete and utter co-ordination. Combining the Arnhem and Grave–Nijmegen air forces into one for the main part of the operation would allow fighter cover and ground aids to be shared.

One issue that faced the British airborne division was that due to the availability of the RAF to lift the division being somewhat restrictive, this could only be accomplished in a two-stage operation, which meant that all the division would not be in theatre until the second day. This would create a timeframe for the enemy's reaction to be heightened and give more time for the Germans to increase their defences. It would thus be necessary to deploy the airborne forces into a tighter pocket, with a smaller perimeter around the Arnhem bridges. Unfortunately, the terrain was unfavourable for this purpose. South of the bridges, between the Neder Rijn and Waal rivers, there was a belt of low-lying fenland with numerous ditches and very few roads. This area was open and exposed, and unsuitable for mass glider landings and rapid troop deployments. North of Arnhem there was a dense belt of woods, where there were some rough heaths and dune lands that would be suitable for paratrooper dropping and insertion, and possible limited glider landings, but again not for mass glider assaults. The airfield at Deelen was another option ruled out. This was heavily defended by a ring of flak and ground defences, and the whole area was a military training zone for the Germans.

The only option for a glider force with the best terrain and near to Arnhem was west-north-west of the town. Its elevation of only a few feet was quite welcome in the Netherlands, the level rising up to and above 20 metres in some areas. Its location did have the advantage of large clearings within a wooded belt, and there were extensive, open areas offering excellent DZs and LZs extending 2.5–8 miles in a straight line from the main objective, the Arnhem road bridge. The initial force when inserted and assembled might have a successful landing front, although the protection that the LZ and DZ might provide may involve some risk for additional landings on day two or three as enemy forces became aware of the zones, and with Allied forces being too thin on the ground. With no suitable alternatives being available, the area near Arnhem was selected and would be used by the 1st Airborne Division, transported by 38 Group.

The DZ/LZ were allocated into L, S, X, Y and Z, all within the usable ground in that area. The furthest easterly DZ was Y and this came within range of the heavy flak from Arnhem and Deelen airfields. A railway line running west-north-west from Arnhem intersected the landing zone group. It had a high embankment carrying a power line, and this information was key to all glider pilots who were directed to avoid it on their landing runs. The runs in general were all good, with distinctive features detailed within the crew's maps to aid upon landing. The allotment of troops to the DZ/LZ for the initial and subsequent days were designed to conform with the movement out towards Arnhem. LZ S, X, Y and Z would not be used after D-Day+1. The following day (D-Day+2) the gliders would be landed at the nearest LZ, which was L; the remaining landing zone being K, which was located immediately south of the river at Arnhem. The forces who were inserted on to L would have to accept that this was unfavourable terrain that consisted of 'polder land'[64] but it was necessary for the saturation and concentration of the area. There was another small but distinctive supply dropping point (SDP V) on the outskirts of Arnhem, chosen for use on D-Day+2. It was hoped that after D-Day+2, or very soon afterwards, the relieving forces from Nijmegen would have made contact with the division at Arnhem. The airborne movement was designed to be in three main lifts by daylight over three successive days, followed by resupply operations as requested.

First Lift: D-Day

DZ X

Six aircraft from 38 Group to drop marker forces of 21st Independent Parachute Company at H-00.20 hours to set up ground aids.

149 Aircraft of IX USTCC. to drop main force of 1st Parachute Brigade at H-Hour.[65]

LZ S

Six aircraft from 38 Group to drop marker force (as above) at 00.20.

130 aircraft of 46 Group, and 23 aircraft of 38 Group, to tow 153 Horsa gliders to release at H-Hour, carrying elements of 1st Air Landing Brigade Group.

LZ Z

167 aircraft of 38 Group to tow 154 Horsa and 13 Hamilcar gliders to release at H-Hour, carrying elements of 1st Air Landing Brigade Group.

Total first lift: 161 parachute aircraft, 297 tug aircraft and 297 gliders.

Second Lift: D + 1

DZY

126 aircraft of IX USTCC[66] to drop the main force of 4th Parachute Brigade.

LZ X

160 aircraft of 38 Group and 48 aircraft of 46 Group to tow 189 Horsas, four Hadrians and 15 Hamilcars gliders carrying elements of 1st Air Landing Brigade Group.

LZ S

62 aircraft of 46 Group to tow 62 Horsas carrying elements of 1st Air Landing Brigade Group.

DZ L

35 aircraft of 38 Group to drop supplies.
  Total second lift: 126 parachute aircraft, 305 tug aircraft and 305 gliders.

Third Lift: D + 2

DZ K

114 aircraft of IX USTCC to drop the main body of the 1st Independent Polish Parachute Brigade group.

LZ L

45 aircraft of 38 Group to tow 35 Horsa gliders carrying elements of 1st Independent Polish Parachute Brigade group and 10 Hamilcars gliders carrying elements of the 878th (US) Aviation Engineer Battalion.

SDP V

100 aircraft of 38 Group and 63 aircraft of 46 Group to drop 163 resupply loads.
  Total third lift: 277 parachute and resupply aircraft, 45 tugs and gliders.
  At mid distance on each sea crossing, a Eureka beacon and coded Holophane light were set up on ships to aid navigation. All DZs and LZs also had Eureka

beacons that were to be set up by the 21st Independent Parachute Company, and these were supplemented by Very signals, ground strips and coloured smoke signals.

Air Support

With such a vast air armada in situ, the need for air support and the means to protect the force was readily apparent. On D-Day the flak positions along the route were attacked by forces belonging to the USAAF Eighth Air Force as well as the ADGB.[67] This was immediately before and during the operation. Throughout the insertion of troops, the Eighth Air Force were to provide light escort cover over the North Sea and the heaviest possible cover over the remaining sections of the route, to and from the DZ and LZ. Once the air landings were under way, there would be light cover maintained by the Eighth Air Force for the landing grounds by day, while night-time cover would be in the hands of the ADGB. Enemy airfields were going to be attacked by aircraft of Bomber Command, including known fixed flak gun emplacements and positions. This would be undertaken on D-1.[68] Bomber Command also had the task of dropping dummy paratroopers from forty aircraft in three areas: west of Utrecht, east of Arnhem and at Emmerich on the night of D-Day plus one. The objective of these was to tie up enemy troops and cause confusion. Also, there were aircraft of 2 Group that were designated to attack barracks in the DZ/LZ area, this task to be completed at -25 minutes of H-Hour. The 2nd Tactical Air Force (TAF) were to carry out armed reconnaissance missions in the DZ/LZ areas and Aircraft of Coastal Command were to carry out diversionary missions outside the area of airborne operations.

RAF station commanders were briefed at TCSP[69] Eastcote on 15 September 1944, with aircrew briefed immediately afterwards. The airborne formations were all set to depart from their various bases from 16 September. D-Day was to be the following day (17th) and H-Hour was designated to be at 13.00. This was the allotted time for the head of the force to reach the DZ/LZ. The weather was issued on the 16th and gave a very positive forecast for the five subsequent days. There was no postponement date or time issued.

In the US sector at Nijmegen, the RAF were given the tasking of delivering the 1st British Airborne Corps. This was entrusted to thirty-eight aircraft from 38 Group towing thirty-two Horsas and six Hadrian (CG-4A) gliders to land on D-Day at H-00.58. Their landing zone was N.

The Flight Plan

The combined flight plan was drawn up by the joint planning staff of 38 Group and IX USTCC at Troop Carrier Command Post, Eastcote. The airfields for the whole operation were formed into two distinctive groups – a southern group of eight British and six US airfields, and an eastern group that consisted of eight US airfields. Aircraft from the southern group were to form up over Hatfield on the outbound leg, those from the eastern group were to form up over March, Cambridgeshire.[70] These initial RV streams for the Arnhem and Grave–Nijmegen sectors would form up over Aldeburgh (northern route), with the Eindhoven sector forming up over North Foreland (southern route). The sea crossing for the northerly route took aircraft directly to the eastern end of Schouwen Island, then on to a final RV at 's-Hertogenbosch. From this point onwards aircraft would diverge to their various DZ/LZ at Arnhem, Grave and Nijmegen. For the aircraft in the southern sector, they would travel from Hatfield in three parallel streams 1½ miles apart. The total time length of the column on D-Day would be roughly sixty-five minutes. The gliders were to be towed and released at 2,500ft, flying above the USTCC aircraft.

For the second lift all aircraft would go via the southern route – North Foreland, Ostend, Gheel and the Eindhoven area – all in similar streams. The time length for the column on D+1 would be about 120 minutes, the RAF gliders and tugs travelling behind the USTCC aircraft. Once all had been released or the troops dropped, aircraft were to turn left and return via reciprocal routes at heights between 5,000–7,000ft. This flight plan was designed to take the force away from, where possible, any known heavy flak areas or emplacements, and after D-Day to provide a known route along the occupied corridor from Eindhoven. It was evident that the initial flight of over 100 miles, both ways, would mean crossing that amount of enemy-held territory would be hazardous to say the least. Flak within the target area was seen to be rapidly built up in the weeks prior to the operation, and although anti-flak sorties had been ordered, appreciable losses were expected.

First Lift: D-Day, 17 September 1944

The early morning fog had lifted at all bases taking part, and all were scheduled for a 09.00 take-off time. Actually, the first combinations did not get airborne until 09.45. Of the 359 gliders that were detailed, all but one failed to go due to it receiving damage before reaching the take off point. Another combination did have to return to base following engine trouble with its tug aircraft. It did try a second time, but to no avail as it had to return again. Both of these loads were transferred to the second lift. The visibility was greatly improved to a range of 4–10 miles. There were patches of stratus cloud at approximately 800ft, but this was clearing by 10.00–11.00. Twenty-four gliders came adrift prior to crossing the English coast, and mainly this had occurred because of difficulties in cloud. One of the gliders crashed, while the remaining twenty-three managed to force-land, with just one load becoming damaged in the landing. The twenty-two undamaged loads were returned to base and added to the second lift.

Once out over the sea there was little cloud, and visibility was 4–8 miles. Four gliders were forced to ditch, two because of broken tow ropes and two due to tug aircraft experiencing engine trouble. The crews who ditched were all rescued. One glider that remained floating was shelled for two hours by a German coastal gun battery, but the rescue launch continued and came alongside while under fire. A fifth glider was forced down on to Schouwen Island due to engine trouble with the towing aircraft. The leading aircraft on the force encountered light flak from a barge when crossing the enemy coast but this was swiftly silenced by the accompanying fighters. There was heavy flak further along the coast but once passed the task force only encountered small arms fire from the ground until they approached the target area. No enemy fighters met the airborne formations, although some Luftwaffe aircraft were engaged by the higher-operating fighters. This force was made up of thirty-three Spitfire, eight Tempest and three Mustang squadrons. Unfortunately one of the Tempests was lost. The weather over the target area was 5–8/10ths clouds, the base was at 2,500–3,500ft with visibility 4–6 miles, falling to 2–4 miles in a few hazy patches. There were light winds that were variable in direction.

On the Nijmegen route, the glider stream was fired upon by light and medium flak emanating from Groesbeek and Cuijk, but this only caused very slight damage to a few gliders and didn't hinder the landing in any meaningful way. One of the gliders did suffer a broken tow rope and had to make a forced landing short of its intended LZ.

On the Arnhem route things were a little more difficult, with eight gliders being lost over the Netherlands. It is estimated that this was due to difficulties with the wake that was being displaced by the towing aircraft. Flak was encountered ranging from light to heavy, especially near to the target area. One of the pathfinder aircraft and six of the tug aircraft were damaged, although none were shot down. Visibility was such that the LZs were easily and clearly recognised. All the ground aids were in operation, as the 21st Independent Parachute Company had carried out their tasks and made the LZ fully operational. The light prevailing winds did affect some of the gliders upon landing, with a few overshooting. It can be said that the landings on one of the LZs was set up downwind! There were close concentrations at the northern end of LZ Z and at the western end of LZ S, with a few gliders receiving damage. Two Hamilcars that landed on soft ground on LZ Z did become bogged down when their wheels sank. With the nose of the aircraft being at an angle towards the ground, they dug further in and overturned, with two of the load of 17-pounder guns lost. During unloading there were some scattered rifle and machine gun fire, which did not interfere too much, although some mechanical difficulties were experienced and the average time to unload approached thirty minutes.

DZ X

The six allocated pathfinder aircraft were successful in deploying the troops on the DZ, later confirmed by the OC, 21st Independent Parachute Company. The main force of the 1st Parachute Brigade dropped by Dakotas from the IX USTCC on to this DZ was also successful, as reported by the aircrew. This was later backed up by photographs and a report from the divisional commander.

LZ S

A total of 153 aircraft towing their respective gliders and carrying elements of the 1st Air Landing Brigade all reported successful release. Following the second lift (D-Day+1) photographs showed all but two of the gliders (134, 87%) on the ground, most within the LZ but also a few very near to the designated target area.

LZ Z

Of 167 towing elements of 1st Air Landing Brigade, 152 (91%) reported successful release. Photographs taken on the day showed 116 gliders landing on the LZ and the remaining twenty-seven landing near to it. Twenty-five of these actually landed on LZ X or the adjoining ground near to the landing zone.

LZ N (Nijmegen Sector)

Thirty-eight aircraft towing thirty-two Horsa and six Hadrian gliders carrying HQ 1st Airborne Corps reported successful release, with thirty-five (91%) actually on to the LZ. The remaining three gliders were lost, one over England, one over the sea and the final one over the Netherlands. Two of the glider pilots were injured in the landings. A report showed that all thirty-five loads were delivered safely. Again, photographic evidence showed that twenty-eight out of the thirty-two Horsas landed on the LZ, but no evidence was available to confirm the Hadrian gliders also landed on the LZ.

Overall, the first lift provided the following figures:

Pathfinder aircraft: DZ X and LZ S. Aircraft despatched twelve, all successfully dropped with no damage incurred by flak or aircraft lost.

Tug aircraft and gliders:

Aircraft despatched – 358
Aircraft reporting successful release – 319 (86%)
Aircraft damaged by flak – six (1.6%)
Aircraft unaccounted for – 0
Unsuccessful sorties – 39 (14%)

Second Lift: D-Day+1, 18 September 1944

The weather had deteriorated slightly and take-off was delayed by fog until 11.00 hours. Thick rain cloud extended from 500 to 12,000ft and was spreading slowly north across Belgium and heading straight for the target area. Because of this shift in weather patterns, the northern route was selected and used as planned. One glider crashed on take-off owing to the tug aircraft experiencing engine failure, but the crew were able to take part in the next lift. Over England and the North Sea cloud cover was at 5/10ths to 8/10ths at 2,000–3,000ft. There were extensive patches of haze in the east of the country, and this weather was as forecast. Some combinations were forced to fly through cloud ,with seven gliders force-landing before reaching the English coast. All the crews from these gliders did take off during the next lift. Conditions did improve once the force were out over the sea but unfortunately two gliders ditched, one breaking up upon impact with the water. Heavy flak was seen as the task force crossed the coast of the Netherlands but this was just south of the track and no casualties were reported. The weather over the Netherlands was better than the forecasters had predicted, there was supposed to be a wall of cloud, but this was around 15 miles to the south of the force.

Flak was a little more intense than the previous day along the route, with frequent bursts of light fire noted. Heavier-calibre guns were noted at 's-Hertogenbosch, where several gliders received some impact. Thirteen gliders were lost over the Netherlands, with an additional two not being accounted for. Three gliders experienced their tow ropes being cut by flak, one glider was shot down and a further three were forced to release from their tug aircraft owing to flak damage on either the glider or towing aircraft. Dakota KG328 from 575 Squadron, 46 Group, operating out of Broadwell, was hit by flak and the pilot, Flying Officer G.E. Henry, killed. The navigator, who was slightly wounded, took over the control of the combination and after a brief moment both he and the glider pilot agreed to carry on with the mission. However, shortly afterwards the glider received further hits and the ailerons were shot away. The combination turned towards friendly territory and the glider released. The tug aircraft made towards Brussels but was prevented from landing because of low cloud. The Dakota continued to Martlesham Heath and there the navigator made a perfect landing, the first one he had ever made in a Dakota!

Nineteen Spitfire, five Tempest and three Mustang squadrons provided support and cover for the main task force, of which two Tempests and four Spitfires were lost with their pilots. Opposition had been met by the marker force, but had managed to get through and set up all the ground aids on the

DZ/LZs. There was little cloud cover, no greater than 3/10ths at 3,000ft, over the target area with a few hazy patches, and the LZs were clearly recognised. Gliders already on the ground provided additional checks if the main force required it. As the main force flew down towards the LZ they encountered heavy to medium flak and small arms fire. The marker force had laid out Ts to indicate a landing direction opposite to that of the previous day, as the wind was a north-easterly at 10mph. Most glider pilots tended to ignore the Ts and landed in the original direction, leading to congestion on the landing zone as well as damaged gliders. Photographs that covered the landings showed 39 damaged out of the 542 plotted.

During the unloading phase a lot of sniping, machine gun and the occasional mortar round did hamper and make things unpleasant for the force. A few of the gliders had landed to close to enemy positions and were either damaged by enemy fire or had to be destroyed to deny the loads to the enemy. The two days had seen a total of forty-seven gliders burnt out on LZ X and Z but not necessarily with their loads.

Sixty-two aircraft were allocated originally to tow gliders with elements of the 1st Air Landing Brigade to LZ S, although it was decided to replace some of these with combinations that had failed to cross the previous day. Seventy-three tug and gliders were despatched with a total of sixty-nine getting to the LZ, a 94% success rate. Tug crews stated that after the second lift there should be a total of 203 gliders on the LZ. Photographs did show that 188 reached the LZ with an additional 13 close to or near the zone, 201 in total.

A total of 208 aircraft were originally allocated to tow gliders to LZ X, again with elements of the 1st Air Landing Brigade. In fact, 223 were actually despatched taking into account the number that did not cross on D-Day. Of these, 203 (91%) reported a successful release. There were no gliders allocated to land on X on D-Day, and photographic evidence showed that 189 gliders landed on or near to the LZ, with twelve landing on LZ, which adjoined X.

On DZ L thirty-five aircraft were despatched to drop supplies, of which thirty (91%) were successful. One crew did do a successful drop but unfortunately it was on LZ S. Two aircraft were unaccounted for. The drop height was 500ft for dropping supplies and of 920 panniers and containers carried, 803 were dropped. The ground report stated that over 80% of these supplies landed on the DZ, which was supported by photographic evidence, although most of the remainder were dropped too high and drifted into the enemy lines due to a north-easterly wind direction at approximately 10mph.

The last DZ Y received the main drop of the 4th Parachute Brigade, which were delivered by Dakotas of IX USTCC, and all reports from aircrew were of a successful drop, as relayed to the divisional commander.

Summary of Results: Second Lift

296 aircraft despatched – Tug and gliders (LZ S and X)
272 aircraft reporting successful release (92%)
30 aircraft Damaged by flak (91%)
1 aircraft unaccounted for (glider possible successful)
24 unsuccessful sorties (8%)
Resupply aircraft (DZ L)
33 aircraft despatched
30 aircraft reporting successful drop (91%)
1 aircraft dropping on wrong DZ
14 aircraft damaged by flak (43%)
2 aircraft unaccounted for (possibly made successful drop)

Third Lift: D-Day+2, 19 September 1944

On the morning of the 19th no communication had been established with the 1st Airborne Division. Later the news emerged that the division had gone into battle at full strength upon landing. Elements of the 2nd Parachute Battalion had reached the road bridge at Arnhem and took to covering the northern approach. The bridge was intact but the southern approach was in the hands of the enemy. The railway bridge had been destroyed and a pontoon bridge was also in enemy hands. The remainder of the 1st Parachute Brigade were engaged in fighting on the western outskirts of the town, although this was in quite a confusing state. The 1st Air Landing Brigade had reached their positions as planned. The DZ/LZ area was subjected to sniping and the occasional mortaring and machine gun fire that was positioned in the south-west of the area, and the unloading of gliders and retrieval of containers and equipment was proving difficult. The road bridge at Grave was taken intact by the 82nd Airborne Division (US) and leading troops of the 5th Guards Armoured

Brigade crossed this bridge before 09.00 on the 19th, but the onward road and rail bridges at Nijmegen were still occupied by German forces. Eindhoven saw elements of the Irish Guards reaching the north end of the town and their armoured brothers from the brigade had made contact with the 101st Airborne Division (US) west of the town, the bridge at Veghel being taken intact.

German resistance was of note and was increasing, so the proposal to fly in airfield engineers and defence units to the north of Arnhem and the insertion of the Polish Parachute Brigade on to DZ K immediately south of the river at Arnhem were postponed. The resupply and glider missions to carry heavy weapons and equipment for the Polish Brigade were ordered. The weather forecast showed that the northern route may offer better flying conditions, but the southern route was to be adopted for tactical reasons; it was thought that to use the same route for a third consecutive day was somewhat unwise! There was an extensive area of low cloud over the Midlands, which did not lift or disperse until nearly midday. Elsewhere, the cloud was broken with a base height of 2,000–3,000ft. Conditions were hazy with visibility 2–5 miles. The winds were east to southeast and were light. While this weather was not forecast, the low cloud was in situ for the whole day in and around the Grantham area, which in turn grounded the gliders allocated for the US and Polish units. This in conjunction with the low cloud in patches along the coast of the Low Countries did hamper operations until the afternoon.

Once airborne the task force set target for the Dutch coast. Seven tow ropes broke, with two gliders ending up in the sea. The flak off the enemy coast was somewhat lighter than the previous two days. This may have been linked to the poor weather, although one tow rope was cut by flak, with the glider ditching. Another glider was hit, with both pilots receiving wounds to their legs. They insisted on completing the flight to the LZ, where a successful landing was made. Flak did increase as crews were making their way to the final RV. A second glider was shot down and came to grief. More gliders had to make forced landings in Belgium and Holland as an additional five were unlucky enough to also suffer from broken tow ropes. Waterborne flak was present along the River Waal, and this was especially prevalent near to bridges. Flak was very heavy near the LZ and DZ on both sides of the corridor. The number of resupply aircraft unaccounted for was thirteen, while a further 106 were damaged by flak out of a total of 165 aircraft. This certainly shows the severity and the accuracy of the flak on the third day! Due to the lateness of the force getting airborne and inadequate communications with fighter squadrons at airfields on the Continent, there was no fighter cover at the RV. Fighters had been despatched to provide cover but much earlier as previously scheduled. On finding no aircraft, they assumed the mission had been cancelled and returned to base. Fourteen Spitfire and one Mustang squadron had operated and suffered no losses. The failure of the fighters to provide cover may have explained why the force of transport/tug and gliders suffered such a marked increase in losses as the flak guns had no opposition during the insertion. Just as the previous day, the DZ and LZ were easily recognisable but ground fire was also an added problem for gliders. No ground aids were ordered for LZ X, which was not the intended target area. LZ L did have ground aids as this was the main landing target for day three.

LZ X was scheduled to receive seven additional gliders, which were available owing to failures from the previous days. These all took off but only two reported successful releases, while another was reported missing.

DZ/LZ L – Thirty-five gliders were despatched to carry elements of the 1st Polish Independent Parachute Brigade. Ten Hamilcar gliders were allotted for the airfield engineers but these were later cancelled. Twenty-eight gliders were reported as releasing successfully, although no confirmation was received that this figure was indeed accurate as partial photographic images only confirmed a figure of nine being visible. Reports were also received that the LZ came under heavy fire from the enemy. Some crews had to abandon their loads upon landing as gliders were on fire and a hasty evacuation was required to get to safety. Two additional parachute aircraft were detailed to drop supplies on to DZ L, with both reporting a successful drop of forty-eight containers and eight panniers.

SDP[71] V – 163 aircraft were despatched to drop supplies for the task force, with 145 (87%) reporting a successful mission. Five dropped their supplies on to DZ S. However, it later emerged that SDP V was in the hands of the German forces, so all the supplied loads fell into enemy hands. This information had unfortunately not been available to pass back to base. Another area had been selected close to Divisional HQ and identified with ground strips and a Eureka beacon[72] had been set up on a high tower close by. The timing of the next drop was uncertain, and the beacon could not be left switched on as this would drain the batteries, so selective use was employed. The strip identification whenever displayed had the undesired effect of attracting enemy fighters, which started strafing the area. The new SDP was far less visible and obscured by trees and less distinctive than SDP V. Very lights were fired but it appears that most of the resupplying crews failed to see or identify these or the ground stripes, with most missions failing in supplying the ground force with much-needed supplies.

During the drop flak was more prevalent and intense. Ground reports tell of one Dakota from 46 Group that was hit on its first run, with its port engine on fire, then going around and completing a second run through the flak to deliver its supplies. The crew were seen hastily throwing panniers from the burning aircraft before it went out of control and crashed. This aircraft was flown by David Lord VC of 271 Squadron. Another report states a 38 Group Stirling was seen to complete its drop of supplies, although one engine had been hit before the crew baled out and the aircraft crashed. A total of thirteen aircraft were unaccounted for during the day. Photographic cover showed that most of the containers fell over an area around 1,000 yards south-south-west of SDP V and a ground report states that 50% fell in the divisional area.

The results for the third lift were as follows:

Tug Aircraft and Gliders: aircraft despatched – 44
Aircraft reporting successful drop – 30 (68%)
Aircraft damaged by flak – 9 (20%)
Aircraft unaccounted for – 0
Unsuccessful sorties – 14 (32%)

Resupply aircraft: aircraft despatched – 165
Aircraft reporting successful drop – 147 (89%)
Aircraft reporting incorrect drop – 5
Aircraft damaged by flak – 97 (58%)
Aircraft unaccounted for (possibly made successful drop) – 13 (8%)

Report from Flying Officer Pattee, 48 Squadron on Experience on 19 September while on Operation Market Garden – D-Day+2

On September 19 1944 at 12.35 we took off in Dakota aircraft 'AP' KG401 in formation from Down Ampney. Bad visibility and deteriorating weather reached its worst in thick cloud over the English Channel and Belgium Coast. We lost sight of our formation about 25 miles before reaching the Belgium Coast and shortly afterwards were forced off course to make way for two Stirlings with gliders. We went underneath the cloud and then climbed through it to be 4,000ft north of Ghent. There were many aircraft above the cloud, but all formations seemed to have been broken up. We investigated three possible pairs but they were not part of our formation. After crossing the enemy lines all aircraft were forced to weave and deviate from course by enemy flak. Nearly all aircraft were now at 5,000ft. In the final approach to the DZ V – on course 056 degrees – nearly all aircraft turned off to starboard to avoid flak and then completed an S turn back to 056 degrees about 5 miles before the DZ. Visibility was poor and as the DZ was extremely small and surrounded by woods it was not seen until we were on top of it. As our height was 2,000ft we could not drop. Two aircraft on my starboard did drop. While turning about some ineffective small arms fire was encountered. We rejoined the stream of aircraft and approached the DZ at 1,200ft ASL and dropped at 15.35. As we pulled away quickly to the left we came under intensive enemy fire. The tail unit was hit and the rudder seemed to be jammed. The port aileron was crumpled in about 6ft from the end. The port engine was hit and the starboard auxiliary tank pierced and drained away except for about 35 gallons. All gyro instruments were unserviceable. Pitch controls, rudder and aileron trim and port engine boost gauge were broken. The fuselage was raked by machine gun fire, and it was at this time that our despatcher Driver Davis was mortally wounded. To get out of this fire I dived the aircraft down and to the left, levelling out with the help of the second Pilot Officer A.C. Kent, at 800ft. We then found it very difficult to pilot the aircraft for it required both our pressures on the starboard rudder and the aileron control was held in a vertical instead of a horizontal position. Our speed was between 95 and 100 mph and we tried to climb on the elevator trim. It took a long while before we could turn starboard on to a course of 225 degrees, and we were hit again before we got to see it. At this time the Wireless Operator, Flying Officer F.J. McIntyre, was at the rear rendering first aid to the wounded despatcher, which was very fortunate because three bullets went through his seat.

   We tried to climb as quickly as possible but could not get any more speed out of the aircraft. I tried throttling back the port engine and discovered that it was still pulling some of its own weight, so I opened the throttle again. We managed to get to 1,500ft but very soon afterwards we were again caught in their fire, and it was necessary to ease off the controls and dive down to the left. They shot a fair hole in the port wing near the roundel and got several hits on the under part of the fuselage. In this pounding the observer Warrant Officer T. Fenwick was saved by his flak suit,[73] which stopped several bullets through the seat.

We levelled off at 700ft to be met by another salvo from in front of us. This time we were able to see the enemy gunners quite plainly. They hit us in several places on the bottom of the fuselage, hit the cross-feed valve and took a good piece out of the starboard leading edge. I think that it was just by luck that we were able to stagger away from them at such close range. The aircraft shuddering a little, but we tried to get some height again. We were not bothered for several minutes and got to about 1,700ft, when we were caught again in comparatively light fire, which hit the aircraft in several places with no noticeable change to control. This did not last long, and very little height was lost, but the radio equipment was riddled. We kept climbing and reached about 3,000ft, where we got a severe pounding. At this point their flak seemed of heavier calibre. From 1 foot to 1.5 ft behind the starboard engine nacelle where it goes into the wing was ripped open about 5ft in length and left flapping over the trailing edge, and fire started here at about 15.50. The leading edge of the fin was hit near the top, wiping off the radio aerials, and a hole put in the starboard wing. When I dived down to the left again they stopped firing and we pulled out at about 1,300ft and used the additional speed to make distance between us.

I went back and looked at the fire and decided that we could stay airborne a while longer and possibly get over the lines. I could not close the starboard engine and stay airborne so I applied the starboard engine fire extinguisher without throttling back. This seemed to do a little good but the fire did not go out. Flying Officer F.J. McIntyre was attending to the wounded despatcher. He and Warrant Officer Fenwick kept me informed of the progress of the fire. Warrant Officer Fenwick was also occupied with navigation on pin pointing. It was not long until we were in it again at about 1,100ft. Then explosive shells hit the bottom of the fuselage in the cockpit area and put smoke in the cockpit. The fire increased in intensity and was burning hard inboard the engine. The intercommunication was gone and electrical circuits broken. The starboard emergency exit was blown off. Flying Officer McIntyre tried a fire extinguisher on the blaze, but it was impossible to direct it on the flames. I went back and looked at the fire again for I feared an explosion, but I planned to risk it and get to Allied territory. Warrant Officer Fenwick informed me that we still had 12 miles to go to the Albert Canal, and I knew of two more possible flak areas for we had been fired at on the way in. However, we imagined that there would be flak all along the Albert Canal so we kept on our course. The fires had increased and there were smoke puffs and shoots of flame in the cabin and around the bulkhead door and wireless operator's seat. Shortly afterwards we were caught in enemy fire again and took several rounds in the bottom of the fuselage and cut out about a square floor of the fuselage floor on the port side. They stopped firing when we dived left slightly. I believe the fire fooled them and they thought we were really going down. When we were crossing the Albert Canal there were two explosions under us which seemed to lift the aircraft about 50ft. This was the last time we were fired upon.

I did not think it could be long now before we exploded and as we were at 1,200ft I gave the despatchers and crew a chance to bail out and at the same time assured the wounded Driver Davis that I would stay with him and put him down. The despatchers considered jumping but changed their minds. We picked out an open area straight ahead and cut the throttles. As soon as the throttles were cut the nose dropped and we now had quite a speed. Houses started materialising out of the mist so I turned to port and got down lower, cutting the engine slowly and getting the tail down with trim. I managed to get the tail down in a small patch of hedge – like trees before an open field. This acted like a brake and we touched down comparatively gently with the tail swinging towards the starboard in about 60 degrees arc. The crew were out in a matter of seconds. Flying Officer McIntyre and Warrant Officer Fenwick carried the wounded despatcher out. I threw out a bit of equipment but got out hurriedly through the exit above my head. Flames were now above the fuselage and the aircraft continued to burn without exploding. We had crash-landed on the outskirts of Kassel at about 16.10 and in no time many helpful Belgians were about. Shortly afterwards the Medical Officer of Rear HQ 83 Group arrived and took the wounded despatcher away but was unable to save his life.

Flight Lieutenant R.B. Austin, Camp Commandant of Rear HQ 83 Group was soon on the scene and offered us every assistance, which greatly relieved the situation. We learnt from the MO that Flying Officer McIntyre had done a marvellous job in as much as he had kept the despatcher alive over an hour with a wound which if left unattended would have meant death in a matter of minutes. The first aid was given under most difficult conditions and under fire when no doubt he had reason to worry about his own safety.

While over the DZ we saw one Dakota going down with flames coming from the starboard side. When last seen it was it was about 700ft and under control. Other aircraft were seen under enemy fire. Although ten to twelve of our fighters were seen at 5,000ft while crossing over the lines on the way in, not a fighter was seen again on the way back that might have shared some of their attention. Throughout the ordeal none of the crew panicked and their words of encouragement were most helpful.

Fourth Lift: D-Day+3, 20 September 1944

Communication with the airborne division was still unsatisfactory. The first situation report had been received by 17.30 on the 19th but this gave the information already mentioned in the ground situation from that day. A further signal stated that the division would require resupplying up to and including D-Day+5 and possibly longer. The 2nd Parachute Battalion were still covering the northern approach to the bridge at Arnhem, which was still intact, though they were no longer in touch with the main body of the unit. At Nijmegen the bridge was still intact but in enemy hands. This was holding up the advance, which was behind schedule. The 5th Guards Armoured Brigade were concentrated in an area 3 miles to the south of Nijmegen, preparing to launch an attack on to the bridge, the (US) 82nd Airborne Division having failed in their original task of capturing it. This was intended to take place on the evening of the 20th with an assault crossing of the Waal to take the bridge defences at the rear. At Eindhoven, the enemy infiltration across the main axis north of the town was causing delay. The 101st Airborne Division were established along the route but enduring strong fighting from enemy forces. The resupply for the 1st Airborne Division was becoming serious; the supply and relief were getting very urgent and becoming a priority to tackle.

A total of 164 aircraft were scheduled to drop supplies, 33 to DZ Z and 131 to a new SDP, which was centred (map reference 691785) about 1 mile south-south-east of LZ L, after information was received that the original SDP V was in enemy hands. The southern route was selected, although there were minor alterations to keep aircraft within the occupied corridor between Eindhoven and Nijmegen. Aircraft were designated to fly at 2,500ft ASL on the outward route and at 4,000ft ASL for the return, in loose pairs as close as possible and as practicable and safe. The height for dropping supplies was increased to 1,000ft. Nos 38 and 46 Group aircraft formed in a left-hand stream in three parallel lines above the US aircraft that were detailed for the Nijmegen area.

Fog was a factor over England during the morning, as well as the target area; this though lifted to low stratus. Noon saw the ceiling level over central England at 1,000–2,000ft and over the SE and SW the afternoon visibility was 3–6/10ths cloud, with the base height at 3,000–4,000ft and visibility out at 1–2 miles. Over the sea in the morning the cloud was at 6–8/10ths with haze increasing as the day progressed to 7–10/10ths with a base height of 2,000–3,000ft, while visibility was the same at 1–2 miles. The target area in the morning was fogged over, the ceiling by noon being 1,000–2,000ft rising in the afternoon to 1,000–3,000ft with 6–8/10ths. Visibility was 1–2 miles.

With the weather being as forecast and with the slow clearance of the cloud, the decision was made to carry out only the glider mission to insert the Polish Parachute Brigade and the resupply missions. Take-off for the US aircraft was postponed because of the weather around the Grantham area, but both sets of aircraft from 38 and 46 Groups did get airborne as scheduled at 11.30. Flak had increased along the route, with heavy fire in the target area being witnessed and reported. Rocket projectiles had been reported along the route. Nine aircraft were reported as missing and a further sixty-two out of the 163 launched suffered from various amounts of flak damage. Twenty Spitfire and three Mustang squadrons provided cover and support. One of each type were lost along with their respective pilots.

Thirty-three aircraft were despatched to DZ Z, with thirty making a successful drop. Two aircraft were reported as missing, but may have successfully dropped prior. It was only after the drops and the analysis of the situation that it emerged that this drop zone was in enemy hands. The total number of panniers and containers that were scheduled to be dropped was 917, and out of these the total number that fell into enemy hands was 809.

SDP 691785 – 131 aircraft had this for their mission and were duly despatched, with 121 reporting successful drops and seven unaccounted for. Again, these aircraft may have dropped. One aircraft did return early after ditching its supplies, but of 291 containers and panniers it was reported that at least 271 were indeed dropped. On the previous day great difficulty had been experienced in putting out ground aids owing to the enemy's mortar and sniping fire. However, a Eureka beacon was installed on the roof of Divisional HQ. Visibility was poor though owing to ground mist, and flak was still intense. The perimeter around the HQ was being reduced further by the enemy, but ground forces did state that a good percentage of supplies fell within the area. Attempts were proposed for the collection of containers and panniers that had fallen outside the perimeter, but this was soon dispelled because of the likelihood that these were possible booby trapped. The indications were that only twenty crews saw Very signals and two reported seeing ground stripes, while one saw a flashing lamp and thirteen others used the Eureka beacon for visual aids.

Summary of Results: Fourth Lift

164 aircraft despatched
152 aircraft reported successful drop (92%)
2 abortive sorties
62 aircraft damaged by flak (38%)
1 no information
9 aircraft unaccounted for (possibly made successful drops) (5.5%)

Fifth Lift: D-Day+4, 21 September 1944

At Arnhem the situation was worsening. The 1st Airborne Division were desperately fighting over an ever-shrinking perimeter under constant heavy fire from the Germans. An urgent request came through at 09.30 on the 21st for reinforcements and supplies for that day. At Nijmegen elements of the 81st Airborne Division and 5th Guards Armoured Brigade had captured the bridge intact. The armoured battalion of the Grenadier Guards had crossed the road bridge and made contact with the 82nd Airborne Division. The 2nd Battalion, Guards Armoured Regiment, who were located to the south of Nijmegen, were expected to advance at dawn but the causeway road to Arnhem was a vulnerable route for all armour taking the 10-mile route because of the low-lying terrain being open to the enemy.

Widespread thick fog and low stratus clouds covered most of England in the early morning. This did begin to clear over the south-west by mid-morning, with visibility improving and giving up to 1–3 miles. The low stratus persisted in the east until early afternoon, when the cloud started to lift and visibility improved. Hazy conditions were common over the country, with patches of low stratus near to coastal areas but no cloud over the rest of the North Sea. Once over the near Continent, cloud was 4–7/10ths with a base foot of 3,000ft and visibility of approximately 4–6 miles. The weather was as forecast so take-offs in the Grantham areas by US aircraft were once again postponed, but 38 and 46 Group aircraft were airborne as planned at 11.00. The southern route was chosen again, but this time instead of one large wave of aircraft, four separate despatches were chosen, totalling 117 aircraft. Instructions had been received that there was a new SDP (693785) only 200 yards to the east of the previous spot. This change did show how a pinpoint drop was targeted for the supplying aircraft. Cover and support were detailed for seventeen Spitfires, three Mustangs and a single Tempest squadron. These were carried out for the initial waves but were grounded later due to the weather. The first wave had a full complement of cover, the second only partial, but the third and fourth had no cover at all. This was further exhibited by the totals of aircraft shot down during that day as enemy fighters (Fw 190s from JG26[74]) downed seven out of ten aircraft from one squadron in the third wave. A total of twenty-three aircraft (20%) were unaccounted for, a further seven were damaged by fighters and thirty-one were damaged by flak, which was again more intense along the entire route and into the target area. Some 52% of the force were lost or damaged; no RAF fighters were lost. Difficulty was again experienced in setting up ground aids. One Eureka beacon had been installed on the top of Divisional HQ and an Aldis lamp[75] was used in flashing a V to all aircrews, but very little was retrieved from this drop.

With the difficulty in obtaining any information as well as the tactical situation in the Arnhem area, the AOC of 46 Group flew over to the area of operations and visited the Air Marshal, 2nd TAF, and headquarters 83 Group and landed at Nijmegen on 22 September. This visit resulted in a decision to send a squadron from 46 Group to Brussels to undertake resupply missions under the local orders of AOC 83 Group. This would give the following advantages: the latest information would be available regarding the tactical situation; the support by fighters and fighter-bombers would be close to hand; shorter flights to the target area and last-minute alterations could be taken to the contents of panniers to be delivered. No. 575 Squadron were selected and made the move from Broadwell to Brussels on the 23rd and started operations on the 24th. Only one aircraft was destroyed during operations on the 24th and 25th but made it to friendly lines before crashing.

Personal Stories – Report on Resupply Mission D-Day+4 Operation Market Garden, 21 September 1944

An aircraft of 48 Squadron, Down Ampney, piloted by Flying Officer Warwick yesterday, 21 September, brought back to England from Brussels four American glider pilots. These four officers were 1st Lieutenant A. West, Flying Officer W.W. Avera, Flying Officer T.C. Campbell, Lieutenant. R.R. Neville of the 9 AEF, 442 Transport Carrier Group, 1st Lieutenant West, Lt Neville, went over on D-Day+1 and the other two on D-Day+2. Three of them landed on the LZ and the fourth, Flying Officer Avera, was forced to cut loose some 12 miles to the north-west owing to circumstances beyond his control and landed in a clear patch surrounded by trees. The actual LZ was to the north of Wilhemina some 16 miles east of Tilburg. Pilot Officer Avera and crew got clear of the glider and rapidly made for cover. After a wait, during which no one of the enemy appearance showed up, the pilot decided to return to the glider and salvage some of the contents. There was a great deal of confusion and noise of guns going on around, which seemed to indicate that a certain amount of disputes were in progress but Pilot Officer Avera felt quite sure that there was no one in his immediate vicinity entertaining any malicious intentions against him. Judge his surprise therefore, when on return to the glider, he was confronted by a small Dutch boy who handed him an apple with every expression of goodwill, but no sooner had he taken the apple than a bullet skimmed past his foot from the rifle of a mean-minded Hun! Avera and boy parted company rapidly and dived into respective ditches. After some further delay he managed to rejoin his comrades, who had been held in reserve at the LZ in case they were wanted for actual participation in the actual fighting. Some of the glider pilots had, in fact, gone off on private wars of their own. These four were eventually pulled out of D-Day+4 and taken to Brussels by British transport. None could be louder in praise for the hospitality given them by the British during their journey back, and they expressed themselves delighted with the treatment they received on all sides. If the scene in the mess in England was any criterion, then the future of Anglo-American relationship is assured.

D-Day+5, 22 September 1944

Two brigades of infantry crossed the Nijmegen bridge but were met with very strong opposition from the German forces; this even included tank forces in the district of Elst midway between Nijmegen and Arnhem. The 1st Airborne Division was still holding out, even though its perimeter was shrinking to approximately 1,000 yards square. The weather was playing its part again and was unsuitable for resupply flights to take place. Although orders had been issued for 123 aircraft of 38 and 46 Groups to fly, no resupply flights were requested by HQ Airborne Corps. An element of 1st Polish Independent Parachute Brigade were dropped south of the river on a newly designated DZ by aircraft of the IX USTCC. This DZ was west of the original DZ K, which had not been used during the entire operation so far.

Sixth Lift: D-Day+6, 23 September 1944

Between Nijmegen and Arnhem during the evening of the 22nd a relief column comprising an infantry battalion of the 43rd Division and an armoured squadron had been cut off by enemy tank forces. As the head of the column approached the River Rijn the enemy opened up and brought the vehicles to a standstill. The boats that they were transporting were quickly ditched and all plans to continue were put on hold until the next day. On the 23rd a brigade with the assault boats did manage to break through, even though they were held up by the enemy forces. By nightfall the leading troops did manage to contact the 1st Polish Independent Parachute Brigade just south of the river, the Poles having been dropped the previous day. All was still desperate as the 1st Airborne Division had reported that they too were in need of air reinforcements. Better weather conditions were still not expected within the whole target area until past midday. A cold front had been anticipated until at least 14.00, giving way to much more favourable conditions. Gliders of the IX USTCC, which had been grounded since the 19th, were able to get airborne for their targets in the Nijmegen and Eindhoven sectors.

Another resupply mission was also scheduled for aircraft from both 38 and 46 Groups, with an over target area of 16.00 in line with the weather forecast, which proved to be accurate. The southern route was once again chosen and RAF were routed in column with the US aircraft. The length of the Allied column was 1½ miles, and 123 aircraft from the 2 RAF groups were detailed. Eighteen Spitfire and three Mustang squadrons were allocated for top cover and support, with two Spitfires lost. Flak was once again very intense, but the RAF fighters made the rendezvous and were very active against the few enemy fighters active. Six aircraft (4.8%) were unaccounted for, with a further sixty-three damaged by flak. This made a total of 56% of the force lost or damaged. Due to the ever-changing situation on the ground and the contraction of the perimeter area, the 21st Independent Parachute Company had been forced to withdraw while leaving a wealth of stores and supplies that had been resupplied for the division. This change in circumstances necessitated the need to abandon any navigational aids and for ground troops to use Very pistols to attract the pilots' attention. Twenty-two crews did report seeing any signals, four reported Aldis lamp signals, seven reported a 'T', one reported a flare and another a coloured smoke signal. Of the 2,847 containers, panniers or other items carried, 2,624 were dropped. The reports coming from the ground gave the results that even though the target area was very restricted the drops were not sufficiently accurate.

Summary of Results: D + 6

123 aircraft despatched
115 aircraft reported successful drop (93%)
2 abortive sorties

63 aircraft damaged by flak (51%)
6 aircraft unaccounted for (possibly made successful drops) (5%)

Seventh Lift: D-Day+7, 24 September 1944

During the evening of the 23rd units that had reached the River Rijn west of Arnhem had ferried supplies to around 100 Polish parachute troops who were located on the north bank. Contact had been made with elements of the 1st Airborne Division, but the main force was still held up fighting near to Elst. The airfield engineer and defence units were meant to be flown in, but this was once again postponed. It was hoped that this may have taken place and scheduled for the 26th at Deelen airfield, with the 52nd Lowland Regiment following on the 27th.

No resupply flights were operated by either 38 or 46 Groups from the UK on the 24th, although twenty-four aircraft of 575 Squadron based out of Brussels were involved in operations over the Arnhem area. All returned safely but there were four with flak damage. All crews reported successful drops were completed.

Eighth Lift: D-Day+8, 25 September 1944

With the situation at Arnhem and the corridor south of Elst not improving, the flight into Deelen was not looking like a feasible proposition and an alternative was planned for the area around Grave, which was eventually carried out by aircraft of the IX USTCC. This was to secure and increase the small bridgehead west of Arnhem that was taken on the 23rd by a battalion of the Dorset Regiment with assault boats, who fought their way to the river by daylight and, joined by elements of four rifle companies, were across the water. These troops then made contact with the 1st Airborne Division and were able to call up artillery support from the south side of the river, which allowed for the evacuation of the division. The final resupply mission of the operation was flown on the 25th with aircraft of 575 Squadron, 46 Group, from Brussels. This was intended to drop food and medical supplies west of Arnhem at Heveadorp (map ref. 682768). Seven aircraft took part and were duly despatched to deliver their supplies. Six reported dropping successfully and one was unaccounted for, with three being damaged by flak. The evacuation of the 1st Airborne Division covered by elements of the Dorset Regiment began at 21.40 on the 25th and was completed by 06.00 the following morning. This curtailed the operations for 38 and 46 Groups in the area.

Casualties

The loss of aircraft to enemy fighters and flak was quite light during the initial phase and did not impact upon the task force in any great numbers. It is fully appreciated though that during the resupply phase of the operation there was increase in losses, damage and aircrew casualties.

The figures of those from 38 and 46 Groups that were missing, killed or wounded, as well as those from the Glider Pilot Regiment and the RASC despatchers, make for sobering reading. The numbers recorded from 30 September 1944 show the following. A total of 120 members of aircrew previously reported as missing had though returned to the UK and are not included in the totals below:

	38 Group	46 Group	Glider Pilot Regiment	RASC Despatchers
Missing	159	66	636	141
		Total Missing 1,002		
Killed	21	10	59	11
		101		
Wounded	12	5	35	20
		72		
Total Casualties	192	81	730	172
		1,175		

46 Group Daks to Arnhem

On the morning of the 17th the weather was overcast, although improving in the afternoon. No. 271 Squadron had allocated twenty-four crews and 48 Squadron another twenty-three out of the expected total of forty-nine. These aircrew were all to be towing Horsa gliders on an operation that was scheduled for take-off at 09.40. Airborne troops started to arrive at their respective gliders roughly twenty-five minutes before take-off. Morale with the troops were very high, with plenty of laughter and humour. This was also witnessed by the chalk markings[76] that were appearing on the side of many gliders, statements like 'It's not Cancelled this time, Horsa the happy Horse, Here we go – we hope, Keeping a date' and 'We'll get his trousers down on the Siegfried line' to name a few. Wing Commander M. Booth DFC, OC 271 Squadron, was first to get airborne at 09.40 and fittingly he was towing Major Jackson (OC Glider Regiment). The take-off was carried out without issue and this first combination set course at 10.20. Both squadrons and their respective gliders all followed, with 48 Squadron's first aircraft lifting at 09.55, followed by the remaining twenty-two. The last left Down Ampney at 10.13.

The weather was fairly cloudy, the formation leader having received instructions to fly below the cloud base. Upon reaching the outskirts of Oxford, 271 Squadron's formation encountered a thick bank of cloud and five of the gliders lost control. Four were released by the glider pilots and one tug captain, but because of these actions one glider pilot (Sergeant Joyce) was killed and another injured. No. 48 Squadron also experienced issues. A glider got into difficulties and was cast off from its tug, with a safe landing taking place 5 miles west of Abingdon airfield. Two gliders were released over the sea when the tug aircraft lost engine performance and had to cut power. Air-sea rescue craft were quickly on station and picked up the crews, as observed from above. The fourth cast off when it experienced difficulties after another towing aircraft developed engine issues. Upon release it landed safely on the Dutch island of Schouwen. The rest of the remaining formation made successful releases at 2,500ft over the LZ. No enemy aircraft were sighted and flak was relatively light, although one soldier in glider number 227 was injured when a piece of shrapnel went into his right lung, causing serious injury. All aircraft made a safe return to base.

As for 233 Squadron's involvement in Market Garden, there were no general flights between 14 and 17 September as this time was needed for preparations. Twenty-two aircraft were detailed to tow gliders containing 309 troops, eighteen handcarts, fifteen motorcycles, ten jeeps, eleven trailers, five wireless sets, eleven bicycles and one 6-pounder anti-tank gun. Their route out was from Blakehill Farm–Hatfield–Aldeburgh–Schwies Island–'s-Hertogenbosch–Arnhem, and the reciprocal course for the return. One of the gliders did manage to break loose near to Chelmsford, Essex. The towing Dakota returned directly to base, while the glider made a successful landing nearby. The remaining aircraft cast their gliders off near to the DZ. Enemy opposition was light and the Dakotas had the benefit of fighter support over the target area and made a safe return.

On the second day of the operation, seventeen aircraft were detailed to transport and tow the same number of gliders. These contained eighty-four troops, fifteen jeeps, seven trailers, eight 6-pounder anti-tank guns, three machine guns, one handcart and four motorcycles, which transited out via the same route as the previous day. Another glider broke loose but landed safely, with the Dakota returning immediately to base. All gliders were inserted with little enemy ground fire and all aircraft returned to Blakehill.

The 19th saw another detail sending gliders into Arnhem that had not been able to operate on the 18th. Flak was very intense, and a Dakota sustained fuselage and port wing damage, but returned safely. The rest of the squadron started flights back into France carrying goods and stores and casualties back to England. The 21st saw eighteen aircraft take part in the resupply flights to Arnhem, their panniers full of food, ammunition and medical supplies. Their route out was via Hatfield–Bramwell–North Fohland–Ghent–Douree–west of Eindhoven–DZ, with the return via the reciprocal. Enemy opposition was intense and flak was severe in the Arnhem area. Six aircraft were damaged and Wing Commander W.R. Coles along with Group Captain H.J. Kennedy (Station Commander, Blakehill Farm) were forced to make an emergency landing at B.56 as their Warrant Officer, Pilot Officer Sharpe was wounded and needed urgent medical treatment. Two aircraft were attacked by nine Fw 190s from JG26 within the area near Eindhoven, one of the aircraft sustaining multiple hits and injuries to crew members. Three aircraft failed to return: Flying Officer Hamilton and crew, Flying Officer Adam and crew and Warrant Officer Punnall and crew.

JG26's records show that they managed to inflict the most damage against the Dakotas on 21 September. Between 17.17 and 17.25 they claim to have shot down twenty aircraft from either 38 or 46 Groups. We know that no Dakotas were operating with 38 Group, so this is incorrect, and that while there were Dakota losses for 46 Group, these were not in the quantities reported, so were there American Dakotas within these figures or was it down to a misidentification of aircraft?

JG26 pilots' claims that day were:

Obfw Teilken – Dakota at Nijmegen 17.17, Confirmed
Oblt Kunz – Dakota at Nijmegen 17.18, Confirmed
Oblt Kunz – Dakota at 's-Hertogenbosch 17.20, Confirmed
Lt Gunther – Dakota at W of Arnhem at 17.23, Confirmed
Ofhr Heindtke – Dakota at Nijmegen at 17.18, Confirmed
Oblt Heckmann – Dakota at Nijmegen 17.17, Confirmed
Oblt Heckmann – Dakota at Nijmegen 17.18, Confirmed
Oblt Heckmann – Dakota at W of Arnhem 17.19, Confirmed
Oblt Heckmann – Dakota at W of Arnhem 17.20, Confirmed
Uffz Herbster – Dakota W of Arnhem 17.20, Confirmed
Uffz Herbster – Dakota W of Arnhem 17.21, Unconfirmed
Gefr Kohler – Dakota at 's-Hertogenbosch 17.22, Unconfirmed
Gefr Kohler – Dakota W of Arnhem 17.25, Confirmed
Uffz Schulz – Dakota W of Arnhem 17.20, Confirmed
Uffz Schulz – Dakota W of Arnhem 17.23, Confirmed
Fw Vandeveerd – Dakota at Nijmegen 17.18, Confirmed
Fw Vandeveerd – Dakota at Nijmegen 17.19, Confirmed
Lt Vogt – Dakota at Nijmegen 17.17, Confirmed
Lt Glunz – Dakota at Nijmegen 17.18, Confirmed
Lt Hoffmann W. – Dakota at Deelen 17.20, Confirmed
Lt Hoffmann W. – Dakota at Zwolle 17.33, Confirmed

No. 437 Squadron were formed on 4 September 1944 at Blakehill Farm, under the leadership of Squadron Leader (Acting Wing Commander) J.A. Sproule DFC and Flight Lieutenant E.L. Joynt as adjutant. This was the first RCAF squadron to be formed in England and come under the direct responsibility of 46 Group. Squadron Leader Sproule had transferred from Down Ampney and 48 Squadron, where he had taken part in D-Day.

Flight Lieutenant E.L. Joynt took over the headquarters offices, operations, living and dispersal sites for the squadron. He had the operational furniture, as well as telephones, installed between 6 and 9 September. There was difficulty in furnishing the whole site as airmen had not been allocated or posted to assist with this work. There were a few members of the RAF Regiment who were seconded, as well as some individuals from the Transport Staging Post who were temporarily at the station, so were allocated to assist. During the 10th to the 14th every effort was made to get accommodation ready for the influx of airmen who were expected to arrive imminently. Two clerks were assigned to man the orderly room, Sergeant Walker and Corporal Kasperski, who had both just returned from France. Also joining was the Squadron Intelligence Officer, Pilot Officer Tuskey, who was working out of a mobile headquarters. On the 15th nine captains and their crews arrived to form the nucleus of 'A' Flight. These were as follows:

Flight Lieutenant R.W. Alexander
Flying Officer G.P. Hagerman
Flying Officer J.A. Delahunt
Flying Officer F.E. Fitzgibbon
Pilot Officer K.Z. Rasmussen
Flying Officer W.E. McLean
Flying Officer R.L. Pearson
Pilot Officer R.S. Purkie
Flying Officer O.A. Simmons

It was believed that these crews would be the only ones available for the squadron until 18 September. All the remaining crews to deploy to Blakehill Farm remained with their current units but operated as a detachment of 437 Squadron until they could physically relocate. On 16 September, 'A' Flight was practically up to strength, with a few more aircrew reporting. Personnel were very busy with an operation set for the 17th, and Blakehill Farm was sealed with nobody allowed to leave or enter without special permission.

The first mission for 437 was Market Garden, led by Squadron Leader Sproule. He took off at 10.15, followed in quick succession by the rest of 'A' Flight, and they then made their way towards the Netherlands. The routing took them from Base–Hatfield–Aldeburgh–Schowen Island–'s-Hertogenbosch–Arnhem and returning via the reciprocal. All gliders were released successfully, and all made the LZ. Some 146 troops, sixteen cycles, ten motorcycles, five jeeps, six trailers, two handcarts, four blitz buggies[77] and three wireless sets were safely on the ground. Enemy activity was practically non-existent as a little light flak was encountered off the coast of the Netherlands, and there were no interceptions from the Luftwaffe. All crews and aircraft started to arrive back at Blakehill Farm from 15.24 onwards. Two Dakotas did operate out of Down Ampney: KG321, captained by R.A. Kenny and loaded with two jeeps, two trailers and equipment, and KG563, captained by G.R. Warrington. KG563 had to abort its sortie as there was an air lock in the fuel system. The engines cut out and the aircraft started to rapidly loose height. The tug pilot managed to maintain flight by manoeuvring the glider but the tow rope got tangled around the nosewheel and the glider pilot requested release. The glider was released and made a successful landing at Martlesham Heath airfield at 12.20.

Another mission to the Netherlands took place on the 18th as six aircraft were detailed to take Horsa gliders into theatre. The same route was chosen and the enemy must have been preparing their defences further as more flak was encountered and concentrated in the Renkum, Wageningen, Rhenen and 's-Hertogenbosch areas. The LZ, which was near to Arnhem, was also more heavily defended, as the placement of the medium-light fire barrage was more apparent. One aircraft flown by Captain Delahunt (KG422) was hit many times with small arms fire. One shell burst in the aircraft just behind the fuel tanks, but the aircraft continued on its tasking. Once again there was no enemy aircraft activity, and it was just the ground fire that the Dakotas had to contain with. All gliders were released and made their allotted LZ. All aircraft made it safely back to base with no further issues. No aircraft from the squadron were tasked to fly on Market Garden on the 19th, but six aircraft flew supplies out to the Continent, either returning empty or carrying personnel that had needed to be back in England.

More aircrew had started to arrive and both 'B' and 'C' Flights were formed. All aircrew that were not scheduled to fly on the 19th were suitable occupied in aiding in getting the station and the facilities to a satisfactory level and were laying linoleum in the flight offices.

There was an incident when Dakota KG589 crash-landed in a field at 13.05 (local) on the 19th when transiting to B.56 Brussels with a load of various freight. The aircraft belly landed after both engines cut out at 1,000ft. The IFF detonated during the impact, but a crash guard was swiftly despatched from Brussels and they managed to remove both the Gee and Rebecca along with the freight of general rations. Flight Lieutenant J.T. Reed arrived on the 20th to take command of 'B' Flight, and Flight Lieutenant A. Hebert reported for duties as the Squadron Medical Officer the same day.

Another Arnhem duty was the order for the 21st, when ten aircraft were to convey and drop panniers for the ground troops of the airborne force in the heat of battle. There main focus of these supplies was to deliver ammunition, which was running low and needed urgently. They routed out from base to Hatfield–Bradwell–N. Foreland–Bourg–Leopold–west of Eindhoven–DZ and the same on the return. The Germans were more attuned to these supply flights and put up a much heavier resistance, including fighter cover from the Luftwaffe. With heavy flak and the Fw 190s, the first loss occurred near to Leopold when Flight Lieutenant R.W. Alexander, flying Dakota KG387, was shot down by German fighters. The aircraft went down in flames, with two of the crew managing to bale out: Flying Officer J. Rechenuc (warrant officer) and Flight Sergeant McHugh (navigator). Flying Officer Rechenuc returned to base the following day, while McHugh remained in an American hospital for treatment of his wounds. Flight Lieutenant Alexander and Flying Officer W.J. McLintock were both reported missing. KG489 was another Dakota that did not make it back, with C.H. Cressman and his crew all reported missing after their aircraft was shot down over the DZ area. The crew of FZ656, flown by Pilot Officer Kenny, were also added to the missing list as they failed to return that same day. The Dakota crashed in Belgium after receiving damage from German flak, and all the crew were taken prisoner. Captain Lane and his Dakota, KG427, was also intercepted by Fw 190s at 6,000ft and 25 miles from the DZ on their homebound leg and light damage was received just above the mainplane on the starboard side. Captain Semple, in KG410, managed to shake off two pursuing Fw 190s when he dived into cloud to escape them.

It was back to delivering general stores on the 22nd as a Brussels trip was assigned to the squadron, with casualties being loaded for the return. Another run to Arnhem were the orders for the 23rd, and this time sixteen aircraft were called upon to partake in the resupply mission for the beleaguered airborne forces who were in desperate need of supplies as many of the previous deliveries had ended up in enemy hands. One Dakota, FZ692, piloted by Flying Officer Roy was cancelled before take-off, while another, KG305,[78] captained by Flying Officer Padgett, was listed as missing and did not return to base. Fourteen aircraft managed to drop their 195 panniers, which was thought had given good results. This was recognised as a good experience as many of the despatchers aboard the Dakotas were on their first operational mission and fairly inexperienced, but the drop did occur within Allied lines. An explosion under the tail of KG345, piloted by Flying Officer Rasmussen, caused the aircraft to dive steeply after two panniers had been dropped from the aircraft. The following Dakota, KG501, flown by Flight Lieutenant Roach, had to take immediate evasive action to prevent a collision with the wayward panniers ahead. This caused his own panniers to come off the rollers and they could not be deployed. They were taken back to Blakehill to try another day. Dakota KG395, flow by Flying Officer Dale, also returned with eight panniers still in his aircraft after the roller system jammed.

The DZ was easily recognised and Very lights and even a sign 'Drop Here' was clearly visible to the crews. There was very little cloud cover overhead at 4,000ft, and the routing was Base–Hatfield–Bradwell–N Foreland–5116N 0300E–5057N 0338E–Bourg–Leopold–West of Eindhoven–DZ–and return, reciprocal. A good fighter cover gave the Dakotas some added protection. It minimised the flak positions west of Eindhoven as the fighters targeted the guns as soon as they opened up on the transports. The Germans decided to use small arms fire on the Dakotas and nearly half of the returning force exhibited small holes. No enemy fighters were seen during the mission. No action was detailed for the 24th and most aircrew took the opportunity to have a rest day. Groundcrew were very busy painting new lettering on to the aircraft. No. 437 Squadron did not take part in any further flights linked to the Arnhem campaign and Operation Market Garden after the 21st.

No. 512 Squadron and their part in Market Garden started much the same as the rest of the units within the group. Twenty-three aircraft were assigned to the first day's operation on the 17th, with three additional aircraft and crews held as reserves. The first Dakota airborne was led by Wing Commander Coventry and was followed in quick succession by the remaining twenty-two. The operation went well and only a small amount of flak was seen or experienced by the crews. They returned to base after despatching the gliders over the LZ with good results.

No. 575 Squadron's September started with aircraft being detailed to fly supplies into Beauvais on the front line, which had extended rapidly since the Allies landed in France back in June. They continued with the general supply of petrol, rations and ammunition. Their main trade was ammunition, and on the 11th twenty of the squadron's Dakotas were each loaded with 5,100lb of ammo for the front line. On the 17th they were also assigned to take part in Market Garden and to drop elements of the 1st Battalion, the Border Regiment, 1st Airborne Division, via Horsa gliders to LZ S in an area north-west of Arnhem between the Arnhem–Utrecht railway and the Arnhem–Ede road. Twenty-four aircraft were assigned and led by Wing Commander Jefferson, who got airborne at 09.45, with the rest of the Dakotas on their way by 10.11. Four of the towed gliders got into difficulty once airborne, and these were cast off and made successful landings. One glider was also cast off near Hatfield when the towing aircraft developed engine issues. The remainder of the force continued, reached LZ S and all gliders released their force of 297 troops, eight jeeps, six motorcycles, seven cycles, nine trailers, twenty-six handcarts, and one 6-pounder anti-tank gun.

The 18th was the second phase for the squadron, and their tasking was once again to release gliders over LZ S loaded with troops and equipment of the 2nd Battalion, South Staffordshire Regiment, 1st Airborne Division, with three aircraft destined for LZ X slightly south of LZ S. Twenty-five aircraft got airborne over the period 10.47–11.23 and headed for the Netherlands. One aircraft was hit by flak and the pilot, Pilot Officer G.E. Henry, was killed, and the navigator, Flying Officer H.J. McKinley, wounded. The second pilot, Warrant Officer A.E. Smith, took control of the Dakota and managed to release the glider (also damaged) and made a safe landing back home, arriving at Martlesham.

The 18th involved all squadrons on the second lift for Market Garden. This time two LZs were in use, LZ S and X. Nos 48 and 271 Squadrons were assigned to release twenty-four gliders each. No. 575 Squadron had twenty-five aircraft detailed and 512 had twenty-four gliders in tow. No. 233 Squadron had seventeen aircraft combinations and 437 Squadron supplied an additional six Dakotas and Horsas.

Gliders that were also assigned to fly on the 17th but for various reasons had to abort were detailed to fly on the 18th. A slight alteration to the routing was detailed:

```
Position B Attu 51,44 00N 00,54 25E
         C Borneo 51,22 25N 01,26 55E
         D Catalina 51,16 20N 03,00 20E
         E Ghent (Airfield) 51,01 25N 03,41 25E
         F Delon 51,06 50N 04,58 37E
         TRV. 51,38 15N 05,18 15E
```

With only six aircraft detailed for the second day of Market Garden, 437 Squadron took six Horsa gliders on the operation. The route was the same as the first day, and the flak was more concentrated in the areas of Renkum, Wageningen, Rhenen and 's-Hertogenbosch, as well as the LZ around Arnhem. One aircraft, KG422, was hit by small arms fire and a shell burst behind the long-range tanks. No enemy aircraft were sighted and all gliders were released and seen to land in their designated areas. All aircraft returned safely to base.

The 19th was the first day of resupply flights to the troops already in theatre for Market Garden. One Dakota had to deploy one of the gliders that was prematurely released on D-Day and had been relocated back to Down Ampney to try again. The aircraft, piloted by Flight Lieutenant G. Whitfield DFM, successfully towed the glider to LZ S and released, returning home after experiencing a little flak north of the LZ. Sixteen other aircraft from 48 Squadron were assigned to take part in the resupply on to DZ V at Arnhem. Once above the DZ it became apparent that the enemy were in partial control of the area. A message had been sent by the airborne forces calling for the cancellation of the drop but this was not received and the drop went ahead. The weather had also played its part because there was a lack of fighter escort over the target, and that coupled with the intensive flak meant that several aircraft were damaged. Two aircraft did not return, those flown by Pilot Officer V.B. Christies and Flying Officer Pattee. The latter crash-landed north west of Kassel after receiving multiple flak strikes. The crew and three of the despatchers were safe, but one died of his injuries. No. 271 Squadron also allocated seventeen aircraft for the resupply mission, again to drop on to

DZ V. As with 48 Squadron, 271 suffered at the hands of the flak gunners, with two more aircraft failing to return. Their captains, Flight Lieutenant D.S.A. Lord DFC and Pilot Officer J.L. Wilson, were both posted missing in action. One aircraft flown by Flight Lieutenant Hollom was hit by flak over the DZ. He managed to initiate a climb to 5,000ft but upon reaching this height the oil pressure and the temperature of the port engine fell and the engine seized. Height was maintained and the aircraft managed to reach B.56 and carry out a successful landing.

Eight aircraft and crews were also detailed to take care of the transport duties carrying fuel to B.56. The weather over the Continent was not the best, with the destination covered in cloud at 10/10ths with a base level as low as 100ft. Seven aircraft managed to land, with the eighth aircraft diverting to B.51.

The resupply missions for Market Garden on 20 September fell upon both Down Ampney's and Broadwell's squadrons to support. Nos 233 and 437 Squadrons at Blakehill Farm resumed their normal freight and passenger duties, something all 46 Group Dakotas had been carrying out throughout the whole period of the Arnhem campaign, albeit in somewhat reduced numbers.

Sixteen aircraft and crews from 48 Squadron were assigned to drop panniers containing food on DZ V near to Arnhem. All the Dakotas reported reaching the drop zone and completed their drops from approximately 1,000ft in hazy conditions with broken cloud. Escort fighters were provided, but no enemy aircraft were seen or engaged. There was heavy flak and some machine gun fire near to the drop, which was in operation between 16.50 and 17.00. One aircraft, KG365, captained by Warrant Officer King, was hit by two cannon shells in the port main plane. Others suffered minor damage but this did not interfere with the mission or the ability of all aircraft to make successful return flights.

Of the fifteen aircraft assigned from 512 Squadron to the resupply mission for the 20th, the flak in and around the DZ was so heavy that most of the aircraft were hit, with two of the fifteen failing to return to Broadwell.

On D-Day+3 the resupply mission was still in operation and both 48 and 271 Squadrons were heavily involved in getting equipment over to the troops. No. 48 Squadron had 16 crews who were to despatch 256 panniers over Arnhem, while 271 Squadron had the same number of aircraft to deliver similar supplies. LZ V was the target, and twenty-seven aircraft successfully reached the drop zone and released their panniers from 1,000ft. No. 48 Squadron did suffer one Dakota receiving heavy flak damage to the starboard engine and the aircraft, piloted by Flying Officer Mackay, had trouble when the engine expired. He managed to regain control and made it back to base, along with the other fifteen from the squadron. No. 271 Squadron aircraft also received damage as they also experienced machine gun fire, light, medium and heavy flak within the area of the DZ.

On the 21st both squadrons again had the objective of resupply to the task force at Arnhem. DZ V was the target and twelve crews were assigned from 271 Squadron, with thirteen allocated from 48 Squadron. Supplies were intended for the 1st Airborne Division and covered much-needed food and ammunition contained in 400 panniers. During previous days the only enemy action came in the form of machine gun and flak, even though this was bad enough with the damage and losses so far incurred. However, today they had to contend with enemy fighters, Fw 190s from Luftwaffe unit JG26. This resulted in many of the Dakotas being attacked with 271 Squadron losing three aircraft. No. 48 Squadron also suffered at the hands of JG26 as well as from heavy flak and tracer in the 's-Hertogenbosch, Boxtel and Keeslen areas and near to the DZ, with several crews lost. One aircraft was reported to have had its port wing torn off due to a pannier striking it after being dropped by another of the squadron flying above. Dakota KG350, piloted by Squadron Leader Duff-Mitchell, had to make an emergency landing at B.56 after being hit by flak, which severed both oil and fuel lines. The landing was a success, and no injuries were incurred. The total aircraft lost by 48 Squadron on the 21st was five, a grim day indeed. These were piloted by Flying Officer Finlay, in KG404, Warrant Officer Webb, in KG579, Flight Sergeant Webster, in FZ620, Captain Campbell, in KG346, and Flying Officer Wills in KG417. Some of the crews did return to base, and their reports were documented and recorded, but two aircraft (KG346 and KG417) were reported missing. A temporary change in the overall command at Down Ampney occurred when Wing Commander M. Booth DFC took control from Group Captain J. Bradbury for a ninety-day period of leave afforded to Bradbury.

There was a stand down day from Operation Market Garden (resupply) for Ampney squadrons on the 22nd. No. 271 Squadron assigned five crews to fly to B.56 carrying petrol, returning with personnel from the Glider Regiment and also Flight Lieutenant C.W. Mott and crew together with their despatchers, who had baled out on the 21st. No. 48 Squadron also assigned four crews and aircraft to cover the scheduled trips carrying medical and tank supplies to B.56. Two aircraft returned to Blakehill Farm carrying casualties and one RAF passenger, One returned with casualties and eight RAF passengers to Broadwell. The remaining aircraft brought back Flying Officer Finlay and crew back to base following his crash the previous day.

On the 23rd, Operation Market Garden resupply continued once again, with thirteen crews from 48 Squadron and only five crews and aircraft available from 271 Squadron, was due to the losses experienced by the squadron on previous resupply flights. The drop was again scheduled for DZ V and panniers and medical supplies were the cargo. There was 5/10ths cloud cover, although most crews reported a successful drop. One captain released his cargo 5–6 miles south of the DZ because of a communication issue with the despatchers. Fighter cover was good, although no enemy aircraft were encountered. One Dakota, KG370, was lost, piloted by Pilot Officer Pring and crew, while another, KG321 piloted by Warrant Officer McLaughlin, was badly damaged and forced to make an emergency landing at Eindhoven. The rest of the crews from both squadrons did make it back to Down Ampney.

Personal Stories – Arnhem: The Abandoning of Dakota FZ620, Flight Sergeant Webster (1434271), 48 Squadron

At approx 1.15 on 21 September we were approaching the DZ and were preparing to drop our load of panniers from 1,000ft. The flak at this time was pretty heavy and I saw two Dakotas in front of me hit and crash! After half of our panniers had been despatched we were hit by flak aft of the cabin. We carried on and after dropping all of the panniers I did a sharp turn left, opened my throttles and started to climb. Very soon afterwards our port wing was hit and a huge hole torn near the trailing edge and several small holes appeared in both wings. The aircraft banked sharply to the right to an angle of 45 degrees and I found it impossible to straighten out. Almost at the same time the cabin began to fill with smoke and flames behind the cabin. Seeing that the situation was hopeless, I gave the order to bale out and opened up the engines to their maximum boost and trimmed back. By this time the aircraft was at 1,000–1,500ft and was still in the down wing position. I left my seat and unclipped my flak suit grabbed my pack and made my way to the rear. By this time the flames were licking up the sides of the fuselage and the aircraft was full of smoke. When I reached the rear door four had already gone, and the others, including myself, followed in quick succession. After jumping the slipstream caught me and I commenced to turn somersaults. I pulled what I thought was the ripcord but after falling for some considerable distance with no results I realised that I was pulling the cloth handle instead. When I did pull the ripcord the chute opened instantly and I experienced a terrific jerk! This was at very low height and although I was last to leave the aircraft, I was first to land. I descended into the Rhine near the northern bank and after discarding my parachute and inflating my Mae West, struck out for the southern bank, where I could see several civilians waving and shouting. The current was very strong and I had difficulty in reaching the bank. However, after several rests I managed it and was pulled out by a youth whom I found later belonged to the Underground Movement. I then saw Corporal Conquest and we were both taken to a house and I was given a change of underclothing and a shirt, shoes and socks, and we were both given hot drinks and sandwiches. About half an hour later I was warned that the Germans were in the vicinity searching and peering out of the window I saw seven of them go by on bicycles. These I was told, were SS troops and were looking for our party. Luckily, they did not carry out a house-to-house search. After dusk, Corporal Conquest and myself were taken to a nearby barn where we met the Warrant Officer, Navigator, and the other three members of the despatching crew. We spent the night in the barn and owing to the incessant fire from big guns and machine guns had very little sleep. The big guns appeared to be firing over our heads and on to somewhere north of the Rhine. At 04.00 the following morning a Dutch youth brought us breakfast consisting of hot milk and pancakes and later this was followed by apples, pears and plums. Later, at about 08.00, we were informed that an English army car had arrived and we were guided to it. The Lieutenant in charge told us to go to a farmhouse on the road to Valborg where we met ten other aircrew, and all of us were to wait there for the arrival of the tanks, which the Lieutenant said would be along shortly. We met the ten others, who turned out to be seven aircrew, two despatchers and one war correspondent, and after a wash, shave, and a meal, we decided to walk along the road to Valborg, which was reported to be in British hands. After walking for a mile along the road we were overtaken and passed by a civilian riding a bicycle. This bloke seemed queer for he passed us in silence while all other Dutch people met, waved, cheered, and clamoured for souvenirs. We were stopped from going any further by other Dutch people who said that this 'Quisling'[79] had gone to warn the Germans. The same people said that 2,400 Tommies were in Driel and so we set off for Driel, but when within sight of the town a sniper opened up at us and a bullet whistled by unpleasantly close. We all took cover in an undulation in the centre of the field while a Dutchman went to find out the situation in the town. After waiting for an hour in vain for his return we decided to retrace our steps and went into hiding in some woods near the road to Valborg. Here we were served tea by a farmer's wife, the meal consisting of eggs, sandwiches, pears, apples, plums, grapes, and tea, and later on, when it went dark we walked in single file to the farmer's house, where we were served a hot meal. We spent the night in the pouring rain in the woods. Once again there was heavy gunfire from all directions, some of it unpleasantly close, and the rumble of tanks could plainly be heard. On the following day a Stirling pilot put on overalls over his uniform and wearing a trilby hat he went scouting along the road to Valborg, retuning later to tell us that the British Second Army was in possession of the town. And so, at 12.00 we set off, still with our Dutch guides, for Valborg and halfway along we met the British moving to take Elst. When we had arrived in the town we were served with tea and sandwiches by some Army blokes and were feeling pretty safe when the camp came under shell fire. One shell landed very close and some Tommies were killed and wounded. We decided to leave Valborg at once and caught an Army truck to Nijmegen. On the way we were sniped at but no one in our party was hit. We were taken to 30 Army Corps, where we spent the night. These people made us very welcome and we were given ample champagne and rum to make up for the shortage of blankets. At 09.45 the next morning our party was taken by truck to Driest. This trip proved uneventful and from Driest we caught another truck to Brussels, arriving at 19.00 hrs. We reported to the RAF police, who told us to call again in the morning. This we did and were instructed to go to B.56. After seeing the IO[80] there we were flown back to Down Ampney by Flying Officer Smith and crew, arriving at 14.35 hrs. We would like to add that all the Dutch people we met, barring the lone 'Quisling', were really marvellous to us, and but for the youths and men of the surrounding countryside our task of reaching the British lines would have been very difficult, if not impossible. Also, we would like to add that our RAF uniforms were often confused with German ones, and this caused considerable embarrassment to us all.

Personal Stories: Report – on Accident to Dakota KG570, 18 September: Flying Officer J.H. Parry

On 18 September 1944, whilst engaged upon a glider-towing operation to the LZ near Arnhem, we were attacked by an anti-aircraft battery at 14.21, 6 minutes before our ETA at the LZ. Upon hearing reports of fire underneath the aircraft, I reported to the captain that the aircraft was indeed on fire beneath the floor of the fuselage. Acting upon his instructions, I released the glider and attempted, assisted by Flight Lieutenant Saunders, to open the emergency escape hatch above the pilot's head, but in vain. The captain then gave the order to bale out and I proceeded, accompanied by the navigator, to the rear of the fuselage and fixed my parachute. The captain of the aircraft then came to the rear and jettisoned the parachute door. It was then obvious to us that we were too low to abandon the machine. The aircraft was then burning fiercely but it was apparent that Flight Lieutenant Saunders still had control. We braced ourselves at the rear and the aircraft made a wheels up landing. Upon impact the machine swung violently to starboard and came to rest facing the way we had landed, close to a wood. I then attempted to get to the front to assist Flight Lieutenant Saunders but this was impossible due to the fire. I left the aircraft through the main door and proceeded to the starboard side of the front of the machine, where I met the navigator and we attempted to assist Flight Lieutenant Saunders, who was still in the cockpit. We found this impossible and after about a minute as I was walking from the aircraft I turned and saw Flight Lieutenant Saunders accompanied by the Navigator and he was badly burned about the head and arms and was cut above the right eye, which was bleeding profusely. The navigator, who speaks Dutch slightly, then contacted some farm labourers, who advised us to hide in the wood. Having been in the wood about 10 minutes we heard footsteps, which turned out to be those of some Dutch peasants. From this point we were taken care of by the Dutch Underground movement and were eventually restored to the British Army and made safe and well. I feel that the safety of the crew was directly due to the outstanding performance of Flight Lieutenant Saunders in as much as his landing of the damaged machine was an epic of heroism which could hardly be surpassed. We were informed by the Dutch Underground that our glider pilots and crew had made their way safely through the enemy lines taking with them twelve prisoners.

Personal Stories – Remember Arnhem!: Lieutenant P.E.A. Gough, Operations Officer, 512 Squadron

Yet again the squadron has had the honour to take a major part in what transpired to be the greatest airborne operation undertaken in history – even of greater magnitude than that carried out on 'D-Day'. On three occasions since that memorable June fifth/sixth an operation was planned for the 1 Para Division. Firstly, to land behind Caen soon after D-Day – next to land near Lambouillet near Paris with the intention of cutting off the main enemy force trapped in the Falaise pocket – and finally an operation in Holland which was cancelled and soon after modified to become the great and magnificent saga of Arnhem. The group's part in the operation was to be a maximum glider lift on each of the first two days, by then the entire Division would have been lifted, and then resupply missions to the 1st Para Division until General Dempsey's Second Army could relieve them. A brief outline of the operation. Come H-Hour and General Dempsey launched an all-out attack from the Bourg–Leapold area, where he had halted two days previously, thrusting north-north-east towards Eindhoven–Nijmegen–Arnhem, with all arms. An American Para Division also reinforced by glider-borne infantry landed near to Nijmegen with the intention of repeating the operation – that of securing the one and only vital bridge. The enemy reacted violently, opening a 48-hour hold-up in the rapid and successful advance of the Second Army's armour. Meanwhile, Pathfinders of the 21st Independent Para Company, were dropped by 38 Group in the region of Arnhem with the intention of securing the bridge across the Lek.[81]

At this stage the squadron entered into the operation. Twenty-two glider combinations were to take part from Broadwell, 575 Squadron led by their CO, Wing Commander Jefferson, followed by 512 Squadron with the remaining gliders. The time for take-off approached with a heavy mist enveloping the aerodrome and as conditions seemed to be the same in the entire area, it boded evil for the operation. Minutes ticked by all too quickly in comparison with the rate of clearance Met had given and although an occasional break appeared in the mist which slowly began to lift, it seemed impossible that the squadrons would be able to take off on time – the most vital factor in the entire operation. Dead on time, however, Wing Commander Jefferson was airborne followed quickly by the rest of the stream from Broadwell, confronted with visibility of about 1 mile at the best and a cloud base of about 200ft, in lifted mist. All got away safely and disappeared into the haze, some climbing and some staying below the cloud base, and just about thirty minutes after the first aircraft was away the lifted cloud began to break very quickly and one could see from the ground the first formations setting course over the aerodrome. From there onwards it proved to be a game of hide and seek in and out of the cloud, which rose to about 3,000ft, and several crews had unpleasantly exciting near misses with a formation of American bombers who were returning at about the same height and on the same track as the outgoing glider stream! Unfortunately, a few gliders had to cast off through getting into difficulties in cloud, but although most landed safely there were unhappily some fatal casualties. The weather improved as the stream flew eastward and after crossing the east coast north of the Thames, it was clear with good visibility all the way. Course was set for Schouwen Island after crossing the coast and by then the various streams from all the other airfields taking part were visible and beginning to link up. Next, the Dutch coast came into sight, but all too slowly was the distance eaten up as the Dakotas laboured on at about 110 mph. A comforting sight appeared in the shape of the ADGB, escort of Spitfires when the enemy-held coast was only a few miles distant and formations of American Dakotas in vics of nine, carrying paratroopers, rapidly began to overhaul the glider stream. They crossed the coast before the glider leader and were met with a heavy concentration of flak from a flak ship and a gun position on the tip of Schouwen. One aircraft was seen to go down in flames but in the next movement two Mosquitoes appeared from nowhere and blew the flakship out of the water, following this by beating up the gun position. No more interference was experienced from this area! The majority of the inland had been flooded and isolated houses could be seen surrounded by water with only the occasional tree visible above the surface. The stream turned east at the neck of the island and set course for the railway junction just south of 's-Hertogenbosch. Visibility was magnificent with no cloud and by this time the sky was literally full of escorting aircraft at all heights. But for an occasional isolated burst of medium flak, no interference was experienced thanks largely due to the low-level escort who were strafing anything and everything they saw. Around 's-Hertogenbosch and then the final run north-east towards Arnhem and the glider LZ, everybody was intact and in high spirits and there were last-minute conversations and messages to and from tug and glider. Just at this time, a burst of flak aimed at the leading aircraft of 575 Squadron exploded under the nose of the glider, unfortunately killing the second pilot outright. The LZ came in sight and one by one the gliders pulled off and were seen to land in the area while the tugs dropped their ropes and turned for home. Next the most incredible sight of all as for the whole journey back to the English coast one was flying over a veritable carpet of glider combinations, Halifaxes, Stirlings, Dakotas and Albemarles with Hamilcars, Horsas and Wacos in train. And to make the scene more fantastic, there now seemed to be thousands of fighters milling around as escorts in close support.

The first day ended with all aircraft returning safely to base, although some bore unpleasant signs of battle with bullet and shrapnel holes dotted over the fuselage and main planes. In fact, the first operation had been a major success and it was obvious that a devastating surprise had been sprung on the enemy. On the next day's lift the same number of combinations were airborne but 512 Squadron leading and, as take-off was delayed for about 4 hours, weather conditions were more favourable than on the previous day. Again local visibility was not very good in haze but shortly after leaving the area it improved and for the most part of the same route was much the same as the day before. By the time the Dutch coast was reached the stream was taking shape and although no escort had yet appeared, no interference was experienced. It was not until turning around 's-Hertogenbosch that the first opposition became apparent in the form of bunches of predicted flak at roughly 2,500ft, the height we were flying, and some of them seemed to be very close. The stream ploughed on, untouched, however, and smoke and a landing tee were identified on the LZ before the gliders pulled off while several fires were seen burning in the woods nearby. A strong escort of Thunderbolts and Mustangs had by this time appeared and seemed to be having a grand old time with ground targets in the vicinity. Again a carpet of tugs and gliders all the way back to the English coast but on this occasion the flak seemed to have increased around the 's-Hertogenbosch area. On the way out one could see the incoming stream underneath getting an occasional peppering and it wasn't until late that evening that it was confirmed that Squadron Leader Southgate and his crew were missing. It was thought that he had force-landed on Schouwen Island with his glider as one had been seen flying very slowly and losing height from roughly his position in the formation when approaching the island.

On the next day, the 19th, the first resupply for the 1st Division took place. The route was changed, crossing the front line near Bruges and on to Arnhem. Nearly all the crews who had been operating on the 17th took part now and it wasn't until the mainland of Holland was reached that the weather deteriorated considerably in lifted fog with bad visibility. From the moment the enemy lines were crossed until the squadron left the coast on the way back home, they were subject to a prolonged attack from all types of flak and nearly all the aircraft were hit, though fortunately, not seriously. To make matters worse, not a single fighter escort was sighted throughout the entire operation which obviously had a lot to do with the incessant interference from flak. The LZ was reached by all aircraft, however, and although the area itself seemed to be clear except for the already landed gliders, the woods and fields surrounding seemed to be either in enemy hands or part of No Man's Land. This was proved when the first aircraft ran in to drop supplies as a terrific barrage of medium and light flak and small arms fire was directed at them and as the squadron was flying in vics of three aircraft most machines received a peppering. Nobody had time to take a proper look around the area but it certainly seemed that the forces on the ground were not in too healthy a position. The stream received the same attention from the enemy gun sites on the way out and they were very tired crews that returned to base at about 19.00 that night.

A word about the military position at this phase. The Second Army had been hold up for about 48 hours at Nijmegen during which fierce fighting was taking place in the hopes of keeping the one and only bridge across the river intact. Not only that but the enemy was constantly breaking through the thin screen left to guard the corridor up to Nijmegen and noticeably harassing the Allied supplies, although the American paratroops carried out a grand job in keeping our lifeline open. Since the bridge at Nijmegen had not yet been taken, the position of the 1st Airborne Division at Arnhem was already becoming precarious since they had been fighting then for three days and every hour were meeting rapidly increasing and overwhelming resistance from tanks and heavy artillery.

On the fourth day the position of the 1st Division was becoming critical and although the bridge at Nijmegen had been captured intact there was no immediate prospect of a link-up. Those crews not operating the previous day took part in the second resupply mission. This time the route was changed at the last moment, to cross the coast near to Ostend, then to Bourg-Leopold and on to Eindhoven, flying over the Allied corridor and from there to strike straight for Arnhem. The DZ had been selected further to the west of the town than on the previous day. Again, the weather was heavy in lifted fog over the area but this time a very strong escort was provided and no flak experienced until the area of the DZ was reached. Then it seemed that everything possible was coming up from the woods around and one could see heavier flak guns with muzzle flashes in the woods to the north of the area. Several aircraft were badly hit and many of them crashed in flames but despite the intense barrage most of the panniers were dropped in the DZ. It is regretted that in this action both Flight Lieutenant Matthews and Pilot Officer Perry were badly hit and have been posted as missing, although some of Perry's crew later baled out with the RASC despatchers and are known to be safe. Flying Officer Campbell had one engine hit and made a successful emergency landing at Brussels in bad weather conditions. By this time the aircraft in the squadron had been peppered so much that it was not possible to put more than a few in the air and on the next two days, which saw the final daylight resupply of the 1st Division, the squadron was standing down.

Unfortunately, on the very next day, several Dakotas from the Group were jumped by Fw 190s and many shot down, among then one of the Canadian crews from the squadron who had just left us to join the Canadian Squadron (233) at Blakehill Farm, Flight Lieutenant Alexander. His Warrant Officer, Flying Officer Rechenuc, happily managed to bale out and lived to tell the tale.

From there the tragic history of that sacrificial stand at Arnhem is known to all. How exhausted and hungry survivors crossed the river at night and the many acts of bravery performed in that pocket, which must have been hell itself. The squadron has more than a working interest in this epic, because our friends were down there fighting; the officers and NCOs and men who came with us on D-Day belonging to the Glider Pilot Regiment. It is impossible to mention all the names but of the officers, Captain Thomas and Captain Ploughman, who have not returned will always be remembered, and Major Tony Murray, who came through with a bullet through his chest.

To close this history we in the squadron pay tribute to the fine men of the RASC who came with us to despatch those well-needed supplies, and who, in the course of these operations suffered heavy casualties.

Well, there usually is a stop press to every story – this without exception. Squadron Leader Southgate and crew have reported back but Flight Lieutenant Saunders had been badly burned about the hands unfortunately but is making good progress. And the latest good news is that Flight Lieutenant Matthews and crew are known to be safe in an enemy hospital. Good Luck to them and we hope we see them soon.

Personal Stories – Statement on Abandoning Aircraft FZ620 over DZ on 21 September 1944 and Escape to British Forces by Sergeant Rushton (1337246)

After all the panniers had been dropped, I received the order to bale out from the aircraft from Captain Flight Sergeant Webster. I jettisoned my flak suit and put my para-pack in position, noting which side the ripcord was and proceeded to the door where the despatchers stood adjusting their 'chutes'. We went out in good order and there was no panic. I remember turning over once, before the canopy filled and there was no unpleasant jerk. At first I thought I would never get down and could feel myself being blown to the north of the river so I dragged on the harness to quicken the fall and cut down the drift. The last 100ft were soon over, and I touched down beside a hedge surrounding a farm. I released myself and pulled the chute in and hid it, with my Mae West, under the hedge. On looking around I saw a lady waving to me, and I ran towards her. She greeted me very warmly and showed me were two of the despatchers were. I ran over to them and found them all unhurt. Our party soon grew owing to the farm people running over. They collected all our chutes etc. and hid them. Then two fellows came along on cycles who spoke English, they told us that the German SS troops were around and took us to the farm explaining the military situation en route. At the farm we had a quick drink of milk and were then taken to a barn in an orchard to hide. In the barn we discussed our chances of escape aided by the map in my purse. The Dutch people said they would try to get us away that night, but we were not sure owing to there being so many Germans about, so we decided to hide and await darkness. About this time a farm worker ran over saying that the Germans were searching for us about 100 metres away, so we hid in the barn. After an hour (approx) we got the 'all clear' from the farmer who said that the 'Underground' people were bringing some of our crew over to the barn, and that we would have to stay in the barn until the British troops arrived. Then a girl brought some excellent sandwiches and plenty of hot milk for us; she also spoke good English. After they'd gone we kept very quiet and kept a careful watch for enemy troops. A few minutes after darkness had fallen the chief man of the Dutch patriots came along bringing Flight Sergeant Fell, our navigator, and another despatcher plus a big bottle of milk. We talked very quietly over getting away and decided to leave ourselves in the hands of our Dutch friends, who obviously knew what they were doing and had the 'guts' to do it. After a short wait the patriots brought Flight Sergeant Webster and the remaining despatcher. From here my story is the same as Flight Sergeant Webster's, who is also making a statement.

Personal Stories – Report on Resupply Mission (D-Day+4) Operation Market Garden, 21 September 1944, Aircraft KG404: Flying Officer Finlay

The panniers were dropped at 16.10 on 21 September, from a height of 800ft. Over the DZ a certain amount of flak was seen bursting at 4,000ft but the aircraft was untouched. The aircraft had turned and was on homeward track at 4,000ft when the first enemy fighters were seen north of Eindhoven. This was at approx 16.15 and despatchers had already warned the pilot that two Dakotas had been shot down by fighters. Flight Sergeant Gray, navigator, went into the astro-dome and saw up to six fighters following about 5,000 yards behind the Dakota. This information was passed to the pilot, who immediately dived for cloud cover. Flying Officer Rice, Warrant Officer, then took over in the astro-dome and saw three Dakotas, each with an engine on fire, with about eight fighters milling around them. One Dakota was losing height, but all seemed to be under control. Two fighters broke away obviously to attack the Dakota KG404 which was then 4,000–5,000 yards ahead and 2,000ft below the fighters. One fighter dived away and disappeared from view, whilst the second turned to make an attack from the port quarter and began to close in. Meanwhile, the pilot of the Dakota was taking evasive action according to directions passed from the astro-dome when hits were registered on the lower starboard side of the fuselage, presumably by another enemy aircraft which remained unseen. The starboard auxiliary tank caught fire as a result, and starboard wing and whole fuselage aft of the cockpit were alight. The starboard motor was put out of action and the aircraft dived further down through cloud at 2,000ft. The port motor showed signs of failing also. The pilot sent back instructions that the despatchers should jump, but they had already gone (it subsequently transpired that the heat of the fire had become too much for them). All attempts to quell the fire were abortive. Pilot then notified crew of impending crash-landing and crew went to crash stations. Navigator Flight Sergeant Gray went behind the bulkhead at rear of navigator's compartment and Warrant Officer Flying Officer Rice braced himself against armour plating to rear of pilot's seat. First and second pilots remained on their seats. At a height of 1,000ft fumes and smoke in the cabin obscured vision for some seconds. Aircraft was set to land in a field but within 500 yards just as vision cleared in the cabin, a fair-sized tree was seen to be right on track of the aircraft. Lateral and horizontal control by this time was almost nil and evasive action could not be taken and aircraft hit a tree about 20ft from the ground in foliage and top branches. Nose of the aircraft caved in, windscreen shattered and one large branch pierced the cockpit, forcing first pilot's rudder pedals back to seat, spraining both ankles of pilot very severely. Aircraft hit ground on more or less even keel – came to rest in turnip field in 200 yards from tree at right angles to track. Starboard wing, port elevator all the fuselage and rudder were alight. Pilot and warrant officer escaped through upper emergency hatch, second pilot and navigator dashed through the flames to rear door as they didn't know then that all the despatchers had already jumped out. Second pilot Flying Officer Walsh entered kite again and shouted for despatchers but intense heat drove him out immediately. The crew were picked up by 58th LAA[82] Regiment of 11th Armoured Division (Captain L.S. Smith) and were treated for injuries sustained and given good hospitality. They were then handed to the 7th British Field Dressing Station, who had already picked up the four despatchers, one of whom (Corporal Matthews) had been wounded and was treated as an air evacuation casualty. Rear Brigade HQ of the 11th Armoured Division transported survivors on 22 September to B.56, whence they were flown to Down Ampney by Squadron Leader Wheatly-Smyth of 48 Squadron.

Personal Stories – by Flying Officer Clark of Warrant Officer Webb's Crew, KG579, on Resupply Mission D-Day+4 Operation Market Garden, 21 September 1944

After the drop, during which slight damage was incurred by the aircraft through flak, aircraft climbed away to 4,000ft. There was difficulty in pulling in straps, warrant officer and navigator went aft to assist. Later, when warrant officer and navigator were going forward, aircraft was hit by cannon fire. Under the impression it was flak, suitable evasion action was taken, but a Fw 190 was seen to fly past aircraft to starboard, and it was realised that Dakota was being attacked by enemy aircraft. Flying Officer Clark got into the astro-dome and saw approximately fifteen Fw 190s on the port quarter at 1,000 yards/200ft to attack. Ten Fw 190s were also on the starboard quarter about 1,000ft above in line astern and the first was peeling off to come in to attack. Evasive action was attempted turning into attacks and out of the total attacking force only four registered strikes, which resulting in fire breaking out underneath centre section of wings. Aircraft entered cloud maintaining approximately same height but after two minutes cloud cover ceased. Almost immediately ten Fw 190s caught up 1,000ft above on port quarter. Evasive action was again carried out, but one aircraft registered a hit and shot away the astro-dome (fortunately at a moment when Flying Officer Clark had ducked down to wave pilot into a steeper turn). Last aircraft of enemy formation registered strikes (approx two-second burst) in starboard engine, causing fire to extend and aircraft went into a steep apparently out of control. Despatchers and warrant officer baled out on instructions from Pilot Officer Clark, who yelled at pilot that aircraft was on fire and was waved back by pilot. Pilot Officer Clark, who had been wounded in legs, made his way to rear door, pulling himself along by means of fuselage ribs owning to the steep angle at which aircraft was diving. Great difficulty was experienced in getting through door, and Clark forced himself out head first until he was far enough out for the slipstream to do the rest. During his way back to the door more hits were registered on Dakota by fighters. On the way down six Fw 190s remained and strafed parachutists. Pilot Officer Clark, realising this, hauled on one side of the lift webs and caused himself to swing violently and evaded the fire from the fighters. Three attempts were made and on the last attempt Clark, who had now got the matter sized up, waited until he saw the fighter turning into attack before adopting his evasive tactics. Fw 190 actually passed within 2ft of parachute and Clark could see the pilot quite clearly laughing. The slipstream from the aircraft caused the chute to collapse but this opened again at 500ft and Clark landed safely.

While disengaging from harness he saw four Fw 190 diving down towards him. He rolled quickly away on to the inside of aircraft turn and saw cannon strikes about 5 or 6 yards away on the grass. During the latter part of descent allied flak engaged the aircraft. Parachute and Mae West[83] were hidden in ditch and Clark made a quick inspection of countryside and saw a girl waving from a farm about a couple of hundred yards away. She took Clark to another farmhouse, where one despatcher had arrived (slightly wounded). First aid was rendered by the Dutch people, who were kindness itself. After a while some Dutch Red Cross workers arrived and dressed their wounds and then it was heard that four other parachutists had landed in the vicinity, and Clark was taken to one spot where two other despatchers were found (one seriously wounded, who subsequently died) and the other wounded in nine places. After fifteen minutes the fourth despatcher arrived slightly wounded in legs. Clark got Dutchmen to intercept transport and a British ambulance arrived and took survivors to Grave, where Warrant Officer Birlison's body was seen riddled with bullets from head to foot! Survivors all landed in village of Zeeland, at Grave survivors were all taken to a medical post and one despatcher detained (with nine wounds). Pilot Officer Clark and two despatchers joined up with the survivors of a Stirling crew from Fairford and hitch-hiked from Grave to

Eindhoven, where they spent the night at the St Francis Hospital just outside the town. The following morning (22 September) they hitch-hiked again to the Escaut Canal, where RAF regiment officer picked them up in two jeeps and drove them to 30 Corps Rear HQ, some 10 miles to the south, where they were hospitably treated. They were then driven in two staff cars to Brussels, where Pilot Officer Clark was brought back to England by Flight Lieutenant Alford of 48 Squadron. Flying Officer Clark states that he kept his crash helmet on when jumping with the result that the buckles on the left web caught under the edge of the helmet and bruised both sides of his jaw and helmet straps nearly strangled him. It was also reported to Pilot Officer Clark that two of the Fw 190s were shot down by Spitfires, but this cannot be confirmed by Pilot Officer Clark, who did not see any friendly aircraft throughout the trip.

Personal Stories – by Warrant Officer Felton in Aircraft KG391 from 48 Squadron – Operation Market Garden (Resupply), 23 September 1944

The aircraft sustained a hit by flak in the tail immediately after dropping the panniers on the DZ. There was a blinding flash, the fuselage was filled with dense smoke, and the aircraft was out of control. There was no rudder control or elevator trim, only downward elevator control. The aircraft climbed rapidly, but after the pilot reduced boost to approximately 20 pounds and exerted considerable forward pressure on the stick, the aircraft assumed a more or less level flying altitude at about 110 mph. The despatchers were moved forward as far as possible to help to keep the nose of the aircraft down. The pilot decided to try to reach B.56, which he succeeded in doing after meeting some light and heavy flak. Warrant Officer contacted Flying Control at B.56 when at 500ft requesting permission to crash-land. This was given. On impact with the ground the port prop sliced the fuselage and starboard prop cut a hole in the starboard wing. This crash-landing had to be an engine-assisted approach almost to the ground as the aircraft was only partially under control but was successful. No one being injured at all. The pilot feels that if despatchers had released panniers sooner, aircraft would not have been hit. The despatchers were not used to manoeuvring panniers in Dakotas – having been in Stirlings previously.

Damage to aircraft:

Two engines U/S[84] (Category B)
Fuselage cut
Starboard wing cut
Tail damaged

Personal Stories – by Warrant Officer McLauglin, 48 Squadron, in AJ KG321 on Resupply Mission D-Day+6, 23 September 1944

While dropping panniers on the DZ the aircraft was hit by flak on the nacelle of the port engine. The pilot took evasive action and got clear of the DZ. The navigator went aft to examine port engine, which was not up to scratch, and found large quantities of oil gushing out. The oil pressure gauge and boost registered zero. The pilot found that it was impossible to feather the prop and tried in vain to throw it off by revving quickly. By this time the aircraft had climbed to 2,000ft but as the engine seized, proceeded to lose height rapidly. The pilot increased the boost to 45 inches, and revs to 2,500, but the starboard engine overheated, and aircraft still lost height. The pilot decided to make for the nearest aerodrome, which happened to be Eindhoven, making a tight turn circuit there at 500ft and received a 'Green'.[85] He intended to crash-land, but at the last moment, when 25ft from touchdown, decided to lower the undercarriage, which was not fully extended when aircraft touched down and landed safely. That night was spent in the officers' mess at Eindhoven, the next morning they joined a convoy going to Brussels at 06.30 and were flown back together with the four despatchers to base by Flying Officer Jones flying aircraft FL614, who is attached to Down Ampney from Doncaster. No injuries were sustained by either crew or despatchers. The pilot reports quite a number of Typhoons on strip at Eindhoven.

Damage to aircraft:

Port tyre punctured
Port engine completely U/S
Some bullet holes in wings

Extract from *Sunday Chronicle*, 3 December 1944 – 'Flaming Pepperbox' Lands Safely

The 'Flaming Pepperbox' is the name they gave to an RAF Transport Command Dakota which landed in the British lines after dropping supplies to Allied troops in Holland. It seemed that every bit of Nazi flak in Holland was flung at the Dakota till it was only a shell. Its tail rudder, port aileron, engine, tank and gyro instruments were either out of action or badly damaged. One of the despatchers, Army men who discharge the supplies, was mortally wounded. The radio operator went to attend to him. As he left his seat it was pierced by three bullets. The plane was down to 700ft by this time and the enemy guns opened up again. Further hits put the radio out of action, ripped open the starboard wing, and set it ablaze. More explosive shells hit the fuselage. The fire in the wing got worse, the inter-com packed up, and all the electrical circuits went dead. Flying Officer L.R. Pattee, a Canadian, and his second pilot, Pilot Officer A.C. Kent, of Fleetwood, Lancashire, struggled on and put the plane down safely in the first open area behind the British lines. 'No sooner were we out,' said Pattee, 'than the flames curled up above the fuselage and the plane continued to burn.'

Personal Stories – Report by Flight Lieutenant Mott, Flying Officer Wells, Flight Lieutenant Packer, Pilot Officer Kennedy from 271 Squadron in aircraft KG516, Operation Market Garden (Resupply), D-Day+4, 21 September 1944

The outward trip was uneventful up to the DZ and all panniers were successfully despatched. The aircraft was then hit in the tail by tracer fire, but this did not interfere with the flight. The captain reports that he saw seven people bale out from one plane and an additional three from another when over the DZ. At a position between Uden and Nijmegen the aircraft was attacked by two Fw 190s. The first came from above astern and the rudder and elevator control were shot away, also both engines went dead. The plane began to descend but was again attacked by an enemy fighter and raked from beam to astern – the last burst set the cockpit panel on fire. The captain then gave the order to abandon the aircraft. The navigator was first out, followed by three despatchers, second pilot, the fourth despatcher and captain and wireless operator. The captain's chute partially opened before he managed to get through the door and was slightly damaged by the tail plane. The landing was made approximately 2 miles west of Uden and the aircraft crashed two miles south-west of the same town. Two men of the Royal Corps of Signals picked up Flight Lieutenant Mott and one despatcher and then contact was made with the navigator and wireless operator. The party then proceeded to Uden, where they discovered that Flight Lieutenant Packer had been taken to Veghel by a Dutch policeman. Flight Lieutenant Mott and Flying Officer Kennedy went to examine the wrecked aircraft, which was a complete 'write off'. They then went back to Uden, contacted Flying Officer Wells and the despatcher and travelled to Veghel, where they found Flight Lieutenant Packer. Accommodation for the night was found and in the morning of 22 September, Flight Lieutenant Mott contacted Colonel Oxley (Operation Commander Control Post). He suggested that all the boys should move to Brussels and advised hitch-hiking as the best method of travel. Brussels Evere aerodrome was reached by 19.00 and the three despatchers who originally lost contact with the remaining party were on the airfield to greet their friends. The complete party flew back to Down Ampney on the morning of 23 September.

Personal Stories – Statement by Flight Sergeant Bayley, 271 Squadron, Regarding the Abandoning of Dakota KG340 and Return to Base of Flight Sergeant Bayley and Flight Sergeant Tipping, Operation Market Garden (Resupply), D-Day+4, 21 September 1944

We dropped all our panniers on the DZ at approximately 15.09 and were turning away to the left when the fuselage was hit by flak. The aircraft immediately caught fire, cutting us off from the despatchers, and as smoke and flames were rushing through towards us, we closed the cabin door and opened the escape hatch. The captain, Warrant Officer Cuer, gave the order to bale out, so I did so, and was immediately followed by Flight Sergeant Tipping. The aircraft seemed to be under control when last seen and I remember seeing four or five parachutes in the sky but as there were several aircraft around could not tell if they were from my aircraft. Both Flight Sergeant Tipping and I landed safely

Above: Dakotas of 233 Squadron lined up on the perimeter track at RAF Blakehill Farm just prior to an exercise with the 6th Airborne Division, 20 April 1944. (Flying Officer Bridge; RAF Official Photographer)

Below: Dakotas of 46 Group at B.2 Bazenville Normandy are loaded with casualties for onward transportation back to the UK. Aircraft that are identifiable are KG432 (H) of 512 Squadron and KG320 of sister 575 Squadron, both home-based at RAF Broadwell. (Flying Officer A. Goodchild; RAF Official Photographer)

Above: Dakotas parked at B.56 Evere Belgium have their freight unloaded. The second aircraft is KG348, coded HC-AO, from 512 Squadron on detachment. (Flight Lieutenant S.A. Devon; RAF Official Photographer)

Below: Some of the Flying Nightingales take a relaxing few moments at Blakehill Farm trying on German helmets that had been souvenired after D-Day. Included in this group are Edna Birbeck and Myra Roberts. (Courtesy of Vince Povey)

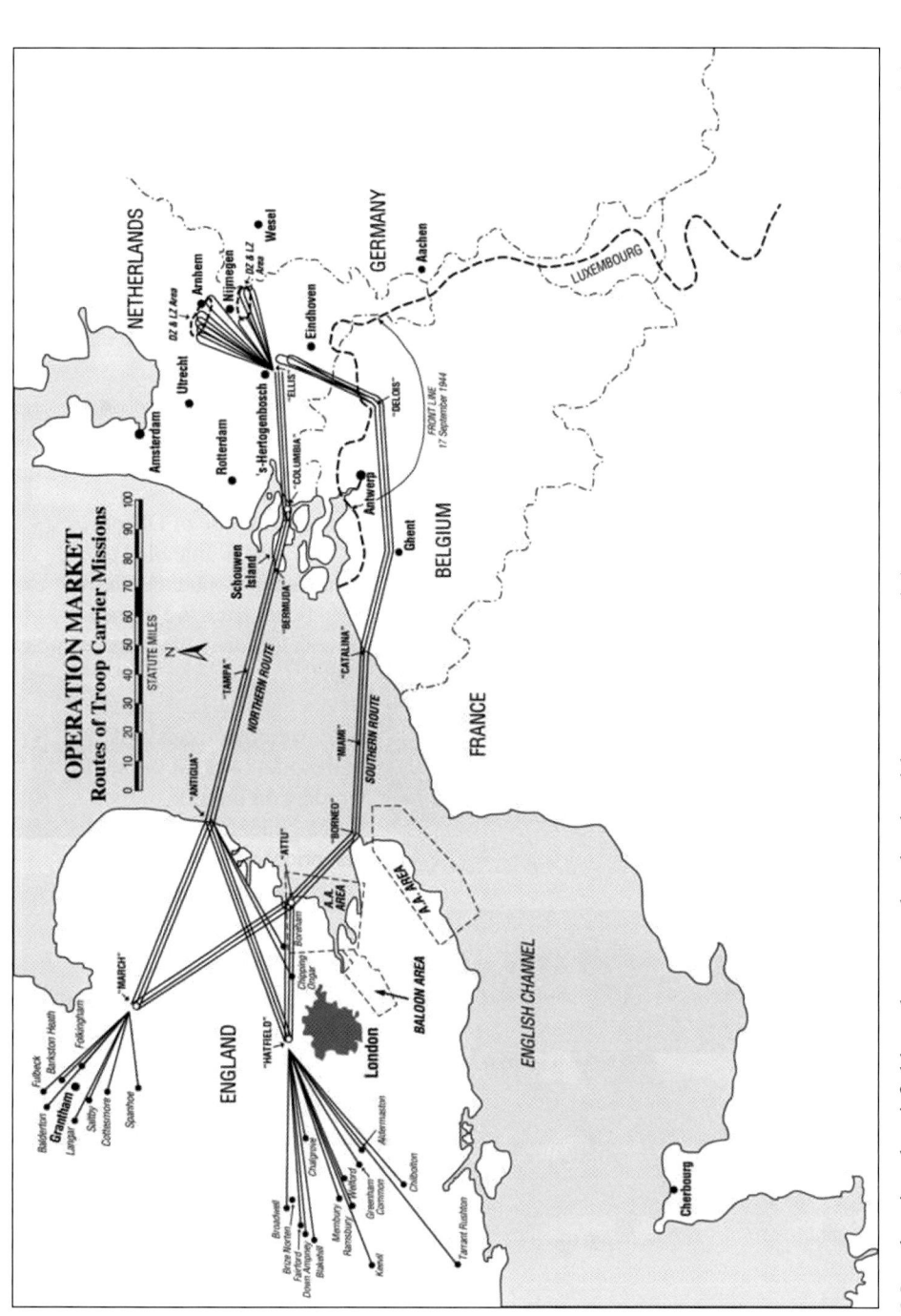

Map showing the airfields and routes taken by the airborne troops and the transport squadrons for both the USAAF and the RAF during Operation Market Garden.

Above: Crews from 233 Squadron chat in front of one of its Dakotas at Blakehill Farm.

Below: A group of glider pilots at Down Ampney just prior to the first lift for Operation Market Garden, September 1944.

Right: Operation Market Garden underway – Dakotas silhouetted against the sky over Oosterbeek, 17 September 1944. (Historic Military Press)

Below: Dakotas lined up at Broadwell prior to an exercise.

Bottom: Another view of Dakotas at Broadwell running up their engines.

Left: A casualty is loaded onto a 46 Group Dakota at B2/Bazenville Normandy for onward transportation to the UK.

Below: Dakota KN427 from 437 Squadron leads others over Copenhagen, Denmark.

A well-worn Dakota Mk.III, KG783 in the foreground, and a Dakota Mk.IV pictured at what is thought to be RAF Hendon, 1945. KG783 still exists and is preserved at Otok, Slovenia. (Courtesy of Jason Holloway)

near to Heteren, where we were looked after by a Dutch farmer and lady doctor who dressed our burns and gave us a meal. We were joined by other aircrew who were in a similar position, Flying Officer Beck, pilot of a Stirling, Flight Sergeant Wheatly and Sergeant R. Percy. We also met an airman called 'Ron' of 48 Squadron who was uninjured. The next day, Friday, 22 September, a German patrol entered the house, gave us the once over and although the Dutch doctor said we were very ill they moved 'Ron' and said they would be back for us later – a guard was left in the house. By this time Sergeant Percy was unconscious and in a bad way. In the afternoon a Polish paratroop force came on the scene but could not help us. One of the officers took our names and they then moved on. Presumably the German guard disappeared when the Polish forces materialised. Next came a patrol from the Hampshire Regiment and a lieutenant saw us and said he would send what help he could. On Sunday morning he sent stretchers for the wounded, who were carried back to a first aid post. Flight Sergeant Tipping, Flight Sergeant Wheatly and myself managed to walk – Sergeant Percy died on arrival. After calling in at another first aid post we were taken by ambulance to Nijmegen. We were then taken to No. 15 Field Dressing Station but Flying Officer Beck was transferred to No. 3 Casualty Clearing Station as he had a compound fracture in one leg and shrapnel in the other. Flight Sergeant Tipping and I remained at the dressing station until the 28 of September, when the MOs advised we should be moved to Grave, expecting to find the landing strip in use, but this was not so. We contacted No. 125 Wing Transport Officer and then moved to a house where we had a bath, changed into clean clothes and were given a hot meal. The following day we were taken to B.56 aerodrome, from where we were flown to Northolt in an ATA Anson. Finally, we wish to state that the Dutch people helped us in every way possible.

Personal Stories – Operation Market Garden (Resupply), 21 September 1944, Aircraft FZ615, Flight Lieutenant Beddow, Flying Officer Dolan, Flight Sergeant Nott, Flight Sergeant Holtom, 271 Squadron

The captain reports that the DZ was reached quite easily, and all panniers were dropped over the target area. When turning, after the completion of the drop the starboard engine and tail plane were hit by flak. The pilot attempted to feather but the engine seized and then the aircraft was flown on one engine at a height of 1,500ft. At a point between Schundel and Veghel the aircraft was hit again by medium flak and the fuselage damaged. This did not upset the flight of the plane and a safe landing was made at B.56 (Brussels Evere) in spite of the fact that the starboard and tail wheel were damaged. The entire crew travelled back to base on the morning of 22 September.

Personal Stories – Operation Market Garden (Resupply), 21 September 1944, Account of the Trip by Major Joubert AFC, 271 Squadron

On arrival over the DZ, I observed that the formation of Dakotas in front commenced to drop their panniers from a height approx. 2–3,000ft. This made it necessary for some aircraft to take evasive action to avoid being hit. A pannier was seen to hit the mainplane of one of the aircraft and the plane was carried away. At a position south of Nijmegen I went to see how my despatchers had fared. A few minutes later one of them came up to me and said, 'Fighters are diving on a Dakota in the rear.' The height at this time was 6,000ft and I was flying immediately over scattered cumulus. There was another bank at 2,000ft below me and when observing an attack being made on a Dakota which immediately burst into flames, I dived for this cloud. I then prepared for an attack which seemed imminent as there were several formations of enemy fighters scattered in various directions. The bank of cloud in which I had taken refuge broke into about 6/10ths cumulus and unfortunately enemy fighters were taking up formations of six and I was observed in an open space between the cumulus. My warrant officer, Flight Sergeant Butterworth, whom I posted in the astro-dome, I must very highly commend for the actions he took in a very calm manner. He gave me the position of the enemy fighters and warned me to stand by for evasive action. As the first fighter peeled off for the attack, I was given the picture immediately and was told which way to dive. I then did a sharp turn to the left and a very steep dive towards the fighters and fortunately the fire was observed missing my tail. I continued the turn and went into the opposite direction to their dive and took cover in the cloud, which was still broken. When I was a safe distance away from this enemy formation, I set course and changed direction on a few occasions when enemy activity was observed until I reached a solid bank of cloud in which I remained. The first Allied fighter support was noticed well after I passed south of Eindhoven. The fighters were then on a course for Nijmegen. After this trip was without incident – in all 3 Dakotas were observed going down in flames.

Personal Stories – Dakota KG374, 19 September 1944, Flight Lieutenant Lord

Dakota KG374 was captained by Flight Lieutenant David Lord DFC to Arnhem on Tuesday, 19 September, during which there was a momentous display of valour during Operation Market Garden.

Leave was resumed and Flying Officer D.I. Macdonnel, navigator to Flight Lieutenant David Lord DFC of 271 Squadron, RAF stationed at Down Ampney, slipped off to Scotland to get married. On Sunday, 17 September Operation Market Garden was finally announced and David Lord was minus a navigator. After enquiring he found out that Flying Officer King was available to navigate his aircraft on Market Garden. King's own crew were standing by as a reserve, and he had flown a few times with David when he first joined the squadron after his Chindit[86] operations, which earned him a DFC, so accepted the request. He did reflect on this decision when the aircraft crossed the enemy coast going into Arnhem and pondered over whether he had made a wise choice though. The paratroopers that they carried on that trip were dropped smack on the DZ, and when they flew back to base their thoughts were of the operational meal waiting for them.

They went out again the following day on the 18th and were towing a glider to the battle area. The difference to the previous day's flight was they were noticing several aircraft and gliders go down in flames and that night the mess was very quiet as they listened to the news broadcast. The next mission for the crew was to be on Tuesday, 19th, for a supply drop. By now they knew things were critical and this drop would be dangerous. Unfortunately, this did prove correct as many aircraft other than Lord's failed to return to many Transport Command airfields later in the day. Flight Lieutenant Lord DFC (posthumous VC), Pilot Officer Dickie Medhurst (son of Air Chief Marshall Sir Charles Medhurst), Flying Officer Alec Balleytine, and four despatchers, Army personnel of the 223rd Company, RASC, Corporal Nixon, and drivers Harder, Ricketts and Rowbotham, were killed. King was to be the only survivor.

Their load that day was eight panniers of ammunition. Dakota KG374 took off at Down Ampney and joined the formation and set course for Arnhem, the weather was deteriorating and within a short time they were navigating solely on 'Gee'; with no visual fixes as they crossed the coast. Arrival was just after 3 p.m. and as the minute hand came to the hour David Lord asked for their position over the intercom. The reply came back 'We should be near the Rhine'. The Dakota broke through the cloud and Nijmegen was visible to starboard and ahead the Needer Rhine and Arnhem. The altitude was 1,500ft with intense flak, and within a couple of minutes they were hit. The aircraft shuddered, with the impact of shrapnel, and it was soon realised they had received a direct hit. Lord checked on the crew – no one was hurt, but KG374 was in trouble. A plume of smoke was flowing back over the starboard main plane, followed by flames. Lord asked Dickie Medhurst, the second pilot, to work the fire extinguisher equipment, followed by asking how far to the DZ. 'Four minutes' came the reply. The fire was increasing and the stream of flame in the slipstream started to engulf the wing. In the wing section was the main fuel tank, and any pilot in this position could have justified his action in turning out of the stream and abandoning the aircraft. Lord quietly told everyone to put on their parachutes. Because the load was badly needed by the ground troops, he would deliver and then everyone could bale out. Normal drill was adopted, and everyone set for the supply drop. Lord continued to fly visually to the DZ and the door opened to help despatch the load. The intercom kept the pilot briefed on when the last pannier was dropped, helping with a kick to push them out through the open door. As the signal flashed green,[87] the first pannier was kicked out. It moved and then jammed – flak had damaged some of the rollers. The crew manhandled panniers out, but this had cost time and the operation was lost and two panniers still remained when the green light switched off and past the DZ. Lord was informed and so the Dakota was sent around again to make another run. It soon became clear that Lord could not keep height, they were going lower and lower. At 600ft they got the green light. The starboard side of the aircraft was well aflame and giving a glow within the fuselage. The last two panniers were pushed out and the order came to bale out. King turned to the despatchers to help them to put their chutes on, the next thing he remembered is that he found himself in space with the ground hurtling up at a great speed. He felt a jerk and found that he was now floating earthbound. Unaware, he had pulled the release ring of the parachute and landed on his back and was badly winded. He never actually knew what had happened, but later he made contact with troops on the ground who informed him that the Dakota just blew up, probably the starboard fuel tank, then the wing separated from the fuselage and the aircraft crashed. There were no other survivors. Lying in the field he looked at his watch: 15.16, only about ten minutes since it all began. Close by was a farmhouse seemingly deserted. He started to move but heard the hiss and whine of bullets. It soon became clear he was in 'no man's land'. He moved into a ditch and lay quietly. He glanced up and saw a glider coming in. All guns turned on to the glider and he took advantage to move along the ditch to the farmyard. From there he made his way over to the glider. It had come from Down Ampney. Captain Elliot was in charge, but one of the airborne troops was killed by flak. His boots fitted King. He moved off to try to make contact with the 10th Battalion HQ, which he duly found. He was given water and some chocolate, and efforts were made to get him to Brigade HQ. He was prevented by mortar fire, so sought cover back with the 10 Battalion HQ. About 19.00 that evening an SS Regiment with tanks overran the 10th Battalion and everything was in turmoil. Through the night resistance continued but in the morning of 20 September the few that remained, including King, were taken prisoner. About midday some seventy including King were marched along the sandy path parallel to the railway to Ede. Everyone was so dog-tired they simply lay down on the cobbled forecourt and fell asleep. King looked at his watch, it was 15.00. He reflected on what had happened in twenty-four hours and muttered a silent prayer.

Flying Officer Macdonnel, the regular navigator of KG374, was given leave to get married when the Arnhem campaign started. Flight Lieutenant Lord co-opted Flying Officer King in his place. However, the squadron report on the flight fails to detail King as a crew member, quoting Macdonnel. King confirmed that he flew with KG374 on the 17th, 18th, and 19th, but this is not shown in the ops report. KG374 is shown to have only flew on the 19th. This may be due to last-minute changes – perhaps one of the planned aircraft went unserviceable and KG374 was used in lieu; this happened regularly. However, you would have expected to see notification of changes recorded in the ops report. That it is not shown suggests that the officer who compiled it failed to verify which aircraft took part, instead using the original flight plan. The ops report for 19 September shows that KG374 was captained by Lord, but with Macdonnel in the crew instead of King. This further anomaly probably happened as suggested above. However, when KG374 was declared 'missing' the usual practice was to notify the crew's next of kin. Who was notified – King's or Macdonnel's family, even though it was known that Macdonnel was with his new wife? King, who was taken prisoner, would have been missing, unless the Red Cross were informed, and details passed back to the British Military. The ops report also states that the resupply drop was foodstuffs, whereas King did state 'eight panniers of ammunition'. This anomaly might be explained by the possibility that the RS/SC split up the 'supplies' to various airfields, and KG374 was given ammo freight instead of foodstuffs.

The impact that Operation Market Garden had on all squadrons from Down Ampney, Blakehill Farm and Broadwell cannot be understated. The losses that were endured from the nine days of sorties did have a huge cost, in both lives and equipment lost. From the first day and the insertion of the force, through to the resupply missions day after day, the crews flew the operations knowing that the troops on the ground needed the supplies to get in theatre to help in their task. To see fellow crews being shot out of the sky must have tested them all, but they kept on flying their unarmed Dakotas into danger. More crews were lost and injured than during D-Day and operations Tonga and Mallard, and it was without doubt the darkest time for the squadrons. As October started and there was the onset of autumn and winter, the writing was definitely on the wall for Hitler and his retreating armies, but the next big push was still to be faced: the crossing of the Rhine and the actual insertion of Allied forces into the Fatherland.

During the late stages of September, all the squadrons started to resume the regular duties they had prior to Arnhem.

Chapter 6

Keeping up the Support (October, November)

October dawned with the weather cloudy but changing to fine conditions later in the day. No. 271 Squadron's first task of the month was for four crews to carry freight out for the Army via B.56 to B.6. A further six aircraft operated out of Blakehill Farm, also taking petrol for B.56, and returning with casualties. No. 48 Squadron also transported petrol from Blakehill Farm to B.56, supplying eight aircraft and crews. No. 437 Squadron also took part, transporting 1,140 cans (containing 4½ gallons each), and on their return journey they had the task of carrying 'Special Secret Fluid (Rocket fuel)' under armed guard. No. 233 Squadron also joined in taking fuel across the Channel, again to the same destination of B.56. No. 512 Squadron had deployed five aircraft to Blakehill for onward transportation to B.56. Three other aircraft made B.6 their arrival point, while four more proceeded to B.59 and a further nine flew directly to B.56. Blakehill Farm was a major hub with the amount of fuel being shipped out that day, care being taken to minimise any potential mishaps. No. 575 Squadron made their way back home from B.56 after the end of Operation Market Garden, with sixteen aircraft making the trip.

More aircraft were made available from various squadrons for the 2nd to take more petrol over to B.56, returning with more casualties on the homeward leg. One of the Dakotas from 271 Squadron transported Major Jackson, CO Glider Regiment, recently returned from the Arnhem operations to give a talk on his experiences during this campaign. The schedule for the rest of the month of October saw all squadrons involved in transporting the wide and varied supplies out to Belgium and France, keeping the front well equipped and stocked with their daily requirements. Transportation back to England still consisted of casualties, as well as general passengers flowing between continental Europe and the UK. B.56 (Brussels Evere) was the main destination for the six squadrons, with nearly all the flights using this as their destination airfield. That said though, a few aircraft did venture to others (B.58 Brussels Melsbroek and B.78 Eindhoven, Netherlands) as and when required. This tended to be more towards the latter half of the month as the ground troops made their way north, advancing through Belgium and on to the Netherlands, constantly making progress up through the Low Countries and towards Germany. This was a difficult and constantly changing situation with the front making greater progress some days than others. A dedicated hub was deemed necessary for all supplies moving into the Continent, as well as a centre for transporting personnel, and Brussels lent itself perfectly for this task as the most widely used airfield in the ETO[88] for the group.

The routine supply of newbies to the squadrons was nothing new, but with the front-line combat squadrons of Fighter and Bomber Command, these tended to be on a far more regular pattern to replace those unfortunately lost in combat. For Transport Command, while there was a replenishment programme, it was the numbers lost during Market Garden that affected the ability to man all squadrons successfully. The number of aircraft lost would have a small effect on squadron strength for the next month or so, although the supplies to continental Europe did not suffer in any major way. Leave was reduced for the remaining crews until replacements were fully integrated within their squadrons and fully operational. Several second pilots were transferred to 107 OTU for captain courses. There was a lot of transfer of personnel within the group along with general 'ins and outs' among the fold. As the ground troops advanced further they started to capture more and more Germans, some of those, mainly injured, started to be taken by Dakotas with Allied troops on the casualty flights, and flown into England to receive medical aid. Most German casualties, though, were transported (again by Dakotas of 46 Group) to the various temporary landing grounds within Europe. The supply of new aircraft to squadrons did continue, even though not in any great numbers, but this did help to furnish wherever there was a shortfall. No. 575 Squadron still had a detachment of Dakotas at B.56, which followed on from the last days of resupply for Market Garden, and it retained these on station for flights required to other landing grounds within the Allies' control. This detachment came to an end on 17 October, with all aircraft, crews and ground staff departing on the 19th and arriving back at Broadwell the same day.

No. 437 Squadron suffered a terrible accident on the 24th when Dakota FZ655 crashed near Saint-Pol-sur-Mer, a suburb of Dunkirk, during a return trip to Blakehill from Antwerp. The reason for the accident is unclear and it took place as the aircraft was making a return flight after delivering freight with eight others from the squadron. All but one member of the crew, Flight Sergeant J.W. Lockwood, perished and they are buried in the Calais Canadian War Cemetery. They were Flight Sergeant Douglas Schneider, Flight Sergeant Sydney Gumbrell and Warrant Officer John Soper. Also on the flight was Flying Nightingale LACW[89] Margeret Campbell, WAAF, who had been assigned for the possibility of needing to nurse wounded personnel on the return leg, but there were no wounded allocated upon arrival in Antwerp.

On the 25th, Major P.S. Joubert of 271 Squadron was posted to HQ Down Ampney and promoted to the rank of Acting Lieutenant General, taking over the duties of Wing Commander Flying. The weather towards the end of the month started turning autumnal, with misty, damp mornings giving way to mostly fine afternoons, so flying was slightly affected, as there were some postponements and cancellations of the regular supply routes across the Channel. Occasionally there were some return flights that did carry a variety of different freight. The Allies were now into the heart of occupied territory and liberated various German equipment and returned it for analysis by the boffins[90] in the UK. These ranged from documents and firearms to a variety of equipment that an occupying army needed to keep it functioning and fighting.

One of the return trips made on the 28th was loaded with 3,500lb of mail from troops at the front line. This went into Blakehill Farm, where the mail was sorted for forwarding on to family on the home front; small comforts for all. During the 28th a Dakota piloted by Flight Lieutenant Cooke 271 of Squadron was returning from B.17 when it crashed immediately after take-off. Cooke fractured a tibia, the second pilot and navigator were also slightly injured, and the nursing orderly received slight abrasions. The warrant officer was luckily unhurt. No. 437 Squadron was by the end of October becoming more an automatous unit with Canadian groundcrew joining and swelling the ranks. This gave the RAF more scope to relocate their personnel to other units within Transport Command. Both Broadwell and Down Ampney squadrons were involved in glider towing training on the 28th when a large-scale exercise was arranged. Fifteen aircraft from both 48 and 271 Squadron, and three from 575 Squadron, were selected to take part. The route for the Down Ampney aircraft was Base, Chippenham, Newbury, base in the morning, followed by another route: base, Stow-on-the-Wold, Wallingford, base. No. 575 Squadron's three aircraft carried out a cross-country route, then returned to base. In the afternoon the Commanding Officer of Broadwell, Major Murray, witnessed and surveyed the glider dropping zone close to the airfield. This was to provide the crews with continuity training and to maintain their capability.

There was a cloudy start to November, a mist hung in the air and all the crews settled down to their continuation flights across the Channel and into mainland Europe. Transport details were the same as October, but there was a bit more focus on the airborne delivery operational side of the squadrons' capabilities and the majority were soon involved with pannier dropping practice on the 3rd to train RASC despatchers.

The resupply flights continued at a pace, and aircraft and crews were fully occupied within this role. The destinations were increasing with the number of airfields served during the month at thirteen, within France, Belgium and the Netherlands, another testimony to the way the Allies were progressing and expanding the area of operations. Their main task was focusing on entering Germany from different points in neighbouring countries. RAF Broadwell did not take part in many of the scheduled trips going forward from the 4th. These flights were now handled by both squadrons at Down Ampney, so reducing the number of aircraft available for special AMB[91] repatriation trips. No. 575 Squadron did have a deployment of aircraft located at B.70 that operated as 'A' Flight and flew local sorties, although this deployment came to an end by 7 November as the temporary duty ceased.

No. 271 Squadron took part in an interesting deployment that commenced on 5 November when a Dakota piloted by Flight Lieutenant Danks was detached to 216 Squadron after they had been sent out to Cairo West. They operated from this airfield and did two return trips to Athens, where they delivered food. The route was via E.l Adem, where they night stopped and then transported passengers from there to Cairo West. A further mission was carried out when two naval officers were taken from Alexandria to Athens with large quantities of food and equipment; no further information was forthcoming. This detachment lasted for three weeks and then the crew returned to Down Ampney.

A surprising announcement on the 9th was the decision to tug all the gliders away to another unit. Even though some of the crews were very pleased to see them go, others had built quite an infinity with their unpowered relations, as well as the men who piloted and crewed these silent warriors. The Glider Regiment would be gone from Down Ampney in roughly one week, but their paths would cross again. A dinner was held on the 15th to honour Group Captain J. Bradbury DFC and the Glider Regiment. He was being posted to 111 Wing RAF BLA[92] and the Glider Regiment was moving the few miles to Blakehill Farm. The new group captain, G.R. Howie DSO, would be the Commanding Officer at Down Ampney and he was duly welcomed at the dinner.

One of 271 Squadron's Dakotas received a hit by enemy flak on 20 November. The aircraft, KG406 captained by Flight Lieutenant G.J. Bailey, was slightly off course and on the return trip from a resupply mission when it received the hit, near Dunkirk. A fire broke out and the crew found it impossible to extinguish it. The pilot elected to make a forced landing, which was successfully made in a waterlogged field, with the mud and water putting put the fire out, as the aircraft came to rest. The captain received injuries to his arm, leg, and left eye, but these were not very serious. The rest of the crew received only slight abrasions, cuts and bruising. The aircraft did have passengers on board but thankfully none of these were injured. Once the plane had stopped, both crew and passengers ran away from the aircraft towards the side of the field, where they were picked up by Czech soldiers and the whole party were taken to a nearby village. Flight Lieutenant Bailey was taken to a field hospital at Saint-Omer, with the rest of the group having arrangements made to get them back to England.

It had been hoped that the war in Europe would be over by the end of 1944, but gritty resistance by the Germans meant that was a little optimistic. The types of supplies being sent out was also changing. With winter soon to be upon the front-line troops, their need for correct kit and clothing were becoming more apparent, Oil cookers, blankets, overcoats, tent heaters, rain covers, and even new boots were being packed along with general freight and medical supplies. Even steel planking[93] was starting to be sent in case of wet weather and the need to be able to continue with operations if the ground got sodden and caused vehicles and aircraft to get stuck.

Nearly every day since the Allies landed on the beaches of Normandy in early June a Dakota from 46 Group had returned to England with a casualty on board. Down Ampney, Blakehill Farm and Broadwell had all been seeing this activity on an all too familiar frequency. Once arriving at any of the three airfields, wounded troops were soon whisked off to hospital, either on base or to a closely located facility. The normal number that the Dakotas could carry was sixteen, this being the stretcher capacity that the aircraft could sensibly fit. If casualties were walking wounded they could carry more, the fit of the aircraft being adjusted to accommodate them accordingly upon arrival on the Continent and once supplies had been unloaded. The addition of nurse orderlies (Flying Nightingales), who accompanied many of the crews on their flights, greatly helped not only with tending to wounds during the flights home, but greatly boosted morale.

Weather cancellations were becoming more frequent. This did not have too much of an impact on the transfer of supplies out, as most flights could get airborne from their respective airfields, but it did start having some effect on aircraft returning to base. Weather diversions became more common, either to Northolt in west London or aircraft night stopping in France or Belgium and returning the following day. The 22nd was particularly bad as severe fog covered the southern part of England, which meant no flying for any squadrons that day. Crews were exceptionally keen to return to the base whenever they could. This was especially so whenever there were casualties aboard, as the crews knew how important it was to get the men back home so they could receive the care and attention they required.

For the remainder of November the squadrons continued with their daily resupply and repatriation flights to Europe, with no main issues being reported. The only slight challenge was the ongoing battle with the deteriorating English weather. The number of casualties carried by 46 Group since the first days of June was impressive. Unfortunately the figure was going to keep on rising before hostilities ceased.

Chapter 7

Winter Tales (December 1944–January 1945)

The weather was generally cloudy but with good visibility, although strong winds were in place and gusting over the airfields of 46 Group. The flights were the same as November, with mixed freight and passengers continuing to being flown to the Continent. One thing that had become more noticeable for all the squadrons was the way that the operational requirements saw various aircraft from the six units all flying to and from the three airfields within group. An example of this came on 4 December, when 437 Squadron's 'A' Flight sent four aircraft to RAF Broadwell to collect a consignment of telephones for movement to B.58, and the subsequent return of casualties to Broadwell. These types of flights were becoming more common and showed a pooling of resources for the whole group of six squadrons.

The 7th saw a 48 Squadron Dakota needing to make an emergency landing at Ford with engine trouble. Its load was transferred to another aircraft while repairs were carried out and the aircraft returned to Down Ampney. HRH the Duchess of Kent visited Down Ampney on the afternoon of the 8th. She was there to receive the 20,000th casualty to be brought back to the station by air, a sobering number indeed. This aircraft was flown by Squadron Leader P. Drummond of 48 Squadron, who touched down at 14.06 precisely. A visit to the sick quarters and the Casualty Evacuation Centre was also on the agenda. The AOC, L. Darvall, was present to welcome the Duchess.

News was also received that the bodies of Flying Officer J.W. Hartley (132698) and Sergeant W.N. Anfield (1450766) from 271 Squadron were buried at Zeebrugge Communal Cemetery. Their bodies had been recovered from the crash site at Ramscapelle, near Bruges, on 21 September after the aircraft crashed. These were the only two members of the crew that were to be recovered, it not being possible to identify or locate anyone further. Another incident took place a couple of days later (10th) when a 271 Squadron Dakota was returning from Gatwick after a night stop, piloted by Pilot Officer E. Gibson. The weather in the vicinity of the airfield was poor, with cloud cover of 10/10ths at 300–400ft and visibility down to 1,000 yards maximum and wind gusts of approximately 30 mph. The aircraft managed to get airborne but soon after take-off crashed into the side of Letch Hill, near Dunsfold, with the crew all being killed. The three crew were: Pilot Officer E. Gibson, Flying Officer S. Holder, and Flying Officer McNeil Smith. Another crash also occurred on the 10th. This time it was an Anson operated by a 575 Squadron crew that came down near Bridgnorth on its way to Belfast. The crew, Flight Lieutenant G.E. Potter and Warrant Officer J.C. Staples, and passenger Flight Lieutenant Campbell (medical) were killed.

RAF Northolt was one of the main points for the majority of passengers returning from the Continent, due to its close proximity to London and the associated agencies or departments that personnel reported to, and it featured nearly every day as a destination or starting point.

The flights into Europe were increasing wherever there was capability for aircraft to fly. Every squadron within 46 Group was involved and the number of flights could easily be into double figures on most days. It was not uncommon for fifteen or sixteen crews per squadron to be carrying out these operations into the continental mainland each day.

A message was received on the 12th that had come from Lady Rachel Davidson, one of the Ladies in Waiting for HRH the Duchess of Kent, it read: 'The Duchess of Kent has asked me to write to say how much she enjoyed her visit to RAF Down Ampney, she was so moved by all she saw and the wonderful atmosphere. Will you convey to everyone concerned her Royal Highnesses' deep appreciation of the wonderful work you are all doing, it was indeed a memorable afternoon.'

Weather played its hand again on 13th and 14 December. All flying was cancelled at Down Ampney, although Broadwell's squadrons managed to get a few aircraft airborne for operations and a couple on local air testing. It took until the afternoon of the 15th before flying operations could fully resume. The funerals of two of the crew who were killed in the Gatwick accident took place in the respective locations of Birmingham (Pilot Officer E. Gibson) and Glasgow (Flight Lieutenant G.W. Baxter). Attendees from the squadron were there to represent the unit and carry the respects of all. The final victim of this incident, Flying Officer S.J. Holder, was buried the day after at Cirencester Cemetery with full military honours. The pall bearers were six Australian officers and the coffin was borne by six senior NCOs[94] of the squadron. The Commanding Officer, Wing Commander Booth DFC, attended the funeral and Flight Lieutenant W.A. Pearce was in command of the parade, the escort party consisting of thirty-five airmen.

Pannier-dropping sorties were increased towards the middle of the month, squadrons carrying out these flights by both day and night. They used the few aircraft that were available due to the intense ferry flights that were key to delivering the supplies that were constantly required at the front, and for the repatriation of casualties on the return.

The weather struck again on the 19th, and once again all airfields were fogged in and all flying was suspended. This was the case for the next few days and it was not until the 21st that the first flight got airborne at Broadwell when 575 Squadron managed to get two Dakotas up on glider tug training. This pause in flying did allow for the time to be well spent, with briefings and instructional films being shown to aircrews. It also allowed ground crews more time for maintenance between flying hours and all aircraft were ready for their next missions. Several flights did manage to get airborne on the 22nd to cover the shortfall in previous days' operations. On this day the return flights to Down Ampney carried record numbers of passengers, including quite a few VIPs who were probably trying to get home for Christmas. They should have gone to Northolt but unfortunately the weather was not going to permit that, so all returned to Down Ampney, additional travel being necessary to get to their final destinations.

A message came through from AOC Transport Command to Air Commodore L. Darvall AOC 46 Group: 'Please accept personal thanks for all the excellent work your personnel both service and civilian have carried out, which has done so much to help us on our way to final victory. My very best wishes to you all for Christmas and the New Year. I can rely on you to keep this splendid effort going until the ultimate aim is assured.'

Another accident befell 271 Squadron on the 23rd when Flight Lieutenant F.R. Riley was killed in an accident while he was on detachment to RAF Shawbury on the staff navigators course. The accident took place at Chicken Rock, Isle of Man, at approximately 10.00.

Christmas Day was a fortunate one for the crews as the weather was foggy so all flying was cancelled. This obviously pleased all crews, who wanted to spend Christmas day on the ground. Festivities for the day were: Blakehill Farm, Christmas lunch served by the officers and senior NCOs for the airmen in their dining hall, followed by a Christmas party for all ranks in the station cinema. Broadwell, Christmas lunch served in both the airmen's and officers' mess, and finally Down Ampney, where the NCOs were entertained in the officers' mess, Christmas lunch and an all-ranks dance in the NAAFI[95] from 20.30.

The Christmas celebrations were soon brought down with a bump as on the 26th crews were once again in the air carrying freight to the Continent. No. 437 Squadron at Blakehill transported American troops to A.83 from Beaulieu on the 26th. This was completed in three flights, A, B and C, which totalled 137 men. C flight was rescheduled to go to Holmsley South as their loads were there. All returned the same day but due to weather had to land at Holmsley South again. They were supported by aircraft from 512 and 575 Squadrons, who also couldn't land back at home base, so also flew into Holmsley South.

January 1945 started with ground frost and mist. This, the seventh year of the war, finally looked like it could be the last. Even though the Germans were in full retreat, the fight was still going to be tough. To highlight this fact, some devastating news was received from the sub 'Sparrow Flight' of 271 Squadron, who were operating out of Brussels Evere with their Handley Page HP.54 'Sparrow' transports on ambulance duties. They were caught in an attack by thirty to forty Bf 109 and Fw 190 fighters that destroyed seven of the aircraft during Operation Bodenplatte,[96] which took place across Belgium, the Netherlands and part of France. LAC[97] J. Hyams, a fitter who was working on one of the aircraft, was killed during the attack. Also, 575 Squadron had three aircraft damaged in a similar attack at Antwerp on the same day. One of the crews, Flying Officer Clegg, received gunshot wounds and was very seriously ill in hospital.

For 46 Group, 1945 also brought a more diverse selection of destinations of operations. The breadth of these saw the Dakotas flying into many newly constructed temporary landing grounds as the Allies made their way further and further into occupied territory, with nearly all return flights coming back with casualties aboard.

Requirements for internal flights within the Continent were such that 233 Squadron were to set up a detachment of Dakotas to operate within theatre, which took effect from the first day of the new year.

The 4th was another notable day as Lieutenant Colonel Joubert from 271 Squadron returned from B.58 with the 50,000th casualty carried by 46 Group to England since its inception back in 1944. This was recorded by the BBC, who made a recording of the event when the aircraft reached the Air Despatch and Reception Unit.[98] This was followed on during the 6th, as the CAEC[99] were the subjects of a film that was being made for the receiving and relocation of casualties at Down Ampney. It is not known where this film was seen, although it may have been shown under the mantle of Pathé News in selected cinemas.

The scope of transport details was widening as even more destinations became available to the Allies to get supplies into theatre, although there were still no troops or forces in Germany at this time. After taking over command of 271 Squadron, one of Lieutenant Colonel Joubert's first tasks was to attend special meetings at station headquarters. The word was that these were related to operations to finally cross the Rhine, but no details were released.

On the 8th scheduled flights had to be cancelled due to snow on the ground and light flurries around the three airfields. It was even worse on the Continent. Dakotas at Broadwell had started the new year with an increased activity in glider towing. These were primarily local flights involving a few crews at a time, but every day where there were aircraft and crews available. Both 512 and 575 Squadrons put aircraft up for this task.

No. 48 Squadron had a close shave on the 9th when six aircraft took off on routings to B.75 carrying mail, newspapers, radar and medical equipment and general freight. Three aircraft returned with mail and two came back empty. The remaining aircraft was completely destroyed while at B.56 as a B-17 Flying Fortress made a crash-landing with a full bomb load and struck it. The Dakota crew were not hurt as they were not near their aircraft when the incident occurred.

There was a need for the creation of a customs Security Control Office at Down Ampney at the ADRU Office to necessitate the increased intake of passengers returning from the Continent. This aided the processing of personnel to ensure that nobody undesirable slipped into the country.

Snow arrived on the 10th, and 512 Squadron's Dakotas that were on their way to B.50 were recalled due to the conditions and icing forming up on the aircraft. The following day the weather was very similar and 512 Squadron aircraft destined for B.50 and B.75 were recalled once airborne. Flying was greatly reduced throughout the group's squadrons. One Dakota from 48 Squadron did get into Northolt but had to night stop due to faulty brakes. It continued on to its destination on the 12th. All scheduled flights were cancelled due to inclement weather on the 12th. Even though 575 Squadron did manage to get two aircraft up for local pannier dropping training and 512 six aircraft for glider towing, Blakehill Farm's and Down Ampney's aircraft remained on the ground.

In the light of this lull in operations, the station commander at Down Ampney took this opportunity to call together all aircrew to discuss the various problems arising from day to day flying and ops. There were many points raised by the crews regarding domestic and flying concerns. All points were duly noted and left in the hands of the CO to muse over. Flight Lieutenant P.A.D. Hollom and crew returned back to Down Ampney after participating in a tour of continental staging posts. This had taken place over the last eight days, consisted of four senior officers and the locations visited were Le Bourget, Rennes, Toulouse, and Istres (Marseilles). Bordeaux was also due to be visited but this was cancelled due to bad weather.

Combined operations at Broadwell saw an increased number of aircraft involved in glider towing, both squadrons putting in a concerted effort in this exercise. Fifteen aircraft were airborne during the morning of the 9th, followed by another eighteen in the afternoon, spending two hours each session honing their skills. This was still an important side to the operations for 46 Group aircraft, with 512 and 575 Squadrons taking the lead in this task. There was obviously something pending in the future.

Nos 233 and 437 Squadrons at Blakehill Farm were not involved with any operations linked to glider towing, and their main operational tasking was still around the transport role and flights into and out of Europe. No. 271 Squadron sent six ground crews and three Sparrow air crews to RAF Leicester East to start training on the Dakota as they were going to be tasked with these flights following the loss of the HP54s at Brussels earlier in the month. The course was due to take nineteen days for the aircrew and seven days for the ground crew. All personnel were to be transferred out to B.56 (Brussels Evere) upon completion of the training.

Twelve aircraft that had been detailed to run the Europe flights on the 17th returned to Down Ampney, with the vast majority being full of American bomber crews who had either had to bale out or who had crash-landed on the Continent. These crews, who had endured these extremely harrowing experiences but had managed to elude capture and make it safely to friendly forces, were very glad indeed to be back on English soil, although they appeared distressed after their ordeal.

Gales were prevalent during the 19th at Down Ampney. At 02.00 a large elm tree came crashing down on to a Nissen hut[100] that was full of airmen from 271 Squadron, but thankfully only five of the inhabitants were slightly injured. Over at Blakehill Farm they were also suffering due to high winds. Both squadrons were stood down for the 19th even though a full day's flying operations were carried out the preceding day. Weather, weather, weather – this was the problem for the 23rd, 24th and 26th, when all scheduled flights were once again grounded because of frost, snow and low cloud. It did pick up and cleared a little on the 25th, and a few flights did manage to make it out to resume some form of the flying requirements. The remaining days of January saw flights taking place every day until the last two days of the month, when once again the dreaded weather curtailed all operations.

Detachment of Dakota FZ697 to Canada and the United States

No. 512 Squadron had the honour to be invited to send a Dakota (FZ697) to Canada to take part in Exercise Eskimo, held at Prince Albert, Saskatchewan, during January 1945. The crew, including four despatchers from the RASC, who loaded the equipment, which included, panniers, roller conveyor and bomb racks, on to the aircraft and set course for North America on the 5th. Their first destination was Dorval, then Ottawa, which was reached by the 9th. Briefed in Ottawa at the AFHW[101] and NDHQ[102] ready for the exercise, they set course for Prince Albert, duly arriving on 14 January. The exercise focused on the movement of a brigade group, and all associated with such a move. Prince Albert was the departure point, with the destination a position within

Labrador. This was to test the extremes and effects of the cold dry conditions on the men and equipment. Routing was using a series of roads and trails though bush country, which was relatively flat and covered with spruce trees and lakes. The range of the air operations was safely set from Prince Albert in a 132-mile radius. The scheduling and operation for the exercise was drawn up before the services and capabilities of the Dakota were widely available, so any tests that were detailed became somewhat surplus to requirements for this aircraft type. Another potentially short-sighted situation was the lack of equipment available, such as spares to enable the Dakota to drop tanks, guns or any other heavier equipment via parachute. A dummy forward operating runway was also meant to have been constructed on a frozen lake for use by Dakotas, as well as a radar site to trial, and finally a LZ to drop paratroopers or land gliders as key points to the exercise. These were quite significant oversights that should have curtailed the whole event. On the positive side was that five supply dropping flights were carried out successfully, as well as eleven local experimental supply dropping sorties, one paratrooper drop and six recce flights. The supply drops did show the capabilities of the Dakota and its ability to carry a wide range of stores, anything from ammunition to food stuff to 45-gallon fuel drums, and that the weather conditions did not have much of an impact on the ability to deliver supplies. The Dakota fared better than expected in snow, which varied from 4–12 inches deep. A decrease in performance of the aircraft due to the lower temperatures did not cause any issues. With a reduced power boost that gave an estimated 1,250hp per engine, the aircraft could still attain an 800-yard take-off distance with a 31,000lb load, and this was also on fairly rough surfaces or a snow-covered runway. All the other key learning points such as map references and LZ identification were covered and the aircraft excelled itself. Even radio communication was very good within the area, although the lack of any potential conflicts with other aircraft was at a minimum.

Once the exercise was over the aircraft and crew relocated to the Royal Military College at Kingston, Ontario, where they were warmly looked after. Finally, there was a visit to the BAC[103] attachment in Washington and a visit to Wright Field, in Dayton, Ohio, followed by an additional stop at the 1st Troop Carrier Command, Stout Field, Indianapolis. It was a very rewarding and enjoyable trip to the continent of North America and a chance to test the Dakota in different weather extremes.

Chapter 8

One Last Hurrah, Operation Varsity (February, March)

It was a brisk start to February, with all squadrons still active taking the ubiquitous freight and passengers out and returning with their casualties, personnel and POW. From this month onwards it was decreed that Down Ampney would be the only station within 46 Group to be involved with casualty evacuation as Broadwell would cease. Canadian casualties would be landed at Redhill and Farnborough and onwards to hospitals. No. 271 Squadron received the last two Sparrow flight Handley Page HP54s, K6987 and K6949, at Down Ampney on the 5th for inspection. K6987 was found to be unfit for further flying and was withdrawn from service.

Many personnel made the short trip over to Blakehill Farm on the 6th as arrangements had been made for the AOC in Command Transport Command, Sir Frederick Bowhill, to make his farewell speech to 46 Group personnel. Unfortunately, due to poor flying conditions the AOC in C was unable to reach the airfield for this special occasion. Maybe road transport should have been the order of the day, as mentioned by a few of the crews assembled. An accident occurred on 6 February when Dakota KG630 crashed near Friston/Beachy Head while on a flight to Europe. The aircraft came down at 11.00, with Warrant Officer Oleinikoff and crew all perishing in an incident that appears to have been caused by bad weather. The Sparrow Flight got a new aircraft as Dakota FZ666 was allocated to it at its Gilze-Rijen base and it was duly collected for onward transportation.

The weather was still playing its part in curtailing operations, but not to the same degree as December and January had seen. February definitely saw a larger amount of rain and poor visibility that hampered ops. This was also seen across the Continent as crews would arrive at airfields with their cargo, only to be stuck and have to night stop until the weather allowed a window to get back home. Flying was cancelled for most on the 15th, 16th and 17th as the weather had closed in once again. Broadwell did manage to get a few aircraft out but most of their activity focused on local flights and glider towing training. The same thing was in place at Blakehill Farm, with no activity at all. This affected the VIP passenger flight that was due to leave on the 15th with General Gale and staff. It remained on the ground at Blakehill instead of proceeding to Northolt to pick up its esteemed guest. General Gale did reach his destination of B.56 via another transport that had routed via A.42,[104] then to B.56 after a pick-up at Northolt and onward transportation.

A Sparrow Flight aircraft from 271 Squadron based out of Brussels came under friendly ground anti-aircraft fire in the Diest–Melsbroek area on the 17th. There was no obvious reason for this attack and the aircraft was full of casualties at the time. Luckily no one was hurt, although the aircraft received some light damage. It made a successful landing, and no further action or enquiries followed this event. A Northolt detachment of five aircraft was created as aircraft were operating empty between there and Down Ampney. This made more sense and would increase efficiency. There was space at Northolt to accommodate the aircraft, and this may have also been on the back of the recent no show of the VIP flight out of Blakehill Farm that failed to reach Northolt. The officer in charge of this detachment was Squadron Leader Pearson.

A record was reached on the 20th when a total of 428 casualties were returned to Down Ampney in one single day, a bittersweet moment for the station. While it was a great achievement in bringing back so many for treatment, it also added a touch of sadness that so many were still getting wounded so late in the war.

March and the weather was rather pleasant over southern England. Although the Continent was having its share of foggy days, it certainly did not stop any flying activity at the beginning of the month. Routings for the continental flights were such that if you looked at them drawn on a map, they would represent a series of lines zigzagging across the UK and into Europe. While the main hubs were still in place, Brussels being the centre for a lot of traffic, the number of destinations were still growing during the first three months of 1945. Crews from 437 Squadron at RAF Blakehill Farm took over the taskings for the scheduled trips to and from mainland Europe on the 9th as crews from 48 and 271 Squadrons (fifteen each) were operating from Blakehill on glider exercises. These were continuity flights, with aircraft getting airborne towing the Horsa gliders at 11.30 and releasing them back on to Blakehill Farm at 12.30, with a subsequent return to Down Ampney for the Dakotas. No. 575 Squadron were busy with a mix of freight flights for B.78 as well as two aircraft on glider towing training. Another two took a trip down to Netheravon to collect gliders and return.

A temporary deployment was put into place on the 14th when two crews from 271 Squadron were scheduled to take freight out to B.56 (Brussels) and set up a semi-permanent flight to cover runs from Brussels to Marseilles. Transport drivers were to be taken from Ghent to Marseilles to collect and return vehicles now that the southern half of France was in Allied control. No. 233 Squadron were still fully employed with transporting various freight and passengers across the Channel, bringing casualties at every available opportunity into Down Ampney on return legs.

Unit censorship came into force at Down Ampney at 23.59 on the 16th. This, of course, raised the alarm and was an indication that there was an impending operation to follow within the next few days. Crews were detailed to travel to Blakehill Farm on the 17th with the intention of flying another 'glider balbo'. In fact, it soon became clear that they would be meeting Glider Regiment crews, whom they would be working with again in the immediate future. More crews were despatched to Broadwell the next morning, again to meet with their glider compatriots. This was the confirmation that was required by crews that there was another major operation in the pipeline. Day to day operational flights on the scheduled runs did continue for some during this time, with none cancelled due to poor weather. The variety of stores and general freight became even wider as the need for constant supply was growing as the Allies' advance was covering more ground as the Germans were being pushed further into their own borders. The new ADRU was officially opened and renamed the P and F.[105] This new facility would be used for security control as well as customs, etc. Any returning 'distressed'[106] airmen would also transit through this facility upon arrival.

Operation Varsity

Exercise Vulture IV looked to be an interesting one and 512 and 575 Squadrons were keen to take part as they believed (like others) that this was going to be another major operation in mainland Europe. For previous months the squadrons had been training quite intensively in their key roles of glider tugging and pannier dropping both by day and night. This became so ingrained that there were almost two aircraft always employed. Every fortnight there was a 'balbo', which meant the squadrons were cleared of any normal resupply taskings. The various training programmes that were in place for both 38 and 46 Groups needed to be coordinated to make a viable proposal under a single scheme and be carried out as joint exercise from all airfields and squadrons to form as a single stream to any point given and return. Vulture IV did accomplish these requirements and was a successful exercise for any upcoming airborne operation being planned.

The final airborne assault of the war was the crossing of the Rhine and the advance into Germany. The Rhine was the last major obstacle for the Allies and their target of getting troops on the ground and on to the soil of the Reich. The targeted area for the river crossing was between the towns of Rees and Wesel. This portion of the land segment was known under the auspices of Operation Plunder, and involved many different crossing points. It came into effect late on 23 March 1945. The overall operation involved over a million men from three Allied countries, Britain, United States and Canada, as well as 4,000 artillery pieces and over 250,000 tons of equipment. Varsity, the airborne operation, was designed to deploy a large force by air insertion as most traditional means of crossing the Rhine had been destroyed by the retreating German Army. It was designated to deploy troops on to the eastern banks of the Rhine and hold positions until the ground troops linked up following their crossing from the western banks. The airborne section still holds the record for the largest single-day airborne operation in history. Some 17,000 British and American paratroopers were released from aircraft above the Rhine during 24 March. The objective was to get the paratroopers within 5 miles north of Wesel on the high ground to act as a bridgehead for the troops crossing the river the previous evening and starting their assault near to Wesel. The British 21st Army Group were to link up with the airborne division and the 6th British Airborne troops and cross the Rhine late on the 23rd and quickly secure nine small bridgeheads. When the airborne troops were released from the 1,128 British aircraft and gliders, the force of over 9,000 troops deploying on to this area and forming an immense fighting force was something the Germans had not seen before and must have sealed the realisation that the war was indeed over. It was now just a matter of time. Escort fighters for the armada totalled approximately 900, including Spitfires, Typhoons, P-51s and P-47s. Even though there were no Luftwaffe fighters flying, the Americans' Fifteenth Air Force flew with a force of 150 heavy bombers and attacked Berlin to potentially occupy any fighters that may have enough fuel[107] to appear. As the paratroopers and the gliders started to land, some encountered sniper and mortar fire as well as concealed flak positions, but this was rather sporadic and somewhat haphazard. It did though have some effect and caused some casualties and damage. Once on the ground, the airborne troops soon fought off attempts by the German forces and took control of their positions, capturing prisoners and securing the ground taken. Varsity was a success as it allowed troops to advance rapidly into northern Germany, capturing bridges, strongholds and towns. British and American casualties were somewhat lower than expected, although they were more than 2,000 split between both divisions. The Allies did go on to capture more than 3,500 German prisoners, although the average German soldier may have decided that the easier option would be to surrender and live than fight and probably die for a lost cause. That does not reflect in any way the bravery that the Allied soldiers who took part in this major operation exhibited during this final phase of the war in Europe.

The Daks Push on to Germany (Operation Varsity)

When the news filtered through that the next main operation would be the crossing of the Rhine, fourteen crews from 271 Squadron were sent to RAF Gosfield. They also sent ground crews by air on the 22nd. This added an additional problem at Down Ampney as there was a shortage of crews to perform the scheduled daily flights, so RAF Hendon and Croydon stepped in to backfill the shortfall while this operation was active. RAF Gosfield was located in Essex about 5 miles north of Braintree, and approximately 40 miles north-east of London. The field had previously been used by the USAAF with the 365th Fighter Group and the 379th Bomber Group taking residence, until they left during April 1944. They were replaced by the 410th Bombardment Group, who stayed until the summer of 1945, eventually being posted to France post-VE Day. Briefings for Varsity were carried out early on the 23rd at Gosfield, twelve crews were down to take part, the other two crews held in reserve. No. 271 Squadron's task would be to tow Horsa gliders to a position north of Wesel and deliver troops from the 6th British Airborne Division along with their equipment.

The route given was:

Gosfield–Altair – 51 06 45 N 01 09 45 E RV
Beta – 50 21 30 N 01 38 30 E
Gemini – 50 30 50 N 02 39 50 E
Marfak – 50 42 45 N 04 37 30 E
Vega – 50 58 50 N 05 04 30 E
Kingston – 51 17 50 N 05 04 30 E
Yalta North 51 38 20 N 06 11 23 E
LZ – north of Wesel

No. 48 Squadron was also employed on Varsity, with twelve crews and two reserves travelling to RAF Birch, also in Essex, 43 miles north-east of London. Their movement from Down Ampney was on the afternoon of the 22nd. The final briefing was held at 04.30 on the 24th, with the Dakotas and Horsa gliders getting airborne between 06.50 and 07.31½. The weather played its part and perfect flying conditions prevailed for the operation.

No. 437 Squadron were employed on Varsity, with twenty-four aircraft deploying to RAF Birch for towing gliders. Their trade was the 1st Ulster Rifles, which consisted of 230 personnel along with fifteen jeeps and trailers, two additional trailers, six separate jeeps, a 6-pounder gun, two handcarts, ammunition, four bicycles and two motor bikes. Their landing zone (U) was reached through a thick haze and allowed for a successful release of all gliders. The routing was from Birch, Dover, Cap Griz-Nez, south-west of Lille, south-east of Brussels to the north-east of the Rhine using the autobahn as a marking point to the DZs 'O' and 'U' near to Hamminkeln.

No. 48 Squadron had two gliders released prematurely due to faulty tow ropes. Dakota KG439, with Flight Lieutenant G. Whitfield (DFM) at the controls, lost its glider over Lille, while Dakota KG364, captained by Squadron Leader L.J. Harries, saw its glider separate 12 miles from the LZ. In both cases the ropes were brought back for inspection and review. The remaining ten aircraft, which were flying at approximately 2,500ft, managed to successfully release their gliders over a seven-minute period (10.19–10.26) close to the DZ/LZ, even though the tug crews did note that there was smoke on the ground obscuring their view. Later came confirmation that all had made successful landings with no issues reported and the ground-based troops had met up successfully with the glider-borne forces.

Two of the Dakotas, piloted by Wing Commander P.D. Squires DFC and Flight Lieutenant R.G.J. Hull, had to make refuelling stops at B.78 (Eindhoven) and B.51 (Lille/Vendeville) respectfully, then returned to base. Concentrated flak was experienced to the east of Ringenberg and to the south-east of Haldern but no damage was reported. There was also scattered flak encountered near Rees from the eastern bank of the Issel Canal but again there was no damage or aircraft losses an all returned safely to base.

No. 271 Squadron's first aircraft got airborne at 06.25 from Gosfield, where again the weather was perfect for flying. They were joined by aircraft from two sister squadrons who had relocated from Broadwell, 512 and 575. Led by Lieutenant Colonel P.S. Joubert AFC, the twelve crews were all airborne and en route at 06.57. No enemy aircraft were encountered on the way to the LZ. Although there was light, intermediate and heavy flak, no damage nor casualties were sustained. One crew reported that their glider was released at position 51 03 N 05 03 E but no reason was known for why this occurred. Once all the gliders had been released, most of the Dakotas landed at Brussels Evere for refuelling. The loads carried within the gliders along with the troops were jeeps, trailers, handcarts, cycles, guns and ammunition.

No. 233 Squadron had allocated twenty-four aircraft for Varsity, each towing a gilder from RAF Birch after relocating there on 23 March. Led by Wing Commander Mellor, all aircraft lifted early on 24 March between 06.18 and 06.49 and successfully released their gliders north of Wessel between 10.17½ and 10.21. They experienced very little in the way of resistance from the Germans, with hardly any flak reported and there were more concerns from the crews that the amount of aircraft in the skies may lead to collisions. One Dakota, KG410, did run short of petrol and had to divert into B.6, where it was found to have received a hit by flak that had caused the fuel issue. The remaining force of twenty-three aircraft continued and released their gliders containing 357 troops of the Oxfordshire and Buckinghamshire Regiment. They then flew on to B.75, where they landed between 10.55 and 11.41. After refuelling, twenty aircraft returned to base, leaving four in theatre in case they were needed for resupply flights. In addition to KG410 receiving slight damage, FZ635 was also hit by flak and suffered damage to the fuselage and electrical circuits.

The operation was deemed a great success, and the advances and inroads made into Germany via both airborne and ground forces alleviated the need to resupply by air. The AOC 38 Group sent the following signal to the AOC 46 Group: 'Please give my thanks to all your Group who took part in the operation whether in the air or on the ground. Your magnificent serviceability was only equalled by your operational success.' While the number of aircraft and crews from the group on Varsity were much lower than for D-Day and Market Garden, the size and importance of the mission was no less important than the main operations of 1944. The significance of the largest airborne operation in history and the lack of any resupply flights go to confirming the superiority of the Allies in both numbers of men and machinery, as well as the realisation that the end was in sight. That said, there was still work to be done and the Allies were still determined to finish the job, with courage being displayed by every service and nationality to a man. More messages of thanks and appreciation came through over the next few days, one from Air Commodore L. Darvall MC: 'Am informed by Commanding General FAAA[108] that dropped the 6 Division both paratroopers and gliders was generally very good. Hearty congratulations to all ranks aircrew and ground staff on their hard work, skill and devotion to duty. I am proud of you all.' On the 30th many glider pilots transitioned through Down Ampney after their participation in Operation Varsity, although they were flown in by Blakehill Farm and Broadwell aircraft.

Exercise Meteor was scheduled for 20 March, operating out of RAF Gosfield. Twenty-four aircraft from 512 Squadron were to be provided, with five spares, with all the aircraft screened from normal transport duties from the 21st. This had the effect of providing the maximum effort required for the operation but did fail to allow time for the crews to prepare and ready their aircraft. This was highlighted by the squadron commander to the station commander, who explained that if insufficient time was allowed there was an immediate danger of aircraft being away from base due to delays in weather and unserviceability, which in turn could lead to a decline in the effort attainable for operations. The date for screening was pulled forward to the afternoon of the 20th, which happened after the squadron commander had been in contact with SASO,[109] HQ 46 Group. It did understand fully that it was necessary for aircraft to be clear one full day to be on top line for ops. This postponed the date to the 21st for aircraft to deploy to Gosfield, the move taking place smoothly with no issues reported. Exercise Meteor, intended to be a security blind for the airborne operation that was Varsity, never ended up taking place.

No. 512 Squadron moved to RAF Gosfield on 22 March, with both aircraft and aircrew making the trip in accordance with RAF Broadwell's instructions. With an early start and breakfast at 06.00, the crews were briefed and detailed to be ready as the first aircraft had to be airborne by 09.30 and the last by 10.04. All leave was cancelled. Twenty-four crews were allocated to deploy, with five reserves. These were then sub-divided into three flights, A, B and C, accordingly. Ground crews were also involved in the deployment, travelling via air and road, dependent on what they had as their responsibility to transport. All leave was suspended, with no calls allowed from or to personnel on base.

No. 512 Squadron had the honour of leading the British stream of aircraft in Varsity. This did place a lot of responsibility on the shoulders of the CO, Wing Commander R.G. Dutton DFC and Bar, who had only taken command of the squadron on 25 January. Timing was of great importance to this operation, and its success was down to accurate timing and scheduling, which Dutton and his crew achieved impeccably. Number two in the formation was the AOC of 46 Group, Air Commodore L. Darvall, flying as co-pilot to Squadron Leader W.A. Mostyn-Brown. To have the AOC of the group take part in the operation did give good cheer and boosted morale for all crews involved. The twenty-four crews and five reserves who took part in Meteor also took part in the operation, and for many this was their first experience of active duty.

The British 6th and the US 17th airborne divisions were scheduled to be dropped some hours after the initial assault. Their destination point was

6 miles east of the Rhine, between Rees and Wesel, and this was to help speed up the build-up of forces, with the airborne lift designed to be carried out in one. The aim was to fool the Germans that the operation would solely be a ground offensive, owing to a possible airborne failure, but in fact the opposite was planned with the aim to draw the remaining main German forces forward and westwards toward the Rhine itself. Launching the airborne assault behind the enemy's lines was the job for both glider-borne and paratrooper forces, to hold key objectives, towns and other positions. This was a lesson learned at Arnhem in September 1944. No. 512 Squadron had the Oxford and Bucks as well as the Royal Ulster Rifles in their gliders and were tasked with delivering them to the LZ just to the east of the Rhine.

With Wing Commander Dutton leading the formation, he got airborne at 06.00 precisely, with the remaining twenty-three Dakotas quickly following and forming up in loose pairs at ten-second intervals. With take-off before dawn and poor visibility being experienced, all aircraft had upward identification and formation lights[110] on, but this still made things difficult for the formation to maintain position. Squadron Leader Clarke, flying number three position in Dakota KG641 (AC), failed to make contact with the lead two aircraft and subsequently turned on to ETA[111] and was followed by the rest of the formation. This had the effect that the lead two aircraft were quite a way down the stream, which put the formation four and a half minutes late at Gosfield. Time was eventually made up at Cap Griz-Nez, with Wing Commander Dutton and Squadron Leader Mostyn-Brownback at the head of the formation, which was now only a minute behind schedule. Onwards to the Rhine, via a south-easterly direction to Bethune, then a southernly turning point followed by a north-easterly direction to Wavre. With no issues or incidents to report, the glider stream continued on course to the ETA. The spacing and formation of the stream was perfect, and with no enemy opposition everything was going to plan. Almost as the lead aircraft was making their turn at Bethune, the first wave of paratroopers aboard the Dakotas of the IXth US Troop Carrier Command passed below and to the port and continued to pass until on the final run-up across the Rhine to the LZ. The last of the US formation were seen discarding their paratroopers approximately 10 miles ahead.

Once Weeze was reached, the operation took on a new phase when compared to the training exercises so far encountered by many of the crews. The Dakota formations ahead started to receive and were repeatably hit by heavy flak, with several of the aircraft witnessed going down in flames or exploding in midair. Luckily for 512 Squadron, most of their Dakotas were low down and partly obscured by a smokescreen that had been laid down by the Second Army, so they were not an easy target for the flak defences. The glider train from Weeze up to the LZ was a distance of 18 miles, which was somewhat hazardous as the tug aircraft had been detailed to fly at 2,500ft and to take no evasive action. Flak was heavy, but thankfully not very accurate and all the Dakotas made it through to the LZ and delivered their respective gliders, except for one whose glider pulled off just before the Rhine. All aircraft turned to port and dropped their towing cables after each of the crews had identified that the ropes would not foul the following aircraft within the stream.

Unfortunately when turning away from the LZ, one of the Dakotas, captained by Flight Lieutenant C.A. Chew, received a flak hit in the port-side fuel tanks and caught fire. Flames spread along the fuselage, and the fabric was seen to be burnt off the rudder and elevators. Aircraft flying near to the burning aircraft reported that they witnessed one of the crew bale out. This was detailed by both Flight Lieutenant Briscoe of Squadron Leader Russell's crew and Flight Sergeant Geisler of Flying Officer Hill's crew. The crew member who baled out was seen to deploy his parachute and float away towards the ground. He was lost from vision though as the aircraft that had been hit broke into two and fell to the ground. No news of Flight Lieutenant Chew and his crew was reported at the time, and all were reported as missing.

There was slight damage to two other aircraft from 512 Squadron, but these made a safe transit back and no other Dakotas were lost from the unit on this day. All aircraft apart from one made a successful landing at Brussels. Squadron Leader Mostyn-Brown landed at Eindhoven due to insufficient fuel levels. At Brussels the crews were debriefed and the possibility of performing any supply drops that may be required by the land forces was discussed. Thankfully these were not needed due to the unprecedented success of the operation.

No. 512 Squadron, like others, had the honour to participate in the three airborne/glider operations: D-Day, Market Garden and the crossing of the Rhine, where they not only had the responsibility of leading the whole glider force, but also carried the AOC from 46 Group, Air Commodore L. Darvill, as a second pilot to Squadron Leader Mostyn-Brown; the AOC proving he was an able member of the crew. The aircraft returned back to RAF Broadwell empty on the 26th from Brussels, although four (KG558, KG373, KG368 and KG344) all flew to Down Ampney with 14,000lb of flak suits and 1,000lb of flak helmets. From Ampney they continued to fly the short distance back to Broadwell.

No. 575 Squadron also supported Operation Varsity, allocating the same number of aircraft as their sister squadron, with twenty-four Dakotas towing Horsa gliders, and operating the same flight profile, routings and similar timings. Carrying elements of the Oxford and Bucks Regiment and the Ulster Rifles, their LZ was also on the east bank of the Rhine near to Hamminkeln, landing back at Brussels.

A Crewman of Chalk 13, 512 Squadron

At 02.00, the final briefing took place and a walk across the airfield and a look at the marshalled aircraft. The moon was low and starting to lose its brilliance as the dawn light started to pierce the night sky. We checked the aircraft and all its equipment, put on Mae Wests and para suits and waited for the first of the engines to start up. At 05.50 we heard number 1 start up and then run them up and back down as the second one burst into life. A whisker after 06.00 we and Chalk thirteen were rolling, speed increased and we staggered into the air with all the associated shuddering, you thought it was only a matter of time until the combination stalled, and you would tumble earthbound! Of course, we didn't tumble, we continued to climb, just skimming the trees with what appeared a few feet to spare. Luckily we saw the tail light of Chalk twelve ahead, and soon eleven came into view after passing Cambridge. Looking out towards Gosfield, we were in position, and we could see the Stirling combinations forming up, thousands of feet above them the Fortresses of the USAAF leaving a trail on their way towards the heart of Germany. Two hours flying time passed relatively quickly, the Thames estuary and the Channel soon behind us. This was a comfort to the glider boys in having a short sea crossing. Below us were the Yanks with their Airborne Division Paratroops. Their flying formations were all together, first class to witness. When the coast of mainland Europe was reached, and approaching Brussels, we saw the great smoke screen that was laid out from the previous days.

Once we got to view the Rhine, things started to liven up, flak was dying down as the last of the Yanks came through, and there was a pause. There were several planes that had been hit and were on fire and going down. Some looked as if they were in control, while others were all over the sky completely out of control. Great plumes of smoke appeared when aircraft hit the ground at near vertical angles. Another was seen to make a gliding approach with its starboard engine and wing ablaze. Suddenly the flak erupted once again and more aircraft were caught in the hail of shrapnel that was filling the skies. A few seconds more and we released our glider, and other squadrons released theirs. Flak bursts were releasing their deadly puffs and we could feel the bottom of our aircraft being peppered on the fuselage.

My mind wondered how the glider pilots would make their way down to the LZ through the smoke, haze and concentrated flak! We had our own job to do getting out pretty fast weaving to avoid a straight flightpath. The jerries certainly had our range and speed, but once we were west of the Rhine we managed to check the aircraft. Luckily for us there was not a hole or severe scratch that we could see. Five hours of flying complete, a cigarette and a cup of tea and ready for the debrief. The reception and hospitality at B.56 was something to behold.

512 Squadron Lands in Germany

The day 27 March was a momentous one. Fourteen Dakotas took off from Broadwell and made their way to Nivelles Aerodrome, Belgium. While this was nothing special, once unloaded two of the aircraft were then ordered to proceed to B.100 to collect casualties. B.100 was a small forward airstrip located 2½ miles from the German town of Weeze and was the hundredth to be used by the Allies since D-Day. The first of the Dakotas to land on German soil was captained by Flight Lieutenant R.A. Davis, with Flying Officer Orchard, Flying Officer Savage and Flying Officer Sowersby. Low cloud of 300–400ft made for a low approach and the aircraft touched down at 13.30. The strip itself was a grass-covered affair that had rows of tents parallel, which housed casualties waiting for airborne evacuation home. All were British troops of the 21st Group and airborne forces who had been involved in the drop and action across the Rhine between Emmerich and Wesel on the preceding Saturday, 24 March. Once loaded the Dakotas took off bound for Brussels, there the casualties were transferred to UK-bound flights.

Chapter 9

War Drawdown, End of Hostilities Within the European Theatre (April, May)

Cloud and light drizzle welcomed the beginning of April, All Fools Day, and the weather was playing its part in embracing the month in typically British style. That said, flying did take place, with the crews from all six squadrons within group actively employed on flights to the European Continent as well as flights throughout the UK. As the Allies fought their way further into the heartland of Germany from the west, and the Russian forces progressed from the east, it was now a matter of when the Reich would finally collapse. This had the effect of increasing the number of passengers that were in need of repatriation back to the UK. Some of these were POWs that were being released either by friendly troops overrunning the camps, or the German guards just vanishing during the night, leaving the prisoners to their own devices. Some of the airfields that were being served by aircraft from Down Ampney, Blakehill Farm and Broadwell were as follows: B.56 Brussels Evere, B.75 Nivelles, B.77 Gilze-Rijen, B.78 Eindhoven, B.120 Hanover, B.150 Hustedt, R.16 Hildesheim, B.100 Goch, B.70 Antwerp, B.108 Rheine, B.114 Diepholz, B.112 Hopsten and B.118 Celle. It was clearly apparent that the number of airfields or Relief Landing Grounds in Germany was increasing in line with the advancing Allies. Northolt's deployment of 271 Squadron was withdrawn at the beginning of the month, with aircraft now deploying to Croydon. This move enabled repair work to be carried out at Northolt, without the need to stop any flights continuing their transportation tasks into Europe. During this time all the squadrons had been operating out of their respective airfields on the scheduled flights, still carrying varied freight and passengers and once again returning with passengers, casualties and POWs.

A change on 9 April saw 271 Squadron returning from Croydon and back in situ at Down Ampney. Now 110 Wing would have a detachment at Croydon and their aircraft would handle the European legs. The 10th was a joyous day as some of the glider pilots who had flown from Ampney on the Arnhem operation and who had been taken prisoner were brought back to the station after being repatriated. While this was a happy occasion for those visiting, the thoughts of all were firmly with their friends who did not make it back.

No. 437 Squadron had been especially busy in the early to middle of the month, operating regular flights to the Continent carrying petrol and Merlin engines. Most of their return flights were transporting released POWs back to the UK as well as casualties back to Down Ampney. No. 271 Squadron were involved in a special exercise on the 12th, with three aircraft assigned to take a party of twenty-three press representatives and war correspondents to see glider tugging and pannier dropping. This was to show some aspects of the work carried out by 46 Group aircraft and crews in support of the front line and how they performed the insertion of troops and resupply with ongoing support. The feedback was positive, and some correspondents went into print for the general populous to read of the exploits of a Dakota squadron and their activities.

While operations took the lion's share of flights, training was also continuing for all the squadrons. Glider towing was still being honed by crews to keep current, as well as for new personnel to master this task in the Dakota. As the month progressed, POWs were being released in great numbers and were taking precedent to be repatriated as a matter of urgency. More German airfields were becoming available for the Dakotas to use as the amount of land held by the enemy was decreasing rapidly. B.108 Rheine was opened to traffic on the 13th, B.114 Diepholz on the 15th and B.120 Langenhagen was open from the 17th. Another message from the AOC 46 Group was received during the 18th. It read, 'Please convey my congratulations to Squadron Leader A.B.J. Pearson AFC, Officers and other men of 271 Squadron detachment, Northolt, on their splendid work during March. The return of flying hours, and the regularity of schedules flown shows that this achievement has been made possible only by untiring work and keenness, displayed by all ranks belonging to this detachment.'

By the 20th the transport details were that intense that all the crews who were away on leave were called back to fulfil the tasks that were uppermost within the group. This amount of traffic was the heaviest the squadrons had experienced, and all future leave was suspended temporarily. There appeared no let-up in the foreseeable future to allow this to be reversed. A slight alteration to this ruling came the following day from 46 Group that one crew from each flight were allowed to be on leave as the timetable of flights could lead to extreme fatigue among the crews. This change of position, while not ideal, did go some way to allowing crews time away from flying operations.

With the rush to get to Berlin, the Allies were making good headway, although the Russians had reached the outskirts of the city by 16 April and had started to attack in force. The Dakotas of 46 Group kept up the supply flights, returning with more and more personnel and POWs. It was a record month as the number of supply flights increased supported by the six squadrons. Casualties were still being brought back to Britain as the fighting was still intense at this late stage of the war.

There was sad news on the 28th when Dakota KG406, operated by 271 Squadron, departed Down Ampney at 06.33 for a routine flight to Brussels and Nivelles. Unfortunately the aircraft never arrived for it was seen to crash into the sea at 07.37, 9 miles east-north-east of Calais. A motor launch was sent to search the area in conjunction with a Walrus aircraft but, no survivors were located. The reason for the crash was not known. The aircraft was carrying photographic materials as well as a nursing orderly. The names of those missing were Flight Lieutenant R.C.J. Southey, Flight Sergeant J.R. Fife-Miller, Pilot Officer J.L. Ives Warrant Officer, Flight Sergeant R.E. Reynolds and Nursing Orderly LACW M.M. Walsh.

Unusual weather conditions affected the flying for Down Ampney and Blakehill Farm on the 29th. It was a cloudy day with sleet showers, so all flying was suspended, although Broadwell did have a couple of inbound and outbound flights. The 30th was another day of poor weather, cloudy with low visibility, and only a few crews managed to get airborne for the continental flights from each of the three airfields. By the end of April 1945, the total number of casualties that 48 and 271 Squadrons had carried amounted to 43,548. It was another fact that since D-Day the number of casualties evacuated by air exceeded the numbers brought back by sea, extolling the virtues of rapid deployment by air over the longer transit time by boat. The total number that survived due to the rapid response of the Dakotas and other aircraft cannot be quantified, but this would be far greater than using a seaborne crossing and subsequent road transportation.

As April rolled into May it was over for the Germans. The Russians were fighting house to house in Berlin and the Allies were making advances from the west. Hitler was dead, the news breaking that he had committed suicide on 30 April, but the Germans were not capitulating. The Dakotas of 46 Group were adding even more destinations within Germany: B.58 Friedrichshafen, Y.75 Frankfurt, R.52 Leipzig and R.102 Virst, to name a few. Crews were being detailed to transport as many POWs back from Europe as possible. The number of casualties was declining, although the number of prisoners released was growing as they wanted to get back to England. No. 271 Squadron's Sparrow flights operating out of Brussels were finally in the hands of Dakotas, with the last of the HP54s, K7000, finally despatched to RAF Kemble after receiving damage at the end of April. The directive made in April about crews and their leave was finally rescinded, to the relief of all.

For VE Day, 8 May 1945, Prime Minister Winston Churchill announced to the nation on the previous evening stating that this day would be one of celebration in defeating Germany and its Allies within Europe.

No. 512 Squadron were again operating as a detachment out of Brussels during early May. This allowed for a hub to be available on the Continent for quicker despatch to transport personnel and goods/supplies within the European field of operations. Once linked with flights to and from the UK, this proved to be a much more practical way for flying operations. Crews would operate to and from Broadwell, then stay and fly a couple of days operating out of Brussels, then return back to Broadwell. The 7th also saw 437 Squadron departing Blakehill Farm for Nivelles, Belgium. Crews were aligned with Three flights, A, B and C, and were scheduled for operations within Europe (as 512) and operated as three or four ship depending on requirements. This detachment now reported through to 111 Wing.

A church service was held in the main hanger at Down Ampney for all and commenced at 10.00. The evening brought both the officers' and sergeants' messes open to all ranks from 20.00. A dance was held in each and free beer was available.

For crews who were still flying, the situation was very different. Scheduled flights still needed to be performed and supplies and stores were still required for those in Europe, as well as those who needed to get back to England. The European Continent was in a mess after six years of war, with millions dead and many, many more displaced. The fighting may have been over, but the rebuilding was going to take years.

On VE Day+1 (9 May) victory celebrations were still continuing throughout the country. While the celebrations were under way, there were still taskings that needed to be carried out. Throughout, there was still a focus for all 46 Group's personnel to remember the tasks required, and there was a new destination added to the flying schedule, Copenhagen. This new tasking did present a few issues as the distance from the UK meant careful routing and planning. Authority was given for a special forty-eight-hour pass to be issued to all personnel following Germany's surrender and defeat. This was not issued en masse, but to ensure that the normal services were adhered to, the leave could be added to longer time periods or taken separately or later.

On 13 May, Flying Officer H.A. King returned to England after time as a POW following his baling out at Arnhem on a resupply mission during September 1944. King had been a part of Flight Lieutenant David Lord's crew when their aircraft was hit by anti-aircraft fire and was the person who filed the recommendation for Lord's VC.[112] Flights continued throughout the month, but on the 25th a crash occurred involving a crew and aircraft from 271 Squadron. This incident involved Warrant Officer Watson T.S. and crew, who had night stopped at Brussels. During the morning the crew were instructed to proceed to R.80 (Salzburg) but the aircraft crashed near to Kell am See, Trier (western Germany), killing all on board. Nobody witnessed the crash, but the aircraft appeared to hit some trees in a forest in a remote part of the country. There was no obvious reason for the crash, although the weather was foggy and cloudy in the region. The names of the aircrew were Pilot Warrant Officer Watson T.S, Warrant Officer A.O. Scherbarth, Pilot Officer N.H. Dixon and Warrant Officer T. Crawford. The burial of the crew took place at Grand-Failly, France, on the 28th. This crew had only been on the squadron for ten days and even though the fighting in Europe had come to an end, it showed the dangers that these crews were still facing while carrying out their resupply duties.

Operations from Down Ampney continued, and 48 Squadron were the first to receive orders to relocate to India in August 1945. However, the Americans dropped the first atomic bomb on to Japan, so their tenure was relatively short lived.

The First Allied Transport Aircraft to Land in Berlin

The mission required the aircraft to proceed to Flensburg in Jutland to take members of the German High Command to Berlin, where they were required at the HQ of Marshal Zhukov[113] of the Russian High Command. So, on 11 May a Dakota from 512 Squadron captained by Squadron Leader McLeod, RAFVR[114] was briefed on the operation and was given clearance by Air Chief Marshal Tedder. Upon arrival at Flensberg, the crew were met by the German High Command, who were in the area with a fully armed Panzer Division and were fully in control of their own activities and actions. Around the airfield were large numbers of German aircraft, which all looked to be in perfect condition with no visible damage, although they were immobilised through a lack of fuel. There were a vast number of German officers around, and again all still appeared to be armed, but all appeared to be complying with the recent unconditional surrender[115] that was put in place on 8 May. There were also 200-plus RAF Regiment soldiers within the area, and the situation appeared slightly strange. Enquiries were made about the identities of the passengers required for transportation to Berlin, and assurances were given that they would be ready and appear within the next five minutes. This became a statement that was heard throughout the whole day.

While the crews waited for their passengers to show, a Russian Dakota landed and the crew made a hasty dash to find the RAF crew and deliver a message that no British planes were allowed to land at Templehof Airport in Berlin. This message was translated through a German interpreter who was available for such instances as this. However, owing to the language difficulties that were experienced by all sides, Squadron Leader McLeod ordered that a wireless contact be established to ascertain exactly what his orders were as he had received no information other than his original orders, which were certainly different to the information supplied by the Russians. It may also be true that during the immediate post-war days there was a little mistrust between some of the Allies. The wireless contact was eventually made, and

War Drawdown, End of Hostilities Within the European Theatre

with some difficulty the original orders did still stand. Demands for the passengers to appear were still ongoing during this time, and once again they said they would be ready in five minutes. However, again nobody appeared. Communication continued in broken German and English by both parties and after a long delay it was ascertained that the Germans would not be ready until the following morning. Even though the orders and instructions to transport them came from the highest command, it was felt that the best option was to comply with the German High Command's proposal. The Dakota returned to base, retracing their route back to Flensburg the next morning to try again to collect their German passengers and complete their mission. Oberstleutnant D. De Maziero of the German General Staff presented himself with his interpreter, and clasped in his hand was a movement order signed by General Jodl that directed him to proceed to the headquarters of Marshal Zhukov. His demeanour was that of a typical junior-ranking German officer: stiff, reserved and extremely non-communicative.

The Dakota took off and headed for Templehof airfield, among the ruins of this once great city, which was duly reached in good time. Berlin was a bustling conurbation, but the populace were mainly Russian soldiers within its heart. The crew were greeted warmly by the Russian ground crews, and once again communications were through a German translator, who appeared to speak fluently in many different languages. Nevertheless, fraternisation with the Russians did take place and there was a lot of small bits and pieces changing hands, such as sixpences, rubles and buttons. There was even a young Yak sergeant pilot who got in on the act.

Once the passengers had deplaned and were handed over to the Russian guards, the crew of the RAF Dakota wanted to leave, but alas they were informed that they had to wait for Russian clearance before they could get airborne. This had also befallen an American crew who had suffered the same fate and had an enforced stay of some days. Some time on a field telephone ensued and the Russian sergeant had difficulties mastering the captain's name but finally permission was granted and the crew could start engines and carry out their departure procedure. Parked next to the RAF Dakota was a Russian VIP Dakota, with the crew sitting in its shade by the main mainplane. Greetings were exchanged, and no language barrier nor difficulties were experienced with this set of Russian military.

The British Dakota took off and set a return course back to their base, a relatively short flight. As the aircraft was circling Tempelhof airfield, the devastation below was an unbelievable site. There appeared to be no building left undamaged, and there were piles of rubble scattered around that were once dwellings or businesses that now were completely destroyed in the fight for the complete capitulation of the German military and its people. There was one building that miraculously did appear to be undamaged. This was the only sign of life from the views afforded from the Dakota in the skies above the city. Dotted around the city there were air raid shelters whose purpose was obvious as they appeared as square concrete panels interspersed within the ruined city landscape. They had flak platforms on their corners, black roofs that made them stand out, and they also looked a bit battered and scarred from the battle. Leafless trees stood in what were once elegant avenues and parks; there were also well-trodden paths through the rubble where locals had created new pathways. Certain landmarks still stood out: the Reichstag and Chancellery, damaged and now flying the Soviet hammer and sickle flag; the Brandenburg Gate and the Sportpalast, which were all significant icons of the Nazi party, the latter one a venue for their grand parades. They could still be recognised in the grim landscape that Berlin now presented along with many other cities throughout Europe. Some of the buildings were still smouldering and one was still on fire. With empty streets and very few vehicles, apart from the occasional military one, Berlin was to all intents and purposes dead. The Dakota continued towards its base, the first transport aircraft of Transport Command to land at Templehof Airfield, Berlin.

Transport Command and Airborne Operations in Europe, 46 Group

No. 46 Group was used in the three most pivotal airborne operations of the war in Europe: Normandy, Arnhem and the Rhine crossing. On the first tasking for D-Day, aircraft from the group managed to carry 2,300 paratroopers, 1,000 glider-borne troops, 200 vehicles as well as panniers filled with arms and equipment. The resupply missions carried further weapons needed to fight the war, including machine guns, mortars and 6- and 17-pounder guns. No. 46 Group were also aligned to casualty evacuation flights, with aircraft flying into theatre delivering their array of supplies and on the return legs utilised for carrying the wounded back to the UK for treatment. The first flight to undertake this task occurred on 12 June, a mere six days after the Allied assault on Normandy, and by the month end hundreds of casualties had been flown home, the total standing at an impressive 3,270 returned. The total freight carried into France over the same time was 253 tons. Dakotas played a significant part in keeping the armoured spearheads supplied, with petrol the most valuable commodity that was needed to keep the advance moving. Staging posts were being set up within France and later Belgium and the Netherlands. These were visited regularly by 46 Group aircraft. Brussels is a good example as the activities around this airfield were key to the Allies, especially seeing how this began only one day after the Germans had been driven out. In a month, there were 3,438 aircraft movements from Britain to Brussels, along with more than 7,000 tons of freight, 4,280 passengers, and 7,200 casualties evacuated, with no mishaps reported or experienced.

The Arnhem operation in September 1944 was the most outstanding to be carried out by 46 Group Dakotas, both the original phase and the resupply flights that followed. Troops from the 1st Airborne Division were taken over in gliders on 17 an 18 September. Dakotas flew glider-towing flights on both days, and these delivered jeeps, handcarts, trailers, bicycles, motorbikes, 6-pounder guns, wireless equipment, ammunition and medical supplies. Once the resupply missions started, panniers were delivered consisting of food and ammunition. These took place on most days for the following week, with the intention of keeping the ground troops supplied with the essentials needed to hold their positions. Flying unarmed aircraft made these missions vulnerable, with relatively slow aircraft flying low making for easy targets for the German flak and fighters who were operating in the perimeter around the British bridgehead. Losses were the heaviest that the Dakotas from the squadrons within 46 Group had suffered so far during the war, but undeterred the pilots and crews still carried out their tasks to resupply the troops on the ground, who praised them for their endeavours. One of the Glider Regiment OCs said that the men on the ground were humbled by the audacity of the resupply pilots.

After the Arnhem campaign the group once again turned its attention to their normal freight operations, and the return of casualties. Air Vice Marshal

Fiddament had become the Senior Air Staff Officer at RAF Transport Command. His successor as AOC of 46 Group was Air Commodore L. Darvall MC, who actually accompanied crews in a Dakota for the operation on 24 March 1945, the Rhine crossing. Operation Varsity is regarded as an exemplary operation in its implementation and execution. Two days before the aircraft were relocated to the eastern side of England. The glider pilots, crews and airborne troops were briefed, during which they were told that the success of the mission would help to speed up the end of the war and deliver final victory. At 02.00 the following day the crews were fed a breakfast of bacon and eggs and received their last briefing (including weather) before being taken out to the aircraft. Aircrew were given revolvers with a warning that if for any reason they found themselves behind enemy lines after needing to bale out, the Germans might not be too keen on taking prisoners due to the disorganised state that the country was now in.

A four-hour flight from England and the Rhine was finally visible, a fairly uneventful journey over in the sunshine of a spring morning. However, when near to the target things started to heat up as a belt of flak and artillery fire came up to greet the airborne force and a layer of smoke started to cover the dropping zone. Some aircraft that were in the middle of the stream passed over and under others, some of which had already cast their gliders away and were returning over the Rhine and heading back. A few had their fuselages and engines on fire. Four hundred glider pilots who had taken part in this great show of force were returned by aircraft of 46 Group, battle weary and exhausted but all in good spirits and greeted back in England by the aircrew who had towed them across to the Rhine. There were some hearty reunions; this being the first time they had seen their comrades since being released 2,000ft above the Fatherland, the glider pilots going down to the smoke and fire of the battle, the Dakotas pilots turning back to England for their next taskings. Glider pilots told of their experiences when they eventually came to a stop and evacuated the glider. The targets for each were dealt with swiftly and all objectives were seized quickly without too much opposition. A fair number of glider pilots were RAF pilots who had volunteered for airborne work and had transferred into the Army. They had been given a short but intensive course in infantry training to enable them to give assistance to the airborne troops while on the ground. This was achieved without taking anything away from their primary role to take the gliders and loads into action, then to aim to get back to their home bases.

One glider pilot said that after release by the Dakota, he put the glider into a turn but immediately lost sight of the landmarks that he intended to use to guide him to the landing zone. 'We ran into a patch of smoke that blotted everything out,' he said, 'and when we emerged, were greeted by a shower of steel from small arms fire. I picked up the landing zone again and made straight for it, about 2,000 yards away. As we came down to land two gliders in front of me collided and crashed – due, I think, to one of them being winged by enemy fire. One or two others crashed near where I was to land and at least one other was on fire. We got down all right, and all got out of the glider safely. Once our party linked up with others and made for the first objective, I was surprised to find that so few of the company appeared to be missing.'

The Rhine missions were complete for the Dakotas of 46 Group, and they were back on to their schedules. Up to just after the end of March they had carried more than 20,000 tons of freight and 1,000 tons of mail to the Continent, as well as more than 35,000 passengers. On the return legs aircraft of the group had brought back more than 600 tons of freight, 1,100 tons of mail and another 35,000 passengers. The group also brought home casualties, with more than 66,000 returned from the Continent for medical treatment.

Chapter 10

The Flying Nightingales

When Corporal Lydia Alford and her two colleagues landed in Normandy on 12 June 1944, they were the first British females to officially put feet onto French soil in over four years and enter a war zone, special operations[116] exempt, and so heralded the birth of the Flying Nightingales and their support for the injured troops.

It is well known that the sooner you administer medical aid to wounded personnel, the greater chance they have of surviving and making a recovery. To this end, 200 nurses from the Women's Auxiliary Air Force were selected to join the Royal Air Force Air Ambulance Unit with the intention of flying out of England on Dakotas from 46 Group, taking supplies etc. out to the front, and bringing wounded personnel back home. The nurses had volunteered to train for the Air Ambulance duties,[117] and the direction of such saw them undertake medical training to deal with the types of injuries they would encounter from the troops that had been in battle and needed treatment. They were given instruction on the administering of oxygen and injections, and this coupled with the general airborne know-how that most had never experienced, put these women into a highly important role, and key within the crew of the aircraft. These nurses flew out on normal scheduled transport flights, carrying normal supplies, so no Red Cross could be displayed on the aircraft. Hence, they were susceptible to attacks from the enemy. Often overlooked, they were just as important as the troops fighting on the front lines. Churchill said the war was being fought by unknown heroes; the Flying Nightingales certainly fitted within these criteria. Heroes, every one of them.

The following stories are taken from the book by K.M. Neave, entitled *A Nightingale Flew*.[118]

Personal Stories: Lydia Alford
I responded to a call asking for volunteers from suitable qualified medical personnel to train for air ambulance duties. Within weeks of applying, I was sent on an intensive air ambulance training course at RAF Hendon. Learning how to cope with the effects of certain types of injuries, such as broken bones, burns and colostomies, and how to cope with the effects of air travel and altitude. When I had completed the course, I was posted to RAF Blakehill Farm, near Cricklade. Training continued with a 'brush up' course at the RAF hospital at Wroughton, dinghy drill in the swimming pool at Bath and several hours of flying experiences often on glider exercises. These were pretty terrifying, as they were carried out with the cargo door removed, and when the glider was released, the whole plane juddered. During the tense days of waiting, we were put through a tough routine of physical training and helped with the building of the new roads on the newly built airfield. It was raining slightly when we boarded our planes at five am on the 13 June, wearing our Mae West life jackets and parachutes and carrying the first aid panniers. Flying over the Normandy coast, we could see the aftermath of the D-Day landings strewn across the beaches, abandoned landing craft, broken tanks, craters and scattered discarded equipment. The thing I remember chiefly about that first time on the ground in Normandy was the dust which was everywhere, coming up in great clouds. Whilst the freight was being unloaded, I tried to make the wounded men as comfortable as possible in all that dust. I had water to give them and panniers of tea. There was a little stray dog that came up from somewhere or other and started to play with the wounded, it cheered them up no end. After the supplies were unloaded, we immediately loaded the wounded on board and took off again. Unfortunately, the weather closed in, and the other two girls had to wait for it to clear. Most of my wounded men were stretcher cases. One man required oxygen, a few hours earlier he had been shot in the chest and back by a German sniper. As the first back, I was overwhelmed by dozens of press men. The story that appeared in the newspaper the following day was the first that my family knew of exactly what I was doing.

Personal Stories: Elsie Beer

I was a nurse when the war began and we used to get into trouble for staying out late, so a few of us packed it in and we joined the Air Force in 1940. I volunteered for the Nursing Orderlies and after training I arrived at Down Ampney, a little village in the Cotswolds in early March 1944, one of the first air ambulance orderlies to be stationed there. It became the main Casualty Air Evacuation Centre and there were two other centres receiving casualties, RAF Blakehill Farm and Broadwell. The whole concept of these air ambulances had been formed in secrecy in the run-up to D-Day, and I was one these nurses selected for training. Aircraft were to ferry urgent medical supplies to the front and return with casualties, who after immediate medical treatment would be transferred to specialist hospitals in the UK. The base at RAF Down Ampney was purpose-built in preparation for the for the invasion of Europe and became the base for 48 and 271 Squadrons, both flying the American DC-3s and C-47s. The Wimpey construction workers were still working on site and as a bit of fun they would allow us to drive their steamroller. We also became friendly with their Irish cook, who would provide the real treat of a fry-up late at night. My first operational flight was on the 18 June 1944.

I recall being called out of church and in a very short time we were on our way to Bény-sur-Mer in France via RAF Tangmere, where we took on freight. The airstrip was in enemy-occupied territory and on our arrival was being shelled. That first flight was very scary. Our plane got hit and shrapnel shot through the Dakota's windows, but we landed safely and managed to unload supplies. We took on casualties and got home safely. This became the routine, landing on fields turned into makeshift airstrips. The enemy were always close by and normally pretty active and as we carried military supplies out the Dakotas didn't have the protection of the Red Cross, even though we were not armed, usually unaccompanied and we could not wear the Red Cross arm bands at any time, so we were often under fire! We were issued with parachutes but if we were attacked on the way home, we were not allowed to use them because we had to stay with the wounded in our care. On a routine parachute check it was discovered mine was bright yellow usually used to drop supplies, probably as well I didn't need to use it.

The Dakotas had been fitted with slings[119] and able to carry eighteen stretcher cases and six sitting wounded plus one air ambulance nursing orderly to treat and care for the wounded. We saw all sorts of things. The soldiers would all ask for cups of tea, and I remember one man saying he wanted a drink, but he couldn't because he didn't have a mouth. That part of his face had just disappeared, I can still see him now. As the only woman it was a little daunting. Sometimes we had to stay overnight, sleeping in a tent with only a hurricane lamp and a stretcher for a bed somehow seemed more frightening than being under fire, and there were no facilities for women.

Towards the end of 1944 I developed glandular fever and didn't fly for a couple of weeks. My next flight was on the morning of 1 January 1945. Whilst on our way we were suddenly diverted to Maldegem near Bruges. Our aircraft came under fire on this trip, but it wasn't until later that we learned that the whole area had been under attack by the Luftwaffe, hence the diversion. On another trip shrapnel had blasted a hole in the fuselage next to our parachutes but luckily Ted Philips's parachute was the only one to fall through. I can also recall being sniped at whilst walking along a lane with members of our Aircrew. We couldn't take off for home immediately for some reason and had been enjoying the break on our way back to the airstrip when the sniper opened fire. One of our crew said to keep walking, so we did. There must have been so many incidents like this, but you just didn't realise the amount of danger you were actually in, managing as well to get home, quite often with badly damaged aircraft. Two of the girls were shot down, one of them, Margaret Walsh was from my hut. A very quiet girl, a little older than us. Earlier that day I had seen her using cards to tell her fortune. I suggested she shouldn't, it was bad luck. She knew that but felt she wanted to. They were never found but we didn't think about the danger. We were very young then and it didn't seem like anything extraordinary. During my time at Down Ampney I flew to France, Holland, Belgium and Germany, logging up around 400 flying hours and brought back many casualties both British and German, often severely injured. I have many fond memories too, the look on the lads' faces when they realised we were over England, the dances, the concerts and on VE Day the whole camp went crazy. People were riding round the perimeter of the camp in all sorts of transport and generally enjoying themselves.

Some of the people I knew flew after the war had ended in Europe to repatriate prisoners of war and soldiers home. All the friendships made during that time made it special.

Personal Stories: Edith Lord
Down Ampney was a well-run and highly organised casualty air evacuation centre and I have many memories of the place and the people I met there, some of who I am still in contact with. I was known as Titch Lord. I was little, and my surname was Lord. I remember my first flight into Normandy on D-Day+3. I was young and didn't know what to expect. I flew into France and Germany bringing back twenty-four stretchers and six walking wounded each trip. I was scared on the journey out, wondering what we would encounter, but we were so busy on the flight coming home, tending to the patients, that I had no time to be scared. We were met by ambulances when we landed and we were driven with our patients to huts, where they were put on blocks. Doctors then checked our patients and decided which hospital they should be moved on to depending on their injuries, such as head, chest, amputation, etc. The majority were transferred to large homes in England that had been turned into hospitals. First the patients were washed, before clean dressings were applied, along with clean clothes where possible – many were in blood-soaked uniforms. They were also fed, and their eyes sure lit up when the waitresses, who did a great job, brought them plates of eggs, bacon, veg and sausages. Often, we had to spoon feed them, but all with a smile, a few jokes and kind words. This was the routine every day, with flights and patients arriving continually. Sometimes we were held up from moving them to their next location or hospital because we were waiting for trains to get a clear run through to the towns and the hospitals. In these situations, we had to help keep their spirits up and try to provide some cheer for those worried about their families and their future. One day Charles 'Paddy' Joyce (my future husband) and Don Tate came into the camp carrying an invisible stretcher with an invisible man on it. They introduced him to the patients, letting him fall off in a funny act, tucking him in, dropping him again, a bit like a Charlie Chaplin mime. It was good to hear the laughter, moments like this helped us all cope.

One time we received about thirty 'bomb happy' boys who had to wait overnight before moving on to their hospitals. My friend Doreen Peffert and I had the job of caring for them during the night. It was so very sad to hear them calling for their mothers, girlfriends, wives etc. We could only hug them, hold their hands and tell them that their next move would be OK. When they left us Doreen and I sat and hugged each other and shed our own tears for these poor men. I have often wondered what happened to them. Later I received a letter from one of the service men who had been there that night and he said he would always remember the 'small blonde' who stayed up with him through the night. I cried when I read his letter but was so glad to think that I had helped him, it seemed so little to me but meant so much.

We did have funny times though. When the patients arrived, if there was a VIP or high-ranking officer among them, you had to let the Matron and Medical Officer know as these patients went into a different hut to the regular airmen. One of the WAAF medics, being a very good Catholic, had rescued a crucifixion statue of Jesus Christ from a church that had been bombed and put it on board. It was a bit knocked from the bombing, but she just had to rescue it and bring it back. Paddy put it on a stretcher and sent word out over the radio that a VIP was arriving on the next flight. Well, you can guess what happened; officials, officers and special ambulances were waiting for the plane. Paddy managed to smuggle the stretcher into the ambulance past the welcoming party. He got the biggest telling off and threatened with disciplinary action, but the Matron and the Doctor had a good sense of humour and luckily a soft spot for him so somehow the 'misuse of equipment and resources' was overlooked this time. Service life could be great, and I have many fond memories of the girls I met there from all walks of life. Some joined to get away or to make a new life for themselves, but we all wanted to do whatever we could to help Britain during the war, although we did miss our families terribly.

Paddy and I married, and he was demobbed in December 1945. I was demobbed a month later in January 1946 but we had kept in touch with many of the nurses and medics, not wanting to lose the friendships we had made. Eventually Paddy and I moved to Australia and had three children. I now have two grandchildren and three great grandchildren, and I celebrated my 100th birthday in September 2016.

Chapter 11

Aircraft and Crews

233 Squadron Allocation on the Night of 5–6 June

KG424 Wing Commander N.E. Morrison, Flight Lieutenant A. Johnstone, Flying Officer R. Cowie, Flying Officer N.S. Sharpe – Airborne 22.50, Landed 02.30.

KG341 Wing Commander G.P. Bailey, Flight Sergeant E.G. Warrington, W/G N.S. Beckett, Sergeant E.C. Pitt – Airborne 22.51½ Landed 02.35½.

KG329 Flying Officer K.E. Wood, Flight Sergeant A.W. Illingworth, Flying Officer W.B. Carr, Sergeant L. Thomas – Airborne 22.52 Landed 02.45.

FZ678 Flight Lieutenant H.J. Barley, Flying Officer W.L. Greenwood, Flying Officer G.N. Taylor, Flight Lieutenant C. Ingleby – Airborne 22.53 Landed 02.40.

KG315 Flying Officer J.H. Fram, Flying Officer N.C. Trigg, Warrant Officer J.C. Pinder, Warrant Officer R.G. Johnstone – Airborne 22.54 Landed 02.50.

KG415 Flying Officer J.F. Haldimand, Flying Officer K.F. Munro, Flight Sergeant B.H. Wallington, Warrant Officer H.P.C. Welch – Airborne 22.55 Landed 03.01.

KG313 Squadron Leader B.A. Miller, Flying Officer F.R. Priestley, Flight Lieutenant L.G.N. Taylor, Sergeant D.G. Morris – Airborne 22.11 Landed 02.45.

KG403 Flying Officer R.R.C. Hyne, Warrant Officer F.W. Evered, Flying Officer J.L. Knapp, Wing Commander G.R. Fotheringham – Airborne 23.11 Landed 02.40.

KG410 Flying Officer P.I. Burden, Flying Officer F.R. Merricks, Flying Officer M.K. Fitspatrick, Wing Commander O.D. Moore – Airborne 23.11 Landed 03.20.

FZ685 Flight Lieutenant A.B.S. Boldsworth, Flight Sergeant K. Cooper, Flying Officer E.S. Smith, Flying Officer V.O.M. Roberts – Airborne 23.11½ Landed 02.50.

KG427 Flying Officer C.D. Hamilton, Flying Officer M. Mensies, Flying Officer F.B. Knight, Flight Sergeant L.J. Firth – Airborne 23.11½ Landed 03.17.

KG399 Flying Officer A.C. MacAuley, Flying Officer A.C. Lord, Flying Officer J. Slater, Warrant Officer W.J. Watt – Airborne 23.12½ Landed 02.43½.

KG440 Squadron Leader G.D. Lane, Warrant Officer M.V. Lee, Flying Officer A.H. Wallace, Flying Officer J.F. Sweeney – Airborne 23.12 Landed 02.37.

FZ686 Warrant Officer E.F. Holliday, Flying Officer W.J.S. James, Warrant Officer W.G.A. Cosens, Flight Sergeant H.J. Richardson – Airborne 23.13 Landed 02.53.

KG400 Wing Commander R. Chesney, Flight Sergeant P. Johnson, Flying Officer G.A. Coppel, Sergeant R.E. Simons – Airborne 23.15 Landed 02.54.

KG430 Flight Lieutenant A.C. Mackie, Flying Officer W.C. Hunter, Flying Officer J.W. Proctor, Sergeant J.L. Anderson – Airborne 23.12 Landed 02.56.

KG433 Warrant Officer R.D. Saunders, Flight Sergeant C.D. Lock, Warrant Officer F.A. Mackay, Warrant Officer N.H.P. Conrad – Airborne 23.13 Landed 03.10.

FZ679 Flying Officer R.S. Down, Flight Sergeant W.R. Neal, Warrant Officer C.H.F. Cousins, Warrant Officer N.M. Elliston – Airborne 23.18 Landed 03.13.

KG356 Flying Officer H.E. Jones, Flight Sergeant J.A. Daldorph, Flying Officer L.N. Williams, Warrant Officer C. Engleberg – Airborne 23.17.

KG429 Warrant Officer M.M. McCannell, Flight Sergeant A.R. Porter, Flight Sergeant A.T. Downing, Warrant Officer N.L. Berger – Airborne 23.16.

KG455 Warrant Officer G.S. Wright, Flight Sergeant L. Cooper, Warrant Officer F.F. White, Sergeant T.H. Lewis – Airborne 23.14 Landed 03.10.

FZ672 Squadron Leader C.J. Mackencie, Flying Officer D.C. Harcus, Warrant Officer L.V. Whitehouse, Warrant Officer J.L. Dods – Airborne 23.14 Landed 02.55.

KG437 Flying Officer J.A. Stewart, Flying Officer D.A. Todd, Flying Officer S.J. Phillips, Flying Officer W.C. Bradley – Airborne 23.14½ Landed 02.54.

FZ688 Flying Officer F.W. Vines, Flying Officer G.B. Wood, Flying Officer J.K.M. Badie, Flying Officer F. Henry – Airborne 23.15 Landed 02.30.

KG448 Flight Lieutenant A. Cody, Flight Lieutenant M.R. Sisley, Flying Officer A.C. Hollingworth, Sergeant G.P.W. Goodfellow – Airborne 23.15 Landed 02.49.

FZ681 Flight Sergeant A.W. Coventon, Flight Sergeant R.L. Beignton, Flight Sergeant J.A. Edwards, Flight Sergeant G.N. Mirfin – Airborne 23.15 Landed 02.49.

KG412 Warrant Officer N. Mills, Sergeant R. Woodgate, Warrant Officer J. Buckton, Sergeant G.G. Sparkes – Airborne 23.15 Landed 03.05.

KG447 Flying Officer F. Norton, Flight Sergeant D.A. Gillings, Flying Officer C.G. Woodruff, Sergeant J.B. Milson – Airborne 23.16 Landed 03.20.

FZ692 Warrant Officer J.P.R. McRae, Flight Sergeant S. Delamare, Warrant Officer W.A. Milne, Warrant Officer S.C. Davidson – Airborne 23.16 Landed 03.24.

KG420 Flight Lieutenant R. McIlraith, Flight Sergeant P.M. Diamond, Flight Sergeant A.J. Phillips, Flying Officer G. Smee – Airborne 23.17 Landed 03.11.

512 Squadron Allocation, Overlord (Tonga), Night of 5 June

KG392 (V) Wing Commander Coventry, Flight Lieutenant Marshall, Flight Lieutenant Williams, Flying Officer Lee – Airborne 23.45 Landed 03.35.

KG390 (E) Squadron Leader Southgate, Flight Lieutenant Saunders, Flight Lieutenant Bryant, Flying Officer Parry – Airborne 23.20 Landed 02.50.

KG422 (B.1) Flight Lieutenant Thomas, Sergeant Dawson, Flying Officer Corlett, Flight Sergeant Bergin – Airborne 23.20 Landed 02.35.

FZ647 (H) Flying Officer George, Sergeant Burgess, Flying Officer Hemming, Flying Officer Hicks – Airborne 23.20 Landed 02.50.

KG322 (C) Flight Lieutenant Clarke, Sergeant French, Flying Officer James, Warrant Officer Anderson – Airborne 23.20 Landed 02.55.

KG314 (C.1) Flying Officer Strens, Sergeant Cunnell, Flying Officer Hurd, Flying Officer Ware – Airborne 23.20 Landed 02.45.

KG480 (G) Flight Lieutenant Carter, Warrant Officer Northall, Flight Sergeant Trewin, Flight Sergeant Woodcock – 23.20 Landed 02.35.

KG373 (B) Flight Lieutenant Hyde, Sergeant Anderson, Flight Sergeant Blundell, Warrant Officer Campbell – Airborne 23.20 Landed 02.35.

KG486 (A1) Flying Officer Garvin, Warrant Officer Seal, Warrant Officer Grant, Warrant Officer Fuller – Airborne 23.24 Landed 02.49.

KG407 (D) Warrant Officer Proctor, Flying Officer Holland, Sergeant Dyer, Warrant Officer Sabourin – Airborne 23.25 Landed 03.40.

KG324 (A) Flight Sergeant Perry, Warrant Officer Gilbert, Flight Sergeant Barritt, Warrant Officer Friend – Airborne 23.25 Landed 03.05.

KG333 (N) Squadron Leader Russell, Pilot Officer Hemmings, Flight Lieutenant Patrie, Flying Officer Briscoe – Airborne 23.15 Landed 02.30.

FZ649 (J1) Flying Officer Buchanan. Sergeant McDonald, Flying Officer Cole, Warrant Officer Hubbert – Airborne 23.15 Landed 02.45.

FZ610 (O) Flying Officer Payne, Sergeant Parratt, Flying Officer Mattocks, Warrant Officer West – Airborne 23.15 Landed 02.35.

FZ694 (R) Flight Lieutenant Reed, Flying Officer O'Connell, Flying Officer Jones, Warrant Officer McLeod – Airborne 23.15 Landed 02.55.

FZ651 (J): Flying Officer Fitzgibbon, Flight Sergeant Parsons, Warrant Officer Fox, Flight Sergeant Herbert – Airborne 23.15 Landed 02.55.

KG344 (L) Flight Lieutenant Gough, Flying Officer McNicol, Flight Sergeant Tibbles, Sergeant Hubbard – Airborne 23.20 Landed 03.35.

KG348 (K) Flight Lieutenant Worts, Sergeant Bruce, Flight Sergeant Bradley, Sergeant Goodall – Airborne 23.15 Landed 02.35.

FZ658 (M) Flight Sergeant Masini, Sergeant Johnson, Flying Officer Dewall, Warrant Officer Kidd – Airborne 23.15 Landed 02.40.

FZ696 (Q) Lt Offenhiser, Flight Sergeant Garvin, Flying Officer Smith, Warrant Officer Bevington – Airborne 23.15 Landed 02.15.

FZ609 (F) Warrant Officer McLaughlin, Sergeant England, Flight Sergeant Houston, Sergeant Placentime – Airborne 23.15 Landed 02.30.

FZ656 (K) Pilot Officer Lewis, Flight Sergeant Robinson, Pilot Officer Coonan, Sergeant Canning – Airborne 23.15 Landed 03.45.

KG377(S) Squadron Leader Smulian, Flying Officer Ring, Flying Officer Tomlinson, Warrant Officer King – Airborne 23.18 Landed 03.15.

KG368 (Y) Flying Officer Pearson, Sergeant Tyson, Flying Officer Vardy, Flying Officer Miechel – Airborne 23.15 Landed 03.15.

KG323 (U1) Flying Officer McLean, Pilot Officer Cox, Sergeant Turner, Warrant Officer Mercert – Airborne 23.15 Landed 03.15.

KG418 (T.1) Flight Lieutenant Alexander, Pilot Officer McLintock, Sergeant McHugh, Flying Officer Rechenuc – Airborne 23.15 Landed 02.45.

KG371 (X) Flying Officer Scary, Warrant Officer Pickering, Pilot Officer Gillette, Warrant Officer Blue – Airborne 23.20 Landed 02.55.

KG330 (T) Flight Lieutenant Matthews, Sergeant Thompson, Warrant Officer Bromige, Warrant Officer Tonner – Airborne 23.15 Landed 03.35.

KG347 (S1) Flying Officer Brennan, Flying Officer Combe, Sergeant Seager, Pilot Officer Toyne – Airborne 23.20 Landed 02.45.

KG361 (U) Flight Lieutenant McLeod, Warrant Officer Corby, Flying Officer Butcher, Sergeant Claydon – Airborne 23.20 Landed 03.33.

KG379 (W) Flight Lieutenant Roberts, Flying Officer Appleton, Flight Lieutenant Starr, Warrant Officer Perry – Airborne 23.14 Landed 02.41.

KG354 (Z) Flying Officer Shaw, Pilot Officer Clone, Sergeant Bryant, Warrant Officer Thayer – 23.35 Landed 03.00.

575 Squadron Allocation 5 June

KG449 Wing Commander T. Jefferson, Flight Lieutenant R. Charlton, Flying Officer C.F. Plimer, Flying Officer E.F. Waight – Airborne 23.29 Landed 03.25.

KG442 Flying Officer R.J. McTeare, Flying Officer L.J. English, Flying Officer Michie, Sergeant J.L. Anderson – Airborne 23.30 Landed 03.00.

KG434 Flying Officer W.A. Simmons, Flying Officer L.C. Sharling, Sergeant G.H. McCrackeh, Sergeant J.S. Lockwood – Airborne 23.30 Landed 03.45.

KG695 Squadron Leader F.T. Cragg, Flight Lieutenant. H.W. Payne, Flight Lieutenant H.H. Hall, Sergeant C.G. Fisher Airborne 23.30 Landed 03.00.

KG431 Flying Officer P.R. Sandford, Flying Officer J.V. Chitty, Warrant Officer P. Siddons, Warrant Officer E.T. Fennell – Airborne 23.30 Landed 02.50.

KG363 Flying Officer E.F. Brown, Flying Officer R. Hay, Pilot Officer F.A. Richards, Sergeant C. Bruce – Airborne 23.30 Landed 03.15.

KG425 Flight Lieutenant P. Hixon, Pilot Officer J.F. Andrews, Flying Officer J.L. Meffat, Flying Officer R.F. Hall – Airborne 23.30 Landed 03.00.

KG311 Pilot Officer S. Baker, Sergeant C.G. Ress, Flying Officer R. Chartres, Pilot Officer J.M. Atkinson – Airborne 23.30 Landed 03.00.

KG640 Pilot Officer K.E. Raemussen, Sergeant R.E. Griffith, Pilot Officer C. Depel, Sergeant E.B. Steele – Airborne 23.30 Landed 02.40.

KG310 Squadron Leader D.C. Pascall, Flying Officer P.L. Newlands, Flying Officer R. Plett, Sergeant G. Bullen – Airborne 23.30 Landed 02.52.

KG328 Flying Officer R.J. Roach, Sergeant P.S. Bell, Warrant Officer G.C. McConachie, Flying Officer J.D. Nadean – Airborne 23.30 Landed 02.45.

KG324 Flight Sergeant E. Imisen, Sergeant N.R. Crew, Sergeant G.L. Campbell, Flight Sergeant F.H. Barnard – Airborne 23.30 Landed 03.10.

KG388 Flight Lieutenant C.E. Slack, Pilot Officer W.S. Menger, Warrant Officer I.L. Holloway, Flight Sergeant G.E. Casuette – Airborne 23.30 Landed 02.45.

KG312 Flying Officer J.W. Atkin, Flight Sergeant D.J. Britten, Flying Officer J.J. Cunliffe, Flying Officer C. Learmont – Airborne 23.30 Landed 02.50.

KG345 Flying Officer J.R. Gambles, Flying Officer E. Clementeen, Pilot Officer W.H. Stapleten, Flying Officer J.E. Howe – Airborne 23.30 Landed 02.50.

KG662 Flying Officer W.T. Player, Flying Officer M.J. Sullivan, Pilot Officer R.M. Partridge, Flight Sergeant E.A. Pahey – Airborne 23.30 Landed 03.05.

KG593 Squadron Leader M.J. Elworthy, Pilot Officer M.F. Porter, Sergeant T.W. Payne, Warrant Officer F.A. Prior – Airborne 23.30 Landed 02.35.

KG359 Flight Lieutenant P.M. Bristow, Sergeant G.D. Burns, Flight Lieutenant W. Dyson, Warrant Officer D.R. Strake – Airborne 23.30 Landed 02.55.

KG332 Flight Lieutenant L.H. Bennets, Flying Officer H.S. Sedgewick, Flight Sergeant W.R. Clunes, Sergeant D.A. Ceep – Airborne 23.30 Landed 02.50.

KG326: Flying Officer P.C. Hakansson, Flying Officer J.A. Morrison, Pilot Officer W. Lemas, Sergeant E.F. Guy – Airborne 23.30 Landed 02.45.

KG355: Flight Sergeant A.L. Dodgson, Flying Officer A.F. Budden, Sergeant P. Joseph. Flight Sergeant W.R. Headifern – Airborne 23.30 Landed 03.00.

48 Squadron Allocation 5 June

AW/FZ671 Warrant Officer V.L. Pearson, Flying Officer G.J. McKenzie, Flight Sergeant H.J. Costen, Pilot Officer A.A Lavoie – Airborne 23.29 Landed 02.59.

AJ/KG321 Squadron Leader C.N. Mcveigh, Flying Officer B. Cobcroft, Flying Officer G.E. Bentley, Flying Officer G.E McNeill – Airborne 23.20 Landed 02.59.

UC/KG337 Pilot Officer R.L. Pearson, Flight Sergeant L.E. Rooke, Flying Officer W. Weatherilt, Pilot Officer V.C. Smith – Airborne 23.20 Landed 02.59.

AH/KG409 Flying Officer J.H. Murray, Flight Sergeant G. Barnes, Flight Sergeant T.R.C. Hayward, Sergeant J. Thompson – Airborne 23.21 Landed 02.57.

AF/KG364 Squadron Leader. T.R.N. Wheatley-Smith, Warrant Officer J.R. Hemsworth, Sergeant C.J. Holmes, Flight Lieutenant W.G.V. Puxley – Airborne 23.21 Landed 02.45.

AD/KG391 Pilot Officer G. Loades, Flight Lieutenant E. Palin, Sergeant W.W. Maxwell, Warrant Officer C.E. Dixon – Airborne 23.20½ Landed 03.09.[120]

WG/KG414 Flying Officer R.G.J. Hull, Flying Officer D. North, Sergeant T. O'Brien, Warrant Officer L.L. Peterson. Hit by flak, rudder, port engine and wing damage – Airborne 23.21½ Landed 03.03.

AG/KG391 Flight Lieutenant P.W. Smith, Warrant Officer J.I. Robinson, Sergeant I. Powell, Flight Sergeant J.H. Golton – Airborne 23.20 Landed 03.00.[120]

UD/KG406 Flying Officer A.J. Williams, Sergeant P. Thompson, Sergeant R.F. Smith, Flying Officer W.B. Gordon – Airborne 23.21 Landed 02.56.

AV/KG499 Sergeant S. Mclaughlin, Flying Officer E.S. Clark, Flight Sergeant L. Bentley, Sergeant R. Diamond – Airborne 23.22 Landed 02.58.

UM/KG416 Squadron Leader P.O.M. Duff-Mitchell AFC, Flying Officer E.J.B. Hobsrawn, Flight Sergeant G.M. Handley, Flying Officer T. Crowley – Airborne 23.23 Landed 02.40.

AK/KG408 Flying Officer S.S. Finlay, Flight Sergeant R.L.T. Gray, Pilot Officer W.J. Walsh, Warrant Officer C.W. Rice – Airborne 23.23½ Landed 03.02.

AL/KG452 Flying Officer H.T. Jones, Sergeant T.K. Brown, Flying Officer H. Fletcher, Sergeant S. Mumford – Airborne 23.23½ Landed 03.00.

AN/KG404 Flight Lieutenant A.C. Blythe, Warrant Officer B.S. Edmonson, Flight Lieutenant N. Iosson, Flight Sergeant P.C Barrett – Airborne 23.23 Landed 02.53.

AM/KG394 Flying Officer G.P. Hagerman, Warrant Officer M.S.R. Mahon, Sergeant J.C. Hackett, Warrant Officer J.P. Deschamplain – Airborne 23.29 Landed 02.55.

UN/KG370 Flying Officer L.R. Pattee, Flight Sergeant R.F Smith, Flight Sergeant A.G. Kent, Flying Officer F.J. Mcintyre – Airborne 23.20 Landed 02.44.

AP/KG401 Flight Lieutenant D.P.M. Whitfield, Flight Lieutenant K.D. Gay, Sergeant J. Jones, Warrant Officer R.W. Button – Airborne 23.24½ Landed 02.48.

AD/KG338 Flying Officer. E.W. McCreanor, Flight Sergeant R. Roberts, Flying Officer D.S. Hodge, Sergeant J. Daniells – Airborne 23.25 Landed 02.46.

AC/KG397 Flight Lieutenant G.M. Metcalfe, Warrant Officer J. Hedges, Flying Officer W.E.J. Bishop, Warrant Officer S. Melidones – Airborne 23.32 Landed 02.46.

AQ/FZ620 Pilot Officer R.K. Walker, Flight Sergeant D.C. Macdonald, Flight Sergeant E. Swallow, Flight Sergeant C. Strange – Airborne 23.27 Landed 02.55.

UL/KG350 Pilot Officer W.R. Pring, Flight Sergeant G.D. Gleave, Flying Officer W.B. Chopping, Warrant Officer J.L. Springsteale – Airborne 23.26 Landed 03.06.

AS/KG436 Flight Lieutenant B. Smith DFC, Warrant Officer R.C. Clarke, Sergeant D.H.R. Plear, Warrant Officer G. Birlisson – Airborne 23.29 Force-landed West Malling 03.26.

UX/KG428 Warrant Officer S.H.J. Carter, Warrant Officer R.F. Carter, Sergeant J. McCullam, Warrant Officer R.W. Nicholson – Airborne 23.27 Landed 03.17.

UY/KG439 Flying Officer M.R.S. Mackay, Flight Sergeant W.A. Lewis, Flight Sergeant W.C. Baynes, Sergeant R. Owen – Airborne 23.26 Landed 03.15.

UV/KG426 Flight Lieutenant P. Drummond, Flight Sergeant H.N. Niven, Sergeant A.G. Johnson, Sergeant S. Saxton – Airborne 23.30 Landed 03.15.

AR/KG417 Flying Officer J.G Wills, Warrant Officer D.G. Hardy, Warrant Officer D.A. Webb, Sergeant D.S. Black – Airborne 23.27 Landed 03.00.

AY/KG346 Warrant Officer V.B. Christie, Flight Sergeant K. Toyne, Sergeant F.E. Fuller, Warrant Officer P.A. Fulmore – Airborne 23.25 Landed 03.12.

AZ/KG423 Flight Lieutenant W.F. Stone, Warrant Officer J.D. Harrison, Sergeant J.P. Clarke, Pilot Officer R.F.J. Hinde – Airborne 23.30 Landed 03.15.

UZ/KG331 Flying Officer G.E. Ruson, Flying Officer G.W. Campbell, Sergeant C.F. Counsell, Flight Sergeant E.A. Graham – Airborne 23.29 Landed 02.59.

UO/FZ624 Pilot Officer J.P Warwick, Pilot Officer A.W. Carfrae, Sergeant C. Tennison, Warrant Officer R.K. Martin – Airborne 23.25 Landed 02.53.

271 Squadron Allocation 5 June

KG545 Wing Commander Booth, Flying Officer Wells, Flight Lieutenant Johnson, Pilot Officer l'Anson – Airborne 22.49 Landed 02.30.

KG500 Major Joubert, Flight Lieutenant Felloivra, Flight Lieutenant Grant, Sergeant Butterworth – Airborne 22.50 Landed 02.40.

KG564 Flight Lieutenant Baddow, Flight Sergeant Nott, Flying Officer Dolan, Sergeant Holt – Airborne 22.50½ Landed 02.42.

KG444 Flight Lieutenant Edwards, Flight Lieutenant Hunter, Sergeant Sarensen, Flight Sergeant Randall – Airborne 22.51 Landed 02.45.

KG512 Flying Officer Wilson, Flight Lieutenant Crocker, Pilot Officer Foster, Pilot Officer Anderson. Airborne 22.50 Landed 03.20.

KG516 Pilot Officer Williams, Warrant Officer Farrar, Flight Sergeant Rainsford, Sergeant Wenaley – Airborne 22.53 Landed 02.48.

KG387 Warrant Officer Wood, Flight Sergeant Tyler, Warrant Officer Garter, Sergeant Laking – Airborne 22.54½ Landed 02.40.

Each glider had twenty paratroopers within from the 3rd Parachute Brigade, and equipment carried included seven jeeps, four trailers, two 6-pounder guns and four motorcycles.

Nine Dakotas were used for the transportation of 165 paratroopers, again from the 3rd Parachute Brigade, to be dropped on to LZ V. All paratroopers jumped from heights ranging from 600–1,200 feet.

KG515 Squadron Leader Squires, Flight Lieutenant Dyke, Flight Lieutenant Plummer, Flying Officer Brown – Airborne 23.29½ Landed 03.25.

FZ639 Flight Lieutenant Cooke, Flight Sergeant Cloutt, Pilot Officer Sergeant, Pilot Officer Robertson – Airborne 23.29½ Landed 03.25.

KG362 Flying Officer Grace, Flying Officer Southey, Flying Officer Blakeney, Warrant Officer Adams – Airborne 23.31 Landed 03.18.

FZ613 Warrant Officer Parfitt, Warrant Officer Reynolds, Warrant Officer Walker, Warrant Officer Richardson – Airborne 23.30½ Landed 03.20.

KG376 Flying Officer Reyeller, Flying Officer Franchum, Flight Sergeant Edwards, Flying Officer Daley – Airborne 23.32½ Landed 03.04.

KG345 Flying Officer Hirst, Flight Sergeant Carmody, Flight Sergeant Bearning, Sergeant Thompson – Airborne 23.32 Landed 03.10.

KG367 Warrant Officer Cuer, Flight Sergeant Sylvester, Warrant Officer Anderson, Sergeant Butler – Airborne 23.29½ Landed 03.25.

KG357 Warrant Officer Wilson, Flight Sergeant Osborne, Flight Sergeant Gaydon, Sergeant French – Airborne 23.30 Landed 03.25.

FZ628 Warrant Officer Quin, Flying Officer Brome, Flight Sergeant Sidebottom, Warrant Officer McDougall – Airborne 23.30 Landed 03.30.

A Flight 271 Squadron Allocation 5 June Blakehill Farm

KG374 Squadron Leader Pearson, Warrant Officer Harrington, Warrant Officer Wemyss, Warrant Officer Gibbons – Airborne 23.19 Landed 02.55.

KG562 Flight Lieutenant Lord, Flying Officer Ager, Flying Officer McDonnell, Pilot Officer Ballintyne – Airborne 23.20 Landed 03.02.

KG378 Flying Officer Flather, Warrant Officer Oakley, Flight Sergeant Hope, Flying Officer Miller – Airborne 23.21 Landed 03.05.

KG365 Flying Officer Hollam, Flight Sergeant Hall, Flight Sergeant Elliott, Pilot Officer Harvey – Airborne 23.21 Landed 03.05.

KG372 Flying Officer Hartley, Warrant Officer Allan, Flying Officer Smith, Sergeant Anfield – Airborne 23.19 Landed 03.27.

KG340 Warrant Officer T. Davies, Flight Sergeant Kimm, Pilot Officer King, Flight Sergeant Brewer – Airborne 23.20 Landed 03.30.

FZ601 Pilot Officer Fletcher, Warrant Officer Owen, Pilot Officer Craik, Sergeant Buckley – Airborne 23.20 Landed 02.50.

KG358 Pilot Officer Pritchard, Sergeant Holt, Pilot Officer Sherval, Sergeant Wilson – Airborne 23.21 Landed 02.53.

KG514 Flying Officer Falconer, Flying Officer Riley, Flying Officer Suter, Flying Officer Tephem – Airborne 23.20 Landed 02.50.

FZ668 Flying Officer Nicholl, Flight Sergeant Dale, Flight Sergeant Marsden, Sergeant Kawes – Airborne 23.20 Landed 03.10.

271 Squadron Allocation 6 June

KG318 Squadron Leader Altman, Flying Officer Wells, Flight Lieutenant Johnson, Pilot Officer I'Anson – Airborne 18.40 Landed 22.45.

KG500 Major Jouhart, Flight Lieutenant Fellows, Flight Lieutenant Grant, Sergeant Butterworth – Airborne 18.40 Landed 22.46.

FZ607 Flight Lieutenant Beddows, Flight Sergeant Nett, Flying Officer Dolen, Sergeant Holt – Airborne 18.41 Landed 22.30.

FZ615 Flight Lieutenant Edwards, Flight Lieutenant Hunter, Sergeant Sarensen, Flight Sergeant Randall – Airborne 18.42 Landed 22.32.

KG512 Flying Officer Wilmot, Flight Lieutenant Crooker, Pilot Officer Fester, Pilot Officer Anderson – Airborne 18.43 Landed 22.40.

KG516 Pilot Officer Williams, Warrant Officer Farrier, Flight Sergeant Rainsford, Sergeant Wensley – Airborne 18.44 Landed 22.28.

FZ367 Warrant Officer Wood, Flight Sergeant Tyler, Warrant Officer Carter, Sergeant Laking – Airborne 18.44 Landed 22.34.

FZ660 Flight Lieutenant Crawford, Flying Officer Orr, Flying Officer White, Flying Officer Jarvis – Airborne 18.45 Landed 22.36.

KG515 Squadron Leader Squires, Flight Lieutenant Dyke, Flight Lieutenant Plummer, Flying Officer Brown – Airborne 18.45 Landed 22.38.

KG387 Warrant Officer Cuer, Flight Sergeant Sylvester, Warrant Officer Anderson, Sergeant Butler – Airborne 18.46 Landed 22.40.

KG389 Flight Lieutenant Robertson, Flying Officer McCashin, Flying Officer Shakes, Flying Officer R. Smith – Airborne 18.48 Landed 22.35.

KG362 Flying Officer Grace, Flying Officer Southey, Flying Officer Blakeney, Warrant Officer Adams – Airborne 18.48 Landed 22.31.

FZ639 Flight Lieutenant Mett, Flying Officer Packer, Flight Lieutenant Rowen, Flight Sergeant Kennedy – Airborne 18.49 Landed 22.30.

FZ628 Warrant Officer Quin, Flying Officer Brown, Flight Sergeant Sidebottom, Warrant Officer McDougall – Airborne 18.50 Landed 22.40.

KG345 Warrant Officer Greenyell, Flight Sergeant Lewis, Flight Sergeant I.R. Brown, Sergeant Aspden – Airborne 18.50 Landed 22.43.

271 Squadron Allocation 6/7 June

KG545 Flight Lieutenant McLeod, Flying Officer Medwin, Flying Officer Shannon, Pilot Officer Mundy – Airborne 22.25 Landed 01.55.

KG489 Flying Officer Delaney, Flying Officer Phillips, Flying Officer Barter, Sergeant Jones – Airborne 22.30 Landed 01.40.

FZ655 Flight Sergeant Carnell, Flight Sergeant Nutt, Flight Sergeant Efratt, Flight Sergeant Moffett – Airborne 22.27 Landed 01.37.

FZ613 Warrant Officer Gibson, Warrant Officer Levy, Pilot Officer Holder, Flight Sergeant Lawrence – Airborne 22.28 Landed 02.26.

'A' Flight operated from Blakehill Farm due to a lack of space at Down Ampney and used the following Dakotas:

KG365 Flying Officer Hollom, Flight Sergeant Hall, Flight Sergeant Elliott, Pilot Officer Harvey – Airborne 22.27 Landed 01.47.

KG514 Flying Officer Falconer, Flying Officer Riley, Flying Officer Sutar, Flying Officer Topham – Airborne 22.27 Landed 01.20.

FZ622 Pilot Officer Fletcher, Warrant Officer Owen, Pilot Officer Craik, Sergeant Buckley – Airborne 22.28 Landed 02.07.

KG376 Flying Officer Flather, Warrant Officer Oakley, Flight Sergeant Hope, Flying Officer Miller – Airborne 22.25½. Aircraft failed to return, all crew members listed as missing.

KG318 Pilot Officer Pritchard, Sergeant Holt, Pilot Officer Sherval, Sergeant Wilson – Airborne 22.26 Landed 01.12 (At Friston).

KG488 Flying Officer Shelley, Flight Lieutenant Howard – Blood, Warrant Officer Connolly, Flying Officer Porter – Airborne 22.27 Landed 01.37.

48 Squadron Allocation 6 June

AJ/KG321 – Squadron Leader R.D. Daniels AFC, Flight Sergeant R.J. Nixon, Sergeant P.O. Walker, Warrant Officer E.E. Bennett Take off 18.51, Landed 22.34.

AV/KG419 – Flying Officer R.A. Kenny, Flight Sergeant R.E. English, Flying Officer P.D. Waring, Warrant Officer A.H. Macaloney, Take off 18.52½, Landed 22.35.

AB/KG395 – Flight Lieutenant R.R. Keiller, Warrant Officer R.T. Barry, Flight Sergeant S.H. Birch, Warrant Officer J.I. Parry, Take off 18.52 Landed 22.35.

AF/KG364 – Flying Officer G.S. Taylor, Flying Officer C. Moore, Sergeant H.A. Perry, Flight Sergeant W.A. Mcquilton, Take off 18.52 Landed 22.40.

UF/KG411 – Flying Officer R.G.J. Hull, Flight Officer D. North, Sergeant T. O'Brien, Warrant Officer L. Peterson, Take off 18.53 Landed 22.34.

AD/KG317 – Flying Officer G. Loades, Flight Lieutenant E. Palin, Sergeant W.W. Maxwell, Warrant Officer C.E. Dixon, Take off 18.45½ Landed 22.33.½.

UD/KG406 – Flight Lieutenant P.W. Smith, Warrant Officer J.I. Robinson, Sergeant I. Powell, Flight Sergeant J.H. Golton, Take off 18.54 Landed 22.41.

AG/KG391 – Warrant Officer F.F. Felton, Flight Sergeant K. Toyne, Warrant Officer G.E. Bentley, Warrant Officer J.A. Chenery, Take off 18.55 Landed 22.35.

AP/KG401 – Flight Lieutenant H,J.G. Alford, Flight Sergeant J.H. Mewis, Sergeant J. Jones, Warrant Officer A.F. Spencer, Take off 18.55 Landed 22.39.

UN/KG370 – Flying Officer G.R. Warrington, Flight Sergeant E.A. Smith, Flying Officer J.E. Cobcroft, Flight Sergeant W. Dahlstedt, Take off 18.56, Landed 22.45.

AK/KG308 – Flying Officer S.S. Finlay, Flight Sergeant R.L.T. Gray, Flight Sergeant W.J. Walsh, Warrant Officer C.W. Rice, Take off 18.57 Landed 22.39.

UL/KG350 – Flying Officer G.P. Hagerman, Warrant Officer M.S.R. Mahon, Sergeant J.C. Hackett, Warrant Officer J.P. Dechamplain, Take off 18.57, Landed 22.40½.

UM/KG416 – Flying Officer E.W. McCreanor, Flight Sergeant R. Roberts, Flying Officer D.S. Hodge, Sergeant J. Daniells, Take off 22.52.

AQ/FZ620 – Pilot Officer R.K. Walker, Flight Sergeant D.C. Macdonald, Flight Sergeant E. Swallow, Flight Sergeant R.K. Strange, Take off 18.59 Landed 21.40.

UO/FZ624 – Pilot Officer J.P. Warwick, Pilot Officer A.W. Carfrae, Sergeant C. Tennison, Warrant Officer R.K. Martin, Take off 18.59 Landed 21.06.

UZ/KG331 – Sergeant S. McLaughlin, Flying Officer E.S. Clark, Flight Sergeant L.T. Bentley, Sergeant R. Diamond, Take off 19.00 Landed 22.47.

AH/KG409 – Flight Lieutenant P. Drummond, Flight Sergeant H.N. Niven, Sergeant A.G. Johnson, Sergeant S. Saxton, Take off 19.01 Landed 22.46.

AY/KG346 – Pilot Officer A.M. Smith, Pilot Officer J.A. Smith, Sergeant F.C.S. Dodson, Sergeant A.D.C. Robertson, Take off 19.02, Forced Landing 22.26 at Ford, wing and fuselage damaged.

AZ/KG423 – Flight Lieutenant W.F. Stone, Warrant Officer J.D. Harrison, Sergeant Clark, Pilot Officer R.F.J. Hinde, Take off 19.02, Landed 22.50.

AR/KG417 – Flying Officer J.G. Wills, Warrant Officer G.G. Hardy, Warrant Officer D.A. Webb, Sergeant D.S. Black, Take off 19.03, Landed 23.42.

UX/KG428 – Warrant Officer V.L. Pearson, Flying Officer G.J. McKenzie, Flight Sergeant H.J.Costin, Pilot Officer A.A. Lavoie, Take off 19.04 Landed 22.51.

UV/KG426 – Flying Officer J. Le.Huray, Flying Officer J.M. Woodcock, Flying Officer H.A. Farrell, Sergeant R. Carr, Take off 18.50 Shot down and crashed 21.10.

Operation RobRoy Re-Supply at DZ 'N' 6/7 June

UY/KG439 – Wing Commander T.F.U. Lang, Flight Lieutenant W.G. Owen, Sergeant D.Anderson, Flying Officer G.E. McNeill, Take off 23.25 Landed 01.35.

AV/KG419 – Warrant Officer V.B. Christie, Flight Sergeant G.W. Campbell, Sergeant G.W.Fuller, Warrant Officer P.H.Fulmore, Take off 22.25 Landed 01.39.

AN/KG404 – Flying Officer L.R. Pattee, Sergeant J.K. Brown, Flight Sergeant A.G. Kent, Flying Officer F.J.McIntyre, Take off 22.25 Landed 01.42.

AZ/KG423 – Flight Lieutenant A.C. Blythe, Pilot Officer B.S. Edmondson, Flight Lieutenant N. Iosson, Flight Sergeant P.C. Barrett, Take off 22.25 Landed 01.40.

UW/KG421 – Pilot Officer R.L. Pearson, Flight Sergeant L.E. Rooke, Flying Officer W. Weatherilt, Pilot Officer V.C. Smith, Take off 22.26½ Landed 01.45.

UC/KG337 – Pilot Officer J.H. Murray, Flight Sergeant G. Barnes, Flight Sergeant T.R.C. Hayward, Sergeant J. Thompson, Take off 22.25 Landed 01.40.

575 Squadron Allocation 6 June

KG442 Squadron Leader J.A. Sproule, Flight Lieutenant R.E. Charlton, Flying Officer C.E. Plimmer, Flying Officer E.F. Waight – Airborne 18.40 Landed 22.30.

KG695 Squadron Leader F.T. Cragg, Flight Lieutenant H.W. Payne, Flight Lieutenant H.H. Hall, Sergeant C.G. Fisher – Airborne 19.10 Landed 22.40.

KG425 Flight Lieutenant J.B. Goodwin, Flight Sergeant G.S. Ravens, Sergeant H. Woodhouse, Warrant Officer W. Sulek – Airborne 19.10 Landed 22.40.

*KG363 Pilot Officer D. Martin, Flight Sergeant J.A. Milner, Flying Officer G.L. Robertson, Flight Sergeant J.S. Tomshak – Airborne 19.10 Landed 22.40.[121]

KG325 Pilot Officer S. Baker, Sergeant C.G. Reed, Flying Officer R. Chartres, Flying Officer J.M. Akinson – Airborne 19.00 Landed 22.40.

KG640 Flying Officer R.J. McTeare, Flying Officer L.J. English, Flying Officer W.A. Michie, Sergeant J.L. Anderson – Airborne 19.20 Landed 22.45.

KG311 Warrant Officer L.D. Eastment, Flying Officer A. Campbell, Flight Sergeant M. Rooney, Sergeant L. Lyne-Hale – Airborne 19.10 Landed 22.35.

KG310 Squadron Leader D.C. Pascall, Flying Officer F.L. Newlands, Flying Officer R. Flatt, Sergeant G. Bullen – Airborne 18.55 Landed 22.30.

KG328 Flying Officer R.J. Roach, Sergeant P.S. Bell, Warrant Officer G.C. McGenachie, Flying Officer J.D. Nadeau – Airborne 18.55 Landed 22.50.

KG334 Flight Sergeant S.E. Inison, Sergeant N.R. Craw, Sergeant G.L. Campbell, Flight Sergeant F.H. Barnard – Airborne 18.55 Landed 22.50.

KG388 Flight Lieutenant C.R. Slack, Pilot Officer W.S. Monger, Warrant Officer I.L. Hollaway, Flight Sergeant G.E. Casuette – Airborne 18.55 Landed 22.35.

KG312 Flying Officer J.W. Atkin, Flight Sergeant D.J. Britten, Flying Officer J.J. Cunliffe, Flying Officer C. Learmont – Airborne 18.55 Landed 22.50.

KG623 Flying Officer J.W. Furley, Flying Officer R.T. Hamlyn, Sergeant W.F. Watts, Pilot Officer W.A. Stacey – Airborne 18.55 Landed 22.50.

KG326 Flying Officer P.C. Makanssen, Flying Officer J.A. Morrison, Pilot Officer W. Lomas, Sergeant E.F. Cay – Airborne 18.55 Landed 22.35.

KG349 Flying Officer F. Dauncey, Flying Officer D.H. Brown, Flying Officer A.B. Evans, Sergeant G.W. Jackson – Airborne 18.55 Landed 22.45.

KG674 Flying Officer H.H. Hague, Flying Officer W.K. Murphy, Pilot Officer G.I. Finlay, Flying Officer R. Pearce – Airborne 18.55 Landed 22.45.

KG355 Flight Sergeant A.L. Dodson, Flying Officer A.F. Budden, Sergeant P. Joseph, F.S.W.R. Headifern – Airborne 19.00 Landed 22.45.

KG311 Flying Officer L.D. Eastment, Flying Officer A. Cambell, Flight Sergeant M. Rooney, Sergeant L. Lyne-Hale, Take off 19.00 Landed 22.50

KG431 Flying Officer P.R. Sandford, Flying Officer J.V. Chitty, Warrant Officer P. Siddons, Warrant Officer E.T. Pennell – Airborne 20.25 Landed 02.00.

KG320 Flight Lieutenant R. Dixon, Pilot Officer J.P. Andrews, Flying Officer J. Moffat, Flying Officer R.F. Hall – Airborne 22.25 Landed 01.30.

KG359 Flight Lieutenant P.M. Bristow, Sergeant G.D. Burns, Flight Lieutenant W. Dyson, Warrant Officer D.R. Struke – Airborne 22.30 Landed 01.30.

KG332 Pilot Officer D. Martin, Flight Sergeant J.A. Milner, Flying Officer G.L. Robertson, Flight Sergeant J.S. Tomshak – Airborne 22.30 Landed 01.30.[121]

KG492 Pilot Officer C.G. McGlene, Pilot Officer W.E. Owen, Flying Officer C. Curry, Warrant Officer R.A. Heading – Airborne 22.30 Landed 01.30.

During 6 and 7 June, 233 Squadron from Blakehill Farm detailed twenty-one aircraft to carry out a resupply mission (Rob Roy) for the 6th Airborne Division at the River Orne.

KG424 Squadron Leader C. Wright, Flying Officer E.Q. Semple, Flying Officer B. Cowie, Flying Officer C.G. Williams – Airborne 22.20. Shot down.

KG341 Wing Commander G.P. Bailey, Flight Sergeant E.C. Warrington, Wing Commander N.S. Beckett, Sergeant E.C. Fitt – Airborne 22.13 Landed 01.22.

KG329 Flying Officer E.E. Wood, Flight Sergeant A.W. Illingworth, Flying Officer W.B. Carr, Sergeant L. Thomas – Airborne 22.30½. Shot down.

KG441 Flight Lieutenant R.N. Lestang, Flying Officer J.C. Dijkstrd, Warrant Officer A.R. Williamson, Pilot Officer A.F. Payne Airborne 22.20 Landed 01.25.

FZ666 Flying Officer W.F. Chambers, Sergeant F.J. Cronk, Warrant Officer F.H. Hill, Sergeant J. Stott – Airborne 22.21½ Landed 01.26.

FZ692 Flying Officer K.M. Dober, Sergeant R.G. Barlow, Flight Sergeant T.F. Bartlett, Flight Sergeant A.A.K. Tyrrel – Airborne 22.21 Landed 01.30.

KG455 Wing Commander G.S. Wright, Flight Sergeant L. Cooper, Wing Commander P.F. White, Sergeant F.B. Lewis – Airborne 22.23 Landed 01.45.

FZ681 Flight Sergeant A.W. Coventon, Flight Sergeant R.L. Beighton, Flight Sergeant J.A. Edward, Flight Sergeant G.F. Mirfin – Airborne 22.23 Landed 01.55.

KG448 Flight Lieutenant A. Cody, Flight Lieutenant M.R. Sisley. Flying Officer A.C. Hollingsworth, Sergeant O.P.W. Goodfellow – Airborne 22.23 Landed 01.40

KG412 Warrant Officer N. Mills, Sergeant R. Woodgate, Warrant Officer J. Buckton, Sergeant G.C. Sparkes – Airborne 22.23 Landed 01.45.

KG566 Squadron Leader C.J. Mackenzie, Flying Officer D.G. Harous, Warrant Officer L.V. Whitehouse, Warrant Officer J.L. Dodds – Airborne 22.25 Landed 01.33.

KG437 Flying Officer J.A. Stewart, Flying Officer D.A. Todd, Flying Officer R.S.J. Phillips, Flying Officer W.O. Bradley – Airborne 22.24 Landed 01.37.

FZ688 Flying Officer F.W. Vines, Flying Officer R.H. Wood, Flying Officer J.R. S. Sadie, Flying Officer F. Saury – Airborne 22.25 Landed 01.36.

FZ669 Flying Officer H.W. Gustafaen, Flying Officer G.R. Fener, Flying Officer S. Allen, Flight Sergeant J. Hickey – Airborne 22.25 Landed 01.53.

FZ680 Flight Lieutenant C.L. Broadley, Flight Sergeant W.H.F. Pirquahiro, Flight Sergeant A.C. Hislop, Flight Sergeant H.C. Plank – Airborne 22.25 Landed 01.45.

KG315 Flight Sergeant P.R. Russell, Flight Sergeant F.H. Samos, Flight Sergeant D.C. Schofield, Warrant Officer A.S. Burgans – Airborne 22.25 Landed 01.40.

512 Squadron Allocation 17 September

KG392 AV Wing Commander H.A. Coventry, Flight Lieutenant J. Williams, Flying Officer W.B. O'Connell – Airborne 10.00 Landed 5.20.

FZ609 AP Squadron Leader T.R. Russell, Flight Sergeant F.R. Pulham, Flight Lieutenant G.S. Petrie, Flight Lieutenant R.T. Briscoe – Airborne 10.10 Landed 5.20.

FZ658 AM Flight Sergeant J.R. Masini, Flight Sergeant J. Johnson, Flying Officer G.E. Dowell, Pilot Officer P.G. Kidd – Airborne 10.05 Landed 5.45.

KG558 UL Flight Lieutenant J.T Reed, Sergeant J.F. Roberts, Flying Officer J.E. Jones, Warrant Officer C.F. McLeod – Airborne 10.00 Landed 5.30.

FZ696 AQ Flying Officer A.P. McCampbell, Flight Sergeant W.E. Pearce, Warrant Officer J.B. Heyes, Pilot Officer R.T. Britton – Airborne 10.10 Landed 5.30.

FZ657 AJ Flying Officer M.G. Kinn, Flight Sergeant D.H. Powell, Flying Officer E. Blaney, Flight Sergeant J. Davidson – Airborne 10.10 Landed 5.30.

KG348 UK Flying Officer P. Murray, Sergeant J.C. Lawson, Warrant Officer R. Shallcross, Flight Sergeant L. Draper – Airborne 10.10 Landed 5.30.

FZ656 AK Flight Lieutenant R.S. Matthews, Flight Sergeant W.C. Thompson, Warrant Officer D.W. Bromige, Warrant Officer P.B. Tonner – Airborne 10.10 Landed 5.25.

KG344 AL Flight Lieutenant A.E. Carpenter, Flying Officer R. Hill, Flight Sergeant J.M. Bowles, Warrant Officer D.R. Miller – Airborne 10.20 Landed 5.15.

FZ649 UJ Flight Lieutenant R.S. Matthews, Warrant Officer D.W. Bromide, Flight Sergeant J.W. McDonald, Pilot Officer E.S. Hubbert – Airborne 10.00 Landed 5.25.

KG407 AD Pilot Officer J. Proctor, Flight Sergeant C.R. Dyer, Flight Lieutenant H. Holland, Pilot Officer J.C.H. Sabourin – Airborne 10.20 Landed 5.05.

KG322 AC Flight Lieutenant P.A. Clarke, Flight Sergeant O.H. French, Flight Lieutenant W.R. James, Flying Officer H.M. Anderson – Airborne 10.15 Landed 5.20.

KG314 UO Flying Officer D.A. Strans, Flight Sergeant F.C. Connall, Flight Lieutenant E.A. Hurd, Flying Officer G.H. Ware – Airborne 10.15 Landed 5.15.

KG570 UF Flight Lieutenant J.C.P. Thomas, Flight Sergeant D.R. Dawson, Flying Officer T. Corlett, Warrant Officer B.F. Bergin – Airborne 10.15 Landed 5.15.

KG324 AA Flying Officer L. Hawdon, Sergeant C. Ridpath, Pilot Officer A.S. Phillips, Flying Officer K. Pearson – Airborne 10.20 Landed 5.10.

KG379 AN Flying Officer F.C. Wright, Flight Sergeant C.J. Parratt, Flying Officer E.T.C. Harris, Flight Sergeant J.C. Ramsay – Airborne 10.20 Landed 5.05.

KG373 AD Flying Officer C.A. George, Flight Sergeant D. Burgess, Flying Officer V.H. Hemming, Flying Officer J.P. Hicks – Airborne 10.15 Landed 5.15.

KG354 AE Flight Lieutenant J.D. Shaw, Flight Lieutenant W.S. Close, Flight Sergeant L. Bryant, Warrant Officer S.E. Thayer – Airborne 10.15 Landed 5.20.

KG361 AV Flight Lieutenant C.H. Mcleod, Pilot Officer H.E.E. Corby, Pilot Officer E.P. Butcher, Flight Sergeant G. Claydon – Airborne 10.15 Landed 5.20.

KG368 AY Flight Lieutenant W.B. Pearson, Flight Sergeant A.M. Tyson, Flying Officer T.L. Vardy, Flying Officer A.E. Miechel – Airborne 10.15 Landed 5.10.

KG544 UV Flying Officer D.R. Lewis, Warrant Officer W. Robinson, Flying Officer A.J. Coonan, Sergeant G. Canning – Airborne 10.00 Landed 5.10.

KG371 AK Flight Sergeant S. Hildrew, Flight Sergeant H.M.V. Birkby, Flight Sergeant W.K. Pattison, Warrant Officer R.F. Platt – Airborne 10.15 Landed 5.25.

Reserves[122] were:

KG422 (B.1) Pilot Officer Perry, Warrant Officer Gilbert, Warrant Officer Barritt, Warrant Officer Friend.

KG333 (B.2) Flight Lieutenant Gough, Flight Sergeant Skitmore, Warrant Officer Tibbles, Pilot Officer Hubbard.

KG377 (B.3) Pilot Officer Benson, Flight Sergeant Williams, Flight Sergeant Harrison, Warrant Officer Oxley.

575 Squadron Allocation 17 September

KG615 Wing Commander T.A. Jefferson, Flight Lieutenant R.E. Charlton, Flight Lieutenant C.F. Plimmer. Flying Officer E.F. Waight – Airborne 10.11½ Landed 15.20.

KG363 Flight Lieutenant R.J. Roach, Flight Sergeant P.S. Bell, Warrant Officer G.C. McConachie, Flying Officer J.G. Nadeau – Airborne 09.46 Landed 10.25.

KG431 Flying Officer P.R. Sandford, Flying Officer J.V. Chitty, Warrant Officer P.N. Siddons, Warrant Officer E.T. Pennell – Airborne 09.47 Landed 15.21.

KG325 Flying Officer D. Martin, Flight Sergeant J.A. Milner, Flying Officer G.L. Robertson, Warrant Officer J.S. Temshak – Airborne 09.48½ Landed 10.29.

KG442 Flying Officer R.J. McTeare, Flying Officer F. Gee, Flying Officer W.A. Michie, Flight Sergeant L.P. Smith – Airborne 09.49½ Landed 15.37.

KG608 Flying Officer S. Baker, Pilot Officer T.F. Andrews, Flying Officer R.W. Chartres, Flying Officer J.M. Atkinson – Airborne 09.50½ Landed 15.08½.

FZ640 Flying Officer I.J. English, Flying Officer I.A. Grahamslaw, Pilot Officer F. Jump, Pilot Officer R.G. Healy – Airborne 09.51 Landed 15.30.

KG334 Pilot Officer E. Inison, Flight Sergeant N.R. Craw, Flying Officer J.L. Moffatt, Pilot Officer P.H. Barnard – Airborne 09.52 Landed 15.50.

FZ698 Flying Officer L.R. Pilshie, Flight Sergeant J.W. Chitty, Flight Sergeant C.J. Turner, Warrant Officer A. Warren – Airborne 09.53 Landed 15.17.

KG602 Squadron Leader D.C. Pascall, Flying Officer F.L. Newlands, Flying Officer R. Flett, Flight Sergeant G. Bullen – Airborne 09.54 Landed 15.50.

KG529 Warrant Officer H. Clark, Warrant Officer D.F. Kerr, Warrant Officer E.R. Wimbridge, Warrant Officer E.W. Townsend – Airborne 10.05 Landed 15.20.

KG520 Flying Officer G.E. Henry, Warrant Officer A.E. Smith, Flying Officer H.H. McKinley, Warrant Officer W. Fowler – Airborne 09.55 Landed 15.20.

KG328 Flight Sergeant L.R. Nunn, Sergeant J. Anderson, Warrant Officer W. Carr, Warrant Officer D.J. Wood – Airborne 09.56 Landed 15.27.

KG312 Flight Lieutenant J.N. Atkin, Warrant Officer D.J. Britton, Flight Lieutenant T.J. Cunliffe, Flying Officer G. Learmont – Airborne 09.56½ Landed 10.40.

KG550 Flight Lieutenant B.P. Legge, Flight Lieutenant V.G. Hogan, Pilot Officer P.C. Ashton, Warrant Officer A. McNahon – Airborne 09.57 Landed 15.37.

KG402 Pilot Officer J.S. McFarlane, Pilot Officer H.W. Beacham, Pilot Officer W.F. Osborne, Warrant Officer M.L. Reardon – Airborne 09.58 Landed 15.25½.

KG359 Flight Lieutenant L.H. Bennets, Flying Officer H.S. Sedgwick, Warrant Officer W.R. Clucas, Flight Sergeant D.A. Coop – Airborne 09.59 Landed 15.20.

KG326 Flying Officer F. Dauncey, Flying Officer D.H. Brown, Warrant Officer A.B. Evans, Flight Sergeant G.W. Jackson – Airborne 10.00 Landed 15.25.

KG327 Flight Sergeant A.C. Martin, Flight Sergeant H.E. Bauer, Flying Officer J.D. Simpson, Pilot Officer M. Blugrind – Airborne 10.02 Landed 15.17.

KG593 Warrant Officer N.D. Batstone, Flying Officer E.W. Newton, Flying Officer D.S. Herd, Warrant Officer R.A. Rolfe – Airborne 10.02 Landed 15.25.

KG355 Pilot Officer A.L. Dodgson, Flight Lieutenant A.F. Budden, Flight Sergeant P. Joseph, Warrant Officer W.R. Headifen – Airborne 10.03 Landed 15.25.

KG390 Flight Lieutenant H.H. Hauge, Flying Officer W.K. Murphy, Flying Officer G.I. Finlay, Flying Officer R. Pearce – Airborne 10.00½ Landed 15.31.

FZ623 Flight Sergeant W.J. Thorn, Flight Sergeant F.N. Griffin, Flight Sergeant H.K. Milton, Sergeant P.R. Manning – Airborne 10.04 Landed 10.47.

KG432 Warrant Officer S. Parker, Sergeant A.C. Smith, Warrant Officer P.L. Hurcomb, Warrant Officer G.H. Wade – Airborne 10.11½ Landed 15.23.

48 Squadron Allocation 17 September

KG452 Flying Officer H.J. Jones, Flying Officer W.J. Cheek, Flight Sergeant J.K. Brown, Flight Sergeant S. Mumford – Airborne 09.57 Landing 15.30.

Aircraft and Crews 221

FZ671 Flight Lieutenant A.C. Blythe, Flying Officer C.G. Dawson, Pilot Officer B.S. Edmonson, Pilot Officer P.C. Barratt – Airborne 09.57 Landing 15.25.[123]

FZ620 Warrant Officer S. Page, Sergeant J. Potts, Warrant Officer P.H. Lee, Warrant Officer R.J. McMichael – Airborne 09.58 Landing 15.35.

KG401 Flight Lieutenant G. Whitfield (DFM), Warrant Officer R.J. Millar, Flight Lieutenant K.D. Gay, Pilot Officer R.W. Button – Airborne 09.58 Landing 15.36.

KG350 Pilot Officer W.R. Pring, Sergeant H.E. Coleman, Flight Sergeant G.D. Gleave, Warrant Officer J.L. Springsteele – Airborne 09.57 Landed 15.27.

KG436 Flight Sergeant S.H. Webster, Flight Sergeant R. Murray, Sergeant W. Fell, Sergeant J.C. Rushton – Airborne 10.00 Landed 15.30.

KG393 Squadron Leader P. Drummond, Flight Sergeant A.G. Johnson, Pilot Officer H.N. Niven, Flight Sergeant S. Saxton – Airborne 10.00 Landed 15.25.

KG428 Pilot Officer S.J.H. Carter, Sergeant J. McCullum, Pilot Officer R.F. Carter, Warrant Officer R.W. Nicholson – Airborne 10.01½ Landed 15.41½.

KG423 Captain V.B. Jury, Flying Officer D.G. Dumper, Warrant Officer D.W. Sanders, Sergeant H.G. Hobbs – Airborne 10.00 Landed 15.30.

KG409 Flying Officer H.M. Tidbury, Flight Sergeant A.S. Thomson, Flying Officer O.H. Lovell, Sergeant D.S. Heliwell – Airborne 10.04 Landed 15.26.

KG439 Flying Officer M.R.S. Mackay, Pilot Officer W.C. Baynes, Warrant Officer W.A. Lewis, Flight Sergeant R. Owen – Airborne 10.04 Landed 15.26.

KG331 Warrant Officer D.A. Webb, Flight Sergeant D.H.R. Plear, Pilot Officer R.C. Clarke, Warrant Officer G. Birlinson – Airborne 10.05 landing 15.37.

KG395 Flight Lieutenant Keiller R.R., Flight Sergeant W.C. Birch, Warrant Officer R.T. Barry. Warrant Officer J.I. Parry – Airborne 10.05½ Landing 15.25.

KG406 Flight Lieutenant P.W. Smith, Flight Sergeant I. Powell, Pilot Officer J.L Robinson, Warrant Officer J.H. Golton – Airborne 10.05 Landing 15.35.

KG346 Captain C.H. Campbell, Flying Officer J.C. Garvey, Flying Officer J.P. Mudge, Flight Sergeant S. Williams – Airborne 10.12 Landed 15.32.

KG391 Flying Officer A.J. Williams, Flight Sergeant R.F. Smith, Pilot Officer J.P. Thompson, Flight Lieutenant W.B. Gordon – Airborne 10.08 Landing 15.30.

KG317 Flying Officer G. Loades, Flight Sergeant W.W. Maxwell, Flight Lieutenant E. Palin, Pilot Officer C.E. Dixon – Airborne 10.11 Landing 15.29.

KG411 (DD) Warrant Officer Felton. F.F, Flight Sergeant A.W. Meecham, Flight Sergeant K. Toyne, Warrant Officer J.A. Chenery – Airborne 10.12 Landing 15.29.

KG414 Flying Officer R.G.J. Hull, Warrant Officer T. O'Brien, Flying Officer D. North, J.L. Warrant Officer Peterson – Airborne 10.12 Landing 15.29.

KG416 Squadron Leader T.R.N. Wheatley-Smith, Pilot Officer J.J. Holmes, Pilot Officer J.R. Hemsworth, Flight Sergeant J.L. Anderson – Airborne 10.09 Landed 13.30.

KG610 Flying Officer J. Le Huray, Flight Sergeant D. Anderson, Flight Lieutenant J.M. Woodcock, Flight Sergeant J.J. Samsun – Airborne 10.03 Landed 10.55.

FZ671 Flying Officer A.M. Smith, Sergeant J. Ambler, Flying Officer J.A. Smith, Flight Sergeant A.D.C. Robertson – Airborne 10.05 Landed 15.37. Same aircraft as detailed above but different crew, suspect aircraft recorded as incorrect serial.[123]

KG364 Flying Officer G.S. Taylor, Warrant Officer H.A. Perry, Flying Officer C. Moore, Warrant Officer W.A. McQuilton – Airborne 10.05 Landed 14.31.

271 Squadron Allocation 17 September

KG545 Wing Commander M. Booth, Flight Lieutenant S. Rowan, Flight Lieutenant R. Johnson, Flying Officer G.C. Topham – Airborne 09.40 Landing 15.20.

KG500 Major P.S. Joubert Flying Officer R. Boasten, Flight Lieutenant R. Fellows, Flight Sergeant D. Butterworth – Airborne 09.41 Landing 15.20.

KG557 Pilot Officer R. Williams, Warrant Officer H. Farrar, Flight Sergeant J.E. Rainford, Flight Sergeant E.E. Wensley – Airborne 09.41½ Landing 15.15.

KG444 Flight Lieutenant K.O. Edwards, Flight Lieutenant G. Hunter, Flight Sergeant H. Saransen, Flight Sergeant N.F. Randall – Airborne 09.43 Landing 15.36.

FZ601 Warrant Officer E. Gibson, Warrant Officer V.M. Levy, Flying Officer S.H. Holder, Flying Officer R.M. Smith. – Airborne 09.44 Landing 15.25.

KG564 Flight Lieutenant A.R.T. Beddow, Flight Sergeant H. Nott, Warrant Officer A.W. Walker, Flight Sergeant A.G. Holt – Airborne 09.44½ Landing 15.30.

KG357 Pilot Officer D. Wood, Flight Sergeant D.F.W. Tyler, Warrant Officer K. Carter, Warrant Officer T.B. Adamson – Airborne 09.45 Landing 15.23.

FZ607 Flying Officer R.D. Anderson, Warrant Officer W. Faircloth, Flight Sergeant F.C. Jenkins, Flight Sergeant L.R. Laking – Airborne 09.45 Landing 15.27.

FZ613 Warrant Officer A.L.F. Bone, Warrant Officer L. Chambers, Warrant Officer M.J. Batstone, Flight Sergeant G.H. Winter – Airborne 09.46 Landing 15.36.

KG340 Pilot Officer J.L. Wilson, Flight Sergeant H. Osborne, Flight Sergeant L.C.C. Gaydon, Flight Sergeant R.F. French – Airborne 09.46 Landing 15.28.

KG516 Flying Officer C.W. Mott, Flight Lieutenant E.J. Packer, Flying Officer R.J. Wells, Warrant Officer T. Kennedy – Airborne 09.48 Landing 15.25.

KG378 Flying Officer J. Reveller, Flying Officer C.J. Frenchim, Flight Sergeant R.D. Howes, Flying Officer H. Daley – Airborne 09.49 Landing 15.29.

KG345 Flight Lieutenant J.G. Cooke, Flight Sergeant L.M. Cloutt, Flying Officer J.S. Sargent, Pilot Officer H.E. Robertson – Airborne 09.50 Landing 15.35.

FZ592 Warrant Officer L. Greenwell, Warrant Officer P.G.H. Reynolds, Warrant Officer F.E. Richardson – Airborne 09.50 Landing 15.34.

KG362 Flight Lieutenant L.J. Grace, Pilot Officer J.D. Cushing, Flying Officer F.T. Blakeney, Warrant Officer R.J. Adams – Airborne 09.50 Landing 15.40.

KG514 Flight Sergeant J.W. Lane, Sergeant G.D. Manson, Pilot Officer G.D. Snider, Flight Sergeant J.E. St Arnlud – Airborne 09.50 Landing 15.21.

FZ625 Flight Lieutenant C.G. Crawford, Flight Lieutenant D.C. Ager, Flying Officer H.E. King, Flight Lieutenant J.C. Jarvis – Airborne 09.52 Landing 15.40.

KG372 Pilot Officer K.P. O'Donnell, Flight Sergeant J.P. Brightling, Pilot Officer T.R. Holdsworth, Flight Sergeant G.J. Watters – Airborne 09.55 Landing 15.20.

KG488 Warrant Officer D. Twiston-Davies, Flight Sergeant H.A. Kim, Warrant Officer T.W. Connolly, Warrant Officer P. Brewer – Airborne 10.13 Landing 15.30.

KG512 Flying Officer K.C. Wilson, Flight Lieutenant D.H. Crocker, Flying Officer J. Foster, Flying Officer F. Anderson – Airborne 09.42 Landing 10.45 – Aborted.

KG515 Squadron Leader P.D. Squires, Flight Lieutenant K.H. Dyke, Flight Lieutenant S.D. Plummer, Flying Officer H.M. Browne – Airborne 09.46 Landing 10.48 – Aborted.

KG562 Squadron Leader A.B. Pearson, Warrant Officer R.D. Harrington, Warrant Officer H.R. Wemyes, Warrant Officer J.S. Gibbons – Airborne 09.52 Landing 12.55 – Aborted.

KG318 Pilot Officer E. Pritchard, Flight Sergeant A.G. Holt, Flying Officer A.H. Sherval, Sergeant W.B. Wilson – Airborne 09.53 Landing 10.56 – Aborted.

FZ622 Flying Officer S.E. Norris, Sergeant G. Foster, Flying Officer D.R. Peiroe, Flight Sergeant P.C. McLaughlin – Airborne 09.53 Landing 10.53 – Aborted.

437 Squadron Allocation 17 September

FZ697 Flight Lieutenant R.S. Down, Flight Sergeant W.R. Neal, Warrant Officer N.S. Beckett, Warrant Officer N.M. Ellington – Airborne 10.03 Landed 15.24.

KG447 Flying Officer J.M. Byrnes, Flying Officer W.E. Simpson, Flying Officer K.E. Hunt, Flight Sergeant J.R. Chambers – Airborne 10.05 Landed 15.35.

KG415 Flying Officer J.F. Haldimand, Flight Sergeant N. Summerfield, Flight Sergeant B.H. Wallington, Flying Officer J. Rechenuc – Airborne 10.11 Landed 15.36.

FZ669 Flying Officer C.N. Roy, Flying Officer B.M. Clarke, Flying Officer D.R. Goodwin, Warrant Officer G.A. Sproule – Airborne 10.12 Landed 15.30.

FZ666 Flying Officer W.F. Chambers, Sergeant J. Pope, Pilot Officer F.H. Hill, Flight Sergeant J. Stott – Airborne 10.13 Landed 15.26.

Aircraft and Crews   225

KG441 Flying Officer E.O. Semple, Flight Sergeant J.A. Daldorph, Warrant Officer F.A.R. MacKay, Warrant Officer M.H.F. Conrad – Airborne 10.15 Landed 15.30.

KG489 Wing Commander J.A. Sproule, Flying Officer R.S. Purkis, Flying Officer E.K. Walker, Flight Sergeant D.B. Fennell – Airborne 10.15 Landed 15.30.

KG389 Flying Officer W.E. McLean, Flying Officer D.A Cox, Flight Sergeant D.A. Turner, Warrant Officer R. Mercer – Airborne 10.15 Landed 15.26.

FZ626 Flying Officer F.E. Fitzgibbon, Warrant Officer E.H. Parsons, Warrant Officer R.W. Fox, Warrant Officer S.E. Thayer – Airborne 10.16 Landed 15.35.

KG422 Pilot Officer J.A. Delahunt, Flight Sergeant D.S. Cooper, Pilot Officer G.L. Breckon, Flying Officer L.D. Hornsby – Airborne 10.16 Landed 15.28.

KG577 Flying Officer O.A. Simmons, Pilot Officer W. Taylor, Warrant Officer G.A.A. Murdock, 1 crew member not detailed – Airborne 10.18 Landed 15.33.

KG452 Flying Officer R.L. Pearson, Flying Officer W.H. Wetherilt, Pilot Officer L.E. Rooke, Pilot Officer J.C. Smith – Airborne 10.15 Landed 15.30.

KG321 Flying Officer R.A. Kenny, Sergeant L. Evans, Warrant Officer 1 R.E. English, Pilot Officer H.H. MacAloney – Airborne 10.06 Landed. Aircraft operated from Down Ampney.

KG563 Flying Officer G.R. Warrington, Flying Officer J. Wilcock, Pilot Officer E.A. Smith, Pilot Officer L.F. Dahlstedt – Airborne 10.00. Aircraft operated out of Down Ampney Airfield, but sortie was abandoned as aircraft developed an airlock in its fuel system. The engines cut out, which led to rapid loss of height. The pilot fought to maintain as much flying profile as possible but the tow rope to the glider got tangled on the glider nosewheel. The glider pilot requested release, which was granted, and the glider landed safely at Martlesham Heath aerodrome, while the Dakota landed back at Down Ampney at 12.20.

233 Squadron Allocation 17 September

KG427 Flying Officer C.D. Hamilton, Flight Sergeant W.G. Sheeler, Pilot Officer F.P. Knight, Flight Sergeant J. Firth – Airborne 09.57 Landed 12.30.

FZ685 Squadron Leader R. Daniell, Flight Sergeant P. Walker, Pilot Officer P.J. Nixon, Warrant Officer E. Bennett – Airborne 09.56 Landed 15.32.

KG399 Flying Officer K. Dober, Flight Sergeant R. Barlow, Flight Sergeant T.V. Barlett, Warrant Officer A.A. Tyrell – Airborne 09.58 Landed 15.31.

KG410 Flight Lieutenant P.I. Burdon, Flight Sergeant C.R. Caic, Flying Officer M.J. Fitzpatrick, Flying Officer C.D. Moore – Airborne 09.57 Landed 15.28.

KG403 Flying Officer R. Hyne, Warrant Officer R. Evered, Flying Officer G.B. Fotheringham, Flying Officer J. Knapp – Airborne 10.00 Landed 15.25.

KG561 Flying Officer G. Clarkson, Flying Officer J.P. Williams, Flight Sergeant N.R.H. Rains, Flying Officer C. Williams – Airborne 09.59 Landed 15.24.

KG341 Pilot Officer G. Bailey, Pilot Officer E.G. Warrington, Flying Officer L.N. Williams, Flight Sergeant R.C. Fitt – Airborne 09.58 Landed 15.25.

KG430 Flight Lieutenant A.C. Mackie, Flying Officer K. Hunter, Flying Officer J. Proctor, Flight Lieutenant D. Goodwin – Airborne 10.01 Landed 15.30.

KG455 Warrant Officer G.S. Wright, Flight Sergeant L. Cooper, Warrant Officer P.S. Wright, Flight Sergeant F.B. Lewis – Airborne 10.01 Landed 15.40.

KG433 Warrant Officer R.D. Sauders, Flight Sergeant C.F. Lock, Warrant Officer C.H.F. Cousins, Flight Sergeant C.A. Hawtyard – Airborne 10.02 Landed 15.37.

FZ665 Flying Officer R. McGowan, Flight Sergeant R.W. Hopkins, Flight Sergeant G. Harmer, Warrant Officer O. Swann – Airborne 10.04 Landed 15.33.

KG400 Flying Officer J.W. Taylor, Flight Sergeant L.A. Edmends, Flying Officer H. Eagles, Warrant Officer W.C.A. Want – Airborne 10.06 Landed 15.34.

KG585 Warrant Officer J.P.R. McRae, Flight Sergeant S. Delamere, Warrant Officer W. Milne, Warrant Officer S.C. Davidson – Airborne 10.07 Landed 15.37.

KG351 Squadron Leader C.J. Mackenzie, Flying Officer D.G. Haroun, Warrant Officer L.V. Whitehouse, Pilot Officer J.A. Dods – Airborne 10.07 Landed 15.34.

Aircraft and Crews 227

KG437 Flying Officer J. Stewart, Flying Officer D.A. Todd, Flying Officer R.S. Phillips, Flying Officer W.C. Bradley – Airborne 10.08 Landed 15.25.

FZ678 Flight Lieutenant H.J. Barley, Flying Officer W.L. Greenwood. Flying Officer G.N. Taylor, Flight Lieutenant C. Ingelby – Airborne 10.09 Landed 15.17.

KG586 Warrant Officer F.R. Bussell, Flight Sergeant F.H. Jones, Warrant Officer C. Schofield, Pilot Officer J. Welch – Airborne 10.10 Landed 15.31.

FZ690 Flight Lieutenant O.L. Broadley, Flight Sergeant W.F. Farquarson, Flight Sergeant A.G. Bishop, Pilot Officer H.C. Plank – Airborne 10.10 Landed 15.35.

FZ681 Warrant Officer K.G. Cranefield, Flight Sergeant B.A. Stapleford, Flight Sergeant T. Holmes, Flight Sergeant D.M.T. Hastings – Airborne 10.10 Landed 15.35.

KG448 Flying Officer P.W. Vines, Flying Officer G.B. Wood, Flying Officer J.K. Eadie, Pilot Officer F. Henry – Airborne 10.12 Landed 15.27.

KG313 Wing Commander W.E. Coles, Flight Lieutenant G.R. Frew, Flight Lieutenant A. Johnstone, Flying Officer E.J. Sharpe – Airborne 09.55 Landed 15.30.

KG412 Flying Officer J.H. Fram, Flying Officer N.C. Trigg, Pilot Officer J.C. Pinder, Pilot Officer R.G. Johnstone – Airborne 10.13 Landed 15.46.

271 Squadron Allocation 18 September

KG545 Squadron Leader R.O. Altman, Flight Lieutenant S. Rowan, Flight Lieutenant R. Johnson, Flight Lieutenant R. Hodgson – Airborne 11.13 Landing 17.05.

FZ692 Pilot Officer C.H. Cressman, Flying Officer J.B. Blair, Pilot Officer P.S. Steffin, Pilot Officer T.J. Brennan – Airborne 11.13 Landing 17.10.

KG515 Squadron Leader P.D. Squires, Flight Lieutenant D.C. Agar, Flight Lieutenant S.D. Plummer, Flight Lieutenant H.M. Browne – Airborne 11.15 Landing 17.00.

KG340 Pilot Officer F.W. Cuer, Flight Sergeant J.M. Bayley, Warrant Officer C.A. Anderson, Flight Sergeant B. Tipping – Airborne 11.15 Landing 17.10.

KG516 Flight Lieutenant C.W. Mott, Flight Lieutenant E.J. Packer, Flying Officer R.J. Wells, – Airborne 11.15 Landing 16.49.

KG362 Warrant Officer C.F. Quin, Warrant Officer P.G.H. Reynolds, Warrant Officer M. Sidebottom, Warrant Officer A. McDougall – Airborne 11.15 Landing 17.05.

KG367 Flight Lieutenant D.K. Hirst, Flight Sergeant C.W. Beckingham, Flying Officer C.T. Bearne, Flight Sergeant R.L. Thompson – Airborne 11.17 Landing 17.07.

FZ613 Warrant Officer A.L.F. Bone, Warrant Officer L. Chambers, Warrant Officer M. Batstone., Flight Sergeant G.H. Winter – Airborne 11.18 Landing 17.19.

KG374 Flight Lieutenant D.S.A. Lord, Flying Officer R.E.H. Medhurst, Flying Officer A.F. Ballantyne, Pilot Officer H.A. King – Airborne 11.17 Landing 17.16.

KG488 Flight Lieutenant P.A.D. Hellom, Sergeant S. Brisk, Warrant Officer A. Elliot, Pilot Officer G.R. Harvey – Airborne 11.19 Landing 17.14.

FZ668 Flying Officer J.R. Nicell, Flying Officer D.I. McDonnell, Pilot Officer C.J. Marsden, Flight Sergeant H.H. Caves – Airborne 11.20 Landing 17.10.

KG514 Flying Officer J.I. McNeil, Flight Sergeant H. Green, Flying Officer A. Whitaker, Warrant Officer F.R. Richardson – Airborne 11.20 Landing 17.20.

FZ625 Warrant Officer G. King, Flying Officer A.T. Donny, Warrant Officer J.F. McManus, Flight Sergeant R.A.V. Faber – Airborne 11.20 Landing 17.00.

KG365 Squadron Leader A.B. Pearson, Pilot Officer R.D. Harrington, Warrant Officer H.R. Wemyss, Warrant Officer J.S. Gibbons – Airborne 11.27½ Landing 17.05.

KG318 Pilot Officer E. Pritchard, Flight Lieutenant F.R. Riley, Flying Officer A.H. Sherval, Sergeant W.B. Wilson – Airborne 11.22½ Landing 17.15.

KG564 Flight Lieutenant A.R. Beddow, Flight Sergeant H. Nott, Flying Officer J.S. Dolan, Flight Sergeant A.G. Holt – Airborne 11.23 Landing 17.10.

FZ601 Flying Officer J.W. Hartley, Flying Officer W.I. Smith, Warrant Officer W.D. Allen, Sergeant W.N. Anfield – Airborne 11.23 Landing 17.06.

KG557 Flight Lieutenant N.T. McLeod, Flying Officer G.P. Bedwin, Flying Officer J. Shannon, Pilot Officer H.T. Mundy – Airborne 11.23 Landing 17.06.

KG357 Flying Officer J. Delaney, Flying Officer H.Z. Rogers, Flight Lieutenant G.W. Baxter, Flight Sergeant M.M. Jones – Airborne 11.25 Landing 17.20.

KG444 Flight Lieutenant K.O. Edwards, Flight Sergeant A.W. Clarke, Flight Sergeant H. Seranson, Flight Sergeant W.J. Randall – Airborne 11.25 Landing 17.12.

FZ607 Pilot Officer R. Williams, Warrant Officer H. Farrer, Flight Sergeant J.E. Rainsford, Flight Sergeant E.E. Wensley – Airborne 11.26½ Landing 17.10.

KG512 Flying Officer K.C. Wilson, Flight Lieutenant D.H. Crocker, Flying Officer J. Foster, Flying Officer F. Anderson – Airborne 11.25 Landing 17.13.

FZ615 Pilot Officer D. Wood, Flight Sergeant D.R.W. Tyler, Warrant Officer K. Carter, Warrant Officer T.B. Adamson – Airborne 11.28 Landing 16.53.

KG372 Flying Officer S.E. Norris, Sergeant C. Foster, Flying Officer D.R. Peirce, Flight Sergeant L.R. Laking – Airborne 11.27 Landing 16.52.

48 Squadron Allocation 18 September

KG416 Squadron Leader P.O.M. Duff Mitchell, Wing Commander M. Haldam, Flying Officer E.J.B. Hobsbann, Flying Officer T. Crowley – Airborne 11.00 Landed 17.00.

KG436 Flight Sergeant S.H. Webster, Flight Sergeant R. Murray, Sergeant W. Fell, Sergeant J.C. Ruston – Airborne 11.00 Landed 17.03.

FZ624 Flying Officer L.R. Patter, Pilot Officer A.C. Kent, Warrant Officer T. Fenwick, Flying Officer F.J. Macintyre – Airborne 11.01 Landed 16.59.

KG386 Flying Officer J.P. Warwick, Flight Sergeant C. Tennison, Pilot Officer A.W. Carfrae, Pilot Officer R.K. Martin – Airborne 11.02 Landed 17.02.

KG408 Flying Officer S.S. Finlay, Pilot Officer W.J. Walsh, Flight Sergeant R.L.T. Gray, Pilot Officer C.W. Price – Airborne 11.03 Landed 16.54.

KG350 Pilot Officer W.R. Pring, Sergeant H.E. Coleman, Flight Sergeant G.D. Gleave, Warrant Officer J.L. Springsteele – Airborne 11.02 Landed 17.02.

KG452 Flying Officer E.W. McGreanor, Flying Officer D.S. Hodge, Flight Sergeant R. Roberts, Flight Sergeant J. Daniels – Airborne 11.04 Landed 17.15.

KG397 Squadron Leader L.R. Harries, Pilot Officer J.J. Holmes, Pilot Officer J.R. Hemsworth, Flight Sergeant J.L. Anderson – Airborne 11.04 Landed 17.00.

KG414 Flying Officer R.G.J. Hull, Warrant Officer T. O'Brien, Flying Officer D. North, Warrant Officer L.L. Peterson – Airborne 11.06 Landed 16.49.

KG406 Flight Lieutenant R.R. Keiller, Flight Sergeant W.C. Birch, Warrant Officer R.T. Barry, Warrant Officer J.I. Parry – Airborne 11.06 Landed 16.50.

KG337 Warrant Officer S. McLaughlin, Pilot Officer L.T. Bentley, Flying Officer E.S. Clark, Pilot Officer S. Melidones – Airborne 11.07 Landed 16.56.

KG317 Captain C.H. Campbell, Flying Officer J.C. Garvey, Flying Officer J.P. Mudge, Flight Sergeant S. Williams – Airborne 11.07 Landed 16.51.

KG364 Flying Officer G.S. Taylor, Warrant Officer H.A. Perry, Flying Officer C. Moore, Warrant Officer W.A. McQuilton – Airborne 11.08 Landed 16.55.

KG587 Flight Lieutenant H.J.G. Alford, Sergeant E.L. Leslie, Flight Sergeant J.H. Mewis, Pilot Officer A.F. Spencer – Airborne 11.08 Landed 16.45.

KG409 Flying Officer H.M. Tidbury, Flight Sergeant A.S. Thomson, Flying Officer H. Lovell, Sergeant D.S. Helliwell – Airborne 11.09 Landed 16.58.

KG423 Flight Lieutenant W.F. Stone, Flight Sergeant J.P. Clarke, Flying Officer J.D. Harrison, Pilot Officer R.F.J. Hinde – Airborne 11.00 Landed 17.00.

KG610 Flying Officer J. Le Huray, Flight Sergeant D. Anderson, Flight Lieutenant J.M. Woodcock, Flight Sergeant J.J. Sansum – Airborne 11.10 Landed 17.00.

KG417 Flying Officer J.G. Wills, Pilot Officer J.W. Erickson, Warrant Officer D.G. Hardy, Flight Sergeant D.S. Black – Airborne 11.10 Landed 17.15.

KG439 Pilot Officer V.B. Christie, Flight Sergeant F.E. Fuller, Pilot Officer F.C.S. Dodson, Warrant Officer P.A. Fulmore – Airborne 11.10 Landed 16.43.

KG331 Warrant Officer D.A. Webb, Flight Sergeant D.H.R. Plear, Pilot Officer R.C. Clarke, Warrant Officer G. Birlison – Airborne 11.12 Landed 17.00.

KG391 Flying Officer A.J. Williams, Flight Sergeant R.F. Smith, Pilot Officer J.P. Thompson, Flight Lieutenant W.B. Gordon – Airborne 11.12 Landed 17.06.

KG395 Flight Lieutenant P.W. Smith, Flight Sergeant L. Powell, Pilot Officer J.L. Robinson, Warrant Officer J.H. Golton – Airborne 11.30 Landed 17.08.

KG404 Flying Officer H.J. Jones, Flying Officer W.J. Cheek, Flight Sergeant J.K. Brown, Flight Sergeant S. Mumford – Airborne 11.31 Landed 17.24.

KG428 Pilot Officer S.J.H. Carter, Sergeant J. McCullum, Pilot Officer R.F. Carter, Warrant Officer R.W. Nicholson – Airborne 11.34 Landed 17.00.

FZ620 Flight Lieutenant G. Whitfield, Warrant Officer W.R. Millar, Flight Lieutenant K.D. Gay, Pilot Officer R.W. Button – Airborne 11.36 Landed 16.54.

All crews successfully released their gliders, although one of 48 Squadron's had its tow rope severed and was forced to land around 5 miles east-north-east of 's-Hertogenbosch, roughly around 10 miles from the LZ. All crews made it safely back to base, no enemy aircraft being observed during the mission.

512 Squadron Allocation 18 September

KG377 AS Squadron Leader P.K. Smulian, Flying Officer D. Tomlinson, Flight Sergeant J.D. Joyce, Warrant Officer L.T. King – Airborne 10.45 Landed 5.45.

KG379 AW, Flight Lieutenant J.R. Roberts, Flight Lieutenant J.S. Starr, Flying Officer D.J. Appleton, Warrant Officer D.L. Perry – Airborne 10.45 Landed 5.40.

KG371 AI, Flying Officer J.H.Seary, Pilot Officer J.E.Gillett, Warrant Officer M.A.S. Pickering, Warrant Officer J.D. Blue – Airborne 10.45 Landed 6.00.

KG544 UV, Flight Lieutenant R.A. Davis, Flying Officer J.K. Ring, Flying Officer D.C. Savage, Pilot Officer W.H. Sowersby – Airborne 10.45 Landed 5.50.

KG368 AY, Flying Officer R.A.S. Benson, Flying Officer R. Harrison, Flight Sergeant D. Williams, Warrant Officer J. Oxley – Airborne 10.45 Landed 5.55.

KG354 AZ, Flight Lieutenant D.W. Marshall, Flight Sergeant H. Jenkins, Flight Sergeant J. Priestley, Sergeant A.R. Hill – Airborne 11.00 Landed 5.50.

KG523 UU, Flight Sergeant S. Hildrew, Warrant Officer W.K. Pattison, Flight Sergeant H.M.V. Birkby, Warrant Officer R.F. Platt – Airborne 10.55 Landed 5.35.

FZ609 AP, Flight Lieutenant R.S. Matthews, Warrant Officer D.W. Bromige, Flight Sergeant W.C. Tompson, Warrant Officer P.B. Tonner – Airborne 11.00 Landed 5.30.

KG361 AU Flying Officer M.G. Pinn, Flying Officer H. Blazey, Flight Sergeant D.H. Powell, Flight Sergeant J. Davidson – Airborne 10.53 Landed 5.20.

FZ649 UJ Flight Lieutenant A.E. Carpenter, Flight Sergeant J.M. Bovies, Flying Officer R. Hill, Warrant Officer D.R. Miller – Airborne 10.50 Landed 5.35.

FZ651 AJ Flying Officer R.D. McNicol, Flight Sergeant C.F. Thomas, Sergeant P.E. Pullan, Sergeant L.F. Christie – Airborne 10.50 Landed 5.25.

FZ658 AM Flying Officer J.E. Masini, Flying Officer G.E. Dewhill, Flight Sergeant J. Johnson, Pilot Officer P.G. Kidd – Airborne 10.55 Landed 5.30.

KG344 AL F.E.A. Gough, Warrant Officer J.E. Tibbles, Flight Sergeant A.R. Skitmore, Pilot Officer J.H. Hubbard – Airborne 10.50 Landed 5.20.

KG558 UL Flight Lieutenant J.T. Reed, Flight Lieutenant J.E. Jones, Sergeant J.F. Roberts, Warrant Officer C.F. McLeod – Airborne 11.00 Landed 5.35.

KG348 UK Flight Lieutenant B.H. Worts, Flight Sergeant J.Brailey, Flight Sergeant K.D. Bruce, Pilot Officer W.C. Bevington – Airborne 10.50 Landed 5.25.

FZ636 AG Lt Flight Lieutenant J.J. Offienhiser, Flight Lieutenant S. Smith, Flight Sergeant W.B. Garvin, Pilot Officer W.C. Bevington – Airborne 10.50 Landed 5.25.

KD314 UG Flying Officer R.A. Garvin, Warrant Officer C.M. Grant, Warrant Officer E. Seal, Warrant Officer G.M. Fuller – Airborne 10.45 Landed 6.00.

KG375 AB Flight Lieutenant D.V.W. Hyde, Warrant Officer W.E. Blundell, Flight Sergeant R. Anderson, Pilot Officer J.R. Campbell – Airborne 10.45 Landed 6.00.

KG422 UB Flight Lieutenant C.F. Thomas, Pilot Officer T. Corlett, Flight Sergeant D.R. Dawson, Warrant Officer B.F. Bergin – Airborne 10.45 Landed 5.30.

KG322 AC Pilot Officer J. Proctor, Flight Sergeant C.R. Dyer, Flight Lieutenant H. Holland, Pilot Officer J.C.H. Sabourin – Airborne 10.415 Landed 5.25.

KG407 AD Pilot Officer W.H. Perry, Warrant Officer I.C. Gilbert, Warrant Officer F. Barritt, Warrant Officer A.B. Friend – Airborne 11.00 Landed 5.30.

KG384 AA Flying Officer L. Hamdon, Pilot Officer A.S. Phillips. Flight Sergeant C. Ridpath, Flying Officer K. Pearson – Airborne 10.50 Landed 5.30.

FZ647 AH Flying Officer H. Chatfield, Pilot Officer P.F Craske, Flight Sergeant K.I. Carson, Pilot Officer R.P. Munson – Airborne 11.15 Landed 5.30.

KG570 UF Squadron Leader G.T. Southgate, Flight Lieutenant S.W. Bryant, Flight Lieutenant A.E. Saunders, Flying Officer J.H. Parry – Airborne 10.45 Landed 3.00.

575 Squadron Allocation 18 September

KG615 Squadron Leader M.J. Elworthy, Flight Lieutenant R.E. Charlton, Flight Lieutenant C.F. Plimmer, Flying Officer E.F. Waight – Airborne 10.47 Landed 19.28.

KG432 Squadron Leader F.T. Cragg, Flight Lieutenant H.W. Payne, Flight Lieutenant H.H. Hall, Flight Sergeant C.G. Fisher –Airborne 11.01 Landed 16.33.

KG320 Flying Officer J.M. Quin, Flying Officer T.G. Young, Flying Officer R.J. Warren, Flight Sergeant A.G. Brown – Airborne 11.07 Landed 16.40.

KG363 Flying Officer E.F. Brown, Flying Officer R. Hay, Flying Officer F.A. Richards, Flying Officer C. Bruce – Airborne 11.02 Landed 16.27.

KG431 Flight Lieutenant R.L. Roach, Flight Sergeant P.S. Bell, Warrant Officer C.G. McConachie, Flying Officer J.G. Nadeau – Airborne 11.03 Landed 16.25.

KG325 Flying Officer D. Martin, Flight Sergeant J.A. Milner, Warrant Officer G.L. Robertson, Warrant Officer J.S. Tamshak – Airborne 11.03½ Landed 16.32.

KG529 Flying Officer R.J. McTeare, Flying Officer F. Gee, Flying Officer W.A. Michie, Flight Sergeant L.P. Smith – Airborne 11.04 Landed 19.07.

KG608 Wing Commander S. Parker, Sergeant A.C. Smith, Warrant Officer P.L. Hurcomb, Warrant Officer G.H. Wade – Airborne 11.06 Landed 16.19.

KG339 Flight Lieutenant A. Bollington, Flight Sergeant P.M. Oleinkoff, Flying Officer G.H. Hall, Flight Sergeant H.E. Hooper – Airborne 11.07 Landed 16.24.

FZ698 Flight Lieutenant C.R. Slack, Pilot Officer W.S. Monger, Pilot Officer I.L. Holloway, Pilot Officer J.E. Caoette – Airborne 11.08 Landed 16.26.

KG602 Flying Officer J.W. Furley, Flying Officer R.T. Hamlyn, Flight Sergeant W.F. Watts, Pilot Officer W.A. Stacey – Airborne 11.09½ Landed 16.20.

KG312 Flight Lieutenant J.W. Atkin, Warrant Officer D.J. Britton, Flight Lieutenant T.J. Cunliffe, Flying Officer G. Learmont – Airborne 11.10 Landed 16.23.

FZ662 Flying Officer W.T. Player, Flight Sergeant A.E. Fahey, Flying Officer R.M. Partridge, Flying Officer M.J. Sullivan – Airborne 11.23 Landed 16.41.

KG380 Flying Officer L.R. Filshie, Flight Sergeant J.W. Chitty, Flight Sergeant C.J. Turner, Warrant Officer A. Warren – Airborne 11.22 Landed 17.00.

KG388 Flying Officer J.R. Gembles, Flying Officer E. Clementson, Pilot Officer W.H. Stapleton, Flying Officer J.E. Howes – Airborne 11.11 Landed 16.20.

KG344 Pilot Officer E. Imison, Flight Sergeant N.R. Craw, Flying Officer J.L. Moffatt, Pilot Officer F.H. Barnard – Airborne 11.11 Landed 16.36.

KG359 Squadron Leader B. Smith, Flying Officer M.F. Porter, Flight Sergeant T.W. Payne, Warrant Officer P.A. Prior – Airborne 11.12 Landed 16.35.

KG326 Flight Sergeant W.S. Clark, Sergeant C.W. Garnett-Botfield, Sergeant R. Seddon, Flight Sergeant B.P. Strickland – Airborne 11.15 Landed 16.40.

KG327 Flying Officer C.G. McGlone, Flight Lieutenant W.E. Owen, Flying Officer C. Curry, Warrant Officer R.A. Heading – Airborne 11.14 Landed 16.29.

KG355 Pilot Officer A.L. Dodgson, Flight Lieutenant A.F. Budden, Flight Sergeant P. Joseph, Warrant Officer W.R. Headifen – Airborne 11.24 Landed 16.40.

KG390 Flight Lieutenant H.H. Hauge, Flying Officer W.K. Murphy, Flying Officer G.I. Finlay, Flying Officer R. Pearce – Airborne 11.16 Landed 16.42.

KG593 Flying Officer F. Dauncey, Flying Officer D.H. Brown, Flying Officer A.B. Evans, Flight Sergeant G.W. Jackson – Airborne 11.19 Landed 16.35.

KG328 Flying Officer G.E. Henry, Warrant Officer A.E. Smith, Flying Officer H.J. McKinley, Warrant Officer W. Fowler – Airborne 11.19 Landed 16.18.

FZ640 Flying Officer I.J. English, Flight Lieutenant A. Grahamslaw, Pilot Officer F. Jump, Pilot Officer R.G. Healy – Airborne 11.20 Landed 16.55.

FZ623 Flight Sergeant W.J. Thorn, Flight Sergeant J.N. Griffen, Flight Sergeant H.K. Milton, Sergeant P.R. Manning – Airborne 11.15½ Landed 16.10.

233 Squadron Allocation 18 September

KG559 Wing Commander W.E. Coles, Flight Lieutenant G.R. Frew, Flight Lieutenant A. Johnstone, Flying Officer E.J. Sharpe – Airborne 10.48 Landed 16.21.

KG415 Flying Officer J. Fram, Flying Officer N.C. Trigg, Pilot Officer J.C. Pinder, Pilot Officer R. Johnstone – Airborne 10.48 Landed 16.32.

KG586 Warrant Officer F.R. Russell, Flight Sergeant F.H. Jones, Warrant Officer D.C. Schofield, Warrant Officer R. Burgess – Airborne 10.46 Landed 16.34.

KG410 Warrant Officer A.L. White, Sergeant J.M. Crossman, Pilot Officer A. Edwards, Warrant Officer O.E.K. Tink – Airborne 10.45 Landed 16.35.

KG399 Flying Officer M.T. Ades, Flight Sergeant J.H. Dorville, Pilot Officer F.S.W. Dyer, Flight Sergeant J. Hickey – Airborne 10.49 Landed 16.38.

KG403 Warrant Officer A.J. Green, Flight Sergeant G.C.A. Jeffery, Flight Lieutenant A.S. Burks, Warrant Officer H. Joshlands – Airborne 10.50 Landed 16.30.

KG441 Warrant Officer H. Curtis, Flight Sergeant L.E. Butcher, Warrant Officer B.N. Caplan, Warrant Officer H.G. Birchnell – Airborne 10.50 Landed 16.35.

KG400 Pilot Officer R. Chessney, Flying Officer N.C. Cummings, Flying Officer G.A. Coppel, Flight Sergeant R.E. Simmonds – Airborne 10.50 Landed 16.35.

KG440 Squadron Leader G. Lane, Flying Officer Proctor, Flying Officer J. Sweeney, fourth crew member information unavailable – Airborne 10.50 Landed 16.25.

FZ686 Warrant Officer R.F. Holliday Flight Sergeant E.J. James, Warrant Officer G.A. Cozens, Warrant Officer H.F. Richardson – Airborne 10.52 Landed 16.35.

KG589 Flight Lieutenant W.A. Jenkins, Flight Sergeant J. Turner, Flight Sergeant H. Lovatt, Flight Sergeant W.A. Lee – Airborne 10.53 Landed 16.28.

KG420 Flight Lieutenant R. McIlraith, Flight Sergeant C.R. Meade, Warrant Officer A.J. Phillips, Flying Officer G. Smee – Airborne 10.53 Landed 16.32.

FZ678 Flight Lieutenant H.J. Barley, Flying Officer W. Greenwood, Flying Officer G.N. Taylor, Flight Lieutenant C. Ingelby – Airborne 10.45 Landed 16.17.

KG412 Warrant Officer N. Mills, Flight Sergeant R. Woodgate, Flight Lieutenant J. Buckton, Flight Sergeant G.G. Sparkes – Airborne 10.44 Landed 16.30.

KG313 Squadron Leader B.A. Miller, Flying Officer F. Priestley, Flight Lieutenant R. Taylor, Sergeant D.G. Morris – Airborne 10.43 Landed 16.31.

KG427 Flying Officer D. Hamilton, Flight Sergeant W.G. Wheeler, Pilot Officer F.B. Knight, Flight Sergeant L.J. Firth – Airborne 10.57 Landed 16.30.

KG448 Flight Lieutenant A. Cody, Flying Officer F.J. Colman, Flying Officer A.C. Hollingsworth, Flight Sergeant C.R. Goodfellow – Airborne 10.50 Landed 16.25.

One of the squadron's aircraft, KG420, was damaged, although only slightly. The navigator, Warrant Officer Phillips, did sustain a cut over one of his eyes. KG448, flown by Flight Lieutenant Cody, had its glider separate over East Anglia. Both managed to land at Andrews Field, Essex, where the glider's load was transferred on to the aircraft and subsequently returned to base.

437 Squadron Allocation 18 September

KG566 Flying Officer N.W. Gustafson, Flying Officer G.R. Tozer, Flying Officer S. Allen, Warrant Officer L.E. Cox – Airborne 10.45 Landed 16.37.

KG489 Flight Lieutenant R.W. Alexander, Flying Officer W.J. McLintock, Flight Sergeant A. McHugh, Flying Officer J. Rechenuc – Airborne 10.53 Landed 16.29.
FZ639 Flying Officer G.P. Hagerman, Flight Sergeant J.C. Hackett, Pilot Officer M.S.R. Mahon, Warrant Officer J.P. DeChamplain – Airborne 10.50 Landed 16.35.
KG568 Pilot Officer K.E. Rasmussen, Flying Officer C. BePol, Flight Sergeant R.E. Griffith, Flight Sergeant P.B. Steele – Airborne 10.55 Landed 16.34.
KG422 Flying Officer J.A. Delahunt, Flight Sergeant D.S. Cooper, Flying Officer G.L. Breckon, Flying Officer L.D. Hornsby – Airborne 10.54 Landed 16.40.
KG452 Flying Officer O.A. Simmons, Flying Officer W. Taylor, Warrant Officer G.A.A. Murdock – Airborne 10.55 Landed 16.30. One crew member not recorded.

Resupply Flights Started on 19 September, 271 Squadron Allocation

KG318 Pilot Officer E. Pritchard, Flight Sergeant A.G. Holt, Flying Officer A.H. Sherval, Sergeant W.B. Wilson – Airborne 12.32 Landing 18.10.
FZ668 Flying Officer J.R. Nicell, Flying Officer J.C. White, Warrant Officer C.J. Marsden, Flight Sergeant H.H. Caves – Airborne 12.30 Landing 17.55.
KG488 Flight Lieutenant P.A.D. Hellom, Sergeant S. Brink, Flight Lieutenant F.R. Riley, Pilot Officer G.R. Harway – Airborne 12.33 Landing (B.56) 16.50.
KG374 Flight Lieutenant D.S.A Lord (posthumously VC), Pilot Officer R.E.H. Medhurst, Flying Officer D.I. McDonnell, Flying Officer A.F. Ballantyne – Airborne 12.32, Shot down. Flying Officer Ballantyne not on aircraft, Flying Officer N.A. King replaced, King the only survivor from the aircraft and captured by the Germans.
KG340 Flight Lieutenant J.G. Cooke, Flight Sergeant I.M. Clout, Flying Officer J.S. Sargent, Pilot Officer H.E. Robertson – Airborne 12.33 Landing 17.50.
KG367 Warrant Officer L. Greenwell, Flight Sergeant W.J. Lewis, Warrant Officer P.G.H. Reynolds, Warrant Officer F.R. Richardson – Airborne 12.35 Landing 17.55.

KG378 Flying Officer J. Reveller, Flying Officer C.J. Frenchum, Flight Sergeant R.D. Howes, Pilot Officer H. Daley – Airborne 12.35 Landing 17.55.

FZ626 Pilot Officer J.L. Wilson, Flight Sergeant H. Osbourne, Flight Sergeant Layden, Flight Sergeant Trent R.F, – Airborne 12.35, Aircraft missing.

KG362 Flying Officer Grace L.J, Pilot Officer Cushing J.D, Warrant Officer Walker, Warrant Officer R.J. Adams – Airborne 12.34 Landing 17.37.

KG357 Flying Officer J. Delaney, Pilot Officer R.Z. Rogers, Flight Lieutenant G.W. Baxter, Flight Sergeant M.M. Jones – Airborne 12.30 Landing 17.55.

FZ601 Flying Officer J.W. Hartley, Warrant Officer W.D. Allen, Flying Officer W.I. Smith, Sergeant W.N. Anfield – Airborne 12.32 Landing 17.57.

KG500 Major P.S. Joubert, Flight Lieutenant R. Fellows, Flight Sergeant D. Butterworth – Airborne 12.30 Landing 17.50. Only three crew detailed.

FZ615 Warrant Officer E. Gilmen, Warrant Officer V.M. Levy, Pilot Officer S.H. Holder, Flying Officer R.M.N. Smith – Airborne 12.31 Landing 17.49.

KG546 Flying Officer R.D. Anderson, Warrant Officer W. Faircloth, Flying Officer F.S. Jenkins, Flight Sergeant L.R. Laking – Airborne 12.30 Landing 18.00.

KG557 Flight Lieutenant N.F. McLeed, Flying Officer G.P. Baldwin, Flying Officer J. Shannon, Pilot Officer H.T. Mundy – Airborne 12.31 Landing 17.43.

FZ613 Flight Lieutenant D.K. Hirst, Flying Officer R.P. Carwody, Flying Officer C.T. Bearne, Flight Sergeant R.L. Thompson – Airborne 12.32 Landing 18.00.

233 Squadron's allocation for the 19th only consisted of one aircraft and glider, which had been non-effective on the 18th. Loaded with six troops one jeep and trailer, the combination deployed on to the LZ, encountering some slight flak damage to the port wing and fuselage in the process.

KG448 Flight Lieutenant A. Cody, Flying Officer F.J. Colman, Flying Officer A.C. Hollingsworth, Flight Sergeant O.P. Goodfellow – Airborne 11.39 Landed 17.52.

48 Squadron Allocation 19 September (Resupply)

KG401 Flying Officer L.R. Pattee, Pilot Officer A.C. Kent, Warrant Officer T. Fenwick, Flying Officer F.J. Macintyre – Airborne 12.35 Crashed 16.10.

KG331 Warrant Officer D.A. Webb, Flight Sergeant D.H.R Plear, Pilot Officer R.C. Clarke, Warrant Officer G. Birlison – Airborne 12.37½ Landed 17.55.

KG395 Squadron Leader T.R.N. Wheatley-Smith, Pilot Officer J.J. Holmes, Pilot Officer J.R. Hemsworth, Flight Sergeant J.L. Anderson – Airborne 12.35 Landed 17.45.

KG391 Flying Officer A.J. Williams, Flight Sergeant R.F. Smith, Pilot Officer J.P. Thompson, Flight Lieutenant W.B. Gordon – Airborne 12.39 Landed 17.56.

KG393 Flying Officer M.R.S. Mackay, Pilot Officer W.C. Baynes, Warrant Officer W.A. Lewis, Flight Sergeant R. Owen – Airborne 12.35 Landed 18.10.

KG338 Flight Lieutenant N. Iosson, Sergeant W. Pritchard, Sergeant H.W. Rose, Flying Officer G.J. Connelly – Airborne 12.36 Landed 18.03.

KG579 Captain V.B. Jury, Flying Officer D.G. Dumper, Warrant Officer D.W. Sanders, Sergeant H.G. Hobbs – Airborne 12.35 Landed 17.50.

KG321 Flying Officer R.A. Kenny, Flight Sergeant L. Evans, Warrant Officer R.E. English, Pilot Officer A.H. Macaloney – Airborne 12.35 Landed 17.47.

KG364 Flying Officer P.D. Waring, Sergeant B. Hessey, Sergeant R.E. Franks, Warrant Officer R. Oliver – Airborne 12.34 Landed 18.05.

KG370 Flight Lieutenant A.C. Blythe, Flying Officer C.G. Dawson, Pilot Officer B.S. Edmonson, Pilot Officer P.L.C. Barrat – Airborne 12.35 Landed 17.46.

KG393 Squadron Leader P. Drummond, Flight Sergeant A.G. Johnson, Pilot Officer H.N. Niven, Flight Sergeant S. Saxton –Airborne 12.35 Landed 17.55.

KG397 Squadron Leader L.R. Harries, Flight Sergeant D. Anderson, Flight Lieutenant B. Cobscroft, Flying Officer G.F. McNeil – Airborne 12.38 Landed 18.20.

KG408 Flying Officer S.S. Finlay, Pilot Officer W.J. Walsh, Flight Sergeant R.L.T. Gray, Pilot Officer C.W. Rice – Airborne 12.38 Landed 17.45.

FZ671 Flying Officer A.M. Smith, Sergeant J. Ambler, Flying Officer J.A. Smith, Flight Sergeant A.D.C. Robertson – Airborne 12.35 Landed 17.47.

KG397 Warrant Officer S. Mclauhlin, Pilot Officer L.T. Bentley, Flying Officer E.S. Clark, Pilot Officer S. Meli Dones – Airborne 12.39 Landed 18.00.

KG428 Pilot Officer V.B. Christie, Flight Sergeant F.E. Fuller, Pilot Officer F.C.S. Dodson, Warrant Officer P.A. Fulmore – Airborne 12.37. Aircraft failed to return to base, crew and aircraft reported missing.

KG416 Flight Lieutenant G. Whitfield, Warrant Officer G.H. Hillard, Flight Lieutenant K.D. Gay, Flying Officer R.W. Butch – Airborne 11.42 Landed 17.59½. Crew detailed to take a Horsa glider to DZ S as the previous day the load was not available to fly. Glider despatched and landed safely as designated, the tug aircraft received minor damage from flak and small arms fire but did make it back to base.

512 Squadron Allocation (Resupply) 19 September

KG382 AV Wing Commander B.A. Coventry, Flight Lieutenant J. Williams, Flying Officer W.B. O'Connell, Flight Lieutenant S.W. Lee – Airborne 12.50 Landed 05.10.

KG333 AN Squadron Leader T.R. Russell, Flight Lieutenant G.S. Petrie, Flight Sergeant P.R. Pulham, Flight Lieutenant R.T. Briscoe – Airborne 12.50 Landed 05.10.

FZ651 AJ Flying Officer R.D. McNicol, Flight Sergeant C.F. Thomas, Sergeant P.E. Pullan, Sergeant L.F. Christie – Airborne 12.50 Landed 05.00.

FZ649 UJ Flight Lieutenant R.K. Buchanan, Flying Officer R.J. Cole, Flight Sergeant J.W. McDonald, Pilot Officer M.S. Hubbert – Airborne 12.50 Landed 05.10.

KG348 UK Pilot Officer P. Murray, Pilot Officer R. Shallcross, Flight Sergeant J.C. Lawson, Flight Sergeant T. Draper – Airborne 12.50 Landed 05.05.

KG361 AU Flight Lieutenant C.H. McLeod, Flying Officer E.F. Butcher, Pilot Officer H.E.H. Corby, Flight Sergeant G. Claydon – Airborne 12.50 Landed 05.15.

KG593 UW Flight Lieutenant D.W. Marshall, Flight Sergeant E. Jenkins, Flight Sergeant J. Priestley, Sergeant A.R. Hill – Airborne 12.50 Landed 05.00.

KG368 AY Flight Lieutenant W.B. Pearson, Flying Officer T.L. Vardy, Flight Sergeant A.M. Tyson, Flying Officer A.E. Miechel – Airborne 12.50 Landed 05.20.

KG407 AD Flying Officer D.R. Lewis, Flying Officer A.J. Coonan, Warrant Officer W. Robinson, Flight Sergeant G. Canning – Airborne 12.50 Landed 05.05.

KG371 AX Flight Lieutenant J.D. Shaw, Flight Lieutenant W.S. Close, Flight Sergeant L. Bryant, Warrant Officer S.E. Thayer – Airborne 12.55 Landed 05.10.

KG322 AC Flight Lieutenant R.A. Shaw, Flight Lieutenant W.S. Close, Flight Sergeant L. Bryant, Warrant Officer S.E. Thayer – Airborne 12.55 Landed 5.05. Details are the same for crew on Dakota KG371, landing time different. Error recording the information at the time.

KG324 AA Flying Officer C.A. George, Pilot Officer V.H. Hemming, Flight Sergeant D. Burgess, Flight Sergeant J.P. Hicks – Airborne 12.50 Landed 05.05.

KG373 AD Flying Officer F.C. Wright, Flying Officer E.T.C. Harris, Flight Sergeant C.J. Parratt, Flight Sergeant J.S. Ramsey – Airborne 12.50 Landed 05.05.

KG314 UC Flying Officer A.C.P. Campbell, Warrant Officer J.R. Haynes, Flight Sergeant W.E. Pearce, Pilot Officer R.T. Britton – Airborne 12.55 Landed 03.40.

FZ696 AQ Flying Officer J. Dauncey, Pilot Officer Jackson, Flying Officer E.H. Brown – Airborne 09.55 Landed 05.55. Only three crew recorded.

FZ609 AP Flight Lieutenant J.J. Offenhiser, Pilot Officer W.C. Envington, Flight Lieutenant S. Smith – Airborne 10.00 Landed 07.10. Only three crew recorded.

KG379 AW Pilot Officer W.H. Perry, Warrant Officer L.C. Gilbert, Warrant Officer F. Barritt, Warrant Officer A.B. Friend – Airborne 10.00 Landed 05.00.

575 Squadron Allocation 19 September

FZ608 Wing Commander T.A. Jefferson, Flight Lieutenant R.E. Charlton, Flight Lieutenant C.F. Plimmer, Flying Officer E.F. Waight – Airborne 12.45 Landed 17.55.

KG437 Flying Officer F.R. Sandford, Flying Officer J.C. Chitty, Warrant Officer P.N. Siddons, Warrant Officer E.T. Fennell – Airborne 12.45 Landed 17.55.

KG432 Squadron Leader F.T. Cragg, Flight Lieutenant H.W. Payne, Flight Lieutenant H.H. Hall, Flight Sergeant C.G. Fisher – Airborne 12.47 Landed 17.50.

FZ640 Flying Officer L.J. English, Flight Lieutenant A. Grahamslaw, Pilot Officer R.G. Healy, Pilot Officer F. Jump – Airborne 12.52 Landed 18.00.

KG320 Warrant Officer H. Clark, Warrant Officer D.M. Kerr, Warrant Officer E.R. Wimbridge, Warrant Officer E.W. Townsend – Airborne 12.47 Landed 17.56.

FZ602 Squadron Leader D.C. Pascall, Flying Officer P.L. Newlands, Flying Officer R. Flett, Flight Sergeant G. Bullen – Airborne 12.47 Landed 17.49.

KG339 Flying Officer J.W. Furley, Flying Officer R.T. Hamlyn, Flight Sergeant W.F. Watts, Pilot Officer W.A. Stacey – Airborne 12.48 Landed 17.58.

KG312 Warrant Officer J.K. Elliott, Flight Sergeant A.M. Sherret, Flight Sergeant G.T. Beck, Flight Sergeant J.K. Conway – Airborne 12.45 Landed 18.00.

KG334 Flying Officer W.T. Player, Flight Sergeant E.A. Pahey, Flying Officer R.M. Partridge, Flying Officer M.J. Sullivan – Airborne 12.50 Landed 18.03.

KG390 Squadron Leader B. Smith, Flying Officer M.F. Porter, Flight Sergeant T.W. Payne, Warrant Officer F.A. Prior – Airborne 12.40 Landed 18.00.

KG326 Flight Sergeant A.G. Martins, Flight Sergeant H.E. Bauer, Flying Officer J.D. Simpson, Pilot Officer M.Blugrind – Airborne 12.50 Landed 17.53.

KG402 Pilot Officer J.S. MacFarlane, Pilot Officer H.W. Beacham, Flying Officer F.W. Osborne, Warrant Officer Warrant Officer M.L. Peardon – Airborne 12.50 Landed 18.00.

KG363 Flying Officer E.F.Brown, Flying Officer R. Hay, Flying Officer F.A. Richards, Flight Sergeant C.Bruce – Airborne 12.52 Landed 18.00.

KG380 Flight Sergeant L.R. Nunn, Sergeant J. Anderson, Warrant Officer W. Cryer, Warrant Officer D.J. Wood – Airborne 12.47 Landed 17.50.

KG550 Flight Lieutenant B.P. Legge, Flight Lieutenant V.G. Hogan, Pilot Officer F.C. Ashton, Warrant Officer A. McMahon – Airborne 12.50. Made a forced landing at RAF Woodbridge due to flak damage.

KG388 Flight Lieutenant C.R. Slack, Pilot Officer W.S. Monger, Pilot Officer I.L. Hollaway, Pilot Officer J.E. Cacette – Airborne 12.48. Reported missing the following day.

48 Squadron Allocation 20 September

KG423 Flying Officer M.R.S. Mackay, Pilot Officer W.C. Baynes, Warrant Officer W.A. Lewis, Flight Sergeant R. Owen, Take off 14.15, Landed 20.16.

KG587 Flight Lieutenant H.J.G. Alford, Sergeant E.L. Leslie, Flight Sergeant J.H. Mewis, Pilot Officer A.F. Spencer, Take off 14.16 Landed 19.40.

Aircraft and Crews 243

FZ624 Warrant Officer S. Page, Sergeant J. Potts, Warrant Officer P.H. Lee, Warrant Officer R.J. McMichael – Airborne 14.15 Landed 19.30.

KG406 Flight Lieutenant P.W. Smith, Flight Sergeant I. Powell, Pilot Officer J.I. Robinson, Warrant Officer J.H. Golton – Airborne 14.12 Landed 19.52.

FZ620 Flying Officer H.J. Jones, Flying Officer J. Cheek, Flight Sergeant J.K. Brown, Flight Sergeant S. Mumford – Airborne 14.14 Landed 19.38.

KG386 Flying Officer J.P. Warwick, Flight Sergeant C. Tennyson, Pilot Officer A.W. Carfran, Pilot Officer R.K. Martin –Airborne 14.14 Landed 19.39.

KG350 Pilot Officer W.R.Pring, Sergeant H.E. Colman, Flight Sergeant G.D. Gleave, Warrant Officer J.L. Sprinsteele – Airborne 14.14 Landed 19.27.

KG411 Flying Officer R.G.J. Hull, Warrant Officer T. O'Brien, Flying Officer D. North, Warrant Officer L.L. Peterson – Airborne 14.12 Landed 19.18.

KG317 Flying Officer G.Loades, Flight Sergeant W.W. Maxwell, Flight Lieutenant E. Palin, Pilot Officer C.E. Dixon – Airborne 14.13 Landed 19.25.

KG391 Warrant Officer F.F.Felton, Flight Sergeant A.W. Meecham, Flight Sergeant K. Toyne, Warrant Officer J.A. Chenery – Airborne 14.13 Landed 19.23.

KG417 Flying Officer J.G. Wills, Pilot Officer J.W. Erickson, Warrant Officer D.G. Hardy, Flight Sergeant D.S. Black – Airborne 14.16 Landed 19.15.

KG346 Captain C.H.Campbell, Flying Officer J.C.Harvey, Flying Officer J.P. Mudge, Flight Sergeant J.L. Anderson – Airborne 14.13, Landed 19.18.

KG579 Captain V.B. Jury, Flying Officer B.G. Dumper, Warrant Officer D.W. Sanders, Sergeant H.G. Hobbs – Airborne 14.16 Landed 19.30.

KG337 Flight Lieutenant N. Iosson, Sergeant W. Pritchard, Sergeant H.W. Rose, Flying Officer G.J. Connelly, Airborne 14.15 Landed 19.32.

KG563 Flying Officer P.D. Waring, Sergeant B. Hessee, Sergeant R.E. Franks, Warrant Officer R. Oliver – Airborne 14.13 Landed 19.34.

KG416 Flying Officer A.M. Smith, Sergeant J. Ambler, Flying Officer J.A. Smith, Flight Sergeant A.D.C. Robertson – Airborne 14.17 Landed 19.21.

271 Squadron Allocation 20 September

KG545 Wing Commander M. Booth, Flight Sergeant N. Rowan, Flight Lieutenant R. Johnson, Flight Lieutenant R. Hodgson – Airborne 14.17 Landed 19.35.

KG557 Pilot Officer D. Wood, Flight Sergeant D.R.W. Tyler, Warrant Officer K. Carter, Warrant Officer T.R. Adamson – Airborne 14.17, Landed 19.27.

KG357 Pilot Officer R. Williams, Warrant Officer H. Farrer, Flight Sergeant J.E. Rainsford, Flight Sergeant E.E. Wensley – Airborne 14.17 Landed 19.25.

FZ615 Flight Lieutenant A.R. Beddows, Flight Sergeant H. Nott, Flying Officer J.S. Dolan, Flight Sergeant A.G. Holt – Airborne 14.17 Landed 19.20.

KG500 Flight Lieutenant K.C. Edwards, Flight Lieutenant G. Hunter, Flight Sergeant H. Sorensen, Flight Sergeant N.F. Randall – Airborne 14.18 Landed 19.20.

FZ607 Flying Officer K.C. Wilson, Flight Lieutenant D.H. Crocker, Pilot Officer J. Foster, Flying Officer F. Anderson – Airborne 14.21 Landing 19.12.

FZ668 Squadron Leader A.B. Pearson, Pilot Officer R.D. Harrington, Warrant Officer Hirrawems, Warrant Officer J.S. Gibbons – Airborne 14.17 Landed 19.15.

KG372 Flying Officer K.P. O'Donnell, Flight Sergeant J.P. Brightling, Pilot Officer T.R. Holdsworth, Flight Sergeant G.J. Watters – Airborne 14.20 Landed 19.20.

FZ622 Flying Officer J.I. McNeil, Flight Sergeant H. Green, Flying Officer A. Whitaker, Warrant Officer F.R. Richardson – Airborne 14.19 Landed 19.35.

KG514 Warrant Officer D. Twiston-Davies, Flight Sergeant H.A. Kimm, Sergeant W. Wilson, Warrant Officer P. Brewer – Airborne 14.20 Landed 19.44.

KG365 Warrant Officer G. King, Flying Officer A.T. Denny, J.F. McManus, Flight Sergeant R.A.V. Faber – Airborne 14.21 Landed 19.38.

KG340 Pilot Officer F.W. Cuer, Flight Sergeant J.M. Bayley, Warrant Officer C.A. Anderson, Flight Sergeant B. Tipping – Airborne 14.18 Landed 19.35.

KG378 Flight Lieutenant C.W. Mott, Flight Lieutenant K.J. Packer, Flying Officer R.J. Wells, Warrant Officer T. Kennedy – Airborne 14.19 Landed 19.25.

KG362 Flight Lieutenant L.J. Grace, Pilot Officer J.D. Cusing, Flying Officer F.T. Blakeney, Warrant Officer R.J. Adams – Airborne 14.19 Landed 19.40.

KG592 Squadron Leader P.D. Squires, Flight Lieutenant D.C. Ager, Flight Lieutenant S.D. Plummer, Flight Lieutenant H.M. Browne – Airborne 14.20 Landed 19.33.

Aircraft and Crews 245

KG516 Warrant Officer A.L.F. Bone, Warrant Officer L. Chambara, Warrant Officer N.J. Batstone, Flight Sergeant G.H. Winter – Airborne 14.21 Landed 19.36.

512 Squadron Allocation 20 September

KG348 UK Squadron Leader J.P. Rae, Flight Sergeant J. Bradley, Flight Sergeant K.D. Bruce, Flight Sergeant J. Goodall – Airborne 14.30 Landed 05.30.

KG333 AN Pilot Officer J. Proctor, Flight Sergeant C.R. Dyer, Flight Lieutenant H. Holland, Pilot Officer J.C.H Sabourin – Airborne 14.20 Landed 05.25.

FZ649 UJ Flying Officer L. Hawdon, Pilot Officer A.S. Phillips, Flight Sergeant C. Kidpath, Flying Officer K. Pearson – Airborne 14.30 Landed 05.30.

FZ651 AI Flight Lieutenant A.E. Carpenter, Flight Sergeant J.M. Bowles, Flying Officer R. Hill, Warrant Officer D.R. Miller – Airborne 14.30 Landed 05.30.

KG344 AL Flight Lieutenant F.E.A. Gough, Warrant Officer J.E. Tibbles, Flight Sergeant A.R. Skitmore, Pilot Officer J.H. Hubbard – Airborne 14.30 Landed 05.05.

FZ658 AM Flight Sergeant J.E. Masini, Flying Officer G.E. Denwell, Flight Sergeant J. Johnson, Pilot Officer P.G. Kidd – Airborne 14.35 Landed 05.30.

KG358 UL Flying Officer M.G. Finn, Pilot Officer E. Flaxey, Flight Sergeant D.H. Powell, Flying Officer J. Davison – Airborne 14.32 Landed 05.30.

FZ694 AR Flight Lieutenant R.A. Davis, Pilot Officer D.C. Savage, Flying Officer J.K. Ring, Pilot Officer W.H. Sowersby – Airborne 14.30 Landed 05.20.

KG422 UB Flight Lieutenant J.C.P. Thomas, Flight Sergeant D.R. Dawson, Flying Officer T. Carlett, Warrant Officer R.F. Bergin – Airborne 14.30 Landed 05.20.

KG544 UV Flight Sergeant S. Hildrew, Flight Sergeant H.A.V. Birkby, Warrant Officer W.K. Pattison, Warrant Officer R.RF. Platt – Airborne 14.30 Landed 05.20.

FZ656 AK Flying Officer R.A.S. Benson, Flight Sergeant D. Williams, Flight Lieutenant J.S. Starr, Warrant Officer J. Oxley – Airborne 14.30 Landed 05.15.

KG379 AW Flying Officer H. Chatfield, Flight Sergeant K.I. Carson, Flying Officer P.F. Crakke, Pilot Officer R.P. Munson – Airborne 14.30 Landed 05.25.

KG354 AL Flight Lieutenant D.V.W. Hyde, Flight Sergeant P. Anderson, Warrant Officer W.B. Blundell, Pilot Officer J.R. Campbell – Airborne 14.30 Landed 05.30.

KG418 UT Flight Lieutenant R.S. Matthews, Flight Sergeant W.C. Thompson, Warrant Officer D.W. Bromige, Warrant Officer P.R. Tonner – Airborne 14.30. Missing failed to return.

KG324 AA Pilot Officer W.H. Perry, Warrant Officer F. Barritt, Warrant Officer L.O. Gilbert, Warrant Officer A.B. Friend – Airborne 14.30. Missing failed to return.

575 Squadron Allocation 20 September

KG449 Flying Officer S. Baker, Pilot Officer T.F. Andrews, Flying Officer R.W. Chartres, Flying Officer J.M. Atkinson – Airborne 14.34½ Landed 20.04.

KG623 Warrant Officer N.D. Batstone, Flying Officer E.W. Newton, Flying Officer D.S. Herd, Warrant Officer R.A. Rolfs – Airborne 14.24 Landed 19.45.

KG339 Flight Lieutenant A. Bollington, Flight Sergeant P.M. Cleinleoff, Flying Officer G.H. Hall, Flight Sergeant H.E. Hooper – Airborne 14.34 Landed 19.47.

KG402 Pilot Officer A.L. Dodgeon, Flying Officer D.H. Brown, Flying Officer A.B. Evans, Flight Sergeant G.W. Jackson – Airborne 14.35 Landed 20.10.

KG312 Warrant Officer J.K. Elliott, Flight Sergeant A.M. Sherret, Flight Sergeant G.T. Beck, Flight Sergeant J.K. Conway – Airborne 14.35 Landed 19.45.

FZ698 Flying Officer L.R. Tillshie, Flight Sergeant J.W. Chitty, Flight Sergeant C.J. Turner, Warrant Officer A. Warren – Airborne 14.35 Landed 19.52.

KG442 Flying Officer J.R. Gembles, Flying Officer E. Clementsorr, Pilot Officer W.H. Stapleton, Flying Officer J.E. Howes – Airborne 14.35½ Landed 19.56.

Aircraft and Crews 247

KG593 Flying Officer C.G. McGlone, Flying Officer W.E. Owen, Flying Officer C. Curry, Warrant Officer R.A. Heading – Airborne 14.36½ Landed 19.45.

KG325 Flying Officer R.J. McTeare, Flying Officer F. Gee, Flying Officer W.A. Michie, Flight Sergeant L.P. Smith – Airborne 14.34 Landed 19.50.

FZ640 Flying Officer D. Martin, Flight Sergeant J.A. Milner, Flying Officer G.L. Robertson, Warrant Officer J.S. Tomshak – Airborne 14.34 Landed 19.36.

KG529 Warrant Officer S.Parker, Sergeant A.C. Smith, Warrant Officer P.L. Hurcomb, Warrant Officer G.H. Wade – Airborne 14.34½ Landed 19.47.

KG327 Flying Officer J.M. Quin, Flying Officer T.G. Young, Flying Officer R.J. Warren, Flight Sergeant A.G. Brown – Airborne 14.34 Landed 20.10.

KG349 Flight Sergeant W.S. Clark, Sergeant C.W. Garnett-Potfield, Sergeant R. Seddon, Flight Sergeant E.P. Strickland –Airborne 14.37 Landed 19.43.

KG615 Pilot Officer E. Imison, Flight Sergeant N.R. Craw, Flying Officer J.L. Moffatt, Pilot Officer P.H. Barnard – Airborne 14.34½ Landed 19.55.

KG380 Warrant Officer H. Clark, Warrant Officer D.M. Kerr, Warrant Officer R.R. Wimbridge, Warrant Officer E.W. Townsend – Airborne 14.34 Landed 19.38.

KG390 Flight Lieutenant J.W. Atkin, Warrant Officer D.J. Britton, Flight Lieutenant T.J. Cunliffe, Flying Officer G. Learmont – Airborne 14.35½ Forced landing at RAF Manston due to severe flak damage.

48 Squadron Allocation 21 September

KG404 Flying Officer S.S. Finlay, Pilot Officer W.J. Walsh, Flight Sergeant R.L.T. Gray, Pilot Officer C.W. Rice – Airborne 13.15 Landed 16.30. Shot down by Fw 190s from JG26.

KG579 Warrant Officer D.A. Webb, Flight Sergeant D.H.R. Plear, Pilot Officer R.C. Clarke, Warrant Officer G. Birlison – Airborne 13.15 Landed 15.25. Shot down by Fw 190s from JG26.

FZ624 Flying Officer E.W. McCreanor, Flying Officer D.S. Hodge, Flight Sergeant J.F. Roberts, Flight Sergeant J. Daniels – Airborne 12.16, Landed 18.35.

KG587 Flight Lieutenant W.B. Stone, Flight Sergeant J.P. Clarke, Pilot Officer J.D. Harrison, Pilot Officer R.F.J. Hinde – Airborne 13.14½ Landed 18.43.

KG337 Warrant Officer S. Mclauglin, Pilot Officer L.T. Bentley, Flying Officer E.S. Clark, Pilot Officer S. Melidones – Airborne 13.15 Landed 18.40.

KG411 Squadron Leader L.J. Harries, Pilot Officer J.J. Holmes, Pilot Officer J.R. Hemsworth, Pilot Officer P.C. Barrett – Airborne 13.15 Landed 18.37.

KG386 Flying Officer J.P. Warwick, Flight Sergeant C. Tennison, Pilot Officer A.W. Carfrae, Pilot Officer R.K. Martin – Airborne 13.13 Landed 19.36.

KG350 Squadron Leader P.O.M. Duff-Mitchell, Wing Commander M. Hallam, Pilot Officer B.S. Edmonson, Flying Officer T. Crowley – Airborne 13.10 Landed 17.15 (crashed).

KG406 Flight Lieutenant R.R. Keiller, Flight Sergeant W.C. Birch, Warrant Officer R.T. Barry, Warrant Officer J.I. Parry – Airborne 13.15 Landed 18.30.

KG393 Squadron Leader P. Drummond, Flight Sergeant A.G. Johnson, Pilot Officer H.N. Niven, Flight Sergeant S. Saxton – Airborne 13.15 Landed 18.40.

FZ620 Flight Sergeant S.H. Webster, Flight Sergeant R. Murray, Sergeant W. Fell, Sergeant J.C. Rushton – Airborne 13.15 Crashed.

KG346 Captain C.H. Campbell, Flying Officer J.C. Garvey, Flying Officer J.P. Mudge, Flight Sergeant J.L. Anderson – Airborne 13.16½. Aircraft and crew reported missing.

KG417 Flying Officer J.G. Wills, Pilot Officer J.W. Erickson, Warrant Officer D.G. Hardy, Flight Sergeant D.S. Black – Airborne 13.14. Aircraft and crew reported missing.

271 Squadron Allocation 21 September

FZ668 Squadron Leader A.B. Pearson, Warrant Officer R.D. Harrington, Warrant Officer H.R. Wemyas, Warrant Officer J.S. Gibbons – Airborne 13.10 Landed 18.29.

KG318 Warrant Officer G.King, Flying Officer A.T. Denny, Warrant Officer J.F. McManus, Flight Sergeant R.A.V. Paber – Airborne 13.12 Landed 18.50.

KG372 Flying Officer K.P. O'Donnell, Flying Officer T.R. Holdsworth, Flight Sergeant J.P. Brightling, Flight Sergeant G.J. Watters – Airborne 13.12 Landed 18.34.

FZ622 Warrant Officer D. Twiston – Davies, Flight Sergeant A.H. Kimm, Warrant Officer T.W. Connolly, Flight Sergeant P.Brewer – Airborne 13.11 Landed 18.41.

KG340 Pilot Officer F.W. Cuer, Flight Sergeant J.M. Bayley, Warrant Officer C.A. Anderson, Flight Sergeant B. Tipping – Airborne 13.11, reported missing.

KG362 Flying Officer J. Beveler, Flying Officer C.J. Frenchum, Flight Sergeant R.D. Howees, Pilot Officer H. Daley – Airborne 13.15 Landed 18.40.

KG516 Flight Lieutenant C.W. Mott, Flight Lieutenant E.J. Packer, Flying Officer R.J. Wells, Warrant Officer T. Kennedy – Airborne 13.15 Landed 16.15 (Crew baled out, aircraft crashed).

FZ613 Warrant Officer C.F. Quin, Flying Officer K.F.C. Brown, Warrant Officer M. Sidebottom, Warrant Officer A. McDougall – Airborne 13.10 Landed 18.35.

KG545 Maj P.S. Joubert, Flight Lieutenant R. Fellows, Flight Sergeant D. Butterworth, Flying Officer R. Boasten – Airborne 13.10 Landed 17.40.

KG444 Flight Lieutenant K.O. Edwards, Flight Sergeant A.W. Clarke, Flight Sergeant H. Serensen, Flight Sergeant N.F. Radall – Airborne 13.11 Crash-landed 16.14 behind enemy lines.

FZ615 Flight Lieutenant A.R.T. Beddow, Flight Sergeant H. Nett, Flying Officer J.S. Dolan, Flight Sergeant A.G. Holt – Airborne 13.12 Landed 17.16 (B.56).

KG557 Flight Lieutenant N.F. McLeod, Flying Officer G.P. Bedwin, Flying Officer J. Shannon, Pilot Officer H.T. Mundy – Airborne 13.10, Landed 18.35.

It was later reported that Flight Sergeant J.M. Bayley and Flight Sergeant R. Tipping from Pilot Officer Cuer's crew had both reported back to base. They reported that once the panniers had been dropped from the aircraft it was hit by flak and caught fire. The captain gave the order to abandon the aircraft immediately. No news was received at the time on the whereabouts and status of P.O. F.W. Cuer and Warrant Officer C.A. Anderson, who remained missing at this stage.

233 Squadron Allocation 21 September

KG559 Wing Commander W.E. Coles, Group Captain W.M.C. Kennedy, Flight Lieutenant A. Johnstone, Flying Officer E.J. Sharpe – Airborne 13.10 Landed 17.00.

KG341 Pilot Officer G. Bailey, Pilot Officer E. Warrington, Flying Officer L.N. Williams, Flight Sergeant R.C. Fitt – Airborne 13.10 Landed 18.35.

KG410 Flight Lieutenant P.I. Burden, Flight Sergeant C.R. Caie, Flying Officer M. Fitzpatrick, Pilot Officer O. Moore – Airborne 13.10 Landed 18.30.

KG351 Squadron Leader C.J. Mackenzie, Flying Officer D.G. Harous, Warrant Officer L.V. Whitehouse, Pilot Officer J.L. Dods – Airborne 13.10 Landed 18.28.

FZ678 Flight Lieutenant H.J. Barley, Pilot Officer W. Greenwood, Flying Officer G. Taylor, Flight Lieutenant C. Ingelby – Airborne 13.11 Landed 18.28.

KG430 Flight Lieutenant A.C.L. Mackie, Flying Officer W.C. Hunter, Flying Officer J. Proctor, Flight Lieutenant D. Goodwin – Airborne 13.12 Landed 18.37.

KG433 Warrant Officer R.D. Saunders, Flight Sergeant G.D. Lock, Warrant Officer C.H.F. Cousins, Flight Sergeant C.A. Hayward – Airborne 13.12 Landed 18.40.

KG455 Pilot Officer G.S. Wright, Flight Sergeant L. Cooper, Warrant Officer P.S. Wright, Flight Sergeant F.B. Lewis – Airborne 13.12 Landed 18.35.

KG441 Squadron Leader R. Daniell, Flight Sergeant P. Walker, Pilot Officer P. Nixon, Warrant Officer E.E. Bennett – Airborne 13.12 Landed 18.30.

KG561 Flying Officer G.T. Clarkson, Flying Officer J.P. Williams, Flight Sergeant N.R.H. Rains, Flying Officer C.J. Williams – Airborne 13.12 Landed 18.31.

FZ681 Flight Lieutenant A. Cody, Flying Officer F.J. Coleman, Flying Officer A.C. Hollingsworth, Flight Sergeant O.R. Goodfellow – Airborne 13.12 Landed 18.34.

FZ680 Flight Lieutenant O.L. Broadley, Flight Sergeant W. Farquharson, Flight Sergeant A.G. Bishop, Pilot Officer H. Plank – Airborne 13.13 Landed 18.41.

FZ665 Flight Lieutenant W.A. Jenkins, Flight Sergeant J. Turner, Flight Sergeant H. Lovatt, Flight Sergeant W.A. Lee – Airborne 13.12 Landed 18.41.

KG585 Flying Officer R.R. McGowan, Flight Sergeant R.W.C. Hopkins, Flight Sergeant G. Harmer, Warrant Officer C.E.P. Swann – Airborne 13.12 Landed 18.37.

FZ686 Warrant Officer J. Taylor, Flight Sergeant L.R. Edmends, Flying Officer H. Eagles, Warrant Officer W.C. Want – Airborne 13.13 Landed 18.37.

KG586 Warrant Officer F.R. Russell, Flight Sergeant F.H. Jones, Warrant Officer D.C. Schofield, Warrant Officer L. Burgess – Airborne 13.12 Failed to return to base.

KG399 Flying Officer M.T. Ades, Flight Sergeant G. Dorville, Pilot Officer F.S.W. Dyer, Flight Sergeant J. Hickey – Airborne 13.13 Failed to return to base.

KG566 Flying Officer C.D. Hamilton, Flight Sergeant W.G. Wheeler, Pilot Officer F.B. Knight, Flight Sergeant L.J. Firth – Airborne 13.12 Failed to return to base.

The squadron met with some fierce resistance, receiving flak from German ground units as well as in the air by the Fw 190s of JG26.

Some 240 panniers were delivered successfully close to the DZ, although nearly every Dakota received damage, some quite heavy. The worst-damaged aircraft that did manage to land was KG559 with holes in both wings and elevator damage. Flying Officer Sharpe was wounded in his right thigh and the crew elected to land at Brussels Evere (B.56) so medical treatment could be administered and the aircraft assessed following the mission. No news was received at the time about the three aircraft that were reported as missing on the day, and all these crews were listed as missing in action.

437 Squadron Allocation 21 September

KG387 Flight Lieutenant R.W. Alexander, W.J. McLintock, Flight Sergeant A. McHugh, Flying Officer J. Rechenuc – Airborne 13.14 Did not return to base.

FZ626 Flight Lieutenant G.R. Warrington, Flying Officer J. Wilcock, Pilot Officer E.A. Smith, Pilot Officer L.F. Dahlstedt – Airborne 13.13 Landed 18.27.

KG437 Flying Officer W.E. McLean, Flying Officer D.A. Cox, Flight Sergeant P.A. Turner, Warrant Officer R. Mercer – Airborne 13.14 Landed 18.32.

KG427 Flight Sergeant J.W. Lane, Warrant Officer T.W. Connolly, Pilot Officer G.B. Snider, Flight Sergeant J.E.R. St Arnaud – Airborne 13.15 Landed 18.28.

KG376 Flying Officer G.P. Hagerman, Flight Sergeant J.C. Hackett. Pilot Officer M.S.R. Mahon, Warrant Officer J.P. Dechamplain – Airborne 13.14 Landed 16.30.

KG469 Flying Officer C.H. Cressman, Flying Officer J.S. Blair, Flying Officer P. Steffin, Flying Officer T.J. Brennan – Airborne 13.14 Did not return to base.

KG410 Flying Officer E.Q. Semple, Flight Sergeant J.A. Daldorph, Warrant Officer F.A.R. MacKay, Warrant Officer M.H.F. Conred – Airborne 13.15 Landed 18.45.

KG351 Flying Officer J.M. Byrnes, Flying Officer W.E. Simpson, Flying Officer K.E. Hunt, Flight Sergeant J.R. Chambers – Airborne 13.35 Landed 18.40.

KG489 Flying Officer W.E. Chambers, Sergeant J. Pope, Pilot Officer F.K. Hill, Flight Sergeant J. Stott – Airborne 13.37 Landed 16.57 (B56).

FZ656 Pilot Officer R.A. Kenny, Sergeant L. Evans, Warrant Officer 1 R.E. English, Pilot Officer H.H. MacAloney – Airborne 13.37 Did not return to base.

Ten aircraft were detailed to drop panniers on to DZ in an effort to get supplies to the airborne troops. Enemy aircraft were encountered in and around the DZ, mainly appearing around the Eindhoven area both on the incoming and outbound legs. KG387, captained by Flight Lieutenant Alexander, KG469, Captain Flying Officer Cressman, and FZ656, Captain Pilot Officer Kenny, did not return to base. KG376 was abandoned when the crew baled out. KG427, Flight Sergeant Lane, received damage from an Fw 190 above the mainplane starboard side after being attacked at 6,000 feet 25 miles from the DZ. KG410, captained by Flying Officer Semple, managed to evade attack by two Fw 190s when he dived into cloud, losing his pursuers in the process. Crew status reported that KG387's pilot and second pilot were killed, even though the warrant officer returned safely, with the navigator believed to be in hospital. KG376's second pilot and navigator were both killed, with the warrant officer and wounded pilot safe. KG489, captained by Flying Officer

Aircraft and Crews 253

Chambers, and FZ656, Kenny, crashed and and all members of the crews were reported missing.

48 Squadron Allocation 23 September

KG391 Warrant Officer F.F. Felton, Flight Sergeant A.W. Meecham, Flight Sergeant K. Toyne, Warrant Officer J.A. Chanery – Airborne 13.44 Landed 17.20.

KG321 Warrant Officer S. McLauglin, Pilot Officer L.T. Bentley, Flying Officer E.S. Clark, Pilot Officer S. Melidones – Airborne 13.58 Landed 16.32 (Eindhoven).

KG317 Flight Lieutenant R.R. Keiller, Flight Sergeant W.C. Birch, Warrant Officer R.T. Barry, Warrant Officer J.I. Parry – Airborne 13.57 Landed 18.43.

KG406 Flying Officer R.G.J. Hull, Warrant Officer T. O'Brien, Flying Officer D. North, Warrant Officer L.L. Peterson – Airborne 13.39 Landed 18.58.

FZ624 Flight Lieutenant G. Whitfield, Warrant Officer W.R. Millar, Flight Lieutenant K.D. Gay, Pilot Officer R.W. Button – Airborne 13.59 Landed 18.44.

KG563 Flight Lieutenant N.J. Steer, Flying Officer J. Bennett, Pilot Officer D.W. McGreagor, Flight Lieutenant R.A. Barker – Airborne 14.03 Landed 19.00.

KG393 Flying Officer M.R.S. Mackay, Pilot Officer W.C. Baynes, Warrant Officer W.A. Lewis, Flight Sergeant R. Owen Take off 13.43 Landed 18.50.

KG416 Warrant Officer S. Page, Sergeant J. Potts, Warrant Officer P.H. Lee, Warrant Officer R.J. McMichael – Airborne 14.20 Landed 19.05.

KG414 Flying Officer A.J. Williams, Flight Sergeant R.F. Smith, Pilot Officer J.P. Thompson, Flight Lieutenant W.B. Gordon – Airborne 13.46 Landed 18.55.

KG337 Squadron Leader L.J. Harries, Pilot Officer J.J. Holmes, Pilot Officer J.R. Hemsworth, Pilot Officer P.C. Barratt – Airborne 13.36 Landed 18.55.

KG364 Flight Lieutenant W.F. Stone, Flight Sergeant J.P. Clarke, Pilot Officer J.D. Harrison, Pilot Officer R.F.J. Hinde – Airborne 13.45 Landed 18.50.

KG587 Flight Lieutenant H.J.G. Alford, Sergeant E.L. Leslie, Flight Sergeant J.H. Mewis, Pilot Officer A.F. Spencer – Airborne 14.19 Landed 18.55.

KG370 Pilot Officer W.R. Pring, Sergeant H.E. Colman, Flight Sergeant G.D. Gleave, Warrant Officer J.L. Sprinsteele – Airborne 13.41, Missing.

Thirteen aircraft were assigned to deliver medical bundles to DZ V. Medium flak was encountered north of the DZ, but all panniers and bundles dropped near to the target. Good fighter cover was present to protect the force of Dakotas, and crews were very pleased with this. One aircraft was hit by flak, which was bad enough for the crew to make a landing at Eindhoven. Another Dakota, KG370, piloted by Pilot Officer Pring, was reported missing and presumed shot down.

271 Squadron Allocation 23 September 1944

KG366 Squadron Leader P.D. Squires, Flight Lieutenant K.H. Dyke, Flight Lieutenant S.D. Plummer, H.M. Brown – Airborne 14.05 Landed 19.00.

KG378 Pilot Officer K.D. Hirst, Flying Officer R.P. Carmody, Flying Officer C.T. Bearne, Flight Sergeant R.L. Thomspon – Airborne 13.50 Landed 19.01.

FZ668 Flying Officer J.R. Nicoll, Flying Officer D.L. McDonnell, Warrant Officer A. Elliot, Flight Sergeant H.H. Cavas – Airborne 13.51 Landed 18.55.

FZ625 Warrant Officer G. King, Flying Officer A.T. Denny, Warrant Officer J.F. McManus, Flight Sergeant R.A.V. Faber – Airborne 13.50 Landed 18.50.

KG500 Flying Officer J. Delaney, Pilot Officer H.Z. Rogers, Flight Lieutenant G.W. Baxter, Flight Sergeant M.M. Jones – Airborne 13.47 Landed 19.05.

Just five crews were assigned to drop panniers to the 1 Airborne Division at DZ V close to Arnhem. The drop took place between 16.13 and 16.20 and all crews reported a successful and accurate drop, which consisted of sixty-one panniers and seventeen medical bundles. A strong fighter escort was provided and thankfully no enemy aircraft were encountered or observed, although there was a degree of medium flak positions that opened up on the Dakotas just north of the DZ. Slight damage was caused to FZ668 piloted by Flying Officer Nicoll, with one of the despatchers receiving a shrapnel wound to his leg. The aircraft made it safely back to base.

233 Squadron Allocation 23 September

KG433 Flight Lieutenant L. Mackie, Flying Officer W.C. Hunter, Flying Officer J. Proctor – Airborne 13.17 Landed 19.07. Only three crew members recorded.

KG440 Flying Officer G.T. Clarkson, Flying Officer J.P. Williams, Flight Sergeant N.R.H. Rains, Flying Officer C.J. Williams – Airborne 13.18 Landed 18.54.

KG400 Pilot Officer R. Chessney, Flying Officer N.C.R. Cummings, Flying Officer G.A. Coppel, Flight Sergeant R. Simmonds – Airborne 13.17 Landed 19.00.

KG403 Flying Officer R. Hyne, Warrant Officer R.W. Evered, Pilot Officer G. Fotheringham, Flying Officer J.L. Knapp – Airborne 13.18 Landed 18.48.

KG410 Warrant Officer A.L. White, Sergeant J.M. Crossman, Pilot Officer A. Edwards, Warrant Officer O.E.K. Tink – Airborne 13.18 Landed 18.50.

FZ666 Warrant Officer A.J. Green, Flight Sergeant G.C. Jeffery, Flight Lieutenant A.S. Burks, Warrant Officer H. Josland – Airborne 13.17 Landed 18.50.

KG351 Flying Officer F.W. Vines, Flying Officer G.B. Wood, Flying Officer J.K.M. Eadie, Pilot Officer F. Henry – Airborne 13.19 Landed 18.41.

KG437 Flying Officer J.A. Stewart, Flying Officer D.A. Todd, Flying Officer R. Phillips, Flying Officer W.C. Bradley – Airborne 13.18 Landed 18.55.

FZ681 Warrant Officer K.G. Cranefield, Flight Sergeant B.A. Stapleford, Flight Sergeant T. Holmes, Flight Sergeant D.M.T. Hastings – Airborne 13.19 Landed 18.50.

KG441 Flying Officer K.M. Dober, Flight Sergeant R.G. Barlow, Flight Sergeant T.V. Bartlett, Warrant Officer A. Tyrell – Airborne 13.19 Landed 18.54.

KG415 Warrant Officer N. Mills, Flight Sergeant R. Woodgate, Flight Lieutenant J. Buckton, Flight Sergeant G.G. Sparkes – Airborne 13.19 Landed 18.57.

KG585 Warrant Officer J.P.R. McRae, Flight Sergeant S. Delamere, Warrant Officer W.A. Milne, Warrant Officer S.C. Davidson – Airborne 13.19 Landed 18.55.

KG313 Flying Officer J.H. Fram, Flying Officer N.C. Trigg, Pilot Officer J.C. Pinder, Pilot Officer R.G. Johnstone – Airborne 13.20 Landed 18.58.

KG341 Pilot Officer G.P. Bailey, Pilot Officer E. Warrington, Flying Officer L.N. Williams, Flight Sergeant R.C. Fitt – Airborne 13.40 Landed 19.05.

FZ685 Flight Lieutenant P.I Burden, Flight Sergeant G.R. Caie, Flying Officer M.K. Fitzpatrick, Pilot Officer O.D. Moore – Airborne 13.40 Landed 18.50.

KG448 Warrant Officer J.W. Taylor, Flight Sergeant L.A. Edmends, Flying Officer H. Eagles, Warrant Officer W. Want – Airborne 13.42 Landed 18.59.

FZ680 Flight Lieutenant H. Barley, Flying Officer L. Greenwood, Flying Officer G.N. Taylor, Flight Lieutenant C. Ingelby – Airborne 13.42 Landed 16.58.

Seventeen aircraft were detailed to drop panniers on to DZ to the west of Arnhem to support the 1st Airborne Division. German opposition was intense, but no fighters were encountered, all the resistance being in the form of flak. This met with strong firepower from Allied fighters, who opened up as soon as the batteries started firing on the Dakotas. Although the flak positions were quite well beaten up, they did still manage to inflict damage on nine out of the seventeen Dakotas from 233 Squadron that made the journey to the Netherlands, the worst hit being FZ681 flown by Warrant Officer Cranefield and crew. Cranefield received a wound to his knee and thigh from a bullet, while the Dakota sustained a 2-foot diameter hole in the starboard wing.

Only fifteen aircraft made it to the DZ and despatched their panniers. FZ685 (Flight Lieutenant Burden) got caught in the slipstream of another Dakota and his aircraft fell suddenly, which caused the load to displace and they had to return to base to protect the crew and aircraft. FZ680 (Flight Lieutenant Barley) lost contact with the formation while evading the flak and taking evasive action. His panniers were jettisoned near to Allied convoys and the Dakota, along with the remaining sixteen aircraft, made a successful return to Blakehill.

437 Squadron Allocation 23 September

FZ545 Flight Lieutenant J.T. Reed, Flight Sergeant J.F. Roberts, Flight Lieutenant S. Smith, Warrant Officer C.F. Macleod – Airborne 13.20 Landed 18.55.

KG422 Warrant Officer H.G. Clegg, Flying Officer F.G. Svendeen, Flight Sergeant G.S.L. Burns, Flying Officer W. Zelicovitz – Airborne 13.20 Landed 18.50.
FZ679 Flight Lieutenant R.S. Down, Flight Sergeant W.R. Neal, Warrant Officer N.S. Beckett, Warrant Officer N.M. Elliston – Airborne 13.20 Landed 18.52.
KG412 Flying Officer F.E. Fitzgibbon, Warrant Officer F.H. Parsons, Warrant Officer R.W. Fox, Warrant Officer S.E. Thayer – Airborne 13.20 Landed 19.05.
KG345 Pilot Officer H.E. Rasmussen, Flying Officer C. Depol, Flight Sergeant R.E. Griffith, Flight Sergeant E.B. Steele – Airborne 13.21 Landed 19.06.
KG565 Squadron Leader C.N. McVeigh, Pilot Officer G.S. Jones, Sergeant H.B. Friedlander, Sergeant C.A. Patenaude – Airborne 13.20 Landed 19.00.
FZ669 Flying Officer R.S. Purkis, Flight Sergeant P. Kowel, Pilot Officer E.K. Walker, Flight Sergeant D.B. Fennell – Airborne 13.27 Landed 19.03.
KG325 Flying Officer R.D. Anderson, Warrant Officer W.H.E. Faircloth, Flying Officer F.C. Jenkins, Flight Sergeant P.C. McLaughlin – Airborne 13.22 Landed 18.47.
KG501 Flight Lieutenant R.J. Rosch, Flying Officer R.S. Coleman, Warrant Officer G.C. McConachie, Flying Officer J.G. Nadeau – Airborne 13.20 Landed 19.10.
KG395 Flying Officer V.J. Dale, Sergeant W.E.L. Manson, Flying Officer L.E. Priest, Sergeant J.V. Harrison – Airborne 13.22 Landed 19.10.
FZ639 Flying Officer N.W. Gustafson, Flying Officer G.R. Tozer, Flying Officer S. Allen, Warrant Officer L.E. Cox – Airborne 13.22 Landed 19.03.
KG338 Flying Officer O.A. Simmons, Pilot Officer W. Taylor, Pilot Officer G.A.A. Murdock – Airborne 13.43 Landed 19.09. Only three crew recorded.
FZ610 Flying Officer J.A. Delahunt, Flight Sergeant D.S. Cooper, Pilot Officer G.L. Breckon, Flying Officer L.D. Hornsby – Airborne 13.46 Landed 18.58.
KG312 Flying Officer E.Q. Semple, Flight Sergeant J.A. Daldorph, Warrant Officer F.A.R. MacKay, Warrant Officer M.F.H. Conrad – Airborne 13.41 Landed 18.48.

KG305 Flying Officer W.R. Pagat, Flying Officer D.L. Jack, Sergeant D.J. O'Sullivan, Flight Sergeant R.I. Pinner – Airborne 13.20 Reported missing.

Sixteen aircraft were scheduled to resupply the airborne elements at Arnhem. The mission was in response to previous resupply flights in which the supplies had fallen into enemy hands. Dakota FZ692, captained by Flying Officer Roy, did not take off and was cancelled, and Dakota KG305, captained by Flying Officer Padgett and his crew did not return to base and were presumed missing in action. Overall, fourteen aircraft made the DZ and were known to have despatched their panniers, although difficulty was experienced by the crews as many of the despatchers were on their first mission. Six panniers were dropped within the Allied lines and proved a useful marker for other aircraft to unload. An explosion occurred under the tail of Dakota KG345 (Flying Officer Rasmussen), which caused the craft to dive just after two panniers had been dropped.

KG501, Flight Lieutenant Roach, had to take immediate evasive action to miss the load from the aircraft ahead, and nine panniers slipped off the rollers and had to be returned to base. The DZ was clearly marked by Very lights and a large 'Drop Here' handmade sign to aid accuracy for the despatchers. As detailed by other squadron this day, the weather was good with excellent visibility, and fighter cover also extremely good. Enemy guns were dealt with promptly and no enemy aircraft were observed.

575 Squadron Allocation 24 September

KG608 Wing Commander Jefferson and crew – Airborne 11.20 Landed 13.25.
KG640 Flight Lieutenant Sandford and crew – Airborne 11.15 Landed 12.40.
KG602 Squadron Leader Pascall and crew – Airborne 11.20 Landed 12.45.
FZ662 Flying Officer Gambles and crew – Airborne 11.42½ Landed 12.50.
KG339 Flight Sergeant Nunn and crew – Airborne 11.25 Landed 12.55.
KG327 Flying Officer MacFarlane and crew – Airborne 11.26 Landed 12.50.
KG332 Flying Officer McGlone and crew – Airborne 11.21 Landed 12.48.
KG349 Flying Officer Dauncey and crew – Airborne 11.25 Landed 12.46.
KG380 Flight Sergeant Thorn and crew – Airborne 11.27 Landed 12.55.
FZ593 Warrant Officer Batstone and crew – Airborne 11.30 Landed 12.53.
KG449 Flight Sergeant Clarke and crew – Airborne 11.22 Landed 12.51.

KG431 Flying Officer Baker and crew – Airborne 11.23 Landed 12.56.
FZ623 Flight Sergeant Martin and crew – Airborne 11.21 Landed 12.55.
KG355 Pilot Officer Dodgson and crew – Airborne 11.25 Landed 12.55.
FZ698 Flying Officer Filshie and crew – Airborne 11.31 Landed 13.00.
KG529 Flying Officer Martin and crew – Airborne 11.25 Landed 12.54.
KG402 Group Captain Morrison and crew – Airborne 13.06 Landed 14.51.

The 16 aircraft that took off on the 24th from B.56 (Brussels), although 17 were allocated, dropped 235 panniers on the DZ that contained food and much-needed ammunition, as well as thirteen bundles of bedding. Some of the panniers did fall into a river slightly north of the DZ, but approximately 75% did land near to or on the DZ and were recoverable for the receiving troops. Two of the Dakotas landed on a grass strip after dropping their supplies. The area for the landings were roughly 1,400 yards long with a good surface. The first to land was Wing Commander Jefferson in KG608, who was followed by G.C. Morrison in KG402. Morrison had taken off later than the main force, at 13.06, dropped sixteen panniers and then proceeded to land. The fighter cover for this flight was good and managed to keep the flak subdued while the drop took place.

KG349 Squadron Leader Cragg and crew – Airborne 17.42 Landed 19.20.
KG339 Flying Officer Quinn and crew – Airborne 17.36 Landed 19.12.
KG327 Flight Lieutenant Legge and crew – Airborne 17.44 Landed 19.08.
KG602 Flight Lieutenant Bollington and crew – Airborne 17.44 Landed 18.40.

Eight aircraft were detailed to take off later in the day on the 24th to drop supplies on the DZ to the west of Arnhem but due to difficulties with loading the Dakotas only four aircraft got airborne. Two of the aircraft experienced flak south-west and north of the DZ and evasive action was taken. The load broke loose in one of the Dakotas and the door of the other aircraft became damaged. Both of these aircraft had to return to base without dropping their supplies and this was recorded as an incomplete mission. The remaining two Dakotas managed to locate the DZ and successfully dropped twenty-eight panniers that contained ammunition and wireless sets. Flak managed to damage both these two Dakotas en route, with KG327's pilot and co-pilot wounded. Both aircraft made a safe return to base.

575 Squadron Allocation for 25 September

KG529 Squadron Leader Smith and crew – Airborne 17.39 Landed 19.25.
KG402 Flying Officer MacFarlane and crew – Airborne 17.40 Landed 19.23.
KG332 Flight Sergeant Martin and crew – Airborne 17.40½ Landed 19.21.
FZ662 Pilot Officer Imison and crew – Airborne 17.41½ Landed 19.20.
KG442 Flying Officer Filshie and crew – Airborne 17.42 Landed 19.30.
FZ640 Flight Lieutenant Hauge and crew – Airborne 17.42½ Landed 19.45.
KG449 Flight Sergeant Clarke and crew – Airborne 17.41 Landed 19.03.
FZ623 Flying Officer Dauncey and crew – Did not get airborne.

Only seven of the eight aircraft detailed from 575 Squadron to take part in the last day of resupply missions to the troops located at Arnhem managed to get airborne on the evening of 25 September. Their route was set as B56 Antwerp Aerodrome, rendezvous with fighter cover thence to Bour–Leopold–Eindhoven–Veghel–DZ and return via the reciprocal route to Eindhoven and then base. Only six Dakotas managed to complete the mission, and despatched seventy-nine panniers containing rations, fourteen panniers containing medical supplies and two bundles of bedding on to the DZ. The fighter cover was very good and allowed the Dakotas to get close on the DZ to deliver the supplies.

German light machine gun fire and flak was experienced from both the north-west and east of the DZ, as well as from Veghel, Zeeland and Dinther. Aircraft KG449, flown by Flight Sergeant Clarke, had to make a forced landing as the aircraft sustained damage from flak at the DZ.

233 Squadron Aircraft Allocated 24 March, Operation Varsity

FZ635 Flying Officer A.L. White, Flight Sergeant J. Crossman, Flying Officer A. Edwards, Flying Officer C.E.K. Tink.
FZ665 Flying Officer R.R. McGowan, Warrant Officer R.W.C. Hopkins, Flight Sergeant G. Harmer, Pilot Officer C.E.P. Swann.
FZ678 Flight Lieutenant H.J. Barley, Flight Lieutenant N.R. Creal, Flight Lieutenant G. Taylor, Flight Lieutenant C. Ingeby.
FZ680 Squadron Leader A.C.L. Mackie, Flight Lieutenant K.E. Young, Flying Officer J.W. Proctor, Flight Lieutenant D.L. Goodwin.

FZ681 Flight Lieutenant F.R. Priestley, Flight Sergeant Bright J.E., Flight Lieutenant R.S. Taylor, Flight Sergeant D.G. Morris.

FZ685 Flying Officer N.R. Holloman, Flying Officer E.F.C. Hopkins, Flight Sergeant C. Harper, Flying Officer G.A.F. Beams.

FZ686 Pilot Officer A.J. Green, Flight Lieutenant D.R. Goodwin, Flight Sergeant J.W. Hayes, Pilot Officer E.G. Sharpe.

KG313 Wing Commander K.G. Mellor, Squadron Leader G.R. Prow, Flight Lieutenant A. Johnstone, Flight Lieutenant E.J. Sharpe.

KG341 Flight Lieutenant G.F. Reid, Pilot Officer W. Heigh, Warrant Officer G.C. Jeffery, Pilot Officer A.A.R. Tyrell.

KG400 Flight Lieutenant J.H. Cheaney, Flying Officer D.R. Greenslade, Flight Lieutenant H. Eagles, Flight Sergeant R.E. Simmonds.

KG403 Flight Lieutenant R.R.C. Hyne, Flight Sergeant J.H. Ellis, Pilot Officer G.B. Fotheringham, Flight Lieutenant J.L. Knapp.

KG410 Flight Lieutenant P.I. Burden, Warrant Officer Caie G.R., Flight Lieutenant L.N. Williams, Pilot Officer O'Connell.

KG415 Pilot Officer N.A.E. Mills, Flying Officer T.A. Clarke, Flight Sergeant R. Anderson, Flight Sergeant G.C. Sparkes.

KG420 Wing Commander J.C. Ridley, Flight Sergeant A. Spence, Flight Sergeant M.J. Russ, Flight Sergeant P.D. Pegg.

KG433 Pilot Officer P.N. Diamond, Warrant Officer F.J. Kenny, Flying Officer F.S. Hewson, Flight Sergeant C.M. Arnold.

KG440 Flying Officer W.C. Hunter, Flight Sergeant S.A.R. Cailes, Pilot Officer A.J. Phillips, Flight Lieutenant G. Smee.

KG441 Pilot Officer G.S. Wright, Flight Sergeant S.S. Lane, Flying Officer P.F. White, Flight Sergeant Lewis F.B.

KG447 Pilot Officer W. Morrison, Flight Sergeant Webb A.F, Flying Officer H.R Diggins, Warrant Officer F.W. Cordes.

KG448 Flight Lieutenant A. Cody, Warrant Officer D.M. Wright, Warrant Officer T.V. Bartlett, Pilot Officer O.R. Goodfellow.

KG455 Squadron Leader A.C. Blythe, Warrant Officer V. Vitte, Flying Officer B.S. Edmondson, Sergeant A. Makin.

KG559 Squadron Leader R.F. Daniell, Flight Sergeant P.O. Walker, Flying Officer P.J. Nixon, Warrant Officer E.E. Bennett.

KG561 Flying Officer G.T. Clarkson, Flight Lieutenant F.T. Thorp, Flight Sergeant N.R.H. Rains, Flying Officer C.L. Williams.

KG585 Flying Officer E.S. Smith, Warrant Officer W.P. Stephens, Flight Sergeant E.W. Allen, Flying Officer A.F. Payne.

KN258 Flight Lieutenant M.S Mass, Flight Sergeant N. Summerfield, Pilot Officer B.M. Wallington, Flying Officer H.P.C. Welch.

437 Squadron Aircraft allocated 24 March, Operation Varsity, All aircraft landed at B.75 Brussels

KG600 (DC) Wing Commander J.A. Sproule, Flying Officer P.J. Andrews, Flight Lieutenant H.C. MacNeil, Flight Lieutenant G.E. MacNeil – Airborne 07.02 Landed 11.56.

KG312 (DG) Warrant Officer R.S. Purkis, Flying Officer P. Kowel, Warrant Officer B.K. Walker, Flying Officer R.F. Platt – Airborne 07.03 Landed 11.51.

KG501 (DT) Flying Officer C.N. Roy, Flying Officer R.A. Chown, Flying Officer W.R. Bellanger, Pilot Officer G.A. Sproule – Airborne 07.04 Landed 11.51.

KG395 (DY) Flying Officer J.H. Phillips, Flight Sergeant R.W. Green, Flying Officer W.J. Hughes, Flight Sergeant R.E. Frank – Airborne 07.04 Landed 11.52.

KG654 (HK) Squadron Leader J.T. Reed, Warrant Officer M. Depew, Flight Lieutenant S. Smith, Warrant Officer J.R. Chambers – Airborne 07.06 Landed 11.52.

KN281 (DR) Flying Officer J.M. Byrnes, Flying Officer M. Kachuk, Flying Officer K.E. Hunt, Warrant Officer J.R. Chambers – Airborne 07.06 Landed 11.33.

KG425 (DM) Flight Lieutenant J.H. Burford, Pilot Officer R.S. Coleman, Flight Lieutenant D.E. Starratt, Flight Lieutenant W.J. Rowanis – Airborne 07.07 Landed 11.35.

FZ694 (DP) Flying Officer G.E. Jones, Flight Sergeant J.R. Knight, Flight Sergeant B. Friedlanger, Flight Sergeant C.A. Patennude – Airborne 07.07 Landed 11.35.

KN276 (DW) Squadron Leader W.C. Sanderson, Flight Lieutenant E.W. Brooks, Flight Lieutenant E.J. Boland, Flying Officer T.C. Hoy – Airborne 07.08 Landed 11.35.

KG412 (NT) Flying Officer H.S. Clarke, Flying Officer R.H. Barnhouse, Flight Lieutenant G.M. Lindsay, Flying Officer D. Kirick – Airborne 07.08 Landed 11.55.

KN269 (DU) Flight Lieutenant C.G. Heirville, Flying Officer H. Liebman, Flying Officer L.F. Crump, Flying Officer T. Weir – Airborne 07.09 Landed 11.36.

KG577 (DS) Flying Officer J.R. Wynne, Flying Officer J.N. Sterling, Flying Officer W.H. Simpson, Flying Officer R.J. Souter – Airborne 07.10 Landed 11.37.

KG389 (DB) Squadron Leader R.G. Joyce, Pilot Officer L.J. Botari, Flying Officer H.J. McKinley, Flying Officer J. Rechanue – Airborne 07.11 Landed 11.33.

KG310 (DD) Flying Officer W.E. McLean, Pilot Officer T.E. Stewart, Flight Lieutenant D.A. Cox, Pilot Officer R. Berger – Airborne 07.12 Landed 11.39.

KG354 (DE) Flight Lieutenant C.F. Payne, Flying Officer J.C. Holborn, Flight Sergeant T.R. Dennison Broad, Warrant Officer H.G. Tennant – Airborne 07.13 Landed 11.59.

KG452 (DF) Flying Officer K.E. Rasmussen, Flight Sergeant S.S. Sutfin, Flying Officer C. DePol, Warrant Officer E.B. Steele – Airborne 07.15 Landed 11.40.

KG529 (DJ) Flight Lieutenant E.Q. Semple, Flying Officer R.H. Dickson, Flying Officer J.P. Mitchell, Warrant Officer R.A. Heading – Airborne 07.17 Landed 11.40.

KG427 (NA) Flying Officer J.E. Seary, Flight Lieutenant E. Roberts, Flying Officer J.E. Gillett, Warrant Officer J.S. Tomshak – Airborne 07.18 Landed 11.41.

KN256 (DL) Flight Lieutenant J.G. Findlster, Flying Officer K.E. Hadfield, Flying Officer J.N. Russell, Warrant Officer J.J. Sargeant – Airborne 07.20 Landed 11.41.

FZ693 (DR) Flying Officer J. Wells, Flying Officer W.H. Porter, Flying Officer F.G. Svendsen, Flight Sergeant E. Chinsky – Airborne 07.21 Landed 11.43.

KK211 (ND) Flight Lieutenant A.A.R. Decks, Pilot Officer L.C. Hoskins, Flying Officer L. Chambers, Flying Officer G.S. McEwen – Airborne 07.32 Landed 11.43.

FZ669 (DQ) Pilot Officer H.G. Clegg, Flight Sergeant P.J. Parrott, Flying Officer J.D. Simpson, Flying Officer W. Selicoyits – Airborne 07.23 Landed 11.43.

KG345 (DV) Flight Lieutenant V.J. Dale, Warrant Officer D.W. MacKay, Flight Lieutenant A.E. Priest, Warrant Officer J.B. Harrison – Airborne 07.24 Landed 11.43.

KG565 (DK) Pilot Officer D.A. Strenz, Warrant Officer R. Laidlaw, Flight Lieutenant E.A. Hurd, Flying Officer F.A. McLeod – Airborne 07.25 Landed 11.43.

Two aircraft were held in reserve but did not take part:

FZ659 (NS) Flying Officer R.J. Durrant, Flying Officer A.B. Armstrong, Flying Officer A.D. Johnston, Pilot Officer W.G. Hardy.

KG394 (DO) Flying Officer T. Lindsay, Flight Sergeant D.J. Greenslade, Flying Officer J.H. Brown, Flying Officer W.H. Morris.

271 Squadron Relocated to Gosfield 24 March 1945

KG622 Lieutenant Colonel P.S. Joubert AFC, Pilot Officer E.R. Hall, Flight Lieutenant R. Johnson, Flying Officer H. Daley – Airborne 06.25 Landed 14.07.

KG562 Flight Lieutenant P.A.D. Hellon, Flight Sergeant N.K. Holmes, Pilot Officer A. Elliot, Flying Officer G.R. Harvey – Airborne 06.25 Landed 14.08.

KG406 Squadron Leader A.R.T. Beddow, Flying Officer H.T. Hearn, Flying Officer J.S. Dolan, Warrant Officer A.G. Holt – Airborne 06.28 Landed 17.12.

KG564 Flight Lieutenant J.I. MacNeil, Warrant Officer H. Green, Pilot Officer A. McHughi, Flight Sergeant H.O.W. Talbot – Airborne 06.29 Landed 17.55.

KG500 Flying Officer K.C. Wilson, Flight Sergeant D. Somerfield, Flying Officer J. Foster, Sergeant W.E.P. Rumble – Airborne 06.30 Landed 14.00.

KG408 Flying Officer D. Wood, Flight Sergeant H.L. Eigele, Pilot Officer K. Carber, Pilot Officer T.B. Adamson – Airborne 06.30 Landed 12.40.

FZ613 Flight Lieutenant R.P. Carmody, Flight Sergeant H.S. Thompson, Warrant Officer R.D. Howes, Flight Sergeant D.R. Fennell – Airborne 06.50 Landed 12.45.

KG378 Pilot Officer T. Parfitt, Flight Sergeant M.B. Flanagan, Flying Officer R.A. Davies, Pilot Officer F. Richardson – Airborne 06.50 Landed 12.50.

KG362 Flight Lieutenant W.K. Murphy, Flight Sergeant F.R. Pearson, Flying Officer R.H. Jungwirth, Flight Lieutenant J.M. Browne – Airborne 06.53 Landed 12.43.

FZ607 Flying Officer K.P. O'Donnell, F. Sergeant L.A. Murray, Flying Officer T.R. Holdsworth, Pilot Officer G.J. Watters – Airborne 06.55 Landed 12.35.

KG357 Flying Officer S.E. Norris, Flight Sergeant G. Foster, Flying Officer D.R. Peirce, Warrant Officer L.R. Laking – Airborne 06.58 Landed 13.45.

KG430 Pilot Officer H. Farrar, Warrant Officer D.J. Lewis, Warrant Officer T.J. Erratt, Flight Sergeant J.A. Proctor – Airborne 06.57, Landed 14.20.

512 Squadron Allocation 24 March

KG590 (AP) Wing Commander R.G. Dutton, Flight Lieutenant J.G.S. Houdret, Flight Lieutenant J. Williams, Flight Lieutenant A.T.S. Porter – Airborne 06.00 Landed 07.30.

KK193 (HK) Squadron Leader W.A. Mostyn-Brown, Air Commander L. Darvall, Flight Lieutenant J.R. King, Flying Officer H.E. Robertson – Airborne 06.01, Landed 07.35.

KG641 (AC) Squadron Leader P.A. Clarke, Flight Lieutenant A.D. Burt, Flight Lieutenant W.R. James, Flying Officer H.M. Anderson – Airborne 06.02, Landed 07.35.

KG322 (UB) Flight Lieutenant C.P. Thomas, Flight Sergeant J.W. Beazley, Flying Officer T. Corlett, Warrant Officer B. Bergin – Airborne 06.03, Landed 07.20.

KG582 (AA) Flight Lieutenant A.E. Carpenter, Flight Sergeant L.O. Cann, Warrant Officer J.M. Bowles, Warrant Officer D.R. Miller – Airborne 06.04, Landed 08.00.

KG323 (AG) Flight Lieutenant D.W. Marshall, Flight Sergeant J. Priestley, Flight Sergeant E. Jenkins, Sergeant A.R. Hill – Airborne 06.05, Landed 07.45.

KG616 (AF) Warrant Officer D.W.E. Smith, Flight Sergeant P.N. Spencer, Sergeant K.C. Thwaites, Flight Sergeant A.H. Doleman – Airborne 06.06, Landed 07.40.

FZ647 (AH) Pilot Officer R.G. Dight, Flight Sergeant S.S. Sanderson, Flying Officer H.J. Batten, Flight Sergeant L.J. Bryce – Airborne 06.07, Landed 07.25.

KG373 (AB) Pilot Officer W.B. Garvin, Flight Sergeant S.L.W. Paddington, F/A D.W. Williams, Flight Sergeant A.J. Williams – Airborne 06.08, Landed 07.30.

KG333 (AN) Squadron Leader T.R. Russell, Squadron Leader K.G. Green-Acre, Flight Lieutenant V.G. Horgan, Flight Lieutenant R.C. Briscoe – Airborne 06.09, Landed 07.40.

FZ649 (AK) Flight Lieutenant C.A. Chew, Flight Sergeant H. Gravett, Warrant Officer G.C. Newman, Warrant Officer P.J. Hughes – Airborne 06.10, Crashed 04.10.

FZ696 (AQ) Lt J.J. Offenhiser, Flight Sergeant S. Delamere, Pilot Officer M.A.S. Pickering, Flying Officer W.C. Bevington – Airborne 06.11, Landed 07.35.

FZ651 (AJ) Flying Officer M.G. Finn, Flight Sergeant W.A. Boyes, Flying Officer E. Blazey, Warrant Officer J. Davidson – Airborne 06.12, Landed 07.45.

KG344 (AL) Flight Lieutenant R.D. McNicol, Flying Officer D.V. Thompson, Warrant Officer C.P. Thomas, Flight Sergeant L.F. Christie – Airborne 06.13, Landed 07.50.

KG348 (AO) Flying Officer P. Murray, Flight Sergeant P.J. Henson, Flying Officer P. Shallcross, Flight Sergeant T. Draper – Airborne 06.14, Landed 07.30.

KG623 (AN) Flying Officer J. Gibson, Flight Lieutenant J. Ismay, Flying Officer P.G. Griffiths, Sergeant J. Sabine – Airborne 06.15, Landed 07.05.

KG361 (AU) Flight Lieutenant C.H. McLeod, Flying Officer N.B. Hopper, Flight Lieutenant E.P. Butcher, Flight Sergeant D. Claydon – Airborne 06.16, Landed 07.40.

KG598 (AZ) Flying Officer H.T.G. Hill, Flight Sergeant O.T. Williams, Flying Officer B.C. Sitch, Flight Sergeant R.L. Geisler (RAAF) – Airborne 06.18, Landed 07.20.

KG330 (AT) Flying Officer R.A.S. Benson, Flight Sergeant S.F. Sargent, Flight Lieutenant J.S. Starr, Pilot Officer J. Oxley – Airborne 06.19, Landed 07.40.

KG377 (AS) Flying Officer L. Flax, Flying Officer A.W. Hatchman, Pilot Officer J. Bradley, Flight Sergeant J. Goodall – Airborne 06.20, Landed 07.40.

KG558 (AW) Flying Officer H. Levin, Flight Sergeant T.E. Symes, Flying Officer H.E.E. Corby, Flying Officer R.T. Britton – Airborne 06.21, Landed 07.40.

KG368 (AY) Warrant Officer S. Hildrew, Flight Sergeant H.M.V. Birkby, Warrant Officer W.K. Pattison, Pilot Officer A.B. Friend – Airborne 06.22, Landed 07.50.

KG371 (AX) Flight Lieutenant G.S. Moss, Flying Officer D.V. Gay, Pilot Officer H. Howarth, Sergeant W.E. Summers – Airborne 06.23, Landed 07.40.

575 Squadron Allocation 24 March

KN290 Wing Commander E.G. Deanesly, Flight Lieutenant Hemsley, Flight Lieutenant R.E. Charlton, Flying Officer Atkinson – Airborne 06.33, Landed 11.17.

KN296 Squadron Leader P.T. Cragg, Flight Lieutenant Cottam, Flight Lieutenant H.H. Hall, Warrant Officer C.G. Fisher – Airborne 06.34, Landed 11.26.

KG431 Flight Lieutenant Clark, Flight Lieutenant Hazelton, Flight Sergeant Arjeant, Flight Sergeant Sheppard – Airborne 06.34½, Landed 11.19.

KG325 Flight Lieutenant C. Wharton, Flight Lieutenant Marsh, Flying Officer Froggatt, Warrant Officer Yates – Airborne 06.35, Landed 11.23.

KG615 Flight Lieutenant Sandford, Warrant Officer Chapman, Warrant Officer Siddons, Pilot Officer Fennell – Airborne 06.36, Landed 11.17½.

KG320 Flight Lieutenant Ellis, Pilot Officer Chitty, Warrant Officer Turner, Flying Officer Warren – Airborne 06.37, Landed 11.26.

KG608 Pilot Officer Parker, Sergeant Willcock, Pilot Officer Hurcomb, Warrant Officer Wade – Airborne 06.37½, Landed 11.24.

KG432 Warrant Officer H. Clark, Sergeant Minton, Warrant Officer Wimbridge, Flight Sergeant P. Thompson – Airborne 06.38, Landed 11.28½.

KG447 Sergeant Goulding, Flight Sergeant Peach, Flying Officer Jeffery, Flight Sergeant Frankland – Airborne 06.39, Landed 11.22.

KG602 Squadron Leader D.C. Pascall, Flight Lieutenant Doig, Flight Lieutenant Fleet, Warrant Officer Bullen – Airborne 06.40, Landed 11.10.

KG328 Flight Lieutenant Beach, Flight Lieutenant Sheridan, Flight Sergeant Griffith, Flight Sergeant Beaver – Airborne 06.40½, Landed 11.10.

KG339 Flight Lieutenant Atkin, Flying Officer Willox, Flying Officer Rostron, Flight Lieutenant Perkins – Airborne 06.41, Landed 11.06.

FZ698 Flying Officer Player, Flying Officer Spinks, Flying Officer Partridge, Flying Officer Taylor – Airborne 06.42, Landed 11.02.

KG620 Flying Officer Imison, Flight Sergeant Scarlett, Flying Officer Stapleton, Warrant Officer Conway – Airborne 06.43, Landed 11.09.

KG344 Pilot Officer Elliott, Flight Sergeant Goodwin, Flight Sergeant Beck, Warrant Officer Wall – Airborne 06.43½, Landed 11.10.

FZ662 Pilot Officer Wallace, Flight Sergeant Harris, Flight Sergeant Marsden, Warrant Officer Seaniger – Airborne 06.44, Landed 11.24.

KN295 Squadron Leader Perry, Pilot Officer Alford, Pilot Officer Porter, Pilot Officer Prior – Airborne 06.45, Landed 11.15.

FZ623 Flight Lieutenant Rees, Flight Sergeant Ashdown, Flight Sergeant M. Thompson, Flying Officer Hoy – Airborne 06.45½, Landed 11.20.

KG326 Flight Lieutenant Macfarlane, Flight Sergeant Soward, Flight Lieutenant Hunter, Pilot Officer Peardon – Airborne 06.46½, Landed 11.20.

KG332 Flying Officer McGlone, Flying Officer McCormick, Flight Lieutenant Curry, Warrant Officer Nicholson – Airborne 06.47, Landed 11.10.

KG327 Flying Officer Dauncey, Flying Officer Sedgwick, Flying Officer Evans, Flight Sergeant Jackson – Airborne 06.48, Landed 11.05.

KG647 – Flying Officer Dodgson, Flight Sergeant Huband, Flight Lieutenant Budden, Flying Officer Headifen – Airborne 06.48½, Landed 11.15.

KG359 Warrant Officer Martin, Sergeant Waite, Flying Officer Jenkins, Pilot Officer Blugrind – Airborne 06.49, Landed 11.12.

FZ593 Warrant Officer W.S. Clark, Warrant Officer Howard, Flight Sergeant Seddon, Pilot Officer Strickland – Airborne 06.50, Landed 11.15.

No. 48 Squadron also participated in Operation Varsity with twelve Dakotas and glider combinations and two spares on 24 March. Unfortunately, no records could be located that details aircraft used and crews that flew. KG439, piloted by Flight Lieutenant Whitfield, and KG364, Squadron Leader L.J. Harries, are the only ones confirmed to date.

Acknowledgements

Seb Davey; Geoff Simpson, *Dakotas at Down Ampney*; Vince Povey; Blakehill Farm, The War to Wildlife Project; Kara Neave, *A Nightingale Flew*; Cricklade Museum; The National Archives; Lee Barton; RAF Historical Branch; RAF Squadron Operational Records; Don Sproule; Jason Holloway; Zaur Eylanbekov; Todd Shugart and R. Bennett.

Endnotes

Chapter 1: Daks Arrive at Down Ampney (February 1944)

1. RAF Hampstead Norris – 1.3 miles north-east of Reading used extensively to train glider pilots.
2. Vic – Three aircraft flying in a V-shaped formation.
3. DZ – Drop Zone – an area where parachutists or supplies are designated to land.
4. Gee – A radio navigation system that measures the time delay between two radio signals to determine a fixed location.
5. Rebecca – An airborne transceiver and antenna system and a short-range radio navigation system used for the dropping of airborne troops and supplies, used in conjunction with Eureka.
6. Eureka – A ground-based transponder that worked in conjunction with Rebecca and calculated the radio signals returned, the recognition of beacons.
7. Roller conveyer – A method of rolling panniers along the aircraft's fuselage.
8. Bomb rack – A small cradle used on the bottom of the wings near to the fuselage for the carriage of small bombs.
9. Oxford (Airspeed) – Training and general support aircraft used in large numbers by various squadrons throughout the RAF.

Chapter 2: Intensive Training and Joint Exercises (March–May)

10. Barrage balloon – Device for stopping enemy aircraft operating over areas due to the cable restricting flying activities and increasing the risks for the attacking aircraft.
11. MI9 – Military Intelligence unit number 9.
12. Star shell – Explosive ordnance designed to burst in the air and light up during the hours of darkness.
13. NF Test – Night flying test plotting.

14. MSL – Mean Sea Level.
15. TRV – Timed Rendezvous Point.
16. OTU – Operational Training Unit.
17. SHEAF – Supreme Headquarters Allied Expeditionary Force.
18. RASC – Royal Army Service Corps (Despatchers).
19. ASR – Air Sea Rescue.

Chapter 3: Something's Afoot (June)

20. ALO – Air Liaison Officer.
21. Sealed – Personnel were confined to camp to maintain security prior to operations.
22. Escape purse – Small bags carrying local currency, compass and other aids.
23. DR – Dead reckoning point.
24. Overlord – Code name for the invasion of France (D-Day).
25. Anti-Air Landing Obstacle – A series of wooden spikes (poles) placed at 45 degrees to prevent gliders landing.
26. Hamilcar – A large British tank-carrying glider.
27. AGL – Above Ground Level.
28. Occults – Lights that flashed a series of Morse coded letters to help crews fix their positions prior to a drop.
29. Pundits – Flashing beacons using Morse to identify a friendly airfield.
30. RV – Rendezvous Point.
31. Station Homing Signals – A series of radio signals that increased in time frequency the closer an aircraft got to the homing beacon.
32. Window – Small foil strips dropped from aircraft to confuse enemy radar.
33. DBST – Double British summertime. Clocks were put forward two hours to increase the amount of daylight to save energy and decrease the amount of blackout time.
34. Sticks – Number of paratroopers per aircraft (fifteen to eighteen).
35. Arrestor parachute – A method of stopping a glider in a short distance.
36. HGSU – Heavy Glider Support Unit.
37. LCI – Landing Craft Infantry.
38. Pull off point – Designated map coordinates where the glider would be released from the towing aircraft.
39. ASI – Air Speed Indicator.

40. RUR – Royal Ulster Regiment.
41. Very cartridges – Used in handheld Very pistols to send a flare.
42. AOC – Air Officer Commanding.
43. ALG – Advanced Landing Grounds, temporary landing strips.
44. FSP – Fixed Steel Planking.
45. WAAF – Women's Auxiliary Air Force.

Chapter 4: Service Français (July, August)

46. BOAC – British Overseas Airways Company.
47. POW – Prisoner of War.
48. Balbo – Formations of a large number of aircraft or gliders.
49. Travel Corridor – Designated route with pre-determined waypoints and map references for flights between England and France/Belgium.
50. VHF – Very High Frequency (Radio).
51. ADRU – Advanced Defence Radar Unit.
52. Palliasse – Thin straw mattress that can be padded out for use, then rolled into a small cylindrical shape for carrying.
53. MI10 – Military Intelligence unit number 10.
54. A12G – British Intelligence Unit.
55. War Dog School – British School for Dog Training.
56. Charleying – Jovial, enjoyment, acting the 'Right Charlie'.
57. PIAT – Projector Infantry Anti-Tank Weapon.
58. Spandau – Colloquial term for a German machine gun emplacement.
59. MT – Motor Transport.
60. RE – Royal Engineers.
61. German miniature tank – Goliath tracked vehicle, remote-controlled unmanned, electric or petrol driven.

Chapter 5: Time to Shine – Market Garden (September)

62. Tropical kit – Lightweight clothing and uniform for hot climates.
63. Operation Comet – The original name for what became Operation Market Garden.
64. Polder land – Low-lying land forms by enclosed embankments known as dykes, usually comprised of peat.
65. H-Hour – The time at which to launch an attack or commencement of an operation.

66. IX USTCC – Ninth Air Force United States Troop Carrier Command.
67. ADGB – Air Defence of Great Britain.
68. D-1 – The day before the first operational flight, D-Day.
69. TCSP – Transport Command Special Planning, located at RAF Eastcote in the London Borough of Hillingdon.
70. March – town in Cambridgeshire.
71. SDP – Supply drop point.
72. Beacon – Hand-held light source powered by a battery pack.
73. Flak suit – All-body covering to aid the protection against flak.
74. JG26 – Jagdgeschwader 26 German Fighter Wing (26) of the Luftwaffe.
75. Aldis lamp – Visual signalling device for optical communications by flashing lamp using Morse code.
76. Chalk markings – Numbers written on the side of gliders in chalk for easy identification, Nose artwork, usually humorous, was applied by troops who would travel on board the glider.
77. Blitz Buggies – Service truck or another name for a Willys jeep.
78. KG305 – Error in reporting this serial as no Dakota had this number allocated. The first batch of Dakotas started at KG310.
79. Quisling – A traitor who collaborated with the enemy forces occupying their country, named after the Norwegian Vidkun Quisling.
80. IO – Intelligence Officer.
81. Lek – River in the western part of the Netherlands.
82. LAA – Light anti-aircraft regiment.
83. Mae West – An inflatable life jacket that was named after the actress, who was known for her generous bust.
84. U/S – Unserviceable.
85. Green (1) – Received a green flare from Control Tower.
86. Chindits – Long-range groups involved in special operations with the British and Indian armies during 1943 and 1944.
87. Green – Signal light to show the despatch of panniers/paratroopers from the aircraft.

Chapter 6: Keeping up the Support (October, November)

88. ETO – European Theatre of Operations.
89. LACW – Leading Aircraftwoman.

90. Boffins – Term for anyone involved in engineering, technical or scientific research and development. Sometimes viewed as quirky or odd.
91. AMB – Ambulance.
92. BLA – British Liberation Army.
93. Steel Planking – Metal strips that would allow movement of aircraft and heavy artillery and trucks over wet or muddy ground.

Chapter 7: Winter Tales (December, January 1945)

94. NCO – Non-commissioned officer.
95. NAAFI – Navy, Army and Air Force Institutes.
96. Operation Bodenplatte – The Germans' last attempt to launch a major attack through the Low Countries, January 1945.
97. LAC – Leading Aircraftman.
98. ADRU – Air Despatch and Reception Unit.
99. CAEC – Casualty Air Evacuation Centre.
100. Nissen hut – A prefabricated steel structure made from cylindrical corrugated iron skin, mainly used as barrack accommodation.
101. AFHW – Air Force Headquarters West.
102. NDHQ – National Defence Headquarters.
103. BAC – Brigade Ammunition Column.

Chapter 8: One Last Hurrah, Operation Varsity (February, March)

104. A, B Relief Landing Grounds – A = American, B = British.
105. P&F – Position and Finder.
106. Distressed airmen – Airmen who were suffering from mental health issues and needed medical treatment.
107. Fuel – At this late stage of the war the Luftwaffe had very little or none available for their aircraft.
108. FAAA – First Allied Airborne Army.
109. SASO – Senior Air Staff Officer.
110. Upward identification and formation lights – A series of different coloured lights, white, red, green and amber, used for formation flying and identification at their home airfield as different combinations of colours to confirm friendly forces.

111. ETA – Estimated time of arrival.

Chapter 9: War Drawdown, End of Hostilities Within the European Theatre (April, May)

112. VC – Victoria Cross, the highest British military medal that can be awarded.
113. Marshal Zhukov – Russia's military commander of the Belorussian front for the attack and eventual success on to Berlin. He accepted the German surrender.
114. RAFVR – Royal Air Force Volunteers Reserves.
115. Unconditional surrender – Allies' requirement for the surrender of Germany, with no negotiated peace.

Chapter 10: The Flying Nightingales

116. Special Operations – SOE, Special Operations Executive, who operated behind enemy lines on covert missions.
117. Air ambulance duties – Casualty evacuation flights.
118. *A Nightingale Flew* – A book written by Karen Neaves about the Flying Nightingales.
119. Slings – Used for supporting stretchers inside aircraft while carrying injured personnel.

Chapter 11: Aircraft and Crews

120. KG391, recorded twice for two different crews, aircraft codes AD/AG for 48 Squadron, on 5 June. Both sets of crews are listed for the same Dakota serial.
121. No. 575 Squadron, 6 June 1944 – A time and crew discrepancy exists with KG363 and KG332. KG363 is recorded as landing at 22.40 and KG332 as getting airborne at 22.30, with the same crew. This must have been a recording error made during this busy day and night of operations.
122. Reserves – Crews that were available to fly if any technical or medical issues affected any of those assigned to fly.
123. Dakota FZ671 – An error in recording the information accurately at the time. The same aircraft is detailed twice but with a different crew. It is suspected that one serial was recorded incorrectly.

Index

1st Division, 6, 8, 138
1 Para Division, 135
1st Airborne Division, 88, 91–2, 94, 104, 111, 113, 116–9, 127, 130, 139, 191
1st Air Landing Brigade Group, 95–6, 100–1, 103–4
1st British Airborne Division, 93
1st British Airborne Corps, 97, 101
1st Battalion, Royal Ulster Rifles, 29
1st Ulster Rifles, 174
1st Parachute Brigade, 95, 100, 104
1st Polish Armoured Division, 86
1st Independent Paratrooper Brigade, Polish, 15, 92, 96, 106, 116–7
1st Battalion, Border Regiment, 127
1st Troop Carrier Command, 168
2nd Army, 29, 93, 135, 138
2nd Battalion Guards Armoured Regiment, 114
2nd Battalion, Independent Paratrooper Brigade, Polish, 15
2nd Air Landing Light A.A Battery, 92–3
2nd Battalion South Staffordshire Regiment, 127
2nd Parachute Battalion, 104, 111
2nd Tactical Air Force, 97
3 Casualty Clearing Station, 149
3rd Parachute Brigade, 5, 22, 26–7, 33–4, 40–2
No3 Commando, 54

4th Parachute Brigade, 96, 104
5th Guards, Armoured Brigade, 104, 111, 113
5th Panzer Group, 86
5 Parachute Regiment, 4
5th Parachute Brigade, 33–4, 39, 41, 83
6th Airlanding Brigade, 31, 33–4
6th British Airborne Division, 26, 31–3, 35, 38, 49, 174, 177
7th British Field Dressing Station, 143
9th Parachute Brigade, 26
9th Parachute Battalion, 43
10th Battalion HQ, 153
15 Field Dressing Station, 149
15th Air Force, 173
17th (US) Airborne Divisions, 177
21st Army Group, 91, 172, 182
22nd Battalion Paratroopers, 15
21st Independent Parachute Company, 95, 97, 100, 117, 135
22nd Independent Parachute Company, 36
30 Corps (Army), 91–2, 133, 145
7 Armoured Division, 67
7 Battalion Paratroopers, 4
8th Battalion, Parachute Regiment, 25
11th Armoured Division, 143
12 Battalion Paratroopers, 4
13th (Lancashire) Parachute Battalion, 26
43rd Division, 116
52nd Infantry Division, 73, 78–9

Index 277

52nd (Lowland) Division, (Airportable), 92–3
52nd Lowland Regiment, 118
58th L.A.A Regiment, 143
81st (US) Airborne Division, 113
82nd (US) Airborne Division, 92, 104, 111, 114
101st (US) Airborne Division, 92–3, 105, 111
223rd Company, RASC, 151
365th Fighter Group, 174
379th Bomber Group, 174
410th Bombardment Group, 174
442 Transport Carrier Group, 115
878th (US) Aviation Engineer Battalion, 92–3, 96
9 A.E.F, 115
91 F.S.P, 60
39 Wing, 69
83 Wing, 57
110 Wing, 184
111 Wing, 159, 186
121 Wing, 61
125 Wing, 149
126 Wing, 59
144 Wing, 57
247 Wing, 60
107 OTU, 16, 156
2 Group, 97
3 Group, 37
11 Group, 19, 37
38 Group, 3, 33, 36–8, 41, 43–4, 46, 49, 92–6, 98, 107, 112, 114, 116–19, 121, 135, 172, 176
46 Group, 2–3, 5, 7, 10, 16–18, 33, 36–8, 41–2, 44, 46, 72, 84, 87–8, 90, 92–3, 95–6, 102, 107, 112, 114–19, 121–2, 129, 156, 160–2, 164–6, 169, 172, 176–7, 179, 184–7, 190–4

48 Squadron, 1–4, 6–9, 11, 13–9, 21–3, 27–9, 38, 54, 56–7, 59–61, 69–73, 77–9, 84–8, 90, 107, 115, 119–20, 122, 127–31, 143, 145–6, 149, 155, 158, 161, 165–6, 171, 174–5, 185, 187, 196
1 Squadron, 60
118 Squadron, 72
165 Squadron, 60
194 Squadron, 37
199 Squadron, 38
216 Squadron, 158
233 Squadron, 2, 6, 8–9, 11, 15, 23–4, 31, 38, 40–1, 57, 69–73, 82, 85–7, 120, 127, 129, 139, 155, 165–6, 171, 175
251 Squadron, 84
271 Squadron, 2–6, 9, 11–19, 21, 23, 27, 29–31, 38, 55–7, 59–60, 69–73, 78, 82–4, 86–8, 90, 107, 113, 119–20, 127–31, 147–51, 155, 157–9, 161, 163–7, 169–71, 173–5, 183–7, 196
295 Squadron, 37, 40
296 Squadron, 37, 39
297 Squadron, 37, 39, 42
298 Squadron, 38–9
299 Squadron, 37
313 (Polish) Squadron, 72
437 (Canadian) Squadron, 90–1, 122–3, 126–9, 155, 157, 161, 164, 166, 171, 174, 184, 186
512 Squadron, 1–2, 4, 6–7, 9–10, 14–18, 20, 26, 31, 38, 52–3, 58, 63, 66, 69, 71–3, 78, 83–4, 88–90, 126–7, 129, 135–7, 155, 164–7, 172, 175–81, 186, 188
575 Squadron, 1–2, 4, 6–7, 9–11, 13–15, 17–8, 26, 38, 58, 69, 71–2, 84, 87–9, 102, 115, 118, 127, 136–7, 155–6, 158, 162–6, 171–2, 175, 180

570 Squadron, 37, 40
644 Squadron, 38–9

A12G, 79
Aachen, 92
Abingdon, 120
Airborne Armoured Reconnaissance Regiment, 34
Airborne Forward Delivery, Airfield Group (AFDAG), 92
Air Ambulance, 194
Air Despatchers, 84
Air Marshal, 2nd TAF, 115
Adam, Flying Officer, 121
ADRU, 74, 165, 171
Agar, Flying Officer D.C., 12
Albert Canal, 91, 110
Alexander, Flight Lieutenant R.W., 123
Altmann, Squadron Leader R.O., 12
Albemarles, 37–42, 44, 54, 92, 137
Aldeburgh, 98, 121, 123
Aldis Lamp, 64, 114, 117
Alexander, Flight Lieutenant R.W., 123, 125, 139
Alford, Corporal Lydia, 194–5
Alford, Flight Lieutenant, 29, 80, 145
ALG, 60
Ampney, 3–4, 6, 10, 20, 29–30, 70, 84, 180, 184
Anderson, Flying Officer (Canadian), 49
Andover, 4, 9
Antwerp, 91, 157, 164, 183
Alcester, 15
Alexandria, 158
Amblie (B.14), 70
Amfreville, 27, 31
Amelles-sur-Mer, 57
Amiens, 89
Anfield, Sergeant W.N., 161

Armoured Division Grenadier Guards, 114
Arnhem, 88–9, 91–5, 97–8, 100, 104–105, 111, 113–14, 116, 118–19, 121–31, 134–5, 137–40, 151–5, 178, 184, 187, 190–1
Asnelles, 32
ASR, 19
Argentan, 12–13
Athens, 158
Australia, 199
Australian, 48, 163
Austin, Fight Lieutenant, R.B, Camp Commandant Rear of HQ 83 Group, 111
Avera, Flying Officer W.W. (US), 115
Avro Anson, 19, 61–2, 71, 73, 84–5, 149, 162
Aylesbury, 4, 9, 18, 84

B-17 Flying Fortress, 165
Bailey, Flight Lieutenant G.J., 159
Bailey, Warrant Officer, 32
Balbo, Operation, 70
Ballater Bridge, 5
Balleytine, Flying Officer Alec, 151
Ballotyne, Pilot Officer E., 12
Banbury, 4, 18
Banville, 75
Barfleur, 69, 85, 87
Barritt, Wing Commander, 77
Basenville, 57
Bath, 195
Bayley, Flight Sergeant, 148
Bazenville (B.2), 59–60
Barkston Heath, 6
Barville, 31
Basingstoke, 2
Battle of Britain, 19
Bayeux, 12, 74, 76

Bayeux, Prefect of, 73
Beachy Head, 169
Beaulieu, 164
Beauvais, 89, 127
Beck, Flying Officer, 5, 149
Beddow, Flight Lieutenant, 149
Beer, Elaine, 196
Berlin, 173, 185–6, 188–90
Belfast, 162
Belgium, 32, 88, 90, 101, 105, 108, 125, 155–6, 158, 160, 164, 181, 186, 191, 197
Benouville, 33–6
Beny-sur-Mer (B.4), 59, 196
Berger, Warrant Officer N.I., 25
Berrow, 15
Berkhamsted, 15
Beta, 174
Bethune, 178
Bf 109, 164
Birch, RAF, 174–5
Birlison, Warrant Officer, 144
Birmingham, 162
Bizz II, Exercise, 5
Blakehill Farm, RAF, 2–3, 7–9, 14, 21, 23, 25, 29, 31, 38, 40, 57–9, 70–3, 79, 82, 84, 88, 90–1, 121–4, 126, 129, 131, 139, 154–5, 157, 159–60, 164, 166–7, 169–171, 176, 183, 185–6, 195–6
Bletchley, 73
BOAC, 71
Bognor Regis, 31
Bomber Command, 97, 156
Booth DFC, Wing Commander M., 12, 16, 27, 120, 130, 163
Bodwin, Flying Officer, 13
Bolthead, 71
Boscombe Down, 18
Bordeaux, 166

Bourg, 125–6, 135, 139
Bowhill GBE, KCB, CMG, DSO, AOC Command Transport Command Sir Frederick, 13, 169
Boxtel, 130
Brackley, 4
Bradbury DFC, Group Captain J., 55, 71, 86, 130, 159
Braintree, 9, 173
Bradwell, 125–6
Bramwell, 121
Brandenburg Gate, 190
Breda, 92
Brennan, Corporal, Nursing Orderly, 83
Bridgnorth, 162
Bridgewood, Squadron Leader, 12
Bridport, 5
British 2nd Army, 29, 32
Brize Norton, 37
Bodenplatte, Operation, 164
Briscoe, Flight Lieutenant, 179
Broadwell, RAF, 1–9, 14, 16–17, 20–1, 27, 31, 38, 53, 57–8, 61, 69, 72, 83–4, 89–90, 102, 115, 129, 131, 136, 154, 156–8, 160–6, 169, 170–1, 175–7, 180–1, 183, 185–6, 196
Brown, Warrant Officer J.A., 11
Browning, Major General, 23
Browning, Lieutenant General F.A.M., HQ1 (British) Airborne Corps, 92
Bruges, 138, 161, 197
Brummwell, Flying Officer, 9
Brussels, 88, 102, 115, 116, 118, 124–5, 133, 139, 145, 148, 156, 166, 170–1, 174, 179, 180–2, 185–7, 191
Brussels Evere, 148, 150, 155, 164, 167, 175, 183
Brussels (Melsbroek B.58), 90, 101, 116, 156
Bury St. Edmunds, 9

Bullseye, Operation, 14
Butterworth, Sergeant M., 12, 150
Byrnes, Flying Officer J., 86

Cabourg, 24, 26
Caen, 24–6, 32–4, 36, 48, 54, 57, 65, 67, 76–7, 79, 135
Caen, canal, 30, 32–4, 50–1, 65
Cairo West, 158
Calais, 185
Cambridge, 180
Campbell, Flying Officer T.C. (US), 115, 139
Campbell, Captain, 130
Campbell, Flying Nightingale LACW, Margaret, WAAF, 157
Campbell, Flight Lieutenant (medical), 162
Camilly, 58
Canada, 167, 172
Cap D'Antifer, 26
Cap de la Hague, 73, 85
Cap Griz Nez, 174, 178
Carantan, 87
Carpiquet (Aerodrome), 77
Carr, Sergeant Charlie, 29, 30, 48, 50–2
Casualty Evacuation Centre, 49, 161
Cauilly, 58
Celle, 183
Cirencester, 18, 73, 83, 163
Chancellery, 190
Charity, Operation, 4
Charlie, Chaplin, 198
Charlie, Exercise, 17
Charlton, Flight Lieutenant R.E., 11
Chatterton DSO, Colonel, G.J.S., Glider Pilot Regiment, 33, 92
Chedworth, 9, 22, 24–5
Chelmsford, 121
Cherbourg, 11, 13, 25, 32, 72, 74

Chew, Flight Lieutenant C.A., 179
Chicken Rock, Isle of Man, 18, 163
Chippenham, 2, 158
Chipping Sodbury, 87
Chitty, Flying Officer J.V., 11
Christchurch, 5, 69, 85
Christies, Pilot Officer V.B., 128
Christie, Warrant Officer, 71
Churchill, Prime Minister Winston, 56, 186, 194
Clark, Flying Officer, 143–5
Clarke, Flight Lieutenant, 61–2
Clarke, Squadron Leader, 178
Clegg, Flying Officer, 164
Cobcroft, Flight Lieutenant B., 86
Cody, Flight Lieutenant, 26
Collier, Air Vice Marshal, 23
Coles, Wing Commander W.R., 121
Comet, Operation, 89–90
Coastal Command, 97
Copenhagen, 187
Cough, Flight Lieutenant, 73
Coulombs (B.6), 60, 69, 89
Colombelles, 25, 33
Colleville-sur-Mer, 84
Confirmation II, Exercise, 14
Conquest, Corporal, 132
Consternation, Exercise, 18
Consternation II, Exercise, 84
Cooke, Flight Lieutenant J.C., 12, 157
Cottesmore, RAF, 6
Cotswolds, 196
Coventry, 52
Coventry, Wing Commander, 26–7, 126
Cragg, Squadron Leader, 1
Crawford, Flight Lieutenant G., 12
Crawford, Warrant Officer T., 187
Cressman, C.H., 125
Cricklade, 173, 195
Croydon, RAF, 173, 183–4

Cuer, Warrant Officer, 148
Cuijk, 99

Daldorph, Flight Sergeant J.A., 24–5
Dale, Flying Officer, 126
Daniells, Squadron Leader, 72
Danks, Flight Lieutenant, 158
Darvall MC, Air Commodore, L., 92, 161, 163, 176–7, 179, 192
Davis, Flight Lieutenant R.A., 181
Davis, Driver, 108, 110
Davidson, Lady Rachel, 162
D-Day (Operation Overlord), 21–3, 34–8, 49, 53, 56–7, 64, 81, 95, 97–9, 100–101, 103–104, 111, 113, 116, 118, 122, 128–9, 135, 140, 154, 176, 179, 185, 190, 195–6, 198
  see also Overlord, Operation
Dean, Flight Lieutenant, 17
Deelen, 94, 118, 122
Delahunt, Flying Officer J.A., 123–4
Dempsey, General, 135
Detling, 60
Didcot, 73
Diepholz, 183–4
Diest-Melsbroek, 170
Dives, river, 33
Dixon, Pilot Officer N.H., 187
Doncaster, RAF, 2–3, 5, 7, 146
Dolan, Flying Officer, 149
Doles Wood, 83
Dollin, Flying Officer, 16
Dorn, Sergeant, 7
Dorset Regiment, 118–19
Dorval, 167
Down Ampney, 1–3, 5, 7–10, 13, 17–18, 20–3, 29–30, 38, 50, 52, 55–7, 59–60, 70–1, 73, 78–9, 82, 84–5, 87, 89–90, 107, 115, 120, 122, 124, 128, 130–1, 134, 143, 146, 148, 151–4, 157–9, 160–7, 169–71, 173–4, 176, 180, 183–7, 196–8
Downham Market, 3
Downing, Flight Sergeant A.T., 25
Douai, 89
Douree, 121
Dover, 174
Dreme, Exercise, 8–9
Driel, 133
Drummond, Squadron Leader, 80, 161
Duff-Mitchell, Squadron Leader, 130
Duhamel, Alice and Arthur, 25
Dundee, 5
Dunkirk, 157, 159
Dunsfold, 162
Dutton DFC and Bar, Wing Commander R.G., 177–8

Early, Pilot Officer W., 12
Eastell, Sergeant, 9
Ede, 127, 153
Edmonds, Air Vice Marshal, 23
Emmerich, 97, 182
Edwards, Flying Officer, 13
Eindhoven, 92–3, 98, 105, 111–12, 117, 121, 125–6, 131, 135, 139, 141, 145–6, 151, 156, 175, 179, 183
Eisenhower, General, 23, 84
El Adem, 158
Eletot, 25
Elliot, Captain, 153
Elst, 116, 118, 133
Emmerich, 97, 182
Engleberg, Warrant Officer C., 24–5
Enstone, 22, 26
Errol, 5
Escaut Canal, 91, 145
Eskimo, Exercise, 167
Essex, 173–74
Exeter, Operation, 17

Extraction, Exercise, 83
Eureka, 5, 28, 36, 38–9, 41–2, 44–5, 72, 83, 96, 106, 113–14
Evesham, 73

Fairford, 38, 144
Fairwood Common, 85
Faith, Operation, 4
Farnborough, 169
Fairoaks, 22, 26
Falaise, 86, 135
Falloon, Flying Officer, 5
Farrell, Flying Officer (Linn), 29–30, 48, 52
Fell, Flight Sergeant, 141
Fellowes, Flight Lieutenant R., 12
Felton, Warrant Officer, 145
Fennell, Warrant Officer E.T., 11
Fennell, Sergeant G.T., 6
Fenwick, Warrant Officer T., 109–10
Fiddament DFC, Air Vice Marshal, AOC, 22–4, 33, 192
Fife-Miller, Flight Sergeant J.R., 185
Finlay, Flying Officer, 80, 130–1, 141
Firefly, Exercise, 14
First Allied Airborne Army, 92
Fitzgibbon, Flying Officer F.E., 123
Flather, Flying Officer, 13
Fleetwood, 147
Flensburg, 188–9
Fletcher, Flight Sergeant, 15
Fletcher, Flight Lieutenant, 19
Flying Nightingales, 18, 160, 194
Ford Airfield, 29
Ford, 55, 57, 69, 161
Fortresses, 180
France, 13, 22–5, 32, 48, 56–60, 63–4, 66, 69–71, 73–4, 83–90, 121, 123, 127, 155, 158, 160, 164, 171, 174, 187, 191, 196–8

Franceville-Plage, 31
Frankfurt, 186
Friedrichshafen, 186
Friston, 169
Fritz, German guard dog, 79
Furley, Flying Officer J.W., 11
Fw 190, 50, 62, 114, 121, 125, 130, 139, 143–5, 147, 164

Gale, General, GOC, 49, 170
Gatwick, 162
Gee, 5, 7, 13–14, 35–6, 40, 125, 152
Geisler, Flight Sergeant, 179
Gemini, 174
German Miniature Tank, 82
German High Command, 188–9
German General Staff, 189
Germany, 19, 32, 91, 156, 158, 165, 172–3, 176, 180–1, 183, 186–7, 197–8
Ghent, 108, 121, 128, 171
Gheel, 98
Gibraltar, 1, 55
Gibson, Pilot Officer E., 162
Gillingham, 15
Gilze-Rijen, 169, 183
Glasgow, 162
Glider Regiment, 56, 120, 131, 155, 159, 171, 191
Glider Pilot Regiment, 92, 119, 140, 162
Gloucestershire, 2, 6, 9
Glunz, Lt, 122
Goch, 183
Gosfield, RAF, 173–8, 180
Gosfield-Altair, 174
Gough, Flight Lieutenant P.E.A., 135
Grand-Failly, 187
Grant, Flight Lieutenant D., 12
Grantham, 105, 112, 114
Grave, 89, 92–4, 98, 104, 118, 144, 149

Index   283

Gray, Flight Sergeant, 141–2
Green, Flight Sergeant, 13
Gregg, Sir James, Secretary of State for War, 72
Groesbeek, 93, 99
Guards, Irish, 105
Gulliver, Exercise, 18
Gumbrell, Flight Sergeant Sydney, 157
Gunther, Lt, 122
Guy, Flight Sergeant, 83

Hadrians, 96, 98, 101
Hagerman, Flying Officer G.P., 123
Hakansson, Pilot Officer, 83
Haldern, 175
Halifax (Aircraft), 38–9, 49, 92, 137
Hallam, Wing Commander, 90
Hamilcars, 34, 38, 43–4, 53–4, 92, 95–6, 100, 106, 137
Hamilton, Flying Officer, 121
Hamlyn, Flying Officer R.T., 11
Hamminkeln, 174, 180
Hampshire Regiment, 149
Hampstead Norris, 4
Handley Page HP54 'Sparrow', 164, 169
Hanover, 183
Harder (driver), 151
Harford Bridge, 9
Harries, Squadron Leader L.J., 175
Harrowbeer, 60
Hatfield, 91, 98, 121, 123, 125–7
Hartland Point, 15
Hartley, Flight Lieutenant, 7
Hartley, Flying Officer J.W., 161
Harwell, 12, 37, 73
Headquarters, 83 Group, 115
Hebert, Flight Lieutenant A., 125
Heckmann, Oblt, 122
Heindtke, Ofhr, 122
Hendon, RAF, 1–3, 7, 17, 173, 195

Henry, Flying Officer G.E, 102, 127
Her Majesty, Queen Mary, 71
Heth V, Exercise, 8
Heveadorp, 118
HGSU, 45
High Wycombe, 4
Highland I, Exercise, 73
Hildesheim, 183
Hill, Brigadier, 22
Hill, Flying Officer, 179
Hirst, Flying Officer, 70
Hitler, 154, 186
Hoffmann, Lt, 122
Holder, Flying Officer, S.J., 162–3
Hollom, Flight Lieutenant, 129, 166
Holland, 105, 135, 138, 147, 197
Hollinghurst CB OBE DFC, Air Vice Marshal, L.N., 33, 92
Holmsley South, 58, 63–4, 164
Holtom, Flight Sergeant, 149
Honeybourne, 4
Hope, Operation, 4
Hope, Sergeant, 13
Hopsten, 183
Horaburgh, Flight Sergeant, 78
Horner, Flying Officer R.H.J., 12
Horsa (glider), 10, 18, 29, 31, 34, 38–9, 42–5, 47, 53–4, 92, 95–6, 98, 101, 120, 124, 127–8, 137, 171, 174, 180
Horsfall, Squadron Leader, 1
Howie DSO, Group Captain G.R., 159
Houlgate, 39
HP54's, 166, 169, 186
HQ 83 Group, 110–11
HQ XVIII (US) Airborne Corps, 92
HQ Airborne Corps, 116
Hull, Pilot Officer, 27
Hull, Flight Lieutenant R.G.J., 175
Houbert, Major P.S., 12
Hungerford, 18, 84

Huntington, 15
Hurn, 60–1, 71
Hustedt, 183
Hyams, LAC J., 164

Independent, Exercise, 73
India, 187
Instone, Captain, 10
Intelligence officers, 5, 7, 16, 20, 22, 52, 123
Isle of Man, 18, 71, 163
Istres (Marseilles) 166
Invasion,19, 28, 47, 52, 55, 70, 196
Ives, Pilot Officer J.L., 185
IX US Troop Carrier Command, 93

Jackson, Major, Commanding Officer of the Glider Regiment, 50–2, 56, 120, 155
James, Flying Officer, 63
Jarvis, Flying Officer J.C., 12
Jefferson, Wing Commander T.A., 11, 127, 136
JG26, 114, 121–2, 130
Jodl, General, 189
Johnson, Flight Lieutenant R., 12
Jones, Flying Officer H.E., 24–5, 41, 146
Joubert, Major P.S., 84, 150, 157
Joubert, Lieutenant Colonel, 165, 175
Joyce, Charles Paddy, 198
Joyce, Sergeant, 120
Joynt Flight Lieutenant E.L., 122
Jurby, Isle of Man, 71
Kasperski, Corporal, 123
Kassel, 110, 128
Keeslen, 130
Keevil, 37
Keiller, Flight Lieutenant 80
Kell am See, 187
Kemble, RAF, 186

Kenny, R.A., 124–5
Kennedy, Group Captain W.M.C., 2
Kennedy, Group Captain H.J., 121
Kennedy, Pilot Officer, 147–8
Kelmscott, Airfield, 15–16
Kent, HRH Duchess, 161–2
Kent, Pilot Officer A.C., 108, 147
King, Flying Officer, 151–4, 187
King, Warrant Officer, 129–30
Kingston (Military College), 168
Kingston, 174
Kohler, Gefr, 122
Kunz, Oblt, 122

Labrador, 167
La Deliveranoc, 76
Lambouillet, 135
Lambourne, 73
Lane, Captain, 125
Lancasters, 26, 36
Lang, Wing Commander T.F.U., 16
Langenhagen, 184
Langford,15
Lantheuil (B9), 60
Laval, 12–3
Lee, Flight Lieutenant, 73
Leicester, East, 16, 166
Leipzig, 186
Lek, 135
Lemon, Exercise, 84
Levings, Flying Officer, 5
Letch Hill, 162
Le Bourget, 88, 166
Le Fresne Camilly (B5), 59
Le Harve, 23–5, 27, 32, 35, 50–3
Le Home sur Mer, 25
Le Huray, Flying Officer, 29–30, 48, 51, 56
Le Mariquet, 27, 31
Leopold, 125–6, 135, 139

Index 285

Leapold, *see* Leopold
Lestang, Flight Lieutenant, 32
Liberator, 67
Lille, 174–5
Linnet, Operation, 88–9
Little Rissington, RAF, 7, 73
Littlehampton, 24–5, 31
Lockwood, Flight Sergeant, J.W., 157
London, 1,9, 56, 74, 79, 160, 162, 174
Lomas, Flying Officer, 83
Lord, Edith (Titch), 198
Lord VC, Flight Lieutenant D.S.A., 12, 107, 129, 151–4, 187
Lord, Trenchard, 83
Luftwaffe, 19, 99, 124–5, 130, 173, 197
Lulworth Cove, 73
Lympne, 72

Maas (River), 91
Maas-Waal Canal, 91
Maastricht, 91
Macdonnel, Flying Officer D.I., 12, 151, 153–54
Mackay, Flying Officer, 28, 80, 130
Mackenzie, Squadron Leader, 2, 32
Mackie, Flight Lieutenant, 25
Malborough, 73
Maldegem, 197
Mallard, Operation, 29–30, 34, 44–5, 48, 52, 56, 154
Mallory, Air Chief Marshal Trafford Leigh, 24
March, Cambridgeshire, 98
Marfak, 174
Market Garden, Operation, 88, 90–1, 107, 115, 120, 123–4, 126–9, 131, 141, 143, 145, 147–51, 154–6, 176, 179
Markey, AC2 J.E., 6
Marseilles, 166, 171

Matthews, Corporal, 143
Matthews, Flight Lieutenant, 139–40
Mattocks, Flying Officer, 78
Martlesham Heath, 102, 124, 127
Mayenne, 13
Maziero, Oberstleutnant, D. De, 189
McCannell, Warrant Officer M.M., 24–5, 41
McLean, Flying Officer W.E., 123
McCreanor, Flying Officer, 27, 80
McKinley, Flying Officer, H.J., 127
McLintock, Flight Sergeant, W.J., 125
McHugh, Flight Sergeant, 125
McIntyre, Flying Officer F.J., 108–11
McLaughlin, Warrant Officer, 131, 146
McLoed, Flight Lieutenant, 13, 62
McLoed, Squadron Leader, 188
McNeil Smith, Flying Officer, 162
McVeigh, Squadron Leader, 28
ME410, 77
Medhurst, Air Chief Marshall Sir Charles, 151
Medhurst, Pilot Officer Dickie, 151–2
Mellor, Wing Commander, 175
Merville, 25, 33–6
Meteor, Exercise, 176–7
Met Office, 23
MI9, 6, 10
MI10, 79
Middle Wallop, 85
Miller, Flying Officer, 13
Miller, Squadron Leader, 24
Mole, Operation, 84
Montebourg, 87
Moody, Fight Sergeant F.E., 6, 11
Morrison, Flight Lieutenant, 83
Morrison, Wing Commander, 2, 24
Mosley, Leonard, 49
Mostyn-Brown, Squadron Leader W.A., 177–9, 180

Mosquito, 136
Mott, Flight Lieutenant C.W., 131, 147–8
Mountford, Flight Lieutenant, 5
Mundy, Flying Officer, 13
Mundell, Wing Commander, medical officer, 57
Murray, Flying Officer, 28
Murray, Major Tony, 140, 158
Mush, Exercise, 11
Mush, Operation, 11
Mustang, 53, 99, 102, 106, 112, 114, 117, 138

Nark, Exercise, 15
Nark II, Exercise, 16
Neave, K.M (*A Nightingale Flew*), 194
Neder Rijn, river, 91, 94
Neptune, Operation, 26, 32–4, 47
Netheravon, 3–7, 9, 14, 18, 33, 70, 83–4, 171
Netherlands, 32, 88–9, 91–2, 94, 100–102, 123–4, 127, 156, 158, 164, 191
Neville, Lieutenant, R.R (US), 115
Newbury, 84, 158
Newhaven, 50–1
Newquay, 18
Nickel, Operation, 12–13, 16
Nijmegen, 89, 92–5, 97–9, 101, 105, 111–17, 122, 133, 135, 138–9, 147, 149–52
Nivelles. 181, 183, 185–6
Nixon, Corporal, 151
Noggin, Exercise, 15
Noggin II, Exercise, 15
Normandy, 21–4, 26, 29, 36, 44, 50, 58–61, 71–3, 77, 79, 80, 85–6, 160, 190–1, 194–5, 198
North America, 167–8
North Foreland, 98, 121, 125–6

Northolt, 58, 61, 70, 73–4, 77, 79, 83–5, 88, 90, 149, 160, 162–3, 166, 170, 183–4
Nott, Flight Sergeant, 149

Oakham, 73
Oakley, Warrant Officer, 13
Occults, 36
Odiham, 69
Oleinikoff, Warrant Officer, 169
Orchard, Flying Officer, 181
Orleans, 85, 87
Orleans-Bricy Airfield, 87
Ormsby-Gore, Captain A.L.O., 20
Orne, river, 27, 31, 33, 50, 57–9, 61–2, 65, 76
Orr, Flying Officer J., 12
Ostend, 98, 139
Ottawa, 167
Otis, Operation, 8
Ouistreham, 26, 32–3, 53, 58, 62, 65
Overlord, Operation, 26, 32–3
Owen, Flight Lieutenant W.G., 86
Oxford, aircraft, 2–3, 7, 19
Oxford, city, 120
Oxfordshire, 1–2, 5
Oxfordshire and Buckinghamshire Regiment, 176, 178, 180
Oxley, Colonel (Operation Commander Control Post), 148

P-51s, 173
P-47s, 173
Packer, Flight Lieutenant, 147–8
Paris, 85, 87, 135
Parry, Flying Officer J.H., 134
Pascall, Squadron Leader, 1
Padget, Flying Officer, 126
Pathfinder Aircraft, 15, 38–9, 93, 101
Pattee, Flying Officer, 107, 128, 147

Payne, Flying Officer, 78
Payne, Flight Sergeant T.W., 83
Pearce, Flight Lieutenant W.A., 163
Pearson, Pilot Officer R.L., 29, 123
Pearson, Squadron Leader A.B.J., 57, 170, 184
Peffert, Doreen, 199
Percy, Sergeant R., 149
Perry, Pilot Officer, 139
Pershore, 2, 18, 20
Perth, 5
Periers-en-Auge, 39
Philips, Ted, 197
Plimmer, Flying Officer C.F., 11
Ploughman, Captain, 140
Plunder, Operation, 172
Pointe de Barfleur, 69, 87
Polder Land, 95
Porter, Flight Sergeant A.R., 25
Porter, Flying Officer M.F., 83
Position B, Antigua, 91
Position C, Bermuda, 91
Position D, Columbia, 91
Potter, Flight Lieutenant G.E., 162
Predannack, 60
Preston, Admiral, 77
Prestwick, 84
Prince Albert, Saskatchewan, 167–8
Princess Elizabeth, 17
Princess Royal, 71
Pring, Pilot Officer, 131
Prior, Warrant Officer F.A., 83
Pundits, 36
Punnall, Flying Officer, 121
Purkie, Pilot Officer R.S., 123
Purton, 6
Quin, Warrant Officer, 69

Rae AFC, Squadron Leader, 53
RAF Regiment, 123, 145, 188
RAF Transport Command, 147, 192
Ralph, Flight Sergeant H.J., 11
Rambouillet, 85
Ramscapelle, 161
Randall, Flight Sergeant, 13
Ranville, 27, 31, 34
RASC, 18, 84, 119, 139–40, 151, 158, 167
Rasmussen, Pilot Officer K.Z., 123, 126
Reading, 74
Rebecca, 5, 14, 20, 28, 36 42, 125
Rebecca II, 36
Rechenuc, Flying Officer J, 125, 139
Red Cross, 144, 154, 194, 196
Redhill, 169
Reed, Flight Lieutenant J.T., 125
Rees, 172, 175, 178
Reichstag, 190
Renkum, 124, 128
Rennes, 166
Renouville, 31
Reykjavik, 84
Rheine, 183–4
Rhenen, 124, 128
Rhine, 89, 91, 132, 152,154, 165, 172–4, 178–9, 180–2, 190–3
Rhyl, 18
Rice, Flying Officer, 142
Ricketts (driver), 151
Rijn, river, 116–18
Riley, Flight Lieutenant, F.R., 163
Ringenberg, 175
Reynolds, Pilot Sergeant, 7
Reynolds, Flight Sergeant R.E., 185
Roach, Flight Lieutenant, 126
Rob Roy, Operation, 30–1, 35, 54–5
Robertson, Flying Officer, 5
Robertson, Warrant Officer H.K., 12
Roger, Exercise, 11
Rothwell, 9
Rowanberry, Exercise, 78

Rowbotham (driver), 151
Roy, Flying Officer, 126
Royal Air Force Air Ambulance Unit, 194
Royal Corps of Signals, 148
Royal Ulster Rifles, 29, 178
Rushden, 2
Russian, 183, 185–6, 188–9
Russian High Command, 188
Rushton, Sergeant, 140
Russell, Squadron Leader, 179

's-Hertogenbosch, 98, 102, 121–4, 128, 130, 137–8
Sackarley, Sergeant R.J.F, 11
Saint-Pol-sur-Mer, 157
Sanderson, Flight Sergeant J.H., 6
Sannerville, 33
Sainte-Croix-sur-Mere (B.3), 85
Saint Martins, 25
Saint-Lo, 13
Saint-Omer, 159
Salisbury Plain, 14
Salzburg, 187
Sandford, Flying Officer P.R., 11
Sargent, Pilot Officer J.S., 12
Sarthe, 13
Saunders, Flight Lieutenant, 134–5, 140
Saunders, Warrant Officer, 32
Savage, Flying Officer, 181
Scherbarth, Warrant Officer, A.O., 187
Schneider, Flight Sergeant Douglas, 157
Schouwen Island, 98–9, 120, 123, 136, 138
Schulz, Uffz, 122
Schundel, 150
Schwies (Island) 121
Scotland, 5, 78–9, 151
Seekout, Exercise, 72
Seine, 36

Selsey-Bill, 57–9, 61, 63, 77–8, 85, 87
Senior Air Staff Officer, 192
Shakespeare, Flight Sergeant F.A., 6
Shannon, Flight Lieutenant, 7
Shannon, Flying Officer, 13
Sharpe, Warrant Officer, 121
Shawbury, 163
SHAEF, 17
Shearwood, Flight Sergeant, 12
Shipton on Stour, 84
Shrewton, 14
Shuttle I, Exercise, 87
Sinclair Bt, KTC MG, MP, The Right Honourable Sir Archibald (Secretary of State for War), 56
Siddons, Warrant Officer P., 11
Simmons, Flying Officer O.A., 123
Skebrae, 72
Sleaford, 73
Smith, Captain L.S., 143
Smith, Sergeant, 9
Smith, Flight Lieutenant, 28, 80
Smith, Squadron Leader B., 83
Smith, Pilot Officer A.M., 55
Smith, Flying Officer B., 83, 134
Smith, Warrant Officer A.E., 127
Snowshoe, Operation, 3
Snowshoe, Exercise, 5
Special Air Service (SAS) Troops, 92
Sommervieu, 69
Soper, Warrant Officer, John, 157
Sossabowski CBE, General Major S., (1st Polish Independent Parachute Brigade Group), 92
South Cerney, 5, 7, 9
Southey, Flight Lieutenant R.C.J., 185
Southampton, 13
Southgate, Squadron Leader, 138, 140
Southrop Airfield, 11, 87
Soviet, 190

Sowersby, Flying Officer, 181
Spitfire, 53, 57–8, 61–5, 67, 99, 102, 106, 112, 114, 117, 136, 145, 173
Sportpalast, 190
Sproule, Squadron Leader, 1, 123
Sproule Wing Commander J.A., 86–8, 90, 122
Squires, Squadron Leader, 69
Squires DFC, Wing Commander P.D., 175
Staples, Warrant Officer, J.C., 162
St Croix sur Mer, 57
St Edmunds, 9
St-Govan's Headland, 15
St Lo, 80
St Mawgan, 3
St Mary's Isle, 18
Stacey, Pilot Officer W.A., 11
Station Intelligence Officer, 7
Stirling (Aircraft), 28, 35, 37–8, 41, 44, 92, 107–108, 133, 137, 144–5, 149, 180
Stone, LAC H.A., 6
Stone, Flight Lieutenant, 28–9
Stout Field, Indianapolis, 168
Stow-on-the-Wold, 158
Strange, Wing Commander, 73–4
Swadlincote, 73
Swindon, 73
Sunbrough, 72

Tain, 84
Tangmere, 58–9, 196
Tarbitten, Flight Sergeant, 54
Tarrant Rushton, 38
Tate, Don, 198
Taunton, 15
Tealing, 78–9
Tedder, Air Chief Marshal, 188
Teed, Pilot Officer, 9

Teilken, Obfw, 122
Tempest, 99, 102, 114
Templehof Airport, 188–90
Tetbury, 18
Thame, 83
Thames, 136, 180
Thomas, Captain (Glider Pilot), 54, 140
Thornbury, 73
Thorney Island, RAF, 57, 73–4, 78, 83, 85
Thunderbolts, 65, 67, 138
Tilburg, 92, 115
Tipping, Flight Sergeant, 148–9
Titanic, Operation, 37
Tonga, Operation, 22–3, 26, 28–9, 43, 48, 154
Touffreville, 24–5
Toulouse, 166
Tournai, 88
Tour, Exercise, 8
Tours, 12–13
Transport Command, 1, 3, 12–13, 147, 151, 156–7, 163, 169, 190, 192
Transfigure, Operation, 85–6
Trenchard, Lord, Marshal of the Air Force, 56, 83
Trier, 187
Troarn, 33–4
Trowbridge, 18
Turnbull, Sergeant, 10
Tuskey, Pilot Officer, Squadron Intelligence Officer, 123
Typhoon, 63, 71, 146, 173

Uden, 147–8
USAAF Eighth Air Force, 97
USAAF, 174, 180
US Airborne Divisions, 93
US Army Air Force, 33
Ubique, Exercise, 87

Urquhart, Major General R.E DSO (1st Airborne Division), 92
Utrecht, 97, 127

Valborg, 132–3
Vandeveerd, Fw, 122
Varaville, 34
Varsity, Operation, 169, 171–7, 179, 180–1, 192
VE-Day, 174, 186–7, 197
Vega, 174
Veghel 105, 148, 150
Vendeville, 175
Ventura, 84
Vince, Flying Officer, 25
Vines, Warrant Officer, 32
Vire (river), 11, 13, 69, 74, 85
Virst, 186
Vitry, 89
Vogt, Lt, 122
Vulture IV, Exercise, 172

WAAF, Medical Orderly, 63, 66–8, 71, 84, 157, 199
Waal (River), 91, 94, 105, 111
Wacos, 137
Wageningen, 124, 128
Waight, Pilot Officer W.F., 11
Wallis, Flying Officer J., 12–13
Walrus, 185
Walsh, Flying Officer, 143
Walsh, Margaret, 197
War Correspondents, 49
War Dog School, 79
Walker, P.H. War Correspondent, 79
Walker, Sergeant, 123
Wallingford, 158
Walsh, Nursing Orderly LACW M.M., 185, 197
Warminster, 18

Watchfield, 5
Watlington, 5
Watts, Flight Sergeant W.F., 11
Warrington, G.R., 124
Warwick, Pilot Officer, 77–8
Warwick, Flying Officer, 115
Watson, Warrant Officer T.S., 187
Washington, 168
Wavre, 178
Webb, Warrant Officer, 130
Webster, Flight Sergeant, 130–1, 140–1
Weeze, 178–9, 181
Wells, Flying Officer, 147–8
West, Warrant Officer, 78, 143
West, 1st Lieutenant A. (US), 115
Wesel, 172, 174, 178, 182
Westbury, 87
Westley, 9
West Malling, 28
Wheatly, Sergeant, 149
Wheatley-Smith, Squadron Leader, 29
Wheatly-Smyth, Squadron Leader, 143
White, Flying Officer J.C., 12
Whitfield, Flight Lieutenant G., 80, 128, 175
Wick, 84
Wilhemina, 115
Williams, Flight Officer I.N., 24–5
Williams, Flight Lieutenant, 52, 73
Wills, Flight Lieutenant, 29
Williams, Major General Paul L., IX US Troop Carrier Command, 93
Wills, Flying Officer, 80, 130
Wilson, Pilot Officer, J.L., 129
Winchcombe, 4
Winder, AC2 J., 6
Winterbourne Stoke, 4
Whitley (Aircraft), 17
Women's Auxiliary Airforce, 194
Wood, Flying Officer, 32

Woodcock, Flying Officer Bill, 30, 48, 50, 56
Worthing, 22, 26
Wotton Basset, 5
Wright Field, Dayton Ohio, 168
Wright, Squadron Leader, 32
Wroughton, 195

Yalta North, 174
Ypreville-Biville, 23, 25

Zeebrugge (Communal Cemetery), 161
Zeeland, 144
Zhukov, Marshal, 188–9
Zwolle, 122